the
action guide
to britain

Rupert Isaacson

THE HARVILL PRESS
LONDON

about the author

Rupert Isaacson is a Londoner of southern African parentage. He has ridden, walked, canoed, climbed, rafted, driven off-road, flown by various means, windsurfed and skied through some of the most rugged areas of the UK, Europe, Africa and North America. He is the author of the Cadogan Guides to South Africa, Goa, South India, Zimbabwe, Botswana and Namibia, and now divides his time between London and Berkeley, California.

please help us update this book

If you find that any of the information contained has changed, please let us know in writing. Contact: The Editors, *The Action Guide to Britain*, The Harvill Press, 84 Thornhill Road, London N1 1RD

The authors, publishers and editors have made every attempt to ensure the accuracy of the information in the book at the time of going to press. However, they cannot accept responsibility for any loss, injury or inconvenience resulting from the use of information contained in this guide.

First published in Great Britain in 1997 by
The Harvill Press, 84 Thornhill Road, London N1 1RD

First impression

A CIP catalogue record for this book is available from the British Library

ISBN 1 86046 194 8

Typeset in Frutiger and Stone Print at Libanus Press, Marlborough, Wiltshire

Printed and bound in Great Britain by Butler & Tanner Ltd at Selwood Printing, Burgess Hill

The author would like to thank Horatio Monteverde of Animage for his page designs; Polly Loxton for her illustrations; Mathew Carter for his work on the water sports chapter; and most of all Kristin Neff, who was responsible for most of the practical sections and without whom the book might never have reached the printers

contents

subactivities

introduction

The Action Guide has selected Britain's best centres for outdoor adventure. Chapters are divided sport by sport, in alphabetical order, with the selected centres also listed alphabetically. Different disciplines of each sport are detailed in the introduction and then indicated, where appropriate, for each centre. Whether you just want to have a go at a sport or intend taking it up seriously, even professionally, the Action Guide tells you what you need to know.

With a description of each centre and what it offers comes detailed practical information on accommodation and food, disabled and children's facilities, other activities on offer, insurance, safety procedures, booking, tariffs, affiliations and access. Finally, each chapter ends with a section called 'kitting yourself out', which gives you an idea of what equipment to buy, how much to pay and which brand names to look for.

The last chapter in the book is organized slightly differently, as it deals with activities related to outdoor action sports, but which do not quite fit the bill – or which are too specialized to be offered in more than one or two places. There are some surprises in this chapter, and it's worth perusing just to get an idea of how eccentric people can be, as well as finding out how to join in.

Centres have been selected by standard of tuition (qualified instructors and low student to instructor ratios), safety and affiliation to governing or representative bodies. In a few cases unaffiliated centres have been listed, owing either to the unique nature of what they offer, or a lack of general availability of other centres in the locality. We have done our best to make sure that these unaffiliated centres have the necessary qualified tuition, but advise that prospective clients should make sure of this before booking.

governing bodies

The Grand National Archery Society
7th Street, Stoneleigh, Kenilworth
Warwickshire CV8 2LG
Tel (01203) 696 631
Fax (01203) 419 662
[sx]Affiliated Regional Governing Bodies

East Midlands Archery Society
Watnall Road, Hucknall
Nottingham NG15 6FB
Tel (0115) 953 8619

West Midlands Archery Society
3 Bredon Close, Albrighton
Shropshire WV7 3PQ
Tel (01902) 374 733

Southern Counties Archery Society
Fordington Road, Winchester
Hampshire SO22 5AL
Tel (01962) 854 932

North Wales Archery Society
20 Elm Grove, Wrexham
Clwyd LL12 7NR
Wales
Tel (01978) 291 170

South Wales Archery Association
53 Cas Troggy, Caldicott
Gwent NP6 4NX
Wales
Tel (01291) 422 229

Grand Western Archery Association
27 Sutherland Avenue, Broadstone
Dorset BH18 9EB
Tel (01202) 692 087

Northern Ireland Archery Society
17 Bridge Road, Kilmore, Lurgan
County Armagh BT67 9LA
Northern Ireland
Tel (01762) 326 987

Northern Counties Archery Society
12 Coeside
York YO2 2XB
Tel (01904) 703 707

Scottish Archery Association
30 Gardner Street, Partick
Glasgow G11 5NJ
Scotland
Tel (0141) 339 9188

archery

Archery has a special place in British history. Evolved in the Welsh Border country, the 6-foot longbow and its 3-foot arrow combined to produce England's most devastating weapon of the Middle Ages. Small companies of Welsh longbowmen successfully routed much greater numbers of French mounted knights at several battles during the Hundred Years War, and until the early 16th century it was compulsory by law for every able-bodied male to practise once a week at the butts (public practice grounds).

With the coming of firearms, the longbow became obsolete and archery was kept alive only by small groups of enthusiasts making their own bows and competing among themselves.

In recent years, however, archery has once again become a national sport, with regular competitions up to Olympic standard. The modern compound bow, made of fibreglass, has replaced the old yew-wood longbow, and designs are becoming increasingly high-tech. The new, shorter bows can exert as much power as the old 6-footers, without the need for such great physical strength.

These days, most multi-activity centres offer archery, but few go beyond the basics. The following chapter therefore only lists clubs where archery is taught as an art, where you can develop your skills sufficiently to think about shooting competitively.

All the above-listed regional bodies have an average of 100 local clubs under their directorship – some many more – making a total of more than 700 in the UK. Ring your local regional body to find out where the club closest to you can be found.

Most clubs meet once or twice a week in local sports fields or sports centres, but a few, which own their own ground, will shoot every evening.

Each club has its own instructors, and 6-week beginners' courses (one session per week over 6 weeks) are usually offered through the summer, at a low cost of £320–350, sometimes refundable if you then decide to join the club. The club supplies all equipment for these beginners' courses.

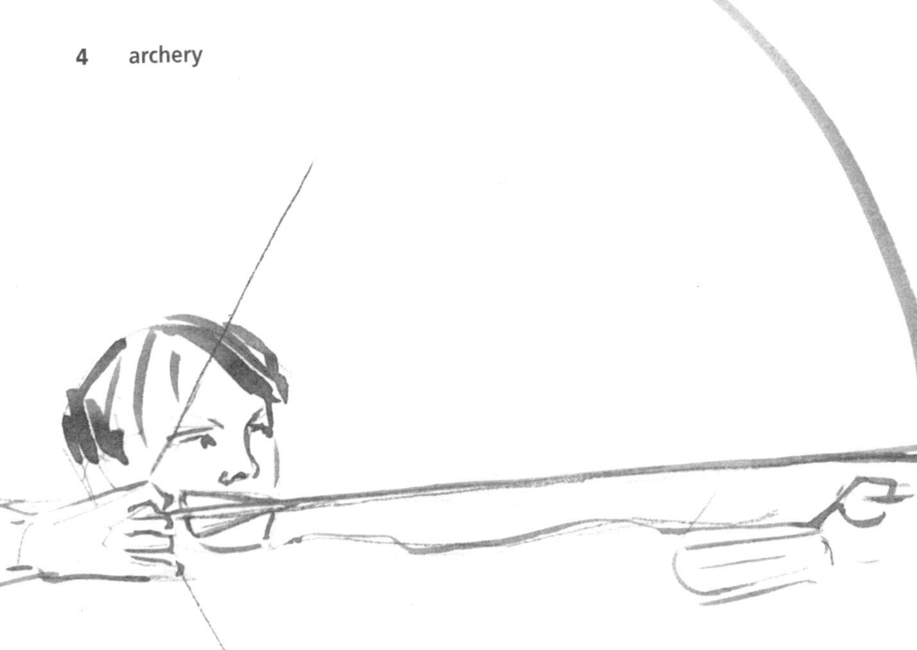

Once you have passed beginner level, you will have to buy your own equipment, which is not cheap (see Kitting Yourself Out, p. 7), and from then on tuition becomes informal and individual. Once you really start to improve, you will be encouraged to begin competing and the coaching sessions become more intensive. Clubs frequently field members up to international competition level, but all coaching fees are included in club membership: apart from occasional inter-club seminars, tuition is unlikely to cost you anything.

The clubs are all affiliated to the Grand National Archery Society in Kenilworth (see above), and insurance is included in the membership fee. The sport is open to most people – women often rise to international standard, and the disabled are often able to compete on equal terms with the able-bodied. Children under 12 can learn on special bows. Doctors often recommend archery to people who suffer from heart conditions for its beneficial expansion of the rib-cage. For the really skilled, and physically fit, the traditional longbow is often taught at club level.

By contrast with the archery clubs, Britain's outdoor centres teach only very superficially, which explains why this chapter has been laid out slightly differently to the others. However, listed below is a selection of centres that use local archery clubs for their beginners' sessions, and through which you can progress to a higher standard if you get hooked.

selected residential centres for beginners' archery sessions

edale yha activity centre

Rowland Cote
Nether Booth
Edale
Sheffield
S30 2ZH
Tel (01433) 670 302
Fax (01433) 670 234

Season: Open all year.

Tariffs: Archery is one of the sports offered in the centre's multi-activity package deals. Prices include equipment, instruction and full-board accommodation: approximately £42 per day in high season (April to August), £32 in low season (November to February).

See Caving (p. 45) for full details.

great glen school of adventure

South Laggan
Nr Spean Bridge
Highland
PH34 4EA
Scotland
Tel (01809) 501 381
Fax (01809) 501 218

Tariffs: 1-hour introductory session: £4.50 per person.

See Paragliding and Parascending (p. 313) for full details.

iris activity breaks

29 Alandale Drive
Pinner
Middlesex
HA5 3UP
Tel (0181) 866 3002

Tariffs: Weekend course includes instruction, equipment, and 2 nights' B&B: from £86–140.

See Ballooning (p. 13–14) for full details.

llangollen yha activity centre

Tyndwr Hall
Tyndwr Road
Llangollen
Clwyd
LL20 8AR
Wales
Tel (01978) 860 330
Fax (01978) 861 709

Seasons: Open all year.

Tariffs: Archery is one of the sports offered in the centre's multi-activity package deals. Prices include equipment, instruction and full-board accommodation: approximately £42 per day in high season (April to August), £32 in low season (November to February).

See Canoeing (p. 24) for full details.

lyncombe lodge

Churchill
Nr Bristol
Avon
BS19 5PQ
Tel (01934) 852 335
Fax (01934) 853 314

Tariffs: Archery is one of the sports offered in the centre's multi-activity package deals (includes equipment, instruction, half-board accommodation). 6-day holiday: £275–315 + VAT (depending on season); 2-day holiday: £110 + VAT. (Discounts for children under 16.)
See Horse Sports (p. 217) for full details.

millfield village of education

Millfield School
Street
Somerset
BA16 0YD
Tel (01458) 445 823
Fax (01458) 840 584

One of the few residential courses on offer in the UK that actually concentrates fully on archery, rather than just using it as part of a multi-activity programme, this one at Millfield offers 6 days of tuition at either beginner or intermediate level. The course is mainly aimed at teenagers, but is open to adults too. It aims to prepare you for competition shooting, with coverage of common mistakes in shooting, the rules of archery, and match and safety procedures. There is also an opportunity to sample compound bows.

Tariffs: Course includes use of equipment and 6 half-day instruction sessions: £68. Full-board accommodation for 1 week: £166 (adult) / £136 (under 12). (5% senior discount.)
See Circus Skills (p. 83) for full details.

whitewave activities

19 Linicro
Kilmuir
Isle of Skye
Highland
IV51 9YN
Scotland
Tel (01470) 542 414

Although the archery offered at Whitewave is aimed at beginners, you can organize more intensive tuition on basic compound bows, by the half-day, day or over a tailor-made course. You have the choice of whether to combine the sport with others such as sea canoeing, kayaking, hill walking and nature studies, or whether to concentrate on archery alone. There is also a choice of accommodation – either in the centre's own renovated croft house, or in a local B&B. Local transport can be arranged for those in alternative accommodation for a small extra charge.

Tariffs: Archery ½-day session (includes tuition and equipment): £8 per person (minimum 2 people). Archery is also included in the multi-activity holiday weeks offered by the centre (includes tuition, equipment, and full-board accommodation): £275. Group, family, and youth rates available.
See Canoeing (p. 36) for full details.

kitting yourself out

Your choice of bow is governed by your height. To give a rough idea of the range available, someone of 5ft 2ins would need a 58in bow, while someone of 6ft 2ins would need a 72in bow. Beginners' bows come in at about £250, while a decent intermediate's bow costs around £400. Advanced shooters can spend up to £800 on a bow. For all levels, the UK manufacturers Marksman and Stylist are recommended by most archers. You may only buy bows and arrows from a registered archery dealer. Contact your local regional body to find out who's close. Compound bows, which are more accurate but harder to shoot, cost much the same as ordinary bows. Their main advantage is that you do not need an arm brace.

Arrows, made of carbon fibre, cost between £50 and £200, and are stored in a quiver. Serious archers often have these hand-tooled and they can cost silly money. However, a regular quiver costs around £20, as does a good leather arm brace. Finally, a finger tab to keep the arrow in place before you shoot costs between £1 and £10.

checklist

- ✔ *quiver*
- ✔ *bow*
- ✔ *arm brace*
- ✔ *set of arrows*
- ✔ *finger tab*

governing body

British Balloon and Airship Club (BBAC)
7 Llewellyn Road, Penllerger, Swansea
West Glamorgan SA4 1BB
Wales
Tel (01792) 899 777

Southampton Balloon Festival

kitting yourself out

Most standard sport balloons carry 4–5 passengers, under an envelope of about 90,000 cubic feet, and cost around £1,200 with basket. The inflator fan is a further £1,000. The quick-release system will set you back around £150. The fuel cylinder with straps and covers costs around £500. Navigation instruments cost from £300 upwards. Remember that you should also add between £15 and £20 per flying hour for fuel and maintenance. Then there will be insurance costs. If all this seems unaffordable, remember that balloons can carry several people; if you form a syndicate the costs per person can be lowered considerably.

Thunder and Colt are one of two manufacturers in Britain and probably the largest in the world. They produce a low-cost package incorporating all the necessary equipment for a first-time buyer which comes in at just under £10,000.

For more specific information ring them on
(01179) 532 772
or fax (01179) 663 638.

further reading

A Beginner's Guide to Airsports, Keith Carey, A & C Black, 1994

checklist

- ✔ *envelope (big bubble thing) and basket*
- ✔ *quick-release and 2 karabiners*
- ✔ *extra fuel cylinder*
- ✔ *navigation instruments*
- ✔ *padded covers*
- ✔ *inflator fan*

governing bodies

British Canoe Union (BCU)
Adbolton Lane, West Bridgeford
Nottingham NG2 5AS
Tel (0115) 982 1100
Fax (0115) 982 1797

National Sea Kayaking Association
5 Osprey Avenue, Westhoughton,
Bolton **Lancashire** BL5 2SL
Tel & Fax (01942) 842 204

Scottish Canoe Association
Caledonia House, South Gyle
Edinburgh EH12 9DQ
Scotland
Tel (0131) 317 7314
Fax (0131) 317 7319

Supersport Photographs / Eileen Langsley

peninsula watersports

Higher Coombe Park
Lewdown
Okehampton
Devon
EX20 4QT
Roadford Lake, Devon
Tel (01409) 211 507
Stithians Lake, Cornwall
Tel (01209) 860 301
Upper Tamar Lake, Cornwall
Tel (01288) 321 712
Siblyback Lake, Cornwall
Tel (01579) 346 522

Open Canadian and Kayaking

Of Peninsula's 4 West Country centres, only Roadford and Siblyback offer canoeing courses and 'taster' sessions, while Tamar offers 'taster' sessions only. Both Roadford and Siblyback offer BCU courses in open Canadian and kayaking at levels 1–2. More experienced canoers can arrange for tailor-made courses. Most BCU courses last 2 days, either over a weekend or spread out over a series of evenings. Group and individual bookings are welcome.

None of the centres have accommodation, but they are happy to help you arrange it locally. You will need your own transport to get to and fro.

Affiliations: BCU.
Tariffs: All prices include tuition and use of equipment. 2-hour taster session: £10; BCU certificate courses: £25. Group and family discounts available.

See Windsurfing (p. 465) for full details.

plas y brenin

The National Mountain Centre
Capel Curig
Gwynedd
LL24 0ET
Wales
Tel (01690) 720 280 / 720 363
Fax (01690) 720 394

Open Canadian, Kayaking and Sea Kayaking

Plas y Brenin's canoeing courses are impressive. They start with a 'taster' weekend for beginner kayakers which takes you through the basic BCU 1 Star level handling skills, paddle strokes and elementary rescue, i.e. rolling. You can then follow up with a 5-day course at the end of which you have the option of being tested for the BCU 1 and 2 Star certificates (kayak). There is also an introductory 2-day open Canadian course with an option of being tested for the BCU 1 Star certificate at the end.

More advanced courses include a 5-day white-water course or specialized 2-day white-water coaching, a BCU white-water and rescue weekend, and a whole selection of instructor courses right up to Coach Award. Sea kayaking is another feature. Introductory weekend courses are followed by 5-day intensive courses for beginners and those ready to go on to wild-water conditions. Really experienced sea paddlers will enjoy the centre's guided 6-day Scottish trip off the west coast.
Affiliations: BCU.
Tariffs: All courses include instruction, equipment, accommodation and full board. A wide range of canoeing courses is available, including: 2-day introductory kayak: £135; 2-day introductory open canoe: £135; 5-day white-water: £320; 5-day sea kayaking: £320; BCU white-water safety and rescue weekend (non-residential): £90; weekend instructor award: £135.

See Mountain Skills (p. 286) for full details.

preseli venture

Parcynole Fach
Mathry
Haverfordwest
Dyfed
SA62 5HN
Tel (01348) 837 709
Fax (01348) 837 656

Sea Kayaking

The Dyfed coast is one of Britain's best for sea kayaking, combining fun stuff like wave paddling with hard-core open–sea crossings to various islands, exploring cliffs and caves, and for the experienced, riding the 'Bitches' of Ramsay Sound, which provides year-round white-water conditions.

There are several courses on offer at Preseli: Introductory Kayaking for the total beginner, which combines tuition with trips to sheltered caves and beaches; Improvers, which builds on the basic skills and introduces you to rock-hopping and kayak surfing; Intermediate, which requires a BCU 3 certificate and takes on more arduous conditions and trips further afield, with some weather forecast interpretation, tidal predictions and chart work; the 'Bitches' – paddling the white water of Ramsay Sound – for people aiming at Advanced Proficiency level. Courses last from 3 to 5 days. The centre is small and friendly, catering for a maximum of 20 people, has 4 instructors (all with relevant BCU instructional qualifications) and will provide local transport to and from the kayaking sites.

Safety: Instructors have first aid and life-saving qualifications.
Tariffs: Prices include instruction, use of equipment, and full-board accommodation. 2-day holiday: £129; 3-day holiday: £189; 5-day holiday: £285. Canoeing is also included as part of the centre's multi-activity packages – 2-day holiday: £129; 3-day holiday: £189; 5-day holiday: £285.

See Cycle Sports (p. 121) for full details.

kitting yourself out

A good family kayak – long, safe and steady – costs about £250–350 new; Kiwi are a tried and trusted manufacturer. More advanced kayakers might progress to a Perception Club Dancer or Club (both £262 new), while fairly serious white-water enthusiasts should try the Ace, Corsica and Pirouette ranges – fancy models start at around £400. For Canadian canoes, Dagger, Pyranha and Old Town are reliable makers, with prices starting at about £250 for a stable beginners' canoe. Good sea kayaks are made by Sea Hawk, Islander, Iceflow, Orion and Sirius, and Iona. Expect to pay between £300 and £500 new for a good standard touring model. The second-hand market is huge. Cruise the classifieds of *Canoe Focus* magazine for bargains, but always take a knowledgeable friend or instructor with you to vet the condition of equipment.

Paddles vary as much as the craft themselves. Kayak paddles by Ace and New Wave are good, as are those by Schlegel. Prices range between £20 and £60. Ace also make very good Canadian paddles for around £20. Sea kayak paddles are a bit more expensive – from £30 up. Helmets by Ace, AP and WW cost between £15 and £30. Buoyancy aids by Field & Trek, WW or Yak range between £40 for the most basic model and £70 for a white-water model with pockets large enough to carry a throw bag.

Palm, Yak and Field & Trek all make reliable spraydecks for kayakers. Prices vary between £30 and £50. Waterproof paddling mittens and boots by Palm, Yak or WW cost about £20 and £30 respectively. Dry bags by Orlieb cost £15–20 depending on the size. A throwline bag to get you out of trouble (Greenslimes is a good maker, despite the name) sets you back around £25, but may save your life.

Field & Trek offer a starter pack for first-time kayakers costing £399 for a Perception Dancer, K100 paddle, Field & Trek spraydeck, buoyancy aid and cagoule, and an AP2000 helmet.

Obviously there is a thriving second-hand market in canoe equipment, but damaged goods are very dangerous. Unless you are already experienced, only buy second-hand stuff through a club or with the advice of an instructor you trust.

further reading

Canoeing, Skills and Techniques, Neil Shave, Crowood Press, 1992.

governing body

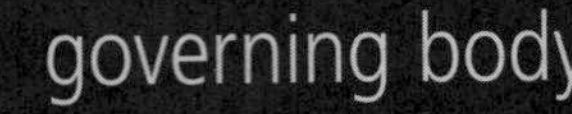

National Caving Association

White Lion House, Ynys Uchaf
Ystrad Glynlais
Swansea
West Glamorgan SA9 1RW
Tel (01639) 849 519

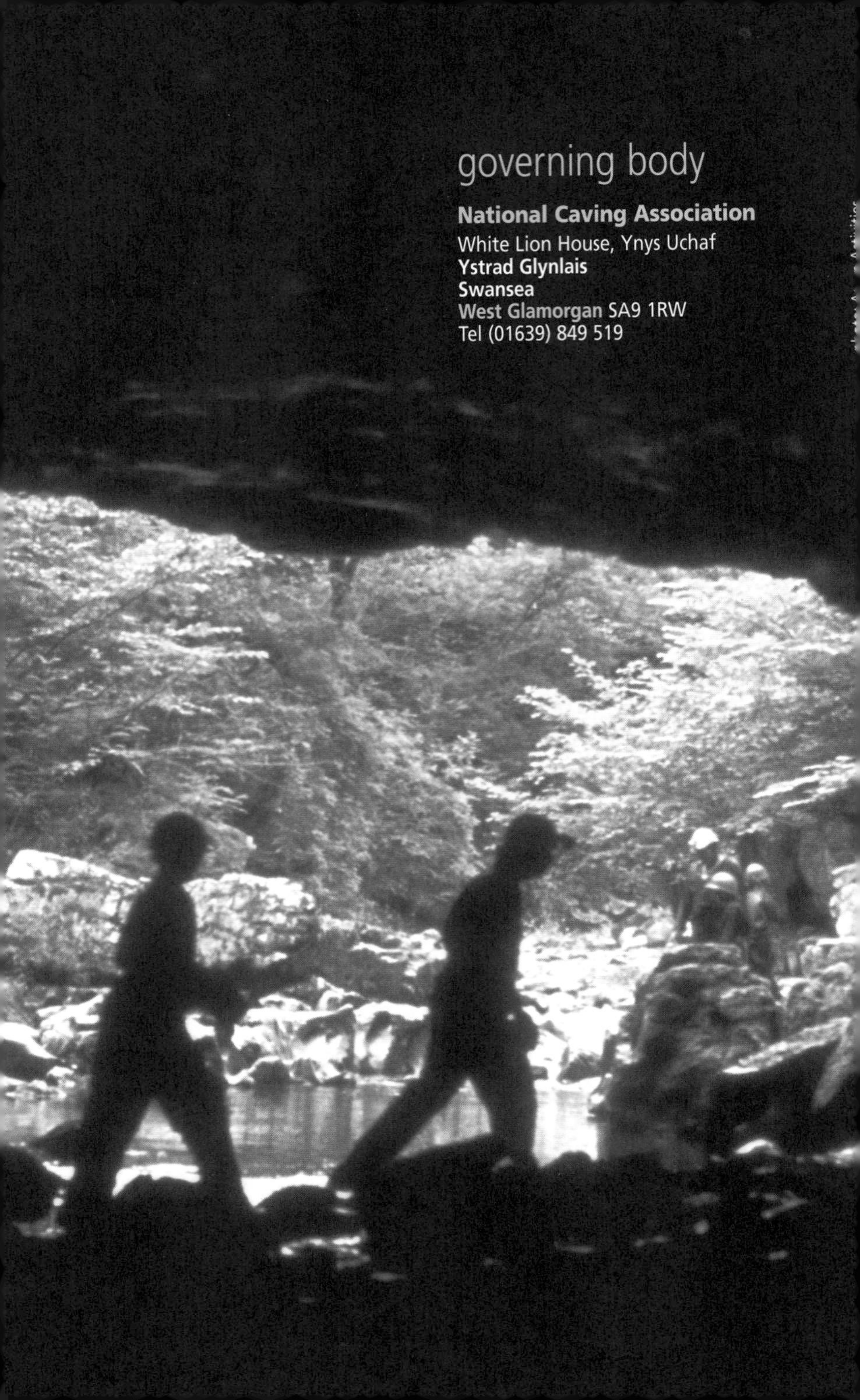

r & l adventures

The Byre
Knotts Farm
Patterdale Road
Windermere
Cumbria
LA23 1NL
Tel (015394) 45104

R&L offer caving and potholing day trips into the limestone cavern systems below the Cumbrian mountains. You can choose at what level you want to do it – cave walking with or without having to twist through the narrow, claustrophobic bits, or, for the more advanced, proper potholing that includes abseiling down to the black void and exploring underground watercourses. Ring the centre for the full range of options.

Tariffs: Prices include instruction and use of equipment. Half-day of caving: £50 for 1 or 2 people, £60 for group of 3–5 people, £10 each for group of 6–8 people.

See Canoeing (p. 32) for full details.

the rock climbing and caving centre

Chudleigh
Devon
TQ13 0EE
Tel & Fax (01626) 852 717

Chudleigh runs trips all over the country as well as on and under its own limestone crag. The caving trips are run with a ratio of 1 instructor to 5 cavers, and the centre is open to beginners and the experienced. Courses vary from undemanding cave walking to ladder-and-line rescue courses, caving instructor courses and Level 1 and 2 cave trips within the locality – to underground systems such as Bakers Pit and Swildon Hole. The owners have 17 years of experience.

The Rock Climbing and Caving Centre also run very good climbing and abseiling courses. If you don't have your own transport the centre will pick you up each morning, but with a small charge dependent on distance from the centre.

Season: Open all year.
Accommodation: Large campsite available (with shower facilities): £1 per person. 6 bunk beds: £32.50 per person. Centre will also provide help in arranging local B&B.
Food: Not provided.
Other Activities: Climbing and Abseiling (see p. 107); Mountain Skills (p. 287).
Children: Instruction for children available.
Disabled Facilities: Courses are run for adults and children with physical or learning disabilities. Clients given 1-to-1 instruction at group rate.
Insurance: centre provides insurance.
Safety: Medic on-site; all staff are trained in mountain first aid and are members of the Devon Cave Rescue Organization.
Affiliations: Association of Mountain Instructors; British Mountaineering Council; British Cave Research Association; Devon Cave Rescue Organization; National Caving Association Training Committee.
Tariffs: Group rate for instruction (includes equipment): £7.50 per person per half-day, £15 per person per day; individual rate: £25 per person per half-day, £50 per person per day. Local Cave Leader Award training courses available by arrangement.
Booking: 25% deposit required, non-refundable if cancellation notice received within 2 weeks of start date. Late bookings sometimes possible if space available.
Access: A38 to the B3344 at Chudleigh. Trains and buses available to Exeter or Newton Abbot; pick-ups can be arranged by centre (charge is cost of fuel only).

rock lea activity centre

Station Road
Hathersage
Peak District National Park
Via Sheffield
S30 1DD
Tel (01433) 650 345
Fax (01433) 650 342

The limestone cliffs and crags of the Peak District National Park are riddled with underground passages carved by water. The Rock Lea Centre has access to several cave systems and runs caving weekends for beginners and experienced potholers. The beginner's course takes you down Giant's Hole, one of the deepest cave systems in England, and the weekend includes ropework techniques and safety procedures. The improvers' course for more experienced cavers teaches more specialist skills such as abseiling, pitch-rigging, rescue and route-finding underground.

The centre is in the village of Hathersage in the middle of the Peaks, so the scenery is outstanding – as are the village's 5 pubs.

Season: Open all year.
Accommodation: 18 dorm beds available in home of centre owners, a Victorian manse.
Food: Half-board included, vegetarian and special diets catered for upon request.
Children: Courses designed for adults. Parties of youngsters only by arrangement (e.g. schools, clubs).
Disabled Facilities: None.
Insurance: Clients are covered by centre's insurance; optional curtailment and cancellation cover can also be arranged.
Safety: Staff and instructors trained and qualified in first aid and rescue procedures.
Affiliations: Derbyshire Association of Residential Education; East Midlands Tourist Board; Institute of Personnel Development.
Tariffs: Prices include instruction, equipment and accommodation. Beginners' Caving Weekend: from £99; Improvers' Caving Weekend: from £99. Caving is also one of the activities offered in the centre's multi-activity package deals: weekends from £99; weeks from £199–399.
Booking: Minimum £20 deposit required. Balance due 8 weeks before holiday. Bookings must be made in advance. Access or Visa cards accepted by phone or post.
Access: Off the A625 near Sheffield. Trains to Hathersage station. Buses to Sheffield and Hathersage. Centre 200 metres from rail and bus stops.

kitting yourself out

Although beginner cavers can get by on old clothes and wellies, if you are planning to get into the sport seriously, spending long hours wet and chilled, you need specialized kit.

Caving suits come in various forms, but almost always involve an under- and an oversuit, similar in design to a diver's dry suit kit, i.e. a furry undersuit inside a rubber outer skin. Daleswear, Bat Products and Caving Supplies all produce good caving suits. Expect to pay about £80 for the inner and outer suits together.

checklist

- ✔ *caving suit*
- ✔ *caving boots*
- ✔ *caving helmet*
- ✔ *knee and elbow pads*
- ✔ *lamp*
- ✔ *Abseil harness, ropes and accessories*

Helmets, made by Lion or Petzl, cost around £25. Lamps, which fit onto the helmet, cost about £25 for an old lead acid model, or £70–100 for the much brighter, more reliable new Essex series.

Boots, although generally referred to as caving boots, are not specialized. Good army combat boots will do fine – but not fancy hiking boots, which will get messed up underground. Make sure your army boots have good ankle support and grip, as well as no metal studs or lace hooks.

Knee and elbow pads cost about £5–10 per pair and good industrial rubber gloves around a fiver. When it comes to abseil harness and equipment, you have to go to a climbing store or specialist caving shop. Petzl is a popular brand name among cavers, but you need very specific models of harness and a more static type of rope than is used by climbers. Seek advice before you buy. Expect to pay over £70 for top-of-the-range ropes and harness. Specialist caving shops are hard to find – they tend to be localized. Buxton in Derbyshire has a few, as does Ingleton in the Yorkshire Dales. Red Dragon in Abercave, near Swansea, South Wales, is also good, as is Bat Products in Wells, Somerset.

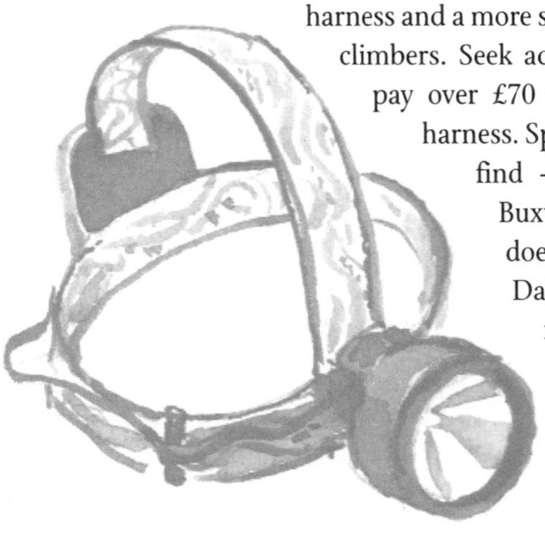

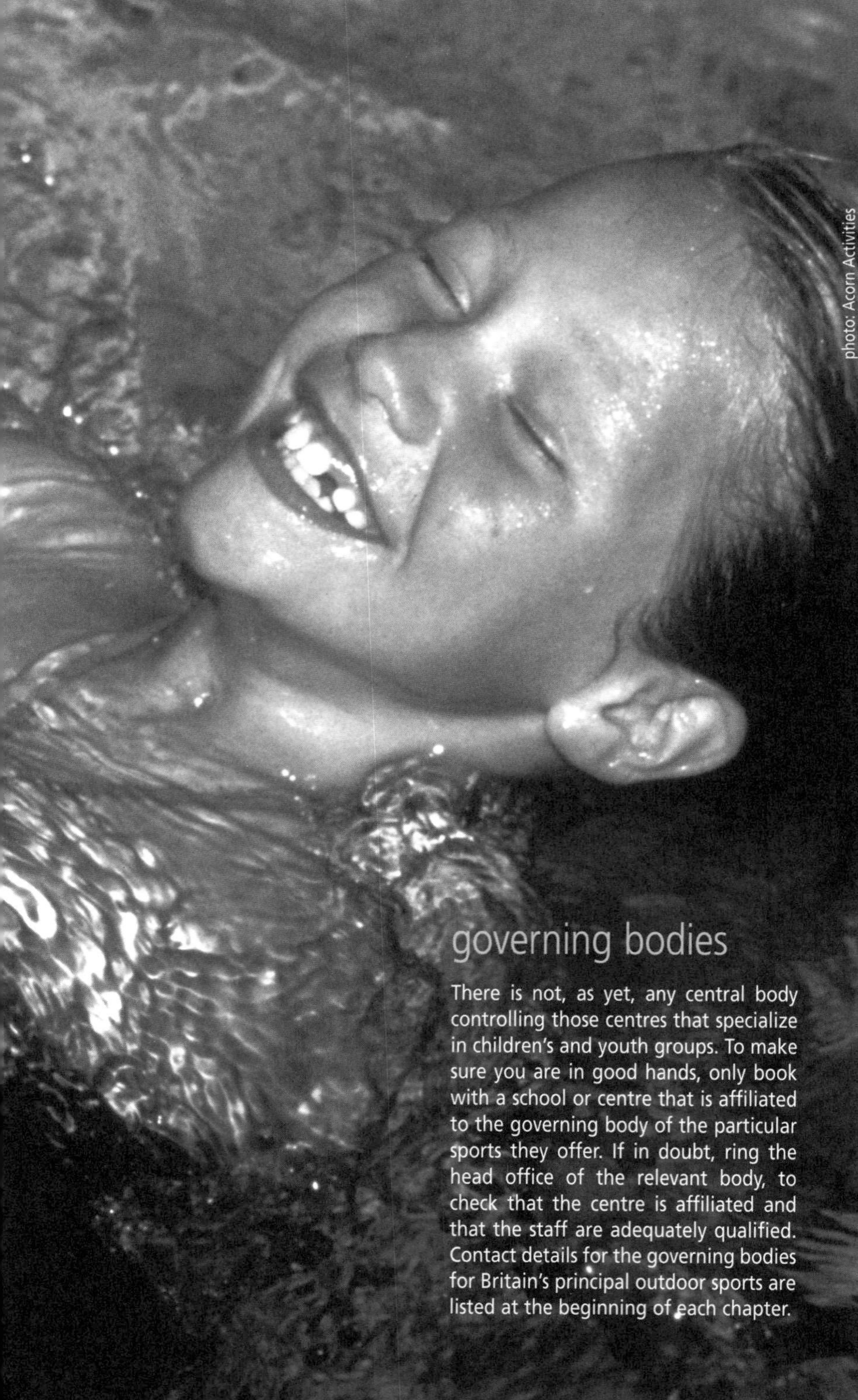

photo: Acorn Activities

governing bodies

There is not, as yet, any central body controlling those centres that specialize in children's and youth groups. To make sure you are in good hands, only book with a school or centre that is affiliated to the governing body of the particular sports they offer. If in doubt, ring the head office of the relevant body, to check that the centre is affiliated and that the staff are adequately qualified. Contact details for the governing bodies for Britain's principal outdoor sports are listed at the beginning of each chapter.

child & youth sports

Although only a few action/adventure sports, such as paragliding or parachuting, actively preclude children from participating, we thought it worth having a section for those centres that cater for children and teenagers specifically, rather than incidentally. Most of these are multi-activity centres, offering packages of several sports over several days – usually a mixture of canoeing, climbing and abseiling, mountain skills and, where possible, wildlife watching. Many of these centres are run by local councils and will cater for special needs and/or disabled children. At least one private centre offers an even greater degree of care if necessary, running courses of up to 6 weeks for children needing a complete change of environment. Apart from the multi-activity courses, a great favourite with children is horse sports – riding camps for children who can already ride, or pony trekking for the complete novice. While there are many riding and trekking centres listed in the Horse Sports section of the guide, a few that cater entirely for children are listed here.

As far as possible we have tried to give full information regarding school groups, supervision and special needs. However, those intending to put together more serious outdoor adventure expeditions for under-16s should contact the Young Explorers' Trust (tel 01628 861 027), which is affiliated to the Royal Geographical Society, 1 Kensington Gore, London SW7 2AR. They can help with putting together trips, whether in Britain or abroad.

selected centres

arethusa venture centre

Lower Upnor
Rochester
Kent
ME2 4XB
Tel (01634) 711 566 / 719 933
Fax (01634) 295 905

Multi-Activity

Catering specifically for special-needs children and youth groups, Arethusa offer week, weekend and day courses in various kinds of activities, with a choice between accommodation at the centre or camping. The centre employs 5 full-time instructors and varying numbers of freelancers as needed. Tuition is generally aimed at beginner level, but can be tailored to suit higher levels of experience.

The activities on offer are: dinghy sailing, canoeing, swimming, climbing, orienteering and archery. Arethusa works with the Shaftesbury group of children's homes and has been operating for 20 years. Accompanied children from as young as 6 can be catered for.

Season: Open all year.
Accommodation: 3 large buildings house up to 90 youths. Camping also available.
Food: Full board included; vegetarian and special diets catered for upon request.
Children: Must be 6 or older. Adventure playground, climbing wall, pool on-site.
Disabled Facilities: Special-needs groups welcome. All equipment, accommodation and vehicles adapted for special-needs use.
Insurance: Clients need their own personal insurance cover.
Safety: Medical centre close by. Staff trained in first aid and rescue skills.
Affiliations: British Canoe Union (BCU); British Mountaineering Council; Royal Yachting Association (RYA).
Tariffs: Prices include full-board accommodation, instruction and use of equipment. Prices vary according to season (lowest from December to January, highest from April to August). 5-day (weekdays) visit: £60–105; 2½-day weekend visit: £45–60; multi-activity day visits (instruction only): £12. Prices higher for groups of less than 25; contact centre for details. Discounts for camping option.
Booking: 25% non-refundable deposit required. Balance due at end of stay. Bookings must be made in advance.
Access: Take the A2 to the A228 (or the M2 to the A289) to Lower Upnor. Trains to Strood station; pick-ups can be arranged by centre.

bowles outdoor centre

Eridge Green
Tunbridge Wells
Kent
TN3 9LW
Tel (01892) 665 665
Fax (01892) 669 556

Multi-Activity

Situated conveniently close to London, Bowles specializes in taking school groups (9 years old and upwards), teaching them canoeing, skiing (on a dry slope), orienteering and climbing, almost all within the same complex – with camping excursions to local tracts of woodland and outdoor canoeing on the Medway. The facilities are impressive – apart from the large, floodlit dry slope, there is a big indoor pool with a water jet to simulate white-water canoeing, and a 50ft natural sandstone outcrop for learning to climb.

Children's groups can book in for weekend, long-weekend and 5-day courses under the supervision of 12 full-time outdoor instructors. All equipment is provided, the centre has an exemplary safety record and can even offer training towards the Duke of Edinburgh's Award (the Duke is patron of the centre).

Children: Minimum age 9. Special rates for student and youth groups. 1 free adult place for every 10 children.
Disabled Facilities: Range of adapted equipment is available. Lodge has full wheelchair access and a lift.
Affiliations: Artificial Slope Ski Instructors; British Association of Ski Instructors; BCU; British Orienteering Federation; English Ski Council.
Tariffs: Instruction in canoeing, climbing, skiing or orienteering is given to organized youth or student groups. There is one fixed charge per group (maximum 12 members): 3-hour daytime instruction session: £108; 2-hour evening instruction session: £82. Residential courses (including instruction, accommodation and full board) are also available – 2 days: £78 per person; 3 days: £88 per person; 5 days: £159 per person. (Surcharges apply to groups with less than 10 members. Cheaper rates from September to February.)

See Skiing (p. 372) for full details.

bradwell outdoor education centre

Bradwell Waterside
Southminster
Essex
CM0 7QY
Tel (01621) 776 256
Fax (01621) 776 378

Dinghy Sailing and Canoeing

This Essex–County–Council–run centre specializes in residential courses for organized youth groups of the 13–19 age group. Rather than being merely centre-based, Bradwell's course holidays try to get the groups out as much as possible, with camping and canoeing weeks and offshore sailing weekends, where each member of the group has to pull their own weight. The centre employs up to 10 instructors in the height of the summer season, so instructor-to-student ratios are kept as low as possible. All levels of competence can be catered for, with 7 hours of tuition per day. Because the centre is run by the local council, it is subsidized and can afford to keep its prices low – see Tariffs overleaf for full details.

Season: April to October.
Accommodation: 40 dorm beds available.
Food: Full board included for residential courses.
Other Activities: Canoeing (see p. 20); Sailing (p. 340).
Children: Minimum age 9, 13 if unaccompanied. Centre specializes in youth instruction.
Disabled Facilities: None.
Insurance: Clients should provide personal insurance cover.
Safety: Staff trained in first aid, safety boat on hand.
Affiliations: BCU; Essex County Council Youth Service; RYA.
Tariffs: 5-day sailing or kayaking course (includes tuition, equipment and full-board accommodation): £78; day activity (includes tuition and equipment): £11.
Booking: Non-refundable deposit required. Bookings normally made in advance, but bookings up to 48 hours in advance accepted if space available.
Access: Off the B1021 north of Southminster at Bradwell Waterside. Contact centre for public transport information.

---

calshot activities centre

Calshot Spit
Fawley
Southampton
Hampshire
S04 1BR
Tel (01703) 892 077
Fax (01703) 891 267

Sailing, Windsurfing, Canoeing, Multi-Activity

Calshot run a variety of special youth courses for 12–16-year-olds in sailing, windsurfing and canoeing, as well as multi-activity holidays in age groupings of 9–11, 12–13, and 14–16 which introduce kids to land-based activities such as dry-slope skiing, climbing, rifle shooting, orienteering, archery, and some water sports too. Alternatively there's a special 'investigating nature' course, teaching about local habitats and wildlife, with field trips into the New Forest and to the shoreline and waters of the Solent.

The children and youth holidays all begin on a Sunday and last until the following Friday. Transport can be provided from Southampton railway station free of charge but must be requested on the booking form. Some of the courses have an optional weekend extension.

The kids are kept entertained in the evenings with table tennis, 5-a-side football, badminton or a barbecue. At the end of the holiday there's a disco. Calshot does ask that, as most of the holidays include water sports, any child coming on holiday should be able to swim 50 metres.

These holidays are not aimed at special-needs children.

Children: Special courses for 9–16-year-olds offered. Birthday parties can be arranged. 1 free adult place for every 12 children belonging to organized groups. Unaccompanied children accepted on adventure holidays and some weekends.
Affiliations: BCU; RYA.
Tariffs: The centre offers a wide range of youth courses. Sample tariffs are provided here; contact centre for full information. Course fees are either non-residential (NR) (includes tuition, equipment, lunch and dinner), or residential (R) (includes tuition, equipment, accommodation and full board): 2-day sailing course: £40 (NR); weekend windsurfing course: £60 (NR) / £72 (R); weekend canoe course: £60 (NR) / £72 (R); 1-week multi-activity course: £165 (NR) / £225 (R).

See Windsurfing (p. 456) for full details.

cornwall outdoors – outdoor education centres

Dalvenie House
County Hall
Truro
Cornwall
TR1 3AY
Tel (01872) 322 448
Fax (01872) 323 806

Multi-Activity

Cornwall Outdoors runs 5 county-council-backed outdoor education centres at different locations in the county, catering mainly for organized school groups. Activities on offer are: dinghy sailing, canoeing, hill and coastal walking, cycling, eco-studies, orienteering, treasure hunting, and introductory horse riding. Groups can use the centres for day courses or residential 3–5-night breaks. You can also choose between full board and self-catering.

Between them the centres have a pool of 28 qualified and experienced instructors who can tailor tuition to suit the child's or teenager's level of experience in any given activity or sport. Cornwall Outdoors has been running for 15 years.

Season: Open all year.
Accommodation: Dormitory accommodation.
Food: Full board and self-catering options. Special diets by arrangement.
Children: Courses designed for school groups from 6–20 years old. 1 free leader place for every 10 students.
Disabled Facilities: Almost all activities can be adapted for disabled youths; contact centre for details.
Insurance: Clients should provide personal insurance cover.
Safety: Staff trained in first aid.
Affiliations: BCU; RYA.
Tariffs: Prices are per person and vary according to centre and whether or not full board is included. Some examples are: multi-activity weekend at Delaware Outdoor Education Centre (full board): £32; 5-day multi-activity week at Roseland Outdoor Education Centre (self-catering): £71; 5 days' accommodation only at Tehidy Woods Camp (self-catering): £15.
Booking: 10% non-refundable deposit required. Bookings must be made well in advance.
Access: Group transport to centres can be arranged; contact centre for more details.

courtland centre

Kingsbridge
Devon
TQ7 4BN
Tel (01548) 550 227
Fax (01548) 550 675

Multi-Activity

Courtland caters mostly for organized school groups (children from 9–16), but will also accept college groups at a slight additional charge. Abseiling, archery, assault courses, initiative tests, climbing, canoeing, sailing, water skiing, caving, mountain navigation and camping are all taught as part of a 1–5-day youth activity holiday. There is also a field studies centre for groups wanting a more ecological slant to their activities, with marine and terrestrial fieldwork offered, whether to fit in with an existing school curriculum, or as part of a general introduction to looking at the natural world.

The courses can be tailored to your requirements. The centre has been running for 21 years and can accommodate up to 70 people, though the individual groups are kept as small as possible.

Season: February to November.
Accommodation: 9 twin rooms, 4 single rooms, 54 dorm beds.
Food: Full board included.
Children: Centre has a variety of courses designed for school and youth groups aged 9–15.
Disabled Facilities: None.
Insurance: Personal insurance for clients can be arranged through centre.
Safety: All staff are trained in first aid.
Affiliations: BCU; British Water Ski Federation; RYA.
Tariffs: Prices include full-board accommodation, tuition and use of equipment. VAT is not included. Prices vary according to season; check with centre for full price listings. 2-day multi-activity weekend: £78–90; 2½-day multi-activity long weekend: £105–118; 3½-day multi-activity mid-week: £142–165; 4-day multi-activity short week: £176–203; 5-day multi-activity budget week: £206–236. (Supplementary charges for riding, water skiing, windsurfing or sailing).
Booking: £10–20 per person non-refundable deposit required at initial booking. 30% of full cost due within 12 weeks, balance due 4 weeks before arrival. Cancellation charges are as follows: less than 4 months in advance – 40%; less than 3 months – 50%; less than 2 months – 75%; less than 1 month – 100%. Late bookings sometimes accepted if space available.
Access: Off the B3194 near Kingsbridge. Nearest mainline station is Totnes on Paddington/Penzance line. Nearest main bus station is Plymouth, branch buses run into Kingsbridge. Centre will arrange pick-up from stations; charge depends on location and group size.

---

cumbria outdoors

Hawse End Centre
Portinscale
Keswick
Cumbria
CA12 5UE
Tel (017687) 72816
Fax (017687) 75108

Multi-Activity

Cumbria Outdoors run 3 different centres – Hawse End, Fellside and Scarness – catering mainly for school and youth groups during the school year, but with adult groups also accepted. During school breaks there are holidays for unaccompanied children, and family holidays as well. Courses and holidays are tailored for children and teenagers between the ages of 9 and 20, with varying levels of tuition available – according to the child or teenager's level of experience in any given sport. Groups are divided by age into 9–14-year-olds and 15–20-year-olds. The centres have been running for about 20 years. Day courses, 2-night, 4-night and week-long holidays are all available with dinghy sailing, canoeing, rafting, climbing, caving and camping as the activities.

Season: Open all year.
Accommodation: Hawse End centre is a large Victorian country house with 48 dorm beds. The Hawse End cottage is a newer building with 24 beds. Fellside centre is in a converted mansion with 38 beds, while Scarness campsite on Bassenthwaite Lake has 40 spaces. Each centre has 2 double rooms for group leaders.
Food: Full board included; vegetarian and special diets catered for.
Children: Centre specializes in courses for school and youth groups of all ages. Many activities specially for small children, e.g. teddy bears' picnic. During school breaks, holidays for families and unaccompanied children.

Disabled Facilities: None.
Insurance: Clients need personal accident insurance cover.
Safety: All instructors qualified in first aid.
Affiliations: BCU; British Cave Research Association; Council for Northern Caving Clubs; Cumbria Association of Residential Providers; Cumbria Tourist Board; Mountain Leaders Training Board; National Trust; Northern Council for Outdoor Education, Training and Recreation; RYA.
Tariffs: Prices include tuition, equipment and full-board accommodation. Family multi-activity holiday (5 days / 4 nights): £158; multi-activity holidays for children 9–14 (6 days / 5 nights): £190. Prices for groups vary depending on group numbers and activities chosen, but an example is – youth group holiday (4 days): £104 per person.
Booking: £50 holding fee required, non-refundable. £20 per person deposit due 8 weeks in advance, balance paid on completion of course. Cancellation charges: less than 3 months' notice, 50% of total; less than 2 months notice, 75% of total; less than 1 month, 100% of total. Late bookings accepted if space available.
Access: Off the A66 at Portinscale. Trains to Penrith, buses to Keswick. Centre can arrange pick-up from station (charge depends on number of people).

---

grenville house

Berry Head Road
Brixham
Devon
TQ5 9AF
Tel (01803) 852 797

Dinghy Sailing and Multi-Activity

This centre has 6 instructors offering 8 hours of tuition per day, aimed at beginner and recreational level, with a maximum of 12 people per learning group. Dinghy sailing, canoeing, climbing, caving and orienteering are taught as part of a Monday–Friday activity break. The tariffs are low, as Grenville House is part of a large charity – the British Seamen's Boys' Home, which has close ties with the Church of England, as well as the local county council, and caters for many schools in the area. However, holiday courses are open to both boys and girls. Evening activities are also offered – arts, music and drama workshops.

Season: Open all year: water-based activities end March–end October; land-based activities available all year.
Accommodation: 2 double rooms, 1 single room, and 42 dorm beds. There is a fixed charge for the hire of Grenville House – £175 per night total. (This cost can be split between multiple groups; contact centre for more details.)
Food: Self-catering, but meals can be arranged. Contact centre for details.
Children: The centre is designed for groups of young people, maximum age 25.
Disabled Facilities: None.
Insurance: Clients must provide their own insurance cover.
Safety: All staff trained in first aid.
Affiliations: BCU; Devon County Council; RYA.
Tariffs: Prices include activity instruction and use of equipment: £42 per morning or afternoon session per each working group of 6 youths (average).
Booking: Non-refundable deposit of £75 required. Cancellation charge of up to 50% of total if notice received less than 12 weeks in advance. All bookings must be made at least one week in advance.
Access: Take the M5 to Exeter, the A380 to Torquay, then the A3022 to Brixham. Trains to BR Paignton station. Buses from Torquay/ Paignton to Brixham. Bus station short walk from centre.

hamble dinghy sailing

Wayfarer Lodge
Welbourn
Lincolnshire
LN5 0QH
Tel & Fax (01400) 273 003

Dinghy Sailing and Multi-Activity

From their head office in Lincolnshire, Hamble run 2 sailing centres, one on the Solent south of Southampton, and another at Falmouth. Children from as young as 5 years old can be catered for on Hamble's special 'Splash Days', which combine an afternoon's picnic for the parents with an introduction for the children to the smallest kind of Optimist dinghies. For kids of 7–12 there are accompanied or unaccompanied Optimist weekends that include the basics of sailing, graduating to races and competitions with small prizes to win. For the 12–16s, the courses aim to get children through their first RYA certificates during a 5-day intensive learning holiday.

Hamble also run multi-activity week-long camps with canoeing, archery, pony trekking, a raft race, wagon ride and a shipwreck during which your craft becomes stranded and you have to build your own den and capture enemy crews also encamped in the woods.

Season: July and August.
Accommodation: Full-board camping available for children's courses (£95 for 5 nights).

Tariffs: Prices include instruction and equipment. 5-day multi-activity course for 7–11-year-olds: £159; 5-day Newtown Creek sailing camps for 10–16-year-olds: £259; 5-day sailing course for under-16s: £169; Optimist sailing weekend for 7–12-year-olds: £69; Optimist sailing day for 5–7-year-olds: £29.

See Sailing (p. 349) for full details.

howtown outdoor centre ltd

Ullswater
Penrith
Cumbria
CA10 2ND
Tel (01768) 486 508
Fax (01768) 486 875

Multi-Activity

Howtown specializes in taking children and youth groups numbering between 10 and 60 and introducing them to a wide variety of outdoor sports. Rock climbing and abseiling, open Canadian canoeing, kayaking, windsurfing, hillwalking, gully scrambling and dinghy sailing are all available. The centre employs up to 16 instructors during the summer, when the youth holidays are run, and can offer more specialized courses in the various sports if the children involved are already experienced, or require specific training. Courses and holidays can run from one day to a week's duration, with single-sex dorm rooms on site.

Season: Open all year. Youth holidays offered in summer only.
Accommodation: 60 dorm beds in 4-person units.
Food: Full board provided; vegetarian and special diets can be catered for.
Other Activities: Canoeing (see p. 23); Climbing and Abseiling (g. 101); Mountain Skills (p. 280); Sailing (p. 350).
Children: Multi-activity and sailing courses offered for unaccompanied youths and children during the summer. School and youth groups welcome year round. Family multi-activity weekends available.
Disabled Facilities: None.
Insurance: Insurance is included for youth holidays and children's courses.
Safety: Staff trained in first aid and mountain rescue.
Affiliations: BCU; Mountain Leaders Training Board; RYA.
Tariffs: Prices include tuition, equipment, insurance and full-board accommodation. VAT is not included. 7-day multi-activity holiday: £195; 1-day introductory sailing course: £45; 5-day sailing course: £250; 7-day sailing course: £295. Family multi-activity weekend (includes VAT): £47 (child), £70 (adult). Group and unemployed discounts available.
Booking: Deposit required, non-refundable. Balance due 8 weeks in advance of course. Cancellation charge if notice received 4–8 weeks in advance: 80% of total; 100% of total if less than 4 weeks in advance. Bookings normally made in advance; late bookings accepted if space available. Visa cards accepted.
Access: South-west of Penrith off the M6. Trains and buses to Penrith; pick-ups from station can be arranged.

killowen outdoor education centre

Killowen Point
Rostrevor
Newry
County Down
BT34 3AF
Northern Ireland
Tel (016937) 38297

Multi-Activity

Killowen, a coastal centre on the border between Northern Ireland and Eire, offers child and youth group courses/ holidays through the summer. Only organized groups can be catered for, not unaccompanied children. The activities taught are dinghy sailing, kayaking, rock climbing and abseiling, and hill walking. Accommodation is in a bunkhouse dormitory and courses include full board (special diets by arrangement), with equipment and instruction as well. Courses last either 3 or 7 days – the 7-day option being a week-long climbing and camping trip to various crags in Northern Ireland and Eire.

Tariffs: 3-day youth break: £30–50; 7-day Irish rock holiday: £60.

See Sailing (p. 352) for full details.

kindrogan field centre

Enochdhu
By Blairgowrie
Perthshire & Kinross
PH10 7PG
Scotland
Tel (01250) 881 286
Fax (01250) 881 433

Eco-Field Studies

Kindrogan occupies an old Victorian manor in Perthshire & Kinross and runs a variety of eco-related courses throughout the year, aimed at everyone – from university level to people simply wanting to identify fungi. Their children and youth courses can be tailored for both school and college groups and for unaccompanied children. Families are also welcome. Children from as young as 6 years old can attend the courses such as Games with Nature, which explores the woods over a weekend in spring, while the Young People's Walks for 10-year-olds and up combine natural history with learning safe hillwalking techniques. Primary and secondary school biology, geology and geography courses are also offered. Accommodation and full board are offered, but clients can arrange their own accommodation nearby as long as they have transport to get to and from the centre.

Tariffs: Prices include tuition, full-board accommodation, and transport during course. Games with Nature (6–10 years, 3 days): £43; Young People's Walks (10–13 years, 3 days): £52; Outdoor Adventure (13+, 3 days): £58; family holiday week: £240 (adults), £180 (children 6+).

See Eco-Sports (p. 147) for full details.

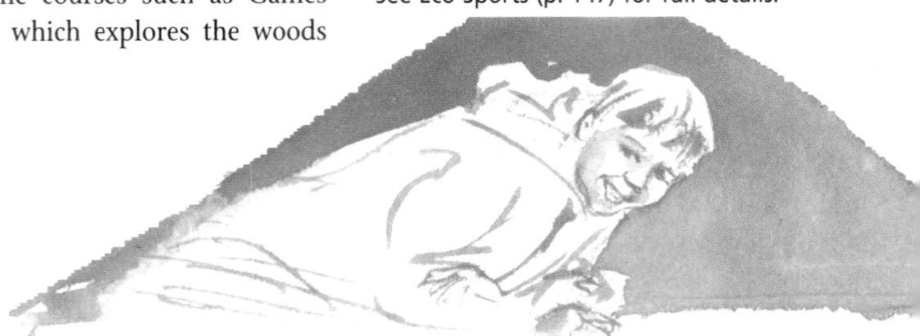

lyncombe lodge

Churchill
Nr Bristol
Avon
BS19 5PQ
Tel (01934) 852 335
Fax (01934) 853 314

Horse-Riding, Multi-Activity

Lyncombe Lodge started life as a riding school about 20 years ago, blossomed into a residential riding centre and now operates as a multi-activity centre, still with a very good riding stables and specializing in unaccompanied children and youth holidays. Situated on a wooded hillside in the Mendips of Somerset and Avon, the centre offers either riding-only holidays for kids of all levels of experience and ability, or multi-activity holidays that include riding, archery, dry-slope skiing, climbing and abseiling, caving in nearby Wookey Hole and Cheddar Gorge, clay pigeon shooting, quad biking and canoeing – certainly enough to keep your kid out of trouble for a week or two. The atmosphere is relaxed but professional – they've been running children's holidays for a long time. For improving your child's riding, this has to be one of the best places in the country.

Children: Special holidays for unaccompanied children ages 6–16.
Affiliations: British Horse Society; British Ski Slope Operators Association.
Tariffs: Prices include accommodation, half-board, equipment and instruction; prices vary according to season. 6-day multi-activity holiday: £255–295 + VAT; 6-day riding holiday: £225–265 + VAT; 2-day riding, skiing or multi-activity breaks: £90 + VAT.

See Horse Sports (p. 217) for full details.

medina valley centre

Dodnor Lane
Newport
Isle of Wight
PO30 5TE
Tel (01983) 522 195
Fax (01983) 825 962

Dinghy Sailing

This is a sailing centre with a difference – a Christian sailing centre. It's very successful – having been open since 1963 – and while its requirements for good behaviour might put off would-be buccaneers, it is nonetheless a well-regarded sailing school. Its junior sailing courses are open both to school groups and unaccompanied children and are run over a week, for groups between the ages of 8 and 16. The holiday courses go from beginner level in Seastars and Optimist boats (8–12) through to RYA Level 5 and beyond into advanced sailing of fast Topper craft (12–16).

Children: Minimum age 8; unaccompanied children must be at least 14. Special youth courses available. Games facilities at centre.
Tariffs: Prices include instruction, equipment, accommodation and full board (unless otherwise noted). 5-day sailing course: £237 (under 16); 5-day non-residential sailing course (includes lunch): £152 (under 16).

See Sailing (p. 354) for full details.

mill on the brue activity centre

Trendle Farm
Bruton
Somerset
BA10 0BA
Tel (01749) 812 307
Fax (01749) 812 706

Multi-Activity

Mill on the Brue offer children's holidays covering a range of activities, with up to 16 instructors in mid-season and 7–8 hours of tuition per day. Canoeing, archery, grass skiing, climbing and abseiling are all offered. The courses/holidays are either residential or by the day. Unaccompanied children, school groups and families can all be catered for. Special courses for teenagers are run out on the Isle of Mull. The Mill on the Brue have over 14 years of experience in running children's holidays and will spot talent where they can, offering the child the opportunity to gain qualifications in whichever sport he or she is best at. There is also the opportunity for children to make their own videos of the holiday and to spend nights camped out in the open. The family-run centre won the National Heartbeat Award for Healthy Eating in 1992 and 1993. All food is home-cooked.

Season: Open all year.
Accommodation: Dorm beds available in a large Victorian farmhouse and converted barn.
Food: Full board included; vegetarian and special diets catered for upon request.
Other Activities: Canoeing (see p. 25); Climbing and Abseiling (p. 103); Orienteering (p. 180).
Children: Courses designed specifically for unaccompanied children (in Somerset) and adolescents (in Scotland).
Disabled Facilities: Special-needs groups can be accommodated, but overnight accommodation is not wheelchair-accessible. Contact centre for more details.
Insurance: Personal holiday insurance can be arranged through centre.
Safety: All staff trained in first aid; centre has written safety policy.
Affiliations: British Activity Holiday Association; BCU; National Association of Outdoor Education; Royal Society for the Prevention of Accidents; West Country and Southern Tourist Boards.
Tariffs: Prices include full-board accommodation, tuition and equipment use. Multi-activity course for children (8–14) in Somerset: £279 per week (16 July–26 August), £236 per week (27 August–2 September); day courses (tuition and equipment only): £20 per day; 10-day multi-activity week for adolescents (14–17) in Scotland: £319.
Booking: Deposit required (amount variable). Balance due 8 weeks in advance of holiday. 50% charge if bookings cancelled. Late bookings accepted if space available.
Access: Off the A359 at Bruton. Trains and buses to Bruton. Free pick-ups from Gillingham in Dorset for trains to Waterloo and Exeter. Taxis from airports can be arranged.

newlands adventure centre

Stair
Keswick
Cumbria
CA12 5UF
Tel & Fax (017687) 78463

Multi-Activity

The Newlands Valley is one of the most beautiful parts of Lakeland, and the Newlands centre operates from an old stone farm with 200 acres of its own land, plumb in the middle of the valley. Scrambling and mountain walking, mountain biking, rock climbing, canoeing and farm and environmental studies are all offered as part of a multi-activity programme running over 2–7 days. The centre offers about 8 hours of tuition per day with evening activities on top and employs up to 16 fully qualified and experienced instructors in the height of summer (this keeps instructor-to-student ratios low – between 1:4 and 1:8). Courses are fully residential and include food and accommodation, equipment, local transport and tuition.

Season: Open all year.
Accommodation: 130 dorm beds plus separate rooms for group leaders.
Food: Full board included. Vegetarian and special diets catered for.
Children: Centre is designed for youth and school groups. Minimum age 8. 1 free adult place for every 10 children.
Disabled Facilities: None.
Insurance: Clients should provide personal insurance cover if desired.
Safety: All staff trained in first aid; first aid facilities on-site.
Affiliations: BCU; British Orienteering Federation; Cumbria Tourist Board.
Tariffs: Prices vary between low season (1 September–30 April) and high season (1 May 1–31 August). Multi-activity courses include full-board accommodation, tuition and use of equipment. VAT must be added. 2 nights: £77 / £84; 3 nights: £109 / £119; 5 nights: £165 / £182; 7 nights: £208 / £231.
Booking: Deposit of £15 per person required. Bookings normally made in advance; late bookings accepted if space available.
Access: Off the A66 near Portinscale. Trains to Penrith, buses to Keswick. Pick-ups from station can be arranged by centre.

outward bound

PO Box 1219
Windsor
Berkshire
SL4 1XR
Tel (01753) 731 005
Fax (01753) 810 666
Outward Bound Scotland, Loch Eil
Tel (01397) 772 866
Outward Bound Wales, Aberdovey
Tel (01654) 767 464
Outward Bound Ullswater, Penrith
Tel (017684) 86347

Multi-Activity

Outward Bound's 3 centres offer superb multi-activity weeks combining canoeing, dinghy sailing, rock climbing and abseiling, hillwalking and orienteering. Both unaccompanied children and school groups are welcome, with children divided into age groups of 11–14, 14–15 and 16–17. Many of the courses are affiliated to the Duke of Edinburgh's Award scheme, with certificates being offered right up to gold standard. There is also a variety of specialist outdoor courses open to over-14s. Ring the central office in Windsor for full details.

Affiliations: RYA.
Tariffs: All prices include tuition, equipment, full-board accommodation, and transport during programme. Prices do not include VAT. Introduction to Dinghy Sailing course (Wales, 5 days): £250; Water Skills course (Wales, 7 days): £325; Introductory Water course (Wales, Ullswater, weekend): £130; Viking Wayfarer expedition (Scotland, 12 days, 16–24): £399; West Coast expedition (Scotland, 7 days, 25+): £325. Sailing is also included as part of the multi-activity holidays offered by centres (for 14–24-year-olds unless otherwise stated). 7-day multi-activity programme (Scotland, Wales, Ullswater): £249; 12-day multi-activity programme (Wales, Ullswater): £399; Outward Bound Classic (Scotland, Wales, Ullswater, 19 days): £499–599; weekend breaks (Wales, Ullswater, 25+): £130; 7-day programme (Scotland, Wales, Ullswater, 25+, 50+): £325; 12-day programme (Wales, Ullswater, 25+): £470.

See Walking (p. 426) for full details.

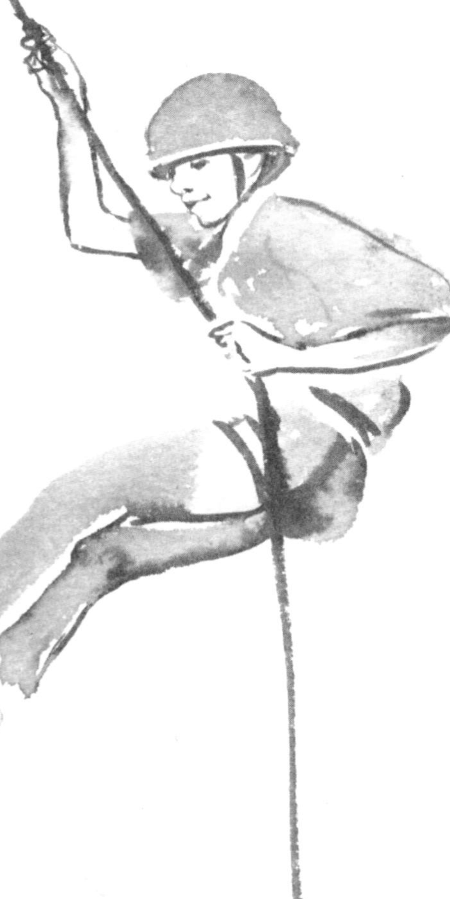

pgl adventure holidays

Alton Court
Penyard Lane
Ross-on-Wye
Hereford & Worcester
HR9 5NR
Tel (01989) 763 511
Fax (01989) 765 451

Multi-Activity

Catering for children and youth groups between the ages of 8 and 16, PGL offer both beginner and advanced tuition in a variety of outdoor sports. It's up to the children to decide whether they want to keep trying different things or concentrate on one or two sports for the time they're on holiday. The activity groups are divided into 3 according to age: 6–9, 8–13 and 12–18. PGL run 13 different centres around the country – in Perthshire & Kinross, Lancashire, Shropshire/Hereford & Worcester, the Welsh Borders, Oxfordshire, Devon and Surrey. They also run children's trips abroad in Normandy, the Dordogne, the Alps and the Mediterranean. A full range of activities is on offer – pony trekking, archery, quad biking, climbing and abseiling, rafting, farming, assault courses, canoeing, caving, windsurfing, surfing, land yachting, mountain biking, falconry, skiing, go-karting, motorbike scrambling – even learning to drive.

There's also a choice of various durations for the holidays – 2 weeks, a week, 4 days, 3 days or a weekend. Unaccompanied children, school groups and families are all welcome – basically things can be tailored to suit your needs.

Season: March to September.
Accommodation: Various centres around the UK offering dormitory accommodation, ranging from tents to converted farmhouses.
Food: All meals provided. Vegetarian and special diets catered for upon request.
Children: Different courses target different age groups, from 6 to 18.
Disabled Facilities: None.
Insurance: Clients must purchase holiday insurance through PGL, £24 per week.
Safety: All instructors trained in first aid.
Affiliations: British Activity Holiday Association; BCU; British Horse Society; British Surfing Association; RYA.
Tariffs: Prices include instruction, equipment and full-board accommodation. A very large selection of courses is available; some sample tariffs are: 1-week multi-activity holiday for 8–11-year-olds at Boreatton Park: £199; multi-activity weekend for 12–16-year-olds at Brecon Beacons campsite: £79; motocross week for 8–13-year-olds in Perth: £269; riding week for 8–13-year-olds at Hay-on-Wye: £289; water sports weekend for 12–18-year-olds near Brecon: £79.
Booking: £25–65 non-refundable deposit required. Balance due 12 weeks before start of holiday. Cancellation charges: 29–56 days in advance: 30% of total; 15–28 days: 45% of total; 1–14 days: 60% of total. Access, Visa and American Express cards accepted. Late bookings accepted if space available.
Access: Depends on site chosen. Escorted travel can be arranged from 27 pick-up points nationwide, and transport to and from railway stations near to centres is available. Charges for these services vary according to location; contact PGL for more details.

pugneys country park

City of Wakefield MDC
Asdale Road
Wakefield
West Yorkshire
WF2 7EQ
Tel (01924) 302 360
Fax (01924) 302 362

Dinghy Sailing, Canoeing, Windsurfing, Multi-Activity Packages

Pugneys Country Park houses one of Britain's best-equipped water sports centres. Courses for children and youth groups are offered in dinghy sailing, open Canadian canoeing and kayaking, windsurfing, or as multi-activity breaks, spiced up with treasure hunting, swimming and games. The specific courses start with 'taster' evenings for those who want to give one of the centre's sports a try, and graduate through all the RYA and BCU's basic certificates (Levels 1–3). Both courses and multi-activity breaks last for 14 hours, split into 2 sessions over both days of a weekend. The centre has no accommodation. They can help you to find local accommodation but you will need your own transport to get to and from the centre. Special-needs groups are welcome.

Children: Specialized junior courses in windsurfing (8–16), canoeing (12–16) and sailing (11–14, 15–18). Multi-activity course for 10–15-year-olds.
Affiliations: BCU; RYA.
Tariffs: All prices include tuition and use of equipment. Multi-activity course (5 3-hour sessions): £35. Introductory windsurfing sessions (2 half-days): £23; RYA windsurfing junior certificate course (5 3-hour sessions): £54; junior windsurfing improvers' coaching session (8 hours): £30; junior introductory canoe sessions (2 half-days): £18; BCU Junior 1 Star Award course (12½ hours): £31; junior RYA Stage 1 & 2 sailing course (20 hours): £38; junior RYA Stage 3 sailing course (40–50 hours): £70; junior improvers' sailing course (40–50 hours): £70. (Note: These are 1996 prices; check with reception for any tariff or course changes.)

See Windsurfing (p. 466) for full details.

queen mary sailsports

Queen Mary Reservoir
Ashford Road
Ashford
Middlesex
TW15 1UA
Tel (01784) 244 776 / 248 881
Fax (01784) 252 772

Sailing, Windsurfing and Canoeing

Children, teenagers and youth/school groups in West London will find this sailsport school convenient to reach. Situated in the industrial suburbs near Hayes, the school runs its courses and fun days on the huge Queen Mary Reservoir. The levels of supervision and tuition are very high, with over 40 qualified instructors and a good safety record. Among the activities offered are sailing or windsurfing courses (mid-week and weekend) with coaching right through to RYA Level 3, and combination days that include both sailing and windsurfing, with kayak canoeing thrown in. Several of these days can be strung together to coach children through their certificates in all 3 sports.

The children's groups are aimed at ages 9–13, and the teenage groups at 14–18, with no mingling of the groups. Unfortunately the school does not take unaccompanied children, and the courses are non-residential. However, school and college groups are most welcome, whether for single days or regular sessions to be included as part of a curriculum.

Children: Minimum age 8. Special courses offered for juniors (8–13) and teens (13–18).
Affiliations: RYA.
Tariffs: Prices include tuition and use of equipment. RYA junior taster days: £25; junior and teen waterfront weeks: £110; junior and teen RYA sailing courses (Levels 1–3, Advanced, Racing): £120. RYA junior and teen Level 1 windsurfing courses: £70; RYA teen level 2–3 windsurfing courses: £120. Group and sibling discounts available.

See Windsurfing (p. 467) for full details

---

raasay outdoor centre

Isle of Raasay
By Kyle
Highland
IV40 8PB
Scotland
Tel (01478) 660 266
Fax (01478) 660 200

Multi-Activity

Although some of the Raasay centre's courses are open to adults too, unaccompanied children and school groups are a speciality. The centre has been open for 11 years and can accommodate up to 60 kids at a time. Multi-activity breaks are offered: climbing and abseiling, windsurfing, dinghy sailing, kayaking, orienteering, archery and hill walking. These are usually weekly packages – there's a free space for an unaccompanied adult if you book for a group of 7 kids or more. The minimum age for a children's/youth holiday is 9 and the maximum 16.

Separate multi-activity and sailing/windsurfing courses are also offered for adults, generally over a week, costing around £330. Alternative workshops and courses in massage, healing and movement may also be arranged, at anything between £30 and £300.

Season: March to October.
Accommodation: Single, twin, family, bunk, dormitory and camping available.
Food: Large and small dining rooms serving breakfast, lunch and evening meals. Café on site serving snacks and hot meals. All dietary requirements catered for.
Children: Programme designed for children under 16. Minimum age for unaccompanied children is 9. 1 free adult place for groups of 7 children or more.
Disabled Facilities: Ground floor is wheelchair-accessible. Sports can often be arranged through centre.
Insurance: Clients are covered by centre's insurance.
Safety: Emergencies dealt with by island doctor and nurse. Helicopter or ferry services available for transportation during emergencies. All staff hold current first aid certificates.
Affiliations: RYA; Scottish Activity Holiday Association.
Tariffs: Rates include instruction, equipment and full-board accommodation: £279 per week. Workshops or special courses from £30–300. Group discounts available on request.
Booking: 25% non-refundable deposit required, balance payable 4 weeks before start date. Full amount lost if cancellation is less than 2 weeks before start date. Visa and Access cards accepted. Although bookings are normally made in advance, late bookings are accepted if space available.
Access: Cars should take the bridge to Skye then the ferry to Raasay (15 minutes). Trains available to Kyle of Lochalsh; regular bus runs to Sconser on Skye. Unaccompanied children will be met at ferry terminal or at train or bus station through prior arrangement.

the ranch

Pensarn Harbour
Llanbedr
Gwynedd
LL45 2HS
Wales
Tel (01341) 241 358
Fax (01341) 241 530

Multi-Activity

Based in a large old farmhouse on the shores of a tidal lagoon, the Ranch enjoys a truly beautiful setting – a tree-covered hill rising behind the stone-built centre to the overhanging mountains of Snowdonia. The sports on offer are circus skills, kayaking, raft building, orienteering, archery, gorge and hill walking. Courses are fully residential and range from a weekend to a week's duration. The Ranch is one of several centres run by a charity called the Northamptonshire Association of Youth Clubs (NAYC) and so is non-profit-making. Preference is given to group bookings from educational establishments, youth organizations, church groups and charities. The philosophy behind the charity is Christian, but it isn't forced down the children's throats. The centre has 17 instructors, 22 years' experience, and a reputation for high standards of tuition.

Season: Open all year.
Accommodation: Accommodation for up to 90 children in 2- to 6-bedded rooms, split between 2 centres. Some en suite rooms available.
Food: Full board included in accommodation tariff. Vegetarian and special diets catered for upon request.
Children: Accompanied groups of children and youths are the centre's speciality. Minimum age 8.
Disabled Facilities: Many years' experience in welcoming disabled groups. Contact centre to discuss special needs.

See Circus Skills (p. 84) for full details.

rockley point sailing school

Hamworthy
Poole
Dorset
BH15 4LZ
Tel (01202) 677 272
Fax (01202) 668 268

Dinghy Sailing

The sheltered waters of Poole harbour make for about as safe an environment as you could wish for in which to learn to sail. Rockley Point, at 20 years old one of Britain's most established sailing schools, run children's dinghy sailing holidays based in fully supervised dorm rooms on the premises, each of which sleeps a maximum of 6 kids. Organized groups and unaccompanied children can both be catered for. When the day's sailing is done, the kids are taken out to the local funfair – Tower Park. This consumer heaven is supplemented by nights spent camping on deserted islands in the bay. The holidays run for 1 to 3 weeks and are open to 10–17-year-olds only. Children can gain their RYA dinghy sailing certificates up to Level 3 during the course.

Season: 29 May–4 June, 3 July–27 August.
Affiliations: RYA – Windsurfing.
Tariffs: 5 nights: £95; 6 nights: £110; 13 nights: £220; 20 nights: £315.

See Sailing (p. 362) for full details.

sealyham activity centre

Wolfscastle
Haverfordwest
Dyfed
SA62 5NF
Wales
Tel & Fax (01348) 840 763

Multi-Activity

With up to 16 instructors during mid-season, Sealyham caters almost exclusively for school or youth club groups, and can accommodate up to 100 children between the ages of 10 and 14, although each learning group is limited to a maximum of 10 kids and 1 instructor. If you book more than 10 children into the centre, a supervising adult can also come along free of charge. Three activities are offered per day, with a choice between pony trekking, orienteering, climbing and abseiling, canoeing, coasteering, dinghy sailing, surfing and archery/air rifle shooting. There is also an environmental studies option.

Season: March to October.
Accommodation: Dormitory accommodation in converted Georgian mansion.
Food: All meals provided.
Children: Course designed for children between 10 and 14. 1 free adult place for every 10 children.
Disabled Facilities: None.
Insurance: Clients are covered by centre's insurance.
Safety: Staff trained in first aid and rescue.
Affiliations: BCU; British Orienteering Federation; Wales Tourist Board.
Tariffs: Fees include 1 week of instruction, equipment and full-board accommodation. Prices vary according to time of year: £159–196.
Booking: £40 non-refundable deposit per person. Balance due 6 weeks before start date. Cancellation charges: 5–8 weeks in advance: 50% of total; 1–4 weeks in advance: 75% of total; less than 1 week: 100% of total. Late bookings accepted if space available.
Access: Off the A40 near Wolfscastle. Trains and buses available to Haverfordwest, pick-ups arranged by centre.

shadwell basin project

Shadwell Pierhead
Glamis Road
London
E1 9EE
Tel (0171) 481 4210
Fax (0171) 481 0624

Canoeing, Climbing, Sailing, Windsurfing, Dragon Boating

This place is something of a godsend for the children of London's East End. Based in the Docklands, with 4 full-time and various part-time instructors, Shadwell operates a youth club. Kids who join have access to multiple activities – sailing, canoeing, climbing, powerboating, windsurfing – alongside specific courses which are designed more for adults (particularly parents) as well as children. Activities are run through the week in the late afternoon and early evening after school. These can be attended either on a random, day-by-day basis, or as part of a structured course gaining BCU, RYA, climbing and other certificates. Training for careers in outdoor instruction is also given, as is competitive coaching. The centre is not residential – kids must come in either accompanied or independently.

Season: Open all year.
Accommodation: Not available.
Food: Light snacks available in vending machines.
Other Activities: Canoeing (see p. 32); Climbing and Abseiling (p. 108); Powerboating (p. 327); Sailing (p. 363).
Children: Club membership designed to allow children to participate in activities for very low cost. Minimum age 9; those under 18 require consent of parent or guardian.
Disabled Facilities: Building and boats are fully accessible for disabled people.
Insurance: Clients must arrange their own insurance cover.
Safety: All staff trained in first aid.
Affiliations: BCU; RYA.
Tariffs: Membership (for those under 18) is charged by sessional or daily rates: £1 per session until £20 is reached, 50p thereafter per session; £1.50 per day until £20 is reached, £1 thereafter per day. Courses focusing on specific sports also available; see chapters listed above under Other Activities.
Booking: Call centre for details.
Access: Short walk from Wapping tube station.

---

shropshire outdoor education centre

Arthog
Gwynedd
LL39 1BX
Wales
Tel & Fax (01341) 250 455

Hillwalking, Kayaking, Open Canadian Canoeing, Rock Climbing and Abseiling, Caving, Gorge Walking and Wave Skiing

Based on the edge of Snowdonia, this centre is run by Shropshire County Council and caters almost exclusively for schools, colleges and other youth institutions of the county. Levels of tuition and safety are high – the centre has been going for 35 years – and groups of as many as 70 people can be catered for on a day, weekend, 5-day or 7-day basis. All levels of competence are accommodated, from beginner to competition standard, and the centre runs a series of certificate courses in the sports it offers, as well as introductory and recreational holidays.

Season: Open all year.

Accommodation: Dormitory accommodation for up to 74 people.
Food: Full board provided. Special diets by arrangement.
Other Activities: Gorge Walking (see p. 183).
Children: Accompanied groups of children from as young as 8 are catered for.
Disabled Facilities: None.
Insurance: Clients must arrange their own personal accident cover.
Safety: All staff trained in first aid.
Affiliations: BCU; Mountain Leaders Training Board; British Mountaineering Council.
Tariffs: These vary with the season and include dormitory accommodation plus all instruction, equipment and food. For peak season (May–July) rates are £66 per weekend and £165 for 5 days. For high season (August–October and March–May) rates are £64 per weekend and £160 for 5 days. For low season (November–February) rates are £60 per weekend and £150 for 5 days.
Booking: Booking should be made 6 weeks in advance with a 25% deposit, refundable only if the course is cancelled on medical grounds (a doctor's certificate will be required as proof). Balance payable on arrival. Late bookings 1 week in advance are possible – ring to see if there are cancellations. Payment by cheque.
Access: The centre is based in the village of Arthog, just south-east of Barmouth on the coast at Cardigan Bay. Those arriving by train should get off at Barmouth or Fairbourne railway stations, from where a pick-up can be arranged.

---

tollymore mountain centre

Bryansford
Newcastle
County Down
BT33 OPT
Northern Ireland
Tel (013967) 22158
Fax (013967) 26155

Rock Climbing and Abseiling, Canoeing, Dinghy Sailing and Multi-Activity

Tollymore is Northern Ireland's best and most professional outdoor centre. It runs several youth courses in specific adventure sports: rock climbing and abseiling, mountaineering, open Canadian canoeing and kayaking, sea canoeing and sailing. These are for able-bodied youths between the ages of 14 and 18 and are run over weekends or 4-day mid-week breaks. The tuition is at introductory level, but can be upgraded if the participants already have some experience.

In addition to these separate courses, Tollymore run their International Youth Camp once a year for 2 weeks in July and August. The emphasis is on dinghy sailing and rock climbing. The weeks are divided between Tollymore and another outdoor centre at Killowen, County Down.

Children: Centre runs special courses for youths between 14 and 18; adult supervision provided.
Tariffs: Instruction, equipment and accommodation (self-catering) are included in prices. 4-day Youth Rock Climbing: £50; 4-day Youth Mountaineering: £32; 3-day Youth Canoeing: £32; 3-day Introduction to Kayaking: £32. Tariffs and bookings for the International Youth Camp through Killowen Outdoor Education Centre, Rostrevor, County Down, tel (016937) 38297.

See Canoeing (p. 35) for full details.

west coast outdoor adventure

63 Swanswood Gardens
Westward Ho!
Devon
EX39 1HR
Tel (01237) 477 637

Speedsailing, Horse-Riding, Surfing, Kayaking, Orienteering, Climbing

West Coast offer 5-day and week-long breaks for unaccompanied and organized groups of children and teenagers. The centre specializes in speedsailing – a kind of windsurfer attached to a skateboard which you sail up and down a beach. Also on offer are riding (for all abilities), surfing, kayaking, orienteering up on the moors behind the centre, rock climbing and abseiling, and surf skiing (also called wave skiing) – a mixture of surfing and kayaking.

Each day at the centre is usually divided between 3 activities. All courses and holidays are fully residential and the centre, which has been going 5 years, aims to keep the instructor-to-student ratio no higher than 1:8.

Season: Open all year.
Accommodation: Clients stay in selected chalets in Westward Ho!
Food: Full board included; vegetarian and special diets catered for.

Other Activities: Land Yachting (p. 236).
Children: Minimum age 8. 1 free adult place for every 8 students in youth group. Unaccompanied children welcome.
Disabled Facilities: None.
Insurance: Clients should provide their own holiday insurance.
Safety: All staff trained in first aid.
Affiliations: British Land Speedsail Association; West Country Tourist Board.
Tariffs: Prices include tuition, equipment and full-board accommodation. Prices vary according to season, and do not include VAT. Land yachting is one of the activities offered in centre's multi-activity packages – weekend holiday: £49–69; 4-day/night holiday: £79–141; 5-day/night holiday: £99–164.
Booking: £35 non-refundable deposit required. Balance due 10 weeks in advance of course. Cancellation charges on sliding scale depending on date of cancellation. Late bookings accepted up to 24 hours in advance if space available.
Access: From Barnstaple, take the A39 then the B3236 to Westward Ho! Trains to Barnstaple, buses to Westward Ho! Pick-ups can be arranged by centre.

west devon outdoor education centre

Martin's Gate
Breton Side
Plymouth
Devon
PL4 0AT
Tel (01752) 253 264
Fax (01752) 255 945

Multi-Activity

This centre offers some of the best children and youth outdoor packages to be found anywhere: dinghy sailing, open Canadian canoeing, kayaking on-site, with rock climbing and caving trips run nearby. Individual groups are limited to 10, with children from 8 to 18 divided into appropriate age groups. The standard of instruction is very high; youth groups above the age of 16 can train for instructor qualifications. You can choose whether to stay at the centre or at a local youth hostel. Organized groups and individual unaccompanied children can be catered for.

The centre employs between 6 and 16 instructors depending on the season, so the courses are flexible – you can concentrate on one sport for anything from a day course to a fortnight or opt for a multi-activity week. All leaders hold national governing body awards and are Devon County Council-registered. Student-to-instructor ratios are kept between 3:1 and 6:1 depending on the sport.

Season: Open all year.
Accommodation: Centre can arrange accommodation at local hostels, from £5–15 per night.
Food: Not available.
Children: Courses designed for children aged 8 and up.
Disabled Facilities: Many sports can be adapted for disabled clients; contact centre for details.
Insurance: Clients are covered by centre's insurance.
Safety: Staff trained in first aid.
Affiliations: BCU; RYA.
Tariffs: Prices include tuition and use of equipment. They vary according to activity; some examples for a group of 12 (maximum) are – half-day sailing: £63; full day kayaking: £126; full day walking: £61; half-day orienteering: £42; multi-activity week (for groups of 10–12): £893 per group. Individuals – £17 per day at peak summer times and £13 per day in autumn and winter.
Booking: 25% deposit required. Deposit lost if cancellation notice received less than 4 weeks in advance. Bookings 2 weeks in advance recommended, but late bookings accepted if space available.
Access: On the A374 at Plymouth. Trains to Plymouth mainline station. Buses to Plymouth, station just opposite centre.

windsport international ltd

Mylor Yacht Harbour
Falmouth
Cornwall
TR11 5UF
Tel (01326) 376 191
Fax (01326) 376 192
Falmouth Centre, Cornwall
Tel (01326) 376 191
Grafham Centre, Cambridgeshire
Tel (01480) 812 288
Rutland Centre, Rutland
Tel (01780) 722 100

Sailing

Windsport is a big concern, running 3 centres, 2 in the East Midlands and 1 in the West Country – at Falmouth, and Grafham and Rutland Waters. Their children and youth programmes mainly offer sailing (dinghies) on its own or combined with a variety of other water sports, the same programme operating at each centre. These are run either by the day or as 5-day packages during which you get around 6 hours of qualified tuition each day, from one of the centres' qualified instructors (each centre has between 4 and 10 depending on the season).

Both unaccompanied children and organized groups can be catered for. All Windsport courses require a minimum age of 8. For sailing courses, children are divided into 2 groups: 8–12 and 13–16.

Children: Must be 8 or older. Special multi-activity courses for children and families. Youth (13–16) and junior (8–12) sailing courses available.

Tariffs: All prices include tuition and use of equipment. A large range of sailing courses is offered; some examples are – Introduction to Cat/Dinghy (1 hour): £25; RYA Cat/Dinghy course Levels 1–5 (5 days): £275; Personal Cat/Dinghy coaching: £25 per hour, £135 per day; Junior Dinghy course (5 days): £245; Youth Cat/Dinghy course (5 days): £245; Professional Cat/Dinghy racing (2 days): £120 per boat; Cat Safari (5 days – Falmouth only): £275. Sailing is also one of the activities offered in the centre's multi-activity packages. 5-day family, child, or adult course: £125 (adult), £95 (child); weekend family course: £48 (adult), £38 (child); 1-day family or child course: £25 (adult), £20 (child); 1-day adult course: £48. Residential packages are also available (including tuition, equipment and accommodation), prices varying according to level of accommodation chosen (hotel, guest house or farmhouse). 5-day courses (6 nights' accommodation): £365–545; 2-day courses (2 nights' accommodation): £220–280. Group discounts available.

See Sailing (p. 366) for full details.

kitting yourself out

Great though the temptation is to make bad jokes about how to kit yourself out with a kid, most of you already know how, and therefore would not find such jokes funny.

From the point of view of specialized equipment, all the centres listed in this chapter supply what is needed as part of the course or holiday package. However, it can be worth buying a few items for your child before sending them off into the void, albeit temporarily. Children going on a riding holiday will be safer if they have a crash cap that really fits; although all riding centres supply hats, they can sometimes be old and ill-fitting. If you buy your offspring his or her own crash cap (make sure it has a Kite mark) with a sure fit, you know that they will be better protected. Such safety does not come cheap – a good child's crash cap costs from £25 to £30.

Similarly, children being sent off into the hills for adventure holidays should be kitted out with effective weatherproof gear. A Gore-Tex jacket (or equivalent) with thermal underwear will do much to prevent hypothermia should your child stray during a hill walking trip, and the right pair of boots, with strong grip and ankle support, is vital. Don't stint on the money for these items – expect to pay about £40 for the jacket and £20–30 for good boots. Adolescents have the advantage of being able to pick up cheap but effective army surplus gear.

If you can prevail upon your child not to wear jeans on the hill – or at least to carry a pair of waterproof over-trousers – then so much the better.

Children going off on sailing courses often come back confirmed enthusiasts. If your child has really got the bug and you live near a sailing club or school, an Optimist child's single-hander dinghy can be bought for about £300 new, or about half that second-hand. Unlike a pony – the other great desire of so many children – an Optimist dinghy requires no feeding and can be easily sold if the child loses interest.

You should be aware of the Association of Sail Training Organizations, a youth-oriented charity that runs crewing courses for older children and teenagers on board large sailing yachts. The courses are run to the requirements of any given group and priority is given to special needs. For more information, contact the Association via the RYA, RYA House, Romsey Road, Eastleigh, Hampshire, SO50 9YA, tel (01703) 629 962, fax (01703) 629 924.

representative body

European Federation of Circus Skills
17 Rue guinard, B 1040 Brussels
Belgium
Tel (0032) 250 2599

Fiddlesticks - photo: Steve Pond

circus skills

juggling
trapeze
unicycling
diabolo
tightrope

clowning
stilt-walking
knife-throwing
whip-cracking and lasso

tumbling
fire-eating & fire-walking
walking on broken glass

Circus is a blanket term that covers a variety of physical skills. Although not all of them are death-defying (for example trapeze or tightrope) they all involve a measure of excitement that qualifies them for inclusion in a guide to adventure sports. Listed in the following chapter are large circus schools where you can learn the full range of skills either for your own interest or vocationally – if you are considering a career in circus or physical theatre – and smaller workshops. Many of the workshops have no fixed location but will travel to a hall or other such venue anywhere in the country.

Circus has a mass appeal in that although the highest level is reserved for able-bodied adults, many of the skills can be learned by just about anyone, regardless of age or physical ability. Skills offered in the following chapter include trapeze, tightrope, tumbling, juggling, diabolo (dancing a two-headed top on a string attached to two sticks, one held in each hand), unicycling, clowning, stilt-walking, knife-throwing, whip-cracking and lasso, clowning, fire-eating and even fire-walking and walking on broken glass – these last two being offered by a travelling workshop.

Other circus skills, such as animal training and horse vaulting do not appear here. For information on these skills contact any working circus (for animal training) or the British Horse Society for horse vaulting (see p. 200). Horse vaulting has taken off as an equestrian sport in its own right over the last few years. No schools operate for horse vaulting as yet; most training is done within riding clubs and pony clubs around the country.

At the time of writing there was no official governing or representative body for circus in Britain, though this looks set to change with the recent resurgence of interest in circus. The only real body is in Europe (listed opposite).

selected centres

circomedia

Unit 14
The Old School House
Kingswood Foundation
Britannia Road
Kingswood
Bristol
Avon
BS15 2DB
Tel (0117) 947 7042

Trapeze, Tightrope, Juggling, Acrobatics, Balance

Based in a refurbished Victorian school and grounds, CircoMedia offer professional training with particular emphasis on blending technique with performance. There are regular weekly sessions in most disciplines, as well as 1-year intensive courses or 11-week foundation courses. A club for children also operates on Saturdays.

Season: Year round.
Accommodation: Not provided.
Food: Not provided.
Children: The Circus Maniacs club meets every Saturday morning for kids of 8 years old and up, but most classes are for 16-year-olds and over.
Disabled Facilities: Contact centre for details.
Insurance: Clients covered by public liability, but should take out their own personal accident policies.
Safety: Staff are first-aid-trained.
Affiliations: None.
Tariffs: Courses in most disciplines are run in hour-long sessions each evening: £10 per person, with 4 people to a class and a half-hour warm-up before the hour's tuition. Specialized 2-day courses: £25–75. For 1-year courses, the cost is £1,200.
Booking: By arrangement – some courses are drop-in. Contact centre for details.
Access: Contact centre for full details.

circus space

Coronet Street
Hoxton
London
N1 6HD
Tel (0171) 613 4141
Fax (0171) 729 9422

Trapeze, Acrobatics, Tumbling, Balance, Juggling, Diabolo, Devil Stick, Stilt-walking, Fire-eating, Unicycle, Tightrope, Knife-throwing, Whip-cracking and Lasso, Clowning

Circus Space operates as both a vocational centre and a place at which to learn part-time. Blessed with Arts Council funding, the school has 12 teachers in various disciplines and offers both structured courses and practice space for regular performers. You can choose between taking classes by the day, or book in for a term. Circus Space also offers a 2-year vocational course, BTEC (Business and Technological Education Council) National Diploma in Performing Arts: Circus, which includes trapeze and acrobatics – though these more advanced skills may be learned informally as well. Write to Circus Space for this year's prospectus of long-term, short-term and drop-in courses.

Season: Year round.
Accommodation: Not provided.

Food: Not provided.
Children: Workshops can be organized for children as young as 3 or 4 years old, but most classes are for 16-year-olds and over.
Disabled Facilities: Courses can be tailored to the physically and mentally handicapped. Wheelchair access and adapted toilet also provided.
Insurance: Clients covered by public liability, but should take out their own personal accident policies.
Safety: Staff are first-aid-trained.
Affiliations: None.
Tariffs: Courses in most disciplines are run in hour-long sessions each evening: £10 per person, with 4 people to a class and a half-hour warm-up before the hour's tuition. Specialized 2-day courses: £25–75. For diploma courses, prices on application.
Booking: By arrangement – some courses are drop-in. Contact centre for details.
Access: Old Street Underground or BR station, or buses 5, 43, 67, 76, 141, 172, 505 – ask the conductor/driver to set you down at Hoxton.

fiddlesticks

Church Farm House
Bacton
Hereford
Hereford & Worcester
HR2 0AR
Tel (01981) 240 568

Juggling, Unicycling, Diabolo, Tightrope and Stilt-walking

Circus skills workshops to order are Fiddlesticks' speciality, though they are generally based in mid-Wales and the Welsh Borders. Children's groups are no problem, but anyone can set up a workshop, whether as a group or individual. Ring them to discuss your exact needs.

Season: Year round.
Accommodation: Not provided.
Food: Not provided.
Children: Workshops can be organized for children as young as 3 or 4 years old.
Disabled Facilities: Courses can be tailored to the physically and mentally handicapped.
Insurance: Clients covered by public liability.
Safety: No particular procedure, but no dangerous skills are taught.
Affiliations: None.
Tariffs: £25 per person per hour for workshops.
Booking: By arrangement with Fiddlesticks.
Access: Workshop sites vary. If Fiddlesticks books a venue, they will supply directions.

great glen school of adventure

South Laggan
Nr Spean Bridge
Highland
PH34 4EA
Scotland
Tel (01809) 501 381
Fax (01809) 501 218

Juggling and Unicycling

The Great Glen School of Adventure is primarily a water sports centre, but it also runs juggling and unicycling workshops, either by the hour or the day or, if you're really keen, over a weekend, giving you the chance to consolidate your skills. Prices are very cheap (see below) and you can choose whether to visit for the day or make it a residential course.

Tariffs: 2 1-hour instruction sessions: £4.50 per person.

See Paragliding (p. 313) for full details.

greentop community circus centre

St Thomas Church
Holywell Road
Brightside
Sheffield
S9 1BE
Tel (0114) 256 0962
Fax (0114) 281 8350

Trapeze, Tightrope, Juggling, Balance and Acrobatics

A charity-run school based in an old church, Greentop run regular workshop sessions from week to week on a range of skills. One of their specialities is acro-balance, moving objects from hand to foot, hand to head, head to foot and so on. Dance and mime can also be combined with courses, and there are special sessions for children.

Season: Open all year.
Accommodation: Provided on weekend workshops.
Food: Provided on weekend workshops, otherwise full self-catering facilities available.
Children: Youth circus 3 times a week (6 years old or over). Centre has an infant circus for toddlers on a Saturday morning.
Disabled Facilities: Centre has disabled access and their workshops and tuition can be tailored to any special needs.
Insurance: Clients should take out their own personal accident insurance.
Safety: Staff are first-aid-trained.
Affiliations: None.
Tariffs: Prices vary, but weekend workshops are normally £40 / £30. 1-hour weekly classes available for £4 / £3 for adults and £3 / £2 for children. Concessionary rates and group discounts available.
Booking: Classes are drop-in. Weekend workshops can be booked in advance by phone.
Access: From the M1, Junction 34. Ring the centre for further directions.
Pick-ups can be arranged from the train or bus stations with prior notice.

millfield village of education

Millfield School
Street
Somerset
BA16 0YD
Tel (01458) 445 823
Fax (01458) 840 584

Unicycling, Tightrope, Stilt-walking, Devil Stick, Diabolo, Balancing, Plate-spinning and Juggling

Sally Maun, an instructor and performer with the Taunton Community Circus, leads this course during the first 2 weeks of August at the Millfield centre. The idea is to find out which of the many circus skills you're best suited for and give you a good enough grounding to get you started on your training. Sally Maun can help you arrange for future tuition should you decide to take the skills further.

The standard of accommodation and food is quite high, and the setting is beautiful, with over 120 acres of private parkland surrounding the school buildings and the greater countryside stretching out on all sides of the village. You will need your own transport to get there.

Season: 28 July–16 August (for 1966).
Accommodation: 33 boarding houses available for guests; children can stay with parents or in separate boarding houses.
Food: Full board included in accommodation tariff. Vegetarian and special diets catered for upon request.
Other Activities: Archery (see p. 6); Eco-Sports (p. 148); Horse Sports (p. 218).
Children: Crèche and baby-sitting facilities available. Special youth clubs and activities at school. Minimum age for circus skills course is 10.
Disabled Facilities: No special facilities.
Insurance: Clients must provide their own holiday insurance; can be arranged through school.
Safety: Medical centre at school.
Affiliations: None.
Tariffs: Course includes use of equipment and 2 half-day instruction sessions: £71. Full-board accommodation for 1 week: £166 (adult), £136 (under-12). (5% senior discount.)
Booking: £40 non-refundable deposit required. Balance due by 30 April. No refunds of fees if cancellation notice received less than 3 weeks in advance. Late bookings sometimes accepted if space available, but courses fill up quickly.
Access: Off the M5 in Street. Trains and buses available to Glastonbury, cabs must be taken to school. Contact school for more details.

the ranch

Pensarn Harbour
Llanbedr
Gwynedd
LL45 2HS
Wales
Tel (01341) 241 358
Fax (01341) 241 530

Juggling, Stilt-walking and Unicycling

Based in a large old farmhouse on the shores of a tidal lagoon, the Ranch has a truly beautiful setting – a tree-covered hill rising behind the stone-built centre to the overhanging mountains of Snowdonia. The circus skills on offer are juggling, stilt-walking and unicycling, which can be learned by themselves or in conjunction with various other sports such as archery, canoeing, rock climbing, gorge walking, raft building, kayaking, orienteering and hill walking. (Team building and development training are also offered.) Courses are fully residential and range from a weekend to a week's duration. The Ranch is one of several centres run by a charity called the Northamptonshire Association of Youth Clubs (NAYC) and so is non-profit-making. Although anyone can book in, preference is given to group bookings from educational establishments, youth organizations, church groups and charities. The philosophy behind the charity is Christian, but it isn't forced down your throat. However, there won't be much après-activity partying – no smoking or drinking are allowed on-site. The centre has been very successful, with 17 instructors, 22 years' experience, and a very good reputation for its high standard of tuition.

Season: Open all year.
Accommodation: Twin, 4-bedded, 6-bedded and 13-bedded rooms for a total capacity of 85–90 guests. En suite rooms available.
Food: Full board included in accommodation tariff. Vegetarian and special diets catered for upon request.
Other Activities: Child and Youth Sports (see p. 70).
Children: Accompanied groups of children and youths are welcome. Minimum age is 8.
Disabled Facilities: Disabled groups are welcome; there is wheelchair-accessible accommodation. Centre has many years' experience working with special-needs guests and those with mobility difficulty. Contact centre to discuss details.
Insurance: Groups should organize their own general accident insurance.
Safety: Staff trained in first aid and water rescue.
Affiliations: British Canoe Union; British Mountaineering Council; British Schools Orienteering Association; National Association for Outdoor Education; Wales Tourist Board.
Tariffs: Course includes use of equipment and full board: weekend £42, long weekend £53, mid-week 5 days £90, full week £126. Seasonal discounts: 20% March–October, 30% off weekends and 40% off longer courses from December to February.
Booking: Deposits required of £10 per person for a 2-day stay or £20 per person for a longer stay. Balance payable 4 weeks prior to course date. Provisional bookings are held for 14 days, after which deposit and registration form are required. Groups may book at 7–10 days' short notice.
Access: To reach the centre by car, head 9 miles out of Barmouth to the north on the A496. The centre is just north of Llanbedr next to the Pensarn railway halt. By train, go from Shrewsbury to Machynlleth and change there for a train to Pensarn halt. As for buses, National Express run to Porthmadog and from there a 38 bus goes via Barmouth to the roadside stop outside the centre's drive.

skidazzle

No contact address
Tel (01300) 321 071

Juggling, Diabolo, Tightrope, Unicycling, Fire-walking and Walking on Glass

Ian Smith's circus workshops have been running since 1989, teaching individuals, groups, children, women's groups, the mentally and physically disabled – just about anyone in fact – the skills of juggling, diabolo, tight-rope, unicycling and clowning. He also runs confidence-building workshops that include such outlandish and spectacular things as fire-walking and walking over broken glass.

Workshops are set up to order, generally in a public hall that is convenient to you, though the business is Dorchester-based.

Season: Year round.
Accommodation: Not provided.
Food: Not provided.
Children: Courses for children as young as 8 by arrangement.
Disabled Facilities: Mentally handicapped and physically disabled courses available. Ring centre to discuss the exact requirements.
Insurance: Clients should have their own personal accident policies.
Safety: All staff first-aid-trained.
Affiliations: None.
Tariffs: These vary from course to course, but prices begin at about £18 per hour for a group.
Booking: By arrangement. Deposits can be agreed between you and Skidazzle.
Access: They come to you, or will book a hall on your behalf, then give you the relevant directions.

zippo's academy of circus arts

174 Stockbridge Road
Winchester
Hampshire
S022 6BW
Tel (01962) 877 600

Trapeze, Acrobatics, Tightrope, Juggling, Fire-eating, Knife-throwing, Stilt-walking, Diabolo, Devil Stick, Balance and other skills subject to availability

Despite a frivolous name, Zippo's is a serious school for would-be professionals. Their intensive 6-month apprenticeship in 'everything' ends up with a BTEC diploma, with training on the road with the school's travelling circus show. Their new Arts Council (aka Lottery) grant has made it possible for this really good school to make bursaries available to some students and to hire specialist tutors. Performance experience is built into the course. More informal courses are also available. Ring Zippo's for a full prospectus.

Season: Year round.
Accommodation: Not provided.
Food: Not provided.
Children: Over-16s only.
Disabled Facilities: Contact centre for details.
Insurance: Clients should have their own personal accident policies.
Safety: All staff first-aid-trained.
Affiliations: None.
Tariffs: These vary from course to course, but prices begin at about £10 per hour for a group of 4. 6-month intensive BTEC diploma course costs £1,200.
Booking: By arrangement. Deposits can be agreed between you and Zippo's.
Access: Contact centre for details.

checklist

- ✔ *juggling balls*
- ✔ *unicycle*
- ✔ *other juggling props*
- ✔ *tight-wire and trapeze equipment*

kitting yourself out

Circus covers such a wide range of skills that it is near-impossible to write a definitive guide to kit in the space available here. For this reason, we will concentrate on the main areas – juggling, unicycling, tight-wire and trapeze. For all other skills, seek advice from your teacher.

Juggling balls come in many forms. The most basic set, which can be bought in any novelty store, costs under £5. However, glow-in-the-dark balls and more specialized juggling props such as clubs, firesticks and so on are produced by Butterfingers in Bristol. You can pay anything from £10 to £70. They also produce devil sticks and unicycles, which cost around £25 and £60 respectively. The Unicyque range is also good for cycles, juggling equipment and devil sticks.

Tight-wire equipment is more tricky to buy. Although a few companies have started producing free-standing rigs, most instructors do not rate them for safety, although the Unicyque rig (which costs about £100) has gained the respect of some. If you want to set up your own rig, get your teacher to help you. You will need to make a solid metal A-frame from which to fix the wire, with pedestals welded to order and specialist non-rotating wire. The whole lot will set you back around £350–400 and will have to be made up by an industrial workshop. It will be safe, however. The right shoes are also vital. Freeds, a company that makes dance and ballet shoes, produce a shoe called the Spartacus, whose suede sole and leather upper gives both protection and sensitivity. Also, remember to wear good, thick material on your legs, so you don't skin yourself when you fall.

Trapeze is trickier still. You can get a single bar and rope made up to your specifications for about £70–80, plus another £100 or so for the swivels and other accessories. Anything larger than this kind of practice bar and you are talking real money – easily £1,000 to set up a really safe high rig with specialist web ropes, a lunge belt to catch you when you fall, and gymnastic safety mats of at least 10ft by 5ft. Unless you plan to go seriously professional it probably works out cheaper to hire equipment and space from one of the circus centres listed in the preceding text.

further reading

The Tight-Rope Walker, Hermione Demoriane, Secker and Warburg, 1989.
Juggling for the Complete Klutz, Klutz Press, 1997

governing bodies

British Mountaineering Council (BMC)
172–179 Burton Road, West Didsbury
Manchester M20 2BB
Tel (0161) 445 4747

Mountain Leaders Training Board (MLTB)
Plas y Brenin, Capel Curig
Gwynedd LL24 0ET
Wales
Tel (01690) 720 280 / 720 363
Fax (01690) 720 394

climbing & abseiling

rock climbing
and abseiling
ice climbing
indoor wall climbing

Few sports seem to grab people the way climbing does. Whether it's the challenge of conquering the fear of heights, the satisfaction of achieving the near-impossible (after all, you're shinning up cliffs), the extreme physical fitness that you can build up, the deep mental concentration and physical co-ordination required, or the exhilaration of looking out from the top of a mountain, climbing seems to attract a greater number of adherents each year than any other adventure sport.

It's a complex and fanatical business. For a start, there's a whole vocabulary of jargon to learn: how to use a chickenhead, how to attach a friend to the rock, when to use a lay-back, a butt-jam or toe-jam, or when to smear. Even the basic gear is complicated; apart from the special climbing boots (which should be so tight that you can feel every detail of the rock's surface through your feet), you need a sit-harness, complete with karabiners (little metal rings through which your basic 11mm rope is passed), a figure-of-eight for abseiling down the rock, and a set of protection pins, or friends (wedges that you push into cracks in the rock-face and fasten your ropes to). Then there is a whole series of specialized knots. You can see why the experienced climbers tend to be a little cliquey – after all, they speak a different language.

However, a good beginner's course will sort you out with all necessary equipment as well as the basic terminology and rope management, and you can get as real a sense of achievement from your early climbs as you will from the more complicated stuff later on. You can also help yourself by going to an indoor climbing wall in your home town (most large sports centres have them) so that you are reasonably fit when you arrive at the real rock-face. The main thing to ensure is that your climbing instructor is affiliated to the British Mountaineering Council (BMC) and has gained a Mountain Instructor's Certificate (MIC) or Single Pitch Supervisor's Award (SPSA).

selected centres

adventure sports

Carnkie Farmhouse
Carnkie
Redruth
Cornwall
TR16 6RZ
Tel (01209) 218 962 / (0589) 427 077

Rock Climbing and Abseiling

Adventure Sports offer rock climbing and abseiling either by the day, over longer courses, or as part of a multi-activity package that includes paragliding, surfing, windsurfing, water skiing and sailing. The farmhouse centre has been running for 12 years and has 3 full-time instructors who offer 8 hours of tuition per day. The average age of the clientele is mid-20s. There is a choice between weekend or 2-day mid-week, 5-day and 7-day trips – at all levels of expertise. However, it should be said that the majority of people coming to Carnkie are dilettante outdoorers, and the centre specializes in taking beginners or those at novice level and building up their confidence and skills. Although more advanced practitioners can be catered for, they would do better to go to a centre specializing in their particular outdoor sport.

Tariffs include accommodation, with varying prices matching varying levels of comfort: double rooms, chalets, caravans or camping. All holidays are self-catering only.

Children: Minimum age 16.
Safety: Instructors are SPSA level.
Tariffs: Climbing and abseiling are 2 of the activities offered in the centre's multi-activity package deals (accommodation included). Prices are variable, depending on season and type of accommodation desired: £44–78 for 2 nights / 2 activities; £150–195 for 5 nights / 5 activities; £154–273 for 7 nights / 7 activities. Group, long-term stay, and previous-customer discounts available. Single persons desiring their own room must pay a 30% surcharge.

See Paragliding and Parascending (p. 310) for full details.

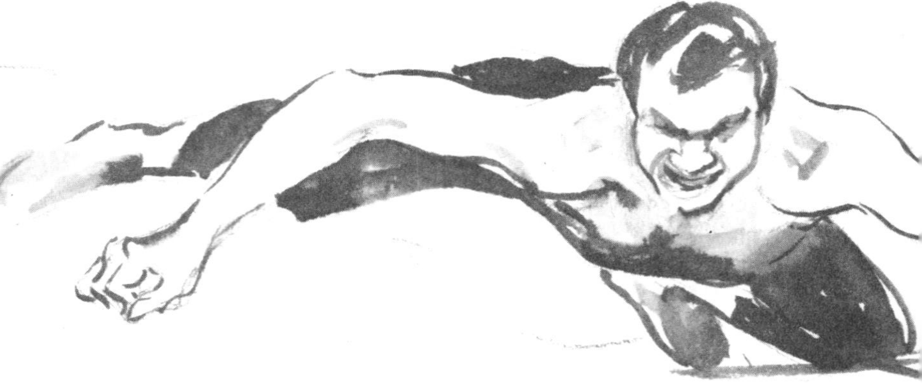

alan kimber professional mountaineering services

Heathercroft
Fort William
Highland
PH33 6RE
Scotland
Tel (01397) 700 451
Fax (01397) 700 489

Rock Climbing and Abseiling, Ice Climbing

Alan Kimber runs his rock climbing courses from May to September in Scotland, then in Italy through October and November. Ice climbing courses run through February and March, with guided trips to the French Alps in the preceding months. Courses are open to all levels of experience and usually last between 5 and 7 days. You choose what kind of accommodation you want. Some of the courses include stack and cliff climbing as well as the Highland west coast's more classic rock routes.

Very experienced climbers can hire Alan Kimber or one of his instructors for individual guiding and tuition outside scheduled course dates.

Tariffs: Fees include instruction and equipment (except boots). A large number of courses are available, including: winter climbing week: £295; winter climbing weekend (includes self-catering accommodation): £130; introductory rock climbing week: £225; classic climbs week: £260.

See Mountain Skills (p. 272) for full details.

alba walking holidays

24 Lundavra Road
Fort William
Highland
PH33 6LA
Scotland
Tel (01397) 704 964

Ice Climbing for Beginners

As well as walking holidays, Alba also organize mountain skills and climbing weeks – winter climbing, that is. With a student-to-instructor ratio of 2:1, this course gives a solid introduction to the skills and grades of winter climbing in all its forms. The course can be taken by summer climbers wanting to develop their skills, with the routes centred in the corries and gullies and up on the ridges and buttresses. Winter belays, climbing styles, route choice and snow conditions are all taught, and students are encouraged to lead wherever possible. You also get a good introduction to the use of the ice axe and crampons and the finer points of winter belaying such as piton placement and ice screw placement.

Tariffs: Introductory winter climbing week (includes 5 days' guiding services, equipment, transport and 7 nights' B&B): £400 (£275 without accommodation). Group discounts available.

See Walking (p. 415) for full details.

ascent travel

20 Mid Causeway
Culross
Fife
KY12 8HS
Scotland
Tel (01383) 880 432

Ice Climbing

Ascent take groups of up to 10 people rock and ice climbing in Scotland, offering courses and expeditions. Their Scottish Ice Climbing 5-day trip is particularly good if you are experienced, with climbing routes ranging from grade 3 to a fearsomely technical grade 7. There is also a beginners' ice climbing course: Scottish Winter Climbing. All climbing courses here have a student-to-instructor ratio of 2:1 or 3:1. Instruction is also given on other aspects of winter mountaineering, such as navigation, assessment of snow conditions, snow-holing, ropework and protection techniques, along with how to use the ice axe and crampons properly. If you want to learn independently of a group, whether as a beginner or an experienced climber, Ascent will also organize individual guiding, but need at least 6 weeks' notice. As with the courses, tariffs for guiding include accommodation and local transport to the climbing sites.

Apart from Scotland, Ascent organize several mountaineering expeditions every year to Nepal and Tibet. These are pretty hard-core – up to 66 days' duration with ascents of Everest, Lhotse, Shishpangma and other serious peaks.

Season: February to March for ice climbing; operational all year.
Accommodation: Clients stay at the Creag Mhor hotel in Onich.
Food: Meals provided.
Children: Not appropriate for children.
Disabled Facilities: None.
Insurance: Clients must provide their own holiday insurance; can be arranged through centre.
Safety: Medic and staff trained in first aid on all expeditions.
Affiliations: BMC.
Tariffs: Rates include instruction, equipment and full-board accommodation. 5-day Scottish Ice Climbing course: £495; 5-day Mountaincraft and Beginners' Ice Climbing course: £395. Individual guiding can be arranged; contact centre for more details.
Booking: £100 non-refundable deposit required. Balance due 6 weeks before start date. Cancellation charges: 20–42 days in advance: 50% of total; 1–20 days in advance: 75% of total; no show: 100% of total. Access and Visa cards accepted. Late bookings sometimes accepted if space available.
Access: Contact centre for details.

black dragon outdoor experiences

7 Ethelbert Drive
Charlton
Andover
Hampshire
SP10 4EP
Tel (01264) 357 313

Black Dragon offer 2 basic climbing courses – Introductory (teaching beginners to set up and manage their own single pitch climbs) and Improver (for those who want to go on to more specialized ropework, anchors, belays, abseiling, escaping from the ropes and a first look at leading). A version of each course is held in the Brecon Beacons and up in Snowdonia. Courses last for 2 days, or you can take a less intensive 1-day course covering the same skills but with less time to put the skills into practice. If you already have some experience and want to develop, you could try the strictly practical Single Pitch Rock Climbs in South Wales and the Wye Valley, or spend a day on a climbing wall. All courses are supervised by fully qualified instructors on an instructor-to-student ratio of 1:4.

Tariffs: Day courses include instruction and equipment, weekend courses also include accommodation and full board. Rock Climbing day course: £33; Single Pitch Rock Climbing day course: £33; Introduction to Indoor Climbing day: £33; Brecon Beacons Rock Climbing weekend: £147; Snowdonia Rock Climbing weekend: £156; Snowdonia Single Pitch Rock Climbing weekend: £156.

See Mountain Skills (p. 274) for full details.

black mountain activities

PO Box 5
Hay-on-Wye
Hereford & Worcester
HR3 5YB
Tel (01497) 847 897

Although Black Mountain are not a BMC-affiliated operator (not at the time of writing, anyway), their staff are BMC-qualified, and the safety standards high enough to warrant inclusion in this guide. Especially good for first-timers wanting to give climbing and abseiling a try, Black Mountain offer climbing either as a day activity on its own or as part of a longer multi-activity break. The Black Mountain staff are also available to act as guides for longer climbing trips in the South Wales area, and can tailor these to any level. They usually require you to find your own way to the starting points, but they will take you there by minibus from a central pick-up point; either way you'll need your own car. They will also book local accommodation at a budget to suit you.

Season: Year round.
Tariffs: A half-day's climbing and abseiling at beginner level costs £20 per person, while a full day costs around £30. For more technical guided climbs prices vary – ring Black Mountain to discuss your requirements.

See White-water Rafting and Coracles (p. 446) for full details.

cobalt total mountain experiences

25 Royal Park Terrace
Edinburgh
EH8 8JB
Scotland
Tel (0131) 652 1794

Ice Climbing

If you already have some winter mountaineering experience and want to get into more technical winter climbing, then Cobalt offer weekend and 5-day courses aimed at helping you make the transition. With a student-to-instructor ratio of 2:1, these 2 courses cover the whole range of winter climbs, from gullies and ice falls through modern buttress climbing. If you have already done some technical winter stuff, then you should try the Classic Cold Climbs trip – 5 days that take you up such famous Scottish winter routes as 'The Curtain', 'Green Gully', and 'Andromeda'. The climbs come after a revision of basic skills. Again the student-to-instructor ratio is 2:1.

More general courses for winter mountaineers offered by Cobalt include a 1-day Snow-hole and Bivvies course and a Winter Belay course designed for both mountaineers and climbers, focusing on specific pieces of equipment such as dead man plates, ice screws, pegs and snow bollards and anything else that can be hammered, bent, pushed or shoved into the mountain for you to attach yourself to, thus increasing your safety margins up there in the Arctic conditions of a winter climb. (Note: at the time of writing, Cobalt's course offerings for 1997 had not yet been finalized. Contact centre for exact course listings.)

Tariffs: Fees cover tuition, in-course transport and use of equipment. Exact course offerings and prices vary, but some examples of past courses are: 2-day Introduction to Snow and Ice Climbing: £120; 5-day Snow, Ice and Buttress Climbing: £280; 5-day Classic Cold Climbs: £285; Snow-holes and Bivvies day course: £30; Winter Belays day course: £45.

See Mountain Skills (p. 276) for full details.

dartmoor expedition centre

Rowden
Widecombe
Newton Abbot
Devon
TQ13 7TX
Tel (01364) 621 249

Rock Climbing and Abseiling

This 25-year-old centre offers rock climbing and abseiling on the tors of Dartmoor and the 150ft rock-faces of the Dewerstone, Chudleigh, or on the sea cliffs of South Devon. Based in an old stone farmhouse in the middle of Dartmoor, the centre takes mainly group bookings for any level of experience – from total beginners through recreational climbers to instructor training courses. Most last for a week, but trips can be tailored to your requirements. You can also try climbing as part of a general multi-activity package. Individuals can fill empty slots in group bookings, or hire one of the centre's 9 instructors for personal guiding and tuition.

The old farm has a bunkhouse and campground. The centre can also book local B&B accommodation and will take you to and fro for a charge of 30p a mile.

Affiliations: BMC.

Tariffs: Prices include tuition, equipment

and full-board accommodation. Rovers course (6 days): £200; climbing instructors' course (6 days): £200. Climbing is included in the multi-activity package offered by centre: £200 per week. An instructor for group climbing trips can be hired for £90 per day.

See Walking (p. 418) for full details.

eagle quest

Lowgrove Farm
Millbeck
Keswick
Cumbria
CA12 4PS
Tel (017687) 75351
Fax (017687) 75763

Rock Climbing and Abseiling for Beginners

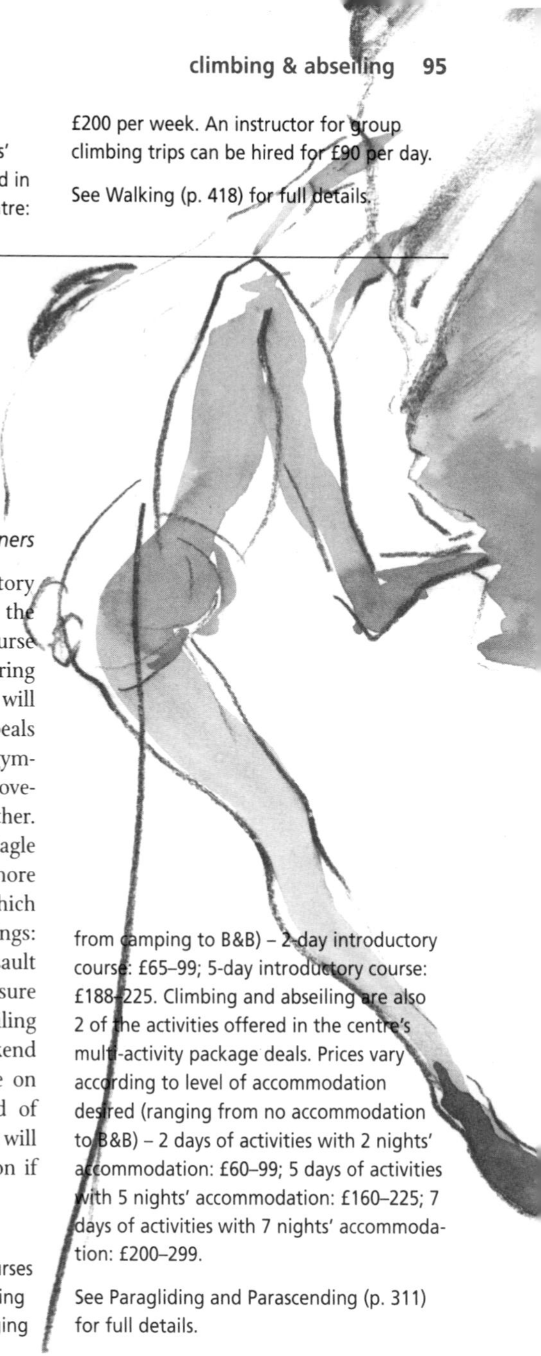

Eagle Quest offer a good introductory course in climbing and abseiling in the Lake District near Blencathra. The course lasts 5 days and is aimed at uncovering where your talents lie, so that you will know which aspect of climbing appeals most, and includes abseiling, rock gymnastics, general mountaineering, movement over screes, navigation, and weather.

If you don't want just to climb, Eagle Quest offer the sport as part of a more general multi-activity holiday, which includes a huge range of other things: rafting, paragliding, go-karting, assault courses, paintball, orienteering, treasure hunting, off-road driving and sailing (phew!). You can choose either a weekend break or a 5-day holiday. Tariffs are on a sliding scale based on what kind of accommodation you want. The centre will pick you up from Keswick bus station if you have no transport.

Children: Courses open to all ages.
Tariffs: Prices for climbing/abseiling courses include accommodation and vary according to level of accommodation desired (ranging from camping to B&B) – 2-day introductory course: £65–99; 5-day introductory course: £188–225. Climbing and abseiling are also 2 of the activities offered in the centre's multi-activity package deals. Prices vary according to level of accommodation desired (ranging from no accommodation to B&B) – 2 days of activities with 2 nights' accommodation: £60–99; 5 days of activities with 5 nights' accommodation: £160–225; 7 days of activities with 7 nights' accommodation: £200–299.

See Paragliding and Parascending (p. 311) for full details.

edale yha activity centre

Rowland Cote
Nether Booth
Edale
Sheffield
S30 2ZH
Tel (01433) 670 302
Fax (01433) 670 234

Rock Climbing and Abseiling

Edale's climbing courses cater for all levels of expertise. With over 16 instructors and a maximum capacity of 80, this multi-activity centre in the Derbyshire Peaks accepts people from 10 years old upwards. For total beginners, there is a 2-day Beginners and Improvers course and for more experienced climbers a Multi-Pitch course, also lasting 2 days, which goes beyond the very basics, through abseiling, belaying, self-rescue and other skills relevant to multi-pitch crags. One step up from this course is the YHA Climbing Club 2-day meet which takes you out to some of the classic climbs of the Peak District, with informal tuition and a more social atmosphere than the regular courses.

Very advanced climbers and aspiring professionals might find the centre's Self-Rescue for Climbers course good value; another 2-day affair, it combines practical instruction on the crags with evening lectures. For would-be instructors only is the Mountain Leaders Training Board (MLTB) Single Pitch Supervisor Assessment (again 2 days), which may only be taken after an approved training course has been completed elsewhere.

The centre offers full board, equipment, tuition and local transport. If you don't want to stay in bunkhouse accommodation, they will arrange alternative quarters elsewhere, but you will have to get to and from the centre yourself.

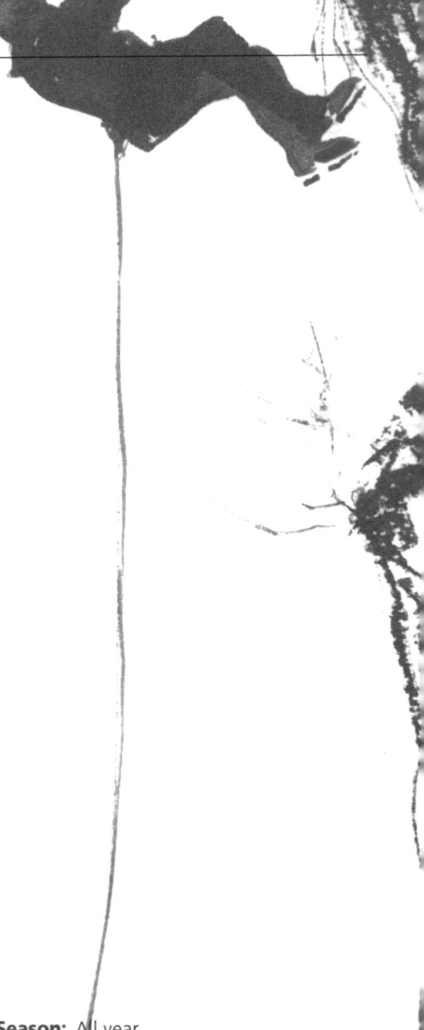

Season: All year.
Tariffs: Price includes equipment, 2 days' instruction and 2 nights' full-board accommodation – Beginners and Improvers courses: £85; MLTB Single Pitch Supervisor training and assessment courses: £95; Self-Rescue for Climbers: £86; Multi-Pitch rock climbing: £86. Climbing is also one of the sports offered in the centre's multi-activity package deals: approximately £42 per day in high season (April–August), £32 in low season (November–February).

See Caving (p. 45) for full details.

first ascent – outdoor experience

Far Cottage
Church Street
Longnor
Nr Buxton
Derbyshire
SK17 0PE
Tel (01298) 83545
Fax (01298) 83897

Rock Climbing and Abseiling

First Ascent organize a number of different climbing courses and holidays, most of them in the southern Derbyshire Peak District. For beginners, there's the aptly named Reassuring Rock Climbing, aimed (in the words of Lizzie and Robin who run First Ascent) at anyone who's thought 'I'd love to try that' but hasn't the confidence. This is run over weekends and introduces beginners to climbing single-pitch routes. A similar course, for women only (sick of all those fit men asserting themselves all over the place), is also run over several weekends through the summer. Progressing on from the beginners' course is Peak Rock, a week of climbing where you put the basic skills to use and progress day by day.

If you have some experience already, try the Learning to Lead 4-day course, which involves leading over routes where the protection is pre-placed and marked out with red pointers. The course also teaches the use of the various safety devices currently available. Multi-pitch climbers will enjoy the Welsh Rock Climbing week which includes some sea cliff climbing as well as several routes in Snowdonia. More sea cliff climbing is offered on First Ascent's August week on Lundy island, with guided climbs offered on an instructor-to-student ratio of 1:2.

Affiliations: BMC; MLTB.

Tariffs: Prices include instruction, equipment and full-board accommodation. Reassuring Rock Climbing weekend: £135; Women's Rock Climbing weekend: £135; Leading Rock Climbing weekend course: £135; Rock Climbing week in Wales: £390; Sea Cliff climbing week: £415. Climbing is also included in the centre's multi-activity packages – adventure weekend: £140; long weekend (3 days): £190; adventure week: £390; women's adventure weekend: £140; women's adventure week: £390; Northumberland adventure week: £415.

See Walking (p. 420) for full details.

go higher

High Dyonside
Distington
Cumbria
CA14 4QQ
Tel & Fax (01946) 830 476

Rock Climbing and Abseiling, Ice Climbing

Go Higher offer group or individual guiding and instruction by the day, with courses by request, and cater for all levels of expertise. Climbing is offered in the Lakes, the Derbyshire Peaks, the Isle of Skye and abroad – France and Spain. You choose at what level you want to be taught – introductory, intermediate or advanced – for both rock and ice climbing. The centre is run from a private house with limited B&B accommodation. If this is full up, Go Higher will book alternative accommodation to suit your budget and lay on local transport free of charge. You get 7 hours of tuition per day and the student-to-instructor ratio is kept as low as possible. Go Higher have been running for 18 years and have a solid following.

Tariffs: Prices are for equipment, guiding and instruction: introductory rock climbing: £40 per day; intermediate rock climbing: £45 per day.

See Mountain Skills (p. 277) for full details.

green rock

20 Castle Hill
Duffield
Belper
Derbyshire
DE56 4EA
Tel (01332) 840 712

Rock Climbing and Abseiling

This is a relatively new school – at the time of writing it had been open just a year. Green Rock offer one of the least expensive climbing services in the country, with a particularly good introductory day course for beginners (see below). Beyond beginner level, they operate as a private guiding and tuition service aimed at all levels of experience. If you want to book as a group, numbers have to be kept very small – Green Rock do not allow a greater instructor-to-student ratio than 4:1.

Although no residential courses are offered, Green Rock will help you book accommodation locally and will help out if you don't have your own transport.

Tariffs: Instruction is £12 per group per hour (any number of people up to 8 maximum). 5-hour introductory courses also available: £20 per person. Helmet and harness hire: £2 per person per day. 25% concessionary discount.

See Gorge Walking (p. 179) for full details.

hadrian mountaineering

19B Carnoch
Glencoe
Argyll & Bute
PA39 4HS
Scotland
Tel (01855) 811 472

Rock Climbing and Abseiling, Ice-Climbing

Hadrian offer intensive climbing courses aimed at preparing novices and rusty climbers to take to the crags independently, with more specialist follow-on courses, such as: supervising single pitch climbs (with a qualification at the end of it) and a snow, ice and mixed climb course aimed either at those totally new to winter climbing or at those with a bit of experience.

The straight rock climbing courses concentrate on sound climbing and rope management techniques applied first on small crags, then advancing, at the student's pace, to multi-pitch courses, with a view eventually to tackling the routes of the Glencoe and Ben Nevis areas. Novice winter climbing courses teach belaying on snow, ice and rock, the selection and use of equipment and climbs up gullies and buttresses to Grade 3 level, with an instructor-to-student ratio of 1:2. Intermediate winter climbs are similar in approach but refine the rope and anchor techniques, take on routes up to Grade 4 and encourage the students to lead where appropriate.

Tariffs: Fees include instruction, equipment and in-course transport; self-catering accommodation or full-board options available. 5-day (6-night) Rock Climbing course: £259 / £419; 2-day (2-night) SPSA: £85 / £125; 5-day (6-night) Snow & Ice Climbing course: £299 / £449.

See Mountain Skills (p. 278) for full details.

---

hendre pursuits

1 Ael-y-Don
Church Street
Barmouth
Gwynedd
LL42 1EW
Wales
Tel (01341) 280 887

Rock Climbing and Abseiling, Ice-Climbing

Hendre offer full- and half-day instruction in rock and ice climbing and abseiling in the mountains of North Wales, from beginner to experienced level, and even cater for unaccompanied children from 9 upwards. The company employs 10 instructors who will give you around 8 hours of tuition per day. You can also arrange for a longer package with Hendre. Individual guiding is offered to people wanting to tackle the more technical routes in the area.

This is one of the better-value climbing schools in Britain, but please note that the tariffs include neither accommodation nor local transport – you will need to be fully independent.

Season: Open all year.
Accommodation: No on-site accommodation. Centre will provide help in obtaining local accommodation.
Food: Not provided.
Children: Minimum age 9.
Disabled Facilities: None.
Insurance: Although centre has third-party insurance, clients are encouraged to take out personal accident cover (£1 per day).
Safety: All staff are trained in first aid.
Affiliations: Wales Tourist Board.
Tariffs: Half-day activity: £9.50 per person; full-day activity: £18 per person. Instruction – half-day: £18; full day: £36. Guiding £70 per day.
Booking: 30% non-refundable deposit required. 5% discount if balance fully paid in advance. Bookings normally made in advance, but late bookings sometimes accepted if space available.
Access: A496 to Barmouth. Trains available from Shrewsbury to Barmouth, buses available from Wrexham to Barmouth.

high trek snowdonia

Tal y Waen
Deiniolen
Gwynedd
LL55 3NA
Wales
Tel & Fax (01286) 871 232

Rock Climbing and Abseiling

Rock climbing is offered by High Trek at beginner and improver level on a student-to-instructor ratio of 2:1. The beginners' course teaches basic equipment, knots, belay and climbing techniques as well as how to abseil, first on a small crag, then something bigger. The improvers' course tackles whole routes in the mountains and on the sea cliffs, honing up on runner placement, belay techniques, general climbing skills, and learning how to lead.

All High Trek's courses are residential, include full board and last four days. If you have no transport they can collect from Bangor train station.

Tariffs: Prices include accommodation, full board, equipment and instruction. 3-day beginners' or improvers' course: £205; 3-day abseiling/scrambling/walking break: £175. Private instruction rates on application.

See Walking (p. 421) for full details.

highlander mountaineering

Highlea
Auchnarrow
Tomintoul
Aberdeenshire
AB37 9JN
Scotland
Tel (01807) 590 250

Rock Climbing and Abseiling

Highlander's climbing courses are mainly aimed at the beginner and improver. The week-long Introductory Rock Climbing course includes gear selection, rope management, belay work, leading, runner placement, and route choice. The weekend Intermediate Rock Climbing course makes a natural progression from the introductory week, revising the basic rope-work and belay techniques and climbing the same crags from several different routes. The course then looks at more complex ropework – multiple anchors, improved runner placement, multi-pitch climbing, double rope techniques, and assisted hoisting (sounds like ballet!). All equipment is provided but participants are encouraged to bring and use their own if they have it.

Tariffs: Courses include guide, equipment, accommodation and meals (either B&B or full board). 1-week Introductory Rock Climbing course: £295 (B&B) / £365 (full board); weekend Intermediate Climbing course: £115 (B&B) / £135 (full board).

See Walking (p. 422) for full details.

howtown outdoor centre ltd

Ullswater
Penrith
Cumbria
CA10 2ND
Tel (01768) 486 508
Fax (01768) 486 875

Rock Climbing and Abseiling

This centre is oriented more towards beginners than experienced climbers, unless you are a would-be instructor in single pitch climbing or mountain first aid. The basics of single pitch are usually taught as part of the centre's multi-activity packages. However, courses can be tailored to suit your requirements – this is a large centre employing up to 16 instructors in the summer months, so chances are they can meet your needs. Ring them up and talk through the kind of climbing you had in mind. All courses are residential.

Affiliations: MLTB.
Tariffs: Prices include tuition, equipment, insurance and full-board accommodation. VAT is not included. Weekend Single Pitch Supervisors' course (training or assessment): £130; mountain first aid course (3-day weekend): £110. Climbing is also one of the sports offered in the centre's youth multi-activity holiday weeks: £195. Group and unemployed discounts available.

See Child and Youth Sports (p. 61) for full details.

john white mountain school

Garden Cottage
High Close
Langdale
Ambleside
Cumbria
LA22 9HH
Tel (015394) 37387

Rock Climbing and Abseiling

John White runs weekend and 4-day courses climbing in the Lakes, North Wales and the Derbyshire Peak District. These are mostly aimed at beginners and improvers – more experienced climbers can join John White's climbing club which organizes climbing meets for more difficult routes and specialist courses by membership demand. He also leads climbing trips to the Austrian and French Alps and in southern Spain. Experienced climbers can hire John White or one of his instructors for one-to-one guiding and tuition by the hour or day.

There are also day courses available for beginners which teach basic climbing and abseiling, often with an ascent of the Middlefell Buttress (about 250–300ft) suitable for beginners and those with very little experience. Improvers can take a day trip to Pillar Rock, via the famous Slab and Notch route – a whole day on the rock-face under instruction. The centre, which has been running for 6 years, has 5 full-time instructors and provides all equipment and local transport. You will need to book your own accommodation.

Season: Open all year.
Children: Minimum age 8.
Tariffs: Day courses include instruction and equipment; weekend or longer courses also include accommodation and breakfast. Abseiling day course: £16.50; Introductory Rock Climbing day course: £16.50; full day's climb of Pillar Rock: £45; Rock Climbing weekend: £90; 4-day Rock Climbing course: £180; Snow and Ice Climbing weekend: £120; 6-day Snow and Ice Climbing course: £295.

See Mountain Skills (p. 280) for full details.

kevin walker mountain activities

74 Beacons Park
Brecon
Powys
LD3 9BQ
Wales
Tel & Fax (01874) 625 111

Rock Climbing and Abseiling

Kevin Walker Mountain Activities has been running for 15 years and comes highly recommended. Climbing courses are offered from novice to instructor level. For the complete beginner there's the 1-, 2- or 5-day Novice Rock Climbing Course which introduces prospective climbers to the basic techniques and use of equipment, and concentrates on building confidence. The 2-day Improvers' Rock Climbing course develops and enhances the basic training and introduces some more problematic climbs. There are 5-day climbing workshops aimed at preparing for exam certificates, and 2-day self-rescue and ropework courses. All the climbing takes place either in the Brecon Beacons or in Snowdonia, with transport from the centre provided. Courses also include equipment, bunkhouse accommodation or camping and full board. The beginners' courses have a student-to-instructor ratio of 4:1, the specialist courses 3:1 and 2:1.

Season: April to October.

Tariffs: A large range of courses is available, all of which include tuition and equipment. Some examples are: 1-day Novice Rock Climbing course: £50; 5-day Novice Rock Climbing course: £235; 2-day Improvers' Rock Climbing course: £95; 5-day specialist climbing workshop: £345.

See Walking (p. 423) for full details.

killowen outdoor education centre

Killowen Point
Rostrevor
Newry
County Down
BT34 3AF
Northern Ireland
Tel (016937) 38297

Rock Climbing and Abseiling

Basic 3-day rock climbing courses for groups and individuals are offered at Killowen, with accommodation in the centre's own bunkhouse. Basic ropework, belaying, equipment and safety are taught, with a few easy climbing routes on local crags. If you are more experienced, try the week-long Irish Rock course, a mobile, tent-based camping tour taking in some of the best crags in Northern Ireland and Eire. Transport, climbing and camping equipment are provided, but you have to supply your own food. Killowen is situated on the Ulster coast, just across the border from Eire, roughly 40 miles south of Belfast as the crow flies.

Tariffs: 3-day basic climbing course: £95 for adults and £53 for children. Prices include bunkhouse accommodation, food, equipment and tuition. Irish Rock course: £60.

See Sailing (p. 352) for full details.

llangollen yha activity centre

Tyndwr Hall
Tyndwr Road
Llangollen
Clwyd
LL20 8AR
Wales
Tel (01978) 860 330
Fax (01978) 861 709

Rock Climbing and Abseiling

Like its sister centre, Edale YHA, in the Derbyshire Peaks, Llangollen offers a set of 2-day climbing courses for all levels of expertise. Complete beginners should start with the Introduction to Climbing course and follow it up with an Improvers' Climbing course which goes beyond the very basics to abseiling and belaying. If you are thinking of beginning a career as an instructor, the SPSA training course teaches you how to lead abseiling and basic climbing trips. Practical sessions on the crag are supplemented by evening lectures.

There are no advanced climbing courses at Llangollen; for YHA courses at this level, please see the Edale YHA entry above.

Season: All year.
Children: Minimum age 16.
Disabled Facilities: None
Tariffs: Prices includes equipment, instruction and full-board accommodation: 2-day beginners' and improvers' courses: £84; 3-day introductory course: £125; 2-day MLTB Single Pitch Supervisor training: £94. Climbing is also one of the sports offered in the centre's multi-activity package deals: approximately £42 per day in high season (April–August), £32 in low season (November–February).

See Canoeing (p. 24) for full details.

mill on the brue activity centre

Trendle Farm
Bruton
Somerset
BA10 0BA
Tel (01749) 812 307
Fax (01749) 812 706

Rock Climbing for Beginners and Instructors Only

You can either try an introduction to climbing during one of this centre's multi-activity breaks or attend one of their non-residential 2-day SPSA training courses – open to experienced climbers (aspiring professionals) only. The centre, which has been going for 14 years, maintains a high standard of tuition, employing around 15 instructors in mid-season. It also has a reputation for good food.

Tariffs: Climbing is one of the sports offered in the centre's adult multi-activity days (tuition and equipment only): £25 per day. 2-day course for SPSA (includes tuition, equipment and meals): £107. Residential packages can also be arranged; contact centre for details.

See Child and Youth Sports (p. 63–4) for full details.

mountain craft

Glenfinnan
Fort William
Highland
PH37 4LT
Scotland
Tel (01397) 722 213
Fax (01397) 722 300

Rock Climbing and Abseiling, Snow and Ice Climbing

Mountain Craft come highly recommended, with flexible courses designed to give as individual a service as possible for climbers at all levels of experience. There are several courses on offer, starting with the basic Rock Climbing week, which kicks off with low-level rock climbing, basic ropework, route finding and some leading, and gradually progresses to more complicated routes. These are full mountain days; you have to walk to the climb sites, so a reasonable level of fitness is required as some scrambling will be encountered. If you are already an experienced climber, try the Classic Rock week which includes climbs on Ben Nevis, the mountains near Applecross, the Skye Cuillins and Glencoe. Again, the course consists of full mountain days with hill walking and scrambling necessary to get to the climb sites.

From January to April, Mountain Craft run several Snow and Ice Climbing weeks for beginners and 2 Advanced Snow and Ice Climbing weeks for the experienced.

All the courses have a student-to-instructor ratio of 2:1 and equipment is thrown in except for boots, which you must already have bought, and preferably broken in, yourself. Local transport is also laid on. You have to book your own accommodation, but Mountain Craft will advise on where to stay. Mountain Craft have been running for 9 years.

Tariffs: Rates include instruction and guiding for 1 week, equipment, and local transport. Snow and Ice Climbing: £315; Summer Mountain Rock Climbing: £295; Classic Mountain Rock Climbing: £305. Private instruction available; contact centre for more details.

See Mountain Skills (p. 282) for full details.

outdoor activities association

Marine Walk
Roker
Sunderland
Tyne & Wear
SR6 0PL
Tel (0191) 565 6662 / 565 7630
Fax (0191) 514 2873

Indoor Climbing

This urban-based centre offers intensive training on its indoor climbing wall, and runs trips out to climbing routes in Northumberland. Beginners' courses and sessions are available most evenings, or as 2-day residential courses, staying in the centre's bunkhouse. More advanced training can also be given in rope handling, improving skills and training and assessment for the MLTB's Single Pitch Supervisor qualification.

Affiliations: MLTB.

Tariffs: Prices include tuition and use of equipment. Introduction to Climbing course: £25; Improvers' Climbing course: £55; BMC SPSA courses are available; contact centre for further details.

See Windsurfing (p. 463) for full details.

outward bound

PO Box 1219
Windsor
Berkshire
SL4 1XR
Tel (01753) 731 005
Fax (01753) 810 666
Outward Bound Scotland, Loch Eil
Tel (01397) 772 866
Outward Bound Wales, Aberdovey
Tel (01654) 767 464
Outward Bound Ullswater, Penrith
Tel (017684) 86347

Rock Climbing and Abseiling

Outward Bound offer courses in climbing as part of their many multi-activity week and weekend holidays, or as part of their longer multi-activity expeditions. Rock climbing and abseiling are included in the Welsh Rover 16-day expedition across the Cambrian mountains, and are combined with hill walking and mountain skills. You must be either 16–17 or 18–24 to qualify for this trip. For people in the younger age category this expedition can contribute towards the Duke of Edinburgh's Gold Award. The same 2 age groups may also take the 16-day Highland Rover, which travels through Lochaber to the west coast and includes the same combination of climbing and mountain skills.

The shorter Welsh Wayfarer (7 days) is open to anyone over 25 and includes 1 day of rock climbing and abseiling along with walking and canoeing. There is also a women-only Trans-Lakeland expedition, with the same combination of activities, open to any female over the age of 25.

Affiliations: MLTB.
Tariffs: All prices include tuition, equipment, full-board accommodation and transport during programme. Prices do not include VAT. Introductory or Intermediate Rock Climbing course (Ullswater, 7 days): £325; Introductory or Intermediate Rock Climbing course (Ullswater, weekend): £130–150. Climbing and abseiling are also included as part of the multi-activity holidays offered by centre (for 14–24-year-olds unless otherwise stated). 7-day multi-activity programme (Scotland, Wales, Ullswater): £249; 12-day multi-activity programme (Wales, Ullswater): £399; Outward Bound Classic (Scotland, Wales, Ullswater, 19 days): £499–599; weekend breaks (Wales, Ullswater, 25+): £130; 7-day programme (Scotland, Wales, Ullswater; 25+, 50+): £325; 12-day programme (Wales, Ullswater, 25+): £470.

See Walking (p. 426) for full details.

pinnacle ridge mountain guiding

Croft 12
Portnalong
Isle of Skye
Highland
IV47 8SL
Tel (01478) 640 330

Rock Climbing and Abseiling, Ice Climbing

Pinnacle Ridge is a 1-man show, run by Colin Threlfall, a qualified instructor who leads small groups (maximum 6 people) or individuals up into the Cuillin Hills of Skye or to Torridon on the mainland. Any level of experience can be catered for – from complete beginners to qualified instructors wanting to develop specific techniques.

The climbing trips last for 5 days, with rock climbing through the summer and snow and ice climbing in March and April. If you come as an individual, trips can be tailored to your requirements, for however long or short a period. Pinnacle Ridge offer guiding and instruction only, with all equipment (apart from ice axes and rock boots) provided. You have to book your own accommodation – Colin Threlfall will advise on what's available – but all local transport to and from the climb sites is laid on.

Tariffs: Prices are for guiding services only – 5-day Snow, Ice and Mixed Climbing course: £210; 5-day Rock Climbing course: £180. Private guiding is available; contact centre for more information.

See Mountain Skills (p. 285) for full details.

plas y brenin

The National Mountain Centre
Capel Curig
Gwynedd
LL24 0ET
Wales
Tel (01690) 720 280 / 720 363
Fax (01690) 720 394

Rock Climbing and Abseiling, Indoor Wall Climbing

Plas y Brenin is widely regarded as the best British school for training to outdoor instructor level across the board of disciplines. At the same time, some people may find the atmosphere a little intimidating – the centre is certainly aimed at serious climbers wanting to improve their skills. Having said this, Plas y Brenin offer a complete beginner's 5-day course that takes in ropework, belay techniques for multi-pitch climbing, protection placement, route selection, equipment selection and elementary rescue procedures. No prior experience is needed to sign up for the course and after the first 2 days the instructor-to-student ratio is 1:2. A less intensive weekend version of this course is also offered.

After taking the beginners' course, you might want to go on to the Rock Improvers 5-day course, which develops the skills learnt in the beginners' course: double rope techniques, rescue on multi-pitch climbs, and a taste of climb leading.

If you have some experience, then you should take the Introduction to Leading 2-day course, for which you should have an understanding of simple ropework and belay techniques. The syllabus covers revision of ropework, belaying and then leading a single or multi-pitch climb under close supervision and guidance. People who have already led climbs will benefit from another 2-day course, the Lead Climbing Coaching weekend, which, again, revises the ropework and then goes on to the mental preparation and psychological effects of leading, coaching in leading skills and technique, the theory and practice of the selection and placement of protection, the leader's rack, theory and practice of anchor selection and placement, stance organization and protecting your second, and route management.

We haven't finished yet – Plas y Brenin also offer more specialist courses: 2 days of Big Wall Climbing for climbers planning to visit the Alps, Yosemite or anywhere else that requires bivouacking on a big wall (i.e. in mid-air – a tent suspended by ropes); 2 days of Self-Rescue, which includes escaping from your own ropes and helping an injured partner; 3 days of Improvised Rescue, which includes retreating, lowering, hoisting, abseiling, escaping the system and dealing with injured climbers; and a variety of climbers' day clinics covering specific techniques such as route setting, abseiling, runners and belays, hazard avoidance and avalanche awareness.

And that's still not all. In addition to all these courses, Plas y Brenin offer a guided 6-day climbing trip to Spain for experienced climbers only, and an indoor climbing wall open 7 days a week from 10 a.m. to 11 p.m. Competitions on the climbing wall are held from October to March and there is a special 2-day course, for those who have only ever climbed on walls, on natural rock-faces.

Tariffs: All courses include instruction, equipment, accommodation and full board. A wide range of climbing courses is available, including – 2-day Rock Climbing: £165; 5-day Rock Climbing: £365; Self-Rescue for Climbers weekend: £180. Various climbing clinics (1 day, non-residential) also held: £30.

See Mountain Skills (p. 286) for full details.

---

r&l adventures

The Byre
Knotts Farm
Patterdale Road
Windermere
Cumbria
LA23 1NL
Tel (015394) 45104

Rock Climbing and Abseiling

Although this centre is not affiliated to any governing body, the staff are fully qualified and the centre has been running for over 15 years. Instruction is by the day only – this is not a residential centre. There are no set courses; everything is tailored to your experience (or lack of it). Choose between single and multi-pitch climbs, for tuition on difficult or basic routes, or put together a trip using the centre's staff as guides. Tuition is of a very high standard, and while groups can be catered for, this is a very good place to come for intensive, one-on-one teaching.

Tariffs: Prices include instruction and use of equipment. Half-day of climbing or abseiling: £50 for 1 or 2 people, £60 for group of 3–5 people, £10 each for group of 6–8 people.

See Canoeing (p. 32) for full details.

---

the rock climbing and caving centre

Chudleigh
South Devon
TQ13 0EE
Tel & Fax (01626) 852 717

Rock Climbing and Abseiling

This Devon centre caters mainly for the 2 extremes of climbing experience – total beginners and would-be instructors. If you are somewhere in between these 2 categories, the centre can still accommodate you, but you should contact them first and tell them what aspect of climbing you would like emphasized so they can put together lessons or a course that suits your needs. The centre does not allow a greater instructor-to-student ratio than 1:4 when climbing.

Unless you have a tent, or are happy to sleep in a bunkhouse, you cannot stay at the centre itself. However, they will help you to book alternative accommodation locally and will pick you up if you don't have a car, for the price of the fuel.

Tariffs: Group rate for instruction (includes equipment): £7.50 per person per half-day, £15 per person per day. Individual rate: £25 per person per half-day, £50 per person per day. 2-day BMC SPSA training or assessment courses: £50.

See Caving (p. 47) for full details.

shadwell basin project

Shadwell Pierhead
Glamis Road
London
E1 9EE
Tel (0171) 481 4210
Fax (0171) 481 0624

Indoor Climbing

Based in London's Docklands, this centre offers city-dwellers a good introductory climbing course on its indoor wall, held over 5 successive evenings. All the basics of equipment choice, ropework, belaying and climbing on single-pitch routes are covered.

Courses are non-residential and you will need to organize your own transport to and from the pierhead.

Tariffs: 5-day introductory course: £50. 5-day multi-activity course (canoeing, climbing, sailing and windsurfing): £75.
Booking: Deposit required (no set amount), non-refundable. 50% of course fee due if cancellation notice received less than 4 weeks in advance. Late bookings accepted if space available.

See Child and Youth Sports (p. 72) for full details.

snowgoose activities

The Old Smiddy
Station Road
Corpach
Fort William
Highland
PH33 7LS
Scotland
Tel & Fax (01397) 772 467

Rock Climbing and Abseiling

Snowgoose run climbing courses and holidays in the mountains of the western Highlands. All levels of experience are catered for, but the place is used regularly by experienced climbers – total novices may feel a little intimidated by the fit bodies and technical talk that goes on in the bunkhouse. However, it is a good place to learn, and many of the more experienced climbers are happy to share tips. The rock climbing and abseiling courses last a weekend or 2 days, or you can come by the day for tuition. Snowgoose will also guide you if there is a particular route you want to climb.

As stated above, the centre has its own bunkhouse and also self-catering flats in Fort William. Alternative accommodation in nearby B&Bs can be arranged.

Tariffs: All prices include instruction and use of equipment. Introduction to Snow & Ice (3 days): £150; Rock Climbing and Abseiling: £35 per day. Climbing is also offered as part of the centre's multi-activity courses (2–5 days): £30 per day. Group discounts available.

See Canoeing (p. 33) for full details.

tollymore mountain centre

Bryansford
Newcastle
County Down
BT33 OPT
Northern Ireland
Tel (013967) 22158
Fax (013967) 26155

Rock Climbing and Abseiling

This is one of the country's most established outdoor centres, having been open more than 30 years. Climbing can either be done as part of a multi-activity package or on its own, and all levels of experience are catered for. Courses include: Introduction to Climbing, Learning to Lead, Multi-Pitch Skills, Self-Rescue and a variety of instructor training and instructor improvement courses. Guided trips to southern Spain are also offered during the winter months. Apart from the trips abroad, almost all Tollymore's climbing courses are of 2–3 days' duration. You can come on a course as an individual or as part of a group, and special courses for children and youth groups and for corporate groups are also offered by arrangement.

The course fees include full board and bunkhouse accommodation as well as local transport.

Season: May to September.
Tariffs: Instruction, equipment, accommodation and full board included in prices. A wide range of courses is available; some sample tariffs are – 3-day Introduction to Rock Climbing course: £84; 3-day Learning to Lead course: £84; Self-Rescue for Rock Climbers course: £84; 3-day Multi-Pitch Training course: £84.

See Canoeing (p. 35) for full details.

uist outdoor centre

Cearn Dusgaidh
Lochmaddy
Isle of North Uist
Western Isles
PA82 5AE
Scotland
Tel (01876) 500 480

Rock Climbing and Abseiling

Although primarily a scuba diving and sea canoeing school, this centre in the Outer Hebrides is a good place to start climbing, rather than a place for the hard-core climbing enthusiast – unless you want to put together a trip to the more climbable terrain of Harris, just across the water, which can be arranged through the centre. There are always between 3 and 5 well-qualified instructors on hand and a variety of climbing routes on moorland crags and sea cliffs is available. Overnight expeditions incorporating survival skills can be included as part of a climbing package, as can hill walking or ridge scrambling.

The centre has its own bunkhouse overlooking a sheltered sea loch, or you can arrange alternative accommodation locally to suit your taste and budget. Climbing breaks can be anything from a half-day or day to a full week. All levels of experience are catered for.

Tariffs: Prices include instruction, equipment and accommodation. 1-week holiday (climbing only or combined with other centre activities): £220 (self-catering), £270 (with full board). Day visitors: £25.

See Sub-Aqua Diving (p. 397) for full details.

kitting yourself out

Good harnesses vary in price from about £30 to £70. A good, cheap lightweight harness is the DMM Alpine – good for beginners and also useful for winter mountain walkers, as its light webbing allows free leg movement. This is suitable for sport routes, where protection already exists in the form of bolts in the rock-face, and the only hardware you need carry is a set of quickdraws. For a little more money, the Mammut Balance (£45) and the Petzl Jump (£58) offer more padding and three gear racks. At the top of the range (£68), the Troll Merlin has five gear racks (suitable for adventure routes where you place all the metal hardware yourself), built-in lumbar support and super-flexible leg and waist straps. The Troll range also includes a harness called a Genie (£68), designed specially for the female waist and pelvis.

Ropes are not cheap. Widely recommended manufacturers are Marlow and Edelrid: 50m of 11mm rope costs about £90 from Marlow, or £100 from Edelrid. If you plan to get into winter climbing, mountain axes and hammers are also quite expensive: Stubai's Blue Star axe is about the cheapest (£50), while DMM's Predator axe comes in at about £126.

Karabiners, or metal rope clips strong enough to take heavy weights, are a must. DMM's Mamba retails at about £10 for a single clip, or £18 for a double. Tracksters, or stretchy climbing trousers (which look very cool, though that is supposed to be beside the point), are useful – loose clothing is a danger when climbing. Ellis Brigham produce lightweight tracksters for about £17, mediums for £18 and heavies for £20.

Climbing shoes vary in price. The Mohawk Tzar costs about £50, and prices rise through the Anasazi Velcro (£56) and Moccasym (£66) to the Boreal range which starts at about £64 and goes up to £70.

The cheapest recommended helmets are the Snowdon Mouldings Alpine (about £36) and Joe Brown Lightweight (around £40). Top of the range is the Edelrid Carbon Fibre helmet for £59.

A set of friends costs anything between £27 and £35, depending on the size and weight you need. Consult an instructor before laying out money for friends, or for ascenders (which cost between £30 and £50), descenders (around £40 each), belay plates (about £10–20 each), check pulleys (around £10) and other rope-control accessories. Good manufacturers for all these are DMM, HB and Petzl.

checklist

- ✔ *waist and leg harness*
- ✔ *11mm rope*
- ✔ *mountain axe or hammer (winter climbers only)*
- ✔ *karabiners*
- ✔ *tracksters*
- ✔ *gear rack – includes nuts/chucks, friends, quickdraws, slings*
- ✔ *climbing shoes*
- ✔ *helmet*
- ✔ *belay units and descenders*

If all this seems too much, send off for a copy of the BMC's New Climber's Pack which outlines the best equipment for beginners, then go to one of the better outdoor shops and ask if they will do you a deal on a special climbing package. For example, at the time of writing, Ellis Brigham of Covent Garden in London were offering a package of a DMM harness, Tzar rock climbing boots, an 11mm x 45m rope, Superbrake and karabiner, plus a container bag at a very reasonable £175.

further reading

The Manual of Modern Rope Technique, Constable Guides, 1990; *The Turquoise Mountain*, Brian Blessed, Bloomsbury, 1991;
The Everest Years – A Climber's Life, Chris Bonington, Hodder and Stoughton, 1986; *Touching the Void*, Joe Simpson, Pan Books Ltd, 1989; *Hard Rock, Extreme Rock*, Ken Wilson, Teach Yourself Press, 1992.

representative body

Cyclists Touring Club

Cottrell House, 69 Meadrow, Godalming
Surrey GU7 3HS
Tel (01483) 417 217
Fax (01483) 426 994

cycle sports

mountain biking
cycle touring

Mountain biking has enjoyed an unprecedented boom of late. Individuals and local clubs have pioneered mountain bike access to Britain's old upland tracks and now some country hotels, outdoor centres and private companies have followed suit, offering guided or unguided mountain biking breaks over great stretches of countryside, many of them on private land that was previously off limits. These companies work out all details of routes, provide bikes, maps or guides, and will organize accommodation for your tour. They may also arrange a pick-up for you if you do not want to take a circular route. Some offer family packages. For the really fit there are tougher mountain treks and even mountain bike point-to-points over boggy moorland.

Such freedom for cyclists is to be welcomed in this age of motorways and car mania. But there are some points to remember: the tracks you cycle on existed before mountain bikes did and, unless you are on private land where you have the right of way, you must give way to walkers (on long-distance footpaths) and horses (on bridleways). Also, shutting gates and walking the bike through very rutted sections, so as not to add further ruts, will endear you to the local community who walk and ride on the tracks regularly, and whose livestock is kept in the surrounding fields. This may seem unnecessary advice for many, but there have been local complaints about irresponsible mountain bikers who have not abided by these rules.

Cycle touring allows you to explore the countryside via quiet country lanes. As with mountain biking, there are now a number of places that organize cycle touring packages, whether on their bikes or your own. And, again, they will often sort out all the details of route, accommodation and pick-ups if you decide to put your own holiday together, at whatever level of distance. Being on the roads, you can cover much more ground on a touring bicycle than on a mountain bike and, in areas of the country where the roads are still uncrowded, to cycle along the lanes above hedgerow height is a real joy. As an inexpensive way of taking an outdoor holiday, mountain biking and cycle touring are rivalled only by hillwalking, as little or no instruction is needed, and a guide is optional.

There are pubs along the way too . . .

selected centres

acorn activities

PO Box 120
Hereford
Hereford & Worcester
HR4 8YB
Tel (01432) 830 083
Fax (01432) 830 110

Cycle Touring and Mountain Biking

The mighty Acorn Activities, whose empire in western England and mid-Wales covers almost every adventure sport you can think of, have several places for both cycle touring and mountain biking, with a choice between short weekend trips and longer breaks, mostly unguided. Accommodation is in B&Bs and your luggage is taken on for you by vehicle. Acorn provides the maps, 18-gear bikes and all other essentials. Go on your own or make up your own group.

For unguided cycle touring, there is a great 7-day tour of the castles of the Welsh Borders (25 miles per day), an easier 7-day trip through the Shropshire hills (10 miles per day), a 2-day Real Ale Trail through south Shropshire (total 50 miles), and shorter cycling weekends in the Shropshire borders (total of 36 miles). There are also some cycle trips in Dyfed – another 7-day castle route; you can choose whether to take a 'leisurely' or 'standard' distance for each day. All these trips go from Saturday to Saturday at any time of year.

If you want to go guided, Acorn run a 7-day group trip for up to 10 people through the first week of August. The trip runs through south Shropshire and covers about 25 miles per day.

For mountain biking, you can head off into the hills of either Snowdonia, mid-Wales or Dyfed unguided (minimum 2 people) for as long as you like, making up your own itinerary, or following one recommended by Acorn. They supply the bikes, which are either 18- or 21-geared, depending on your preference. You should have some experience of hill weather and how to use gears before heading off independently. Otherwise you can hire a guide for an all-inclusive fee of £40 per day, again with a minimum booking of 2 people for the trip.

Season: All year.
Accommodation: Accommodation is in B&Bs arranged through Acorn, with the exception of the unguided mountain bike trips where you can choose your budget (from camping to luxury hotels).
Children: No unaccompanied children.
Tariffs: Cycle touring: all 7-day breaks are £350 including equipment and accommodation and all 2-day breaks are £100 including equipment and accommodation. Mountain biking: bike hire is £25 per day, but you must pay for accommodation on top, whether booked through Acorn or yourself. Of course, you can always camp . . .

See Walking (p. 414) for full details.

bideford bicycle hire

Torrington Street
East The Water
Bideford
Devon
EX39 4DR
Tel (01237) 424 123
Fax (01579) 351 113

Mountain Biking and Cycle Touring

The Tarka Trail runs along the disused Southern Railway line north of Dartmoor – a beautiful, relatively undemanding ride along the banks of the River Torridge and on to its estuary, a stretch of country made famous by Henry Williamson's novel *Tarka the Otter*. You can hire bicycles to pedal this route by yourself, on 3-speed tourers, 18-gear mountain bikes, trailer bikes (allowing you to carry a child with you), tandems and even a wheelchair tandem that allows you to push a wheelchair-bound friend along in front of the handlebars. You can comfortably do the Tarka Trail in a day, and so hire rates are by the day only. If you want to break the trail up and explore the surrounding country, hire over several days – there is a pound off the cost for a second day's hire. Bideford will help you book accommodation in the area you want to explore.

Bideford Bicycle Hire are associated with 2 other cycle hire companies in the West Country offering similar rates for daily explorations of the Camel Trail in Cornwall, which follows an old railway line from Bodmin to Wadebridge: tel Wadebridge Bike Hire on (01208) 813 050, or of the country around St Austell, also in Cornwall: tel Pentewan Bike Hire on (01726) 844 242.

Season: Open all year.
Accommodation: Centre will provide help in arranging local accommodation.
Food: Light refreshments.
Children: All ages welcome. Children's bikes, trikes, seats and trailers available. (A trailer for dogs also available.)
Disabled Facilities: Wheelchair tandem bike and other special equipment for disabled clients.
Insurance: Clients should provide personal insurance cover if desired.
Safety: Staff trained in first aid.
Affiliations: None.
Tariffs: A variety of bikes available for use on the Tarka Trail; some examples are – children's mountain bike: £6 per day; children's trailers: £6.50 per day; recumbent bikes: £20 per day; tandem bikes: £18 per day; adult tourer: £7.50 per day; adult mountain bike: £8.50 per day; hybrids £8.50 per day. Group and school rates available.
Booking: No deposit required. Advance bookings recommended in summer. Visa and Access cards accepted.
Access: Off the A386 in Bideford. Trains to Barnstaple, buses to Bideford, easy walk to centre from station.

black mountain activities

PO Box 5
Hay-on-Wye
Hereford & Worcester
HR3 5YB
Tel (01497) 847 897

Mountain Biking

Black Mountain run mountain biking trips (guided and self-guided) aimed at all levels of fitness – they have over 50 routes on their list and will tailor them to suit the client as much as possible. All routes run through either South Wales or the Black Mountains and Hay-on-Wye area. Most last a day or half-day, but it is possible to put together a longer break if you want to – the longest route is a full 7 days. Longer trips are all self-guided, with accommodation booked in advance in farmhouse B&Bs. All bikes come with 21 gears, a puncture repair kit and pump. Black Mountain usually require you to find your own way to the starting points, but they will take you there by minibus from a central pick-up point; either way you'll need your own car. They will also book local accommodation at a budget to suit you.

Season: Year round.
Tariffs: Guided mountain biking costs £15 per half-day and £25 per full day. Prices are slightly lower for unguided long trails – apply to Black Mountain for their latest tariffs. Camping packs, which include a 2-man tent, 2 karrimats, a stove and fuel, may also be hired at £8 per day.

See White-water Rafting and Coracles (p. 446) for full details.

calshot activities centre

Calshot Spit
Fawley
Southampton
Hampshire
S04 1BR
Tel (01703) 892 077
Fax (01703) 891 267

Mountain Biking

Although it's primarily a water sports centre, Calshot offers excellent mountain biking day trips into the New Forest, usually on Sundays. You can choose between an introductory course with half a day in the Forest, or a full day that includes map reading tuition and specific off-road techniques. There's also a weekend course aimed at training would-be group leaders, with a syllabus covering group control, safety, repairs and navigation.

Calshot provide bikes and helmets but suggest you bring your own gloves. You can either stay in their shared bunkrooms or arrange outside accommodation to suit your budget.

Season: February to October.
Children: 13 and over.
Affiliations: British Cycling Federation.
Tariffs: 1-day introductory or intermediate course: £35 (includes lunch); weekend Preliminary Coaching Award course: £90 (includes tuition, equipment, lunch and dinner), or £105 (includes tuition, equipment, accommodation and full board). Special courses for children available at reduced rates.

See Windsurfing (p. 456) for full details.

clive powell mountain bikes

The Mount
East Street
Rhayader
Powys
LD6 5DN
Wales
Tel & Fax (01597) 810 585

Mountain Biking

Clive Powell has been running Dirty Weekends for about 10 years now, along with longer biking trips up into the wild splendour of the Elan Valley of mid-Wales, where you can still see shepherds working sheep on horseback, and where red kites are a common sight. Clive and his 2 full-time guides tailor their routes around your ability and give advice and tuition if you want it, or you can head off by yourself (i.e. in your own group) if you want to. Either way, you are promised 'lung-bursting climbs and exhilarating descents', and by night you sleep in a handsome old stone farmhouse and eat very good food cooked by Clive's mum – who also drives the support vehicle bringing the picnic lunch out to the guided trips: the Dirty Weekend, a 3-day option or a Wild Wales week.

Season: End of April to beginning of October.
Accommodation: Double and single rooms in family house.
Food: Home-cooked meals by Clive Powell's mother; lunches provided on trails.
Children: Minimum age 12; those under 18 require consent of parent or guardian.
Disabled Facilities: None.
Insurance: Clients are covered for third party but not for personal accident or injury.
Safety: Staff are trained in first aid.
Affiliations: Wales Tourist Board; Welsh Canoe Union; Association of British Cycle Coaches.
Tariffs: 2-day weekend (includes 2 days' guided riding, 2 nights' accommodation and meals): £106; 3-day weekend: £147; Wild Wales week (5 days' riding, 6 nights' accommodation and meals): £258.
Booking: Non-refundable deposit required. Balance due on arrival, or 2 weeks before commencement for groups. Booking normally made in advance, but late bookings accepted if space available.
Access: In Rhayader off the A44. Trains available to Llandrindod Wells, buses available to Llangurig; pick-up from stations can be arranged by centre.

cotswold cycling company

Hallery House
48 Shurdington Road
Cheltenham
Gloucestershire
GL53 OTE
Tel (01242) 250 642
Fax (01242) 529 730

Cycle Touring

Old stone medieval villages, high uplands, deep-cut wooded valleys, dry-stone walls, hedge and ditch country and wide ploughlands – the Cotswolds are picture-postcard-perfect England. Cycling is a good way to get around the area as you are above hedge height and travel at a natural enough speed to take in the landscape. The side roads are quiet and many of the pubs serve real ale . . .

The Cotswold Cycling Company have put together several itineraries lasting from day or weekend trips to 10 days, and taking in a Roman villa, medieval packhorse routes, ruined abbeys, a wildlife park and a rare-breeds farm. You stay in good period hotels, eat hearty meals with good wine and have your luggage sent on ahead of you by vehicle each day. The tariffs are not cheap for these holidays, but the quality of board and accommodation is very high. The company has been going for 4 years, steadily gaining popularity, and now offers guided trips by arrangement as well as the self-led itineraries. Mountain bike trips are also being planned; ring the centre for more details.

Season: Open all year.
Accommodation: Accommodation in a variety of inns and hotels (most with en suite facilities), depending on choice of tour.
Food: Breakfast included.
Children: 50% rate reduction for children under 12 when sharing with both parents. Guided trips can be arranged for children 6 and over.
Disabled Facilities: None.
Insurance: Clients should provide personal insurance cover.
Safety: Emergency back-up provided. Staff trained in first aid.
Affiliations: None.
Tariffs: Prices include B&B accommodation, luggage transfers, cycling equipment, routes and maps. A large number of tours is offered; some examples are – 5-day/4-night Classic Cotswolds tour: £300; 10-day/9-night Cotswold Explorer tour: £450; 2-day/1-night Cheltenham break: £99; 3-day/2-night Banks of the Severn break: £144; 3-day guided mountain bike weekend from Bourton-on-the-Water: £159; 2-day guided Cheltenham weekend: £91; pre-ski 'get in shape' weekend: £21 per day.
Booking: £50 non-refundable deposit required. Balance due 8 weeks before holiday. Cancellation charges if notice received 28–55 days in advance: 40% of total; 8–27 days in advance: 75% of total; less than 8 days: 100% of total. Access, Visa, American Express and JCB cards accepted. Late bookings accepted if space available.
Access: Trains and buses to Cheltenham Spa. Free pick-ups from station can be arranged by centre.

outward bound

PO Box 1219
Windsor
Berkshire
SL4 1XR
Tel (01753) 731 005
Fax (01753) 810 666
Outward Bound Wales, Aberdovey
Tel (01654) 767 464

Mountain Biking

Outward Bound Wales offer a 7-day mountain bike trip through the hills and forests of the Cambrian Mountains. Open to anyone over 14 years old, this is a great introduction to off-road cycling, with supervised coaching over various types of terrain. Maintenance is also taught, along with navigation, access laws and conservation (how not to bugger up the tracks). Most of the biking days return to the centre each night, but the course finishes with a night in a log cabin in the remote Dovey Forest.

Tariffs: Price includes tuition, equipment, full-board accommodation and transport during programme. Price does not include VAT. Mountain biking course (7 days): £249.

See Walking (p. 426) for full details.

pedal away

Trereece Barn
Llangarron
Ross-on-Wye
Hereford & Worcester
HR9 6NH
Tel (01989) 770 357

Mountain Biking and Cycle Touring

The Welsh Borders are superb biking country, with several hundred miles of old drovers' roads (the locals call them green roads) that cross over and run along the hills dividing Wales from England. Pedal Away have 2 centres in the Welsh Borders, one in the hill country near Ross-on-Wye, another in the Forest of Dean.

The Ross centre offers off-road mountain biking or cycle touring round the lanes, while the Forest of Dean centre works as a bike hire centre. Both centres hire bikes and accessories to suit all ages (including child seats, trailers and junior-size bikes) and well-planned routes either off-road or on farm tracks, drovers' and forestry roads and the occasional tarred lane. Rides can be easy or as technical as you wish, and last from 2 to 7 days, with accommodation to suit your budget. Most are self-guided, but Pedal Away can supply guides if needed.

Season: Open all year.

Accommodation: B&B arranged in local lodges.

Food: Breakfast only.

Other Activities: Combination canoeing/biking holidays can be arranged.

Children: Junior bikes, kiddy seats and trailers available. Children under 14 must be accompanied by an adult.

Disabled Facilities: Tandem bikes, buddy bikes, wheelchair tandems and tricycles available.

Insurance: Clients must arrange their own insurance.

Safety: Staff are trained in first aid.

Affiliations: Forest of Dean & Wye Valley Activity Operators; Wales Tourist Board.

Tariffs: Prices vary according to type of accommodation desired – 2-day tour (includes 2 nights' B&B): from £35 per person; 4-day tour (includes 4 nights' B&B): from £66 per person; 6-day tour (includes 6 nights' B&B): from £115 per person. Bike hire additional, ranging from £10–15 daily, £50–75 weekly.

Booking: Non-refundable deposit required: £15 for 2-day tour; £25 for 4 days; £35 for 7 days. Balance due 28 days before week-long holidays, 14 days before weekend breaks. 66% of total returned if notice of cancellation received more than 28 days in advance (14 days for weekend breaks).

Access: From Ross-on-Wye, take the A40 to the A4137 towards Hereford. Trains to Gloucester station, buses to Ross. Pick-ups from stations can be arranged by centre.

preseli venture

Parcynole Fach
Mathry
Haverfordwest
Dyfed
SA62 5HN
Tel (01348) 837 709
Fax (01348) 837 656

Mountain Biking

The Dyfed coast is a beautiful outdoor playground – rugged hills, jewel-like sheltered valleys, cliffs and beaches, all now preserved as a national park. Preseli Venture hire bikes for guided or unguided mountain biking holidays. The guided trips run as weekend or 3-day breaks with routes along the coastal region and into the Preseli Hills. The unguided trips can also be based on maps prepared by the centre, or you can just follow your own nose. All food and accommodation are included for each type of holiday, meaning that you return to the centre each night.

The bikes here are good – 21-gear Saracens – as are the hot showers and plentiful food. Being a small, family-run centre, the atmosphere is friendlier and more personal than at the larger, more go-get-'em centres. Preseli is recommended if you want to avoid the macho, competitive side of outdoor pursuits.

Season: Open all year.
Accommodation: Double room, family room and dorm beds accommodating up to 16 people in converted Welsh stone barn.
Food: Full board included (self-catering options available).
Other Activities: Canoeing (see p. 30); Coasteering (p. 182); Walking (p. 428).
Children: Must be 11 or older.
Disabled Facilities: None.
Insurance: Clients should provide their own holiday insurance; can be arranged through centre.
Safety: Staff qualified in first aid and life-saving techniques.
Affiliations: British Canoe Union; Wales Tourist Board; Welsh Canoeing Association.
Tariffs: Prices include instruction, use of equipment and full-board accommodation. 2-day holiday: £129; 3-day holiday: £189. Mountain biking is also included as part of the centre's multi-activity packages – 2-day holiday: £129; 3-day holiday: £189; 5-day holiday: £285.
Booking: Deposit required, non-refundable. Credit cards accepted. Late bookings accepted if space available.
Access: Just outside the village of Mathry, off A487. Trains and buses to Fishguard or Haverfordwest. Pick-ups arranged by centre.

red kite activity centre

Neuadd Arms Hotel
Llanwrtyd Wells
Powys
LD5 4RB
Wales
Tel (01591) 610 236

Mountain Biking

This has got to be one of the most fun places to go biking. The Neuadd Arms Hotel hosts Britain's annual 20-mile mountain bike bog-leaping point-to-point, held in conjunction with its bog snorkelling championship every July (see p. 334). If you don't want to get quite so frantic, the hotel offers guided and self-guided (on your bike or theirs) mountain biking in the local Cambrian Mountains, from short pootles in the forest to 50-mile-a-day epics. The hotel has gone to the trouble of waymarking routes through the moors and forests and provides maps as well as bikes and guides by the full or half-day, over weekend or mid-week breaks, or for longer, 4-day rides. One of the best is the 'Real Ale Wobble' in November, held in conjunction with the mid-Wales beer festival – where you actually work off flab after downing pints, piloting your way unsteadily over the off-road trails between the pubs.

In the second week of every August, the hotel also organizes its Red Kite Bash, with a bike-dismantling limbo contest, bike footy and bike polo and, for the really suicidal, chainless downhill.

Accommodation: 14 double, 6 single rooms. B&B from £18 to £23 per day. Full board £30 per day. Discounts for children and groups available. Dormitory-style attic accommodation also available at reduced rates.
Tariffs: There is usually no additional fee for participation in guided rides or cycle events for guests of the Neuadd Arms Hotel. Bike hire is £14 per day, £50 per week.
Booking: £25 deposit per person required, balance due 6 weeks before holiday starts. Cancellation charge of 50% of total cost if notice received more than 4 weeks in advance, 75% if less than 4 weeks in advance. Although bookings normally made in advance, late bookings are accepted if space available.

See Walking (p. 429) for full details.

roundabout scotland cycling holidays

4 Observatory Lane
Glasgow
G12 9AH
Scotland
Tel (0141) 337 3877
Fax (0141) 334 8411

Cycle Touring

Scotland by bike is arduous but very rewarding – both for the spectacular scenery and for the physical fitness you cannot but help getting, even in a few days. Itineraries are run for cycling round Argyll and the Isles, Speyside and Nairn, and Dumfries and Galloway.

Your luggage is transferred each day by vehicle, and the routes include castles, distilleries, ancient churches, prehistoric sites, battlefields and nature reserves – as well as the smithy where the first-ever bicycle was made 150 years ago (at least according to the Scots) and the bike museum at Drumlarig. You stay in B&Bs and can ride either your own or one of the company's bikes. All tours are week-long, starting in Glasgow on Saturday evening and finishing in Glasgow the following Saturday afternoon. Transport by minibus to the start and finish of the tour is included in the package and groups of up to 20 can be catered for. Average daily cycling distance is 35–45 miles.

Season: June to September.
Accommodation: Various hotels and B&Bs, depending on tours chosen.
Food: Only breakfast provided.
Children: All ages welcome.
Disabled Facilities: None.
Insurance: Clients should provide their own holiday insurance.
Safety: Staff trained in first aid; first aid kit carried by guide.
Affiliations: None.
Tariffs: All tours are a week long, and prices include guide, bikes, luggage transfer, and B&B accommodation. Tours are available to the Island of Arran, Dumfries and Galloway, or Speyside and Nairn: £300–375.
Booking: Non-refundable deposit required; cancellation charges apply if notice received less than 8 weeks in advance. Contact centre for details. Late bookings up to 48 hours in advance accepted if space available.
Access: All tours start and end in Glasgow, which is easily accessible by car, train or bus. Centre can arrange free pick-ups from station/airport if notice given 7 days in advance.

---

saddles and paddles

4 Kings Wharf
The Quay
Exeter
Devon
EX2 4AP
Tel (01392) 424 241
Fax (01392) 430 370

Cycle Touring and Mountain Biking

Explore the Devon countryside by bike, by yourself, with pre-planned route maps and cycles (either a tourer, tandem or mountain bike) equipped with helmets, locks, pumps, pannier racks, tool kits and lights – even a child seat if you need it. Routes include gentle pootles round the country lanes, visits to ancient sites, or rugged, physically challenging mountain bike trails on Dartmoor.

The centre will book accommodation to suit your budget along the route and the hire/route map(s) can be tailored to anything from 1 hour to 2 weeks.

A full range of Canadian canoes is also available for hire from the centre on an hourly or daily basis, hence the name Saddles and Paddles.

Season: Open all year.
Accommodation: Local B&Bs or YHA hostels around Devon and Cornwall.
Food: Breakfast included in B&B option. Most youth hostels offer breakfast and dinner.
Children: Children under 16 must be accompanied by adults.
Disabled Facilities: Tandem bicycles available for the disabled.
Insurance: Full insurance included for cycling holidays and cycle hire.
Safety: Staff trained in first aid.
Affiliations: West Country Tourist Board.
Tariffs: Prices include accommodation, bike rental, maps and routes. 2-day Exeter cycling break: £55; 1-week YHA cycling holidays: from £86.
Booking: 10% deposit required. Bookings normally made in advance, but late bookings accepted if space available. Credit cards and Switch cards accepted.
Access: Take the M5 to Exeter. Trains and buses available to Exeter; easy walk from city centre.

share holiday village

Smiths Strand
Lisnaskea
County Fermanagh
BT92 OEQ
Northern Ireland
Tel (013657) 22122 / 21892
Fax (013657) 21893

Mountain Biking

The lake country of County Fermanagh has hundreds of miles of good turf tracks and forestry roads, all perfect for mountain biking. The Share Holiday Village is not so much for the serious sportsman as for the weekender who wants to try something different. For this reason mountain biking is usually included as part of a general multi-activity package. However, you can arrange with the centre to hire bikes and take off on your own through the hills – especially in low season when business is quiet.

Tariffs: Mountain biking is one of the sports included in the multi-activity holidays offered by centre. Prices vary according to season. Full-board accommodation packages (dormitories) – weekend: £40–60; mid-week (5 days): £75–88; full week: £150. Clients can also stay in self-catering chalets or camp, and pay for activities separately – each 2½-hour activity session (including tuition and equipment): £4.50. See Disabled Activities (p. 136) for full details.

snowgoose activities

The Old Smiddy
Station Road
Corpach
Fort William
Highland
PH33 7LS
Scotland
Tel & Fax (01397) 772 467

Mountain Biking

Get yourself good and exhausted in the mountains of the western Highlands on one of Snowgoose's guided mountain bike treks. You'd better be fit, or it'll be hell. If you are fit, this holiday combines technical challenges (*really* steep, muddy descents), hills that threaten to shut down your respiratory system, and some of the most exhilarating ridge riding in Britain. If you go self-guided you can choose slightly easier routes – and of course guided trips can be tailored to be less demanding too. Rather than an all-in package, you can either go out from Fort William every day, or stay overnight in different places, in which case accommodation is not included in the price. For a small extra fee you can get the centre to drop you off and pick you up from easily accessible trail-heads away from Fort William. Ring Snowgoose and tell them what you want to do.

Tariffs: Guided mountain bike treks (includes equipment and guiding): £30 per day. Self-guided mountain bike treks (includes equipment and route map): £12 per day. Transport to and from route points: £20 (up to 8 bikes). Group discounts available.

See Canoeing (p. 33) for full details.

wheely wonderful cycling holidays

Petchfield Farm
Elton
Nr Ludlow
Shropshire
SY8 2HJ
Tel & Fax (01568) 770 755

Cycle Touring

Despite the appalling name, this bike centre in the wonderful Welsh Borders offers good things – self-guided cycle touring holidays through Shropshire and Hereford & Worcester or over the hills into Powys. These tours are not for hard-core mountain bikers; the routes are planned to about 20 miles maximum, and take between 2 and 4 hours to ride. Accommodation can be booked either in quite luxurious farmhouse inns and the odd manor house, or in local youth hostels. You can choose between a 2-day, 3-day, or week-long trip.

The choice of routes is wide: there is a Black and White Villages tour along the lanes, a Forest Tracks tour which gets you a little more tired and dirty, a Real Ale Trail, which would get you fatter if you weren't cycling between pints (at least, that's the idea), and a Border Castles tour through the Teme and Clun valleys. There is also a tour through the early industrial heartland of Ironbridge and its surrounding country.

The Welsh Borders are home to a whole bunch of festivals through the summer and autumn, including the famous Hay Book Fair, Ludlow Jazz Festival, various local arts festivals, and more local events such as coracle regattas and harness racing (horse trotting races). If you want to take in some of these, Wheely Wonderful (yikes!) will do their best to book your route and accommodation nearby.

If you only want to cycle for the day, the centre offers daily bike hire. Or, if you don't feel like cycling at all, you can try one of their walking holiday packages.

Season: Open all year.
Accommodation: Depends on cycle tour chosen, either B&B or hostel accommodation.
Food: Breakfast included (except for hostel options), evening meals optional.
Children: Child seats available for toddlers 10 months or older. Riders should be old enough to be competent cyclists. Reduced rates for children 14 or under.
Disabled Facilities: Holidays can sometimes be arranged for disabled clients – contact centre for details.
Insurance: Clients should provide their own holiday insurance. Details available from centre.
Safety: Back-up service provided for emergencies; first aid box included in equipment.
Affiliations: South Shropshire Tourism Association.
Tariffs: Prices include accommodation, transport of luggage, bikes and equipment, routes and maps. A variety of tours is available; some samples are – 2-day Quietest Cycle Tour under the Sun (includes 2 nights' B&B): £89; 3-day Black and White Villages tour (includes 2 nights' B&B): £106; 8-day Castle Tour (includes 7 nights' B&B): £326; 8-day YHA Ironbridge tour (7 nights in hostels): £195. Discounts for children.
Booking: £40 non-refundable deposit required. Balance due 6 weeks in advance of holiday. Charge if cancellation notice received 14–42 days in advance: 50% of total; under 14 days: 100% of total.
Access: Off the A49 in Ludlow. Trains to Ludlow station; pick-ups from station arranged by centre (£5 per person).

wight water

19 Orchardleigh Road
Shanklin
Isle of Wight
PO37 7NP
Tel & Fax (01983) 866 269

Mountain Biking

High Adventure operate from a handsome old Victorian hotel and offer guided mountain biking, or unguided bike hire, either as part of a sailing/water sports or paragliding/hang gliding package, or on its own.

The Isle of Wight is criss-crossed with bridleways and farm tracks: there are over 20 different trails within a 15-mile radius of the hotel, which provides the bikes – Saracen Tuff Trax Extremes, which will take you easily over the hill tracks and coastal paths of the island. If you fancy biking with a bit more of a purpose, High Adventure also organize mountain bike orienteering and treasure hunts. You can book in for a week, a 5-day holiday, a weekend or hire by the day – it's up to you.

Children: All ages welcome. Child seats available.
Insurance: Clients should obtain personal insurance cover.
Affiliations: Association of Cycle Traders.
Tariffs: Bike hire – half-day: £5; full day: £9; 2 days: £15; 7 days: £32. Guide/instructor – half-day: £13; full day: £26. Group discounts available.

See Windsurfing (p. 469) for full details.

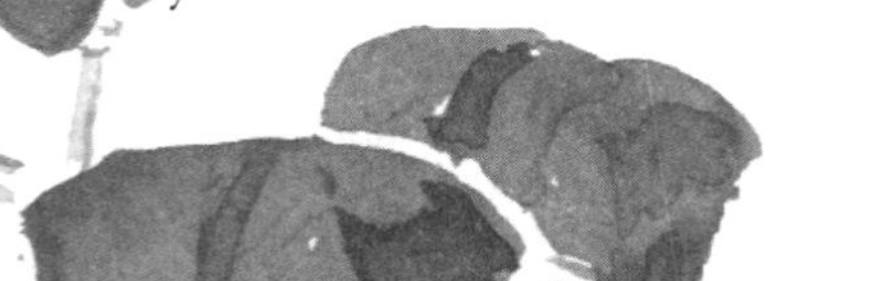

checklist

- ✔ *mountain bike (21-gear) or t bike (10-gear)*
- ✔ *sponge saddle*
- ✔ *saddlebags and rack*
- ✔ *adjustable spanner*
- ✔ *pump, or mini-pump*
- ✔ *tyre levers*
- ✔ *puncture repair kit*
- ✔ *chain tool*
- ✔ *D-lock*
- ✔ *inner tube*
- ✔ *1 in 6 Allen key set*
- ✔ *cycling shorts or leggings*
- ✔ *gore-tex jacket*
- ✔ *helmet*

further reading

Britain by Bicycle, Rob Hunter, Weidenfeld and Nicolson, 1985; *Learn Mountainbiking in a Weekend*, Andy Bull, Dorling Kindersley, 1992.

kitting yourself out

A good bike isn't cheap if you buy it new – a decent mountain bike by Trek, Ridgeback, Muddy Fox, British Eagle, Claude Butler, Barracuda, Gary Fisher or Saracen, or a Dawes, Peugeot, Puch, Orbit or Raleigh tourer, will set you back at least £200 fresh from the shop, and might well cost up to £400. However, bicycles are one of the specialist sports items that even a complete beginner is relatively safe in buying second-hand for about half the shop price. Page through *Loot* in London, or one of the equivalent regional free-ad papers. A brief glance through *Loot* at the time of writing revealed several bargains – for example, a 17-inch-frame Claude Butler 18-gear mountain bike (unwanted present) for £150, an 18-inch-frame Muddy Fox 21-gear bike for £160, and another 18-inch-frame, this time a Barracuda with 18 gears, at £100. A Puch 10-gear gent's tourer was going for £50.

Having bought your bike, take it to a bike shop for a full service. Even if there's a lot wrong with it and minor parts have to be replaced, a service is unlikely to cost more than about £30, probably much less.

Then there are the accessories: a gel saddle for extra comfort costs anything from about £14 to £35; a rack for saddlebags costs at least £25, and saddlebags between £20 and £50. You'll need a maintenance/repair kit (available from any bike shop): adjustable spanner at between £5 and £10, a chain tool for about the same money, tyre levers and Allen key set for the same money again, a puncture repair kit (same price) and an inner tube for under £5. A mini-pump that can be zipped away in your saddlebag costs between £12 and £20.

Riding a bike is safer if you wear a helmet. At the cheaper end of the recommended range are the New Rhode helmets, which start at about £20. Mid-range are the Trek helmets at around £50, with extra breathability and air flow. Right at the top are the Specialized Sub 6 Pros, used by competitive riders, at around £80. As regards other cycling gear, a pair of stretchy shorts by Bellwether or Caratti costs between £25 and £35. A good Gore-Tex jacket that will keep out both cold and rain costs £100–150, but the Calange or Breezebloc lighter-weight touring jackets cost about £50. If you want to wear special cycling shoes, Shimano do a fine range, starting at about £50 and going up to £80.

main governing bodies

British Sports Association for the Disabled
Mary Glen Haig Suite, Solecast House,
13–27 Brunswick Place
London N1 6DX
Tel & Fax (0171) 490 4919

Scottish Sports Association for the Disabled
FIPRE, Viewfield Road, Glenrothes
Fife KY6 2RA

British Amputee & Les Autres Sports Association
30 Greaves Close, Arnold
Nottingham NG5 6RS
Tel (0115) 926 0220

British Blind Sports
67 Albert Street, Rugby
Warwickshire CV21 2SN
Tel (01788) 536 142

British Deaf Sports Council
7a Bridge Street, Otley
West Yorkshire LS21 1BQ
Tel (01943) 850 214

British Paralympic Association
Delta Point, Room G13A
35 Wesley Road, Croydon
Surrey CR9 2YZ
Tel (0181) 666 4556
Fax (0181) 664 4617

British Wheelchair Sports Foundation
Ludwig Guttmann Sports Centre
Harvey Road, Stoke Mandeville
Buckinghamshire HP21 8PP
Tel (0129) 684 848
Fax (0129) 624 171

Cerebral Palsy Sport
11 Churchill Park, Colwick
Nottingham NG4 2HF
Tel (0115) 940 202

RADAR
Unit 12, City Forum, 250 City Road
London EC1 8AF
Tel (0171) 250 3222

RADAR give advice on disabled-oriented activity holidays in Britain and abroad.

Riding for the Disabled
Avenue R, National Agricultural Centre
Kenilworth
Warwickshire CV8 2LY
Tel (01203) 696 510
Fax (01203) 696 532

Sailability
16 Church Street, Wanlip
Leicester LE7 8PJ
Tel (01162) 677 138

The United Kingdom Sports Association for People with Learning Disability
Solecast House,
13–27 Brunswick Place
London N1 6DX
Tel (0171) 250 1100
Fax (0171) 250 0110

The Uphill Ski Club of Great Britain
c/o Scope, 12 Park Street
London W1 4EQ
Tel (0171) 636 1989

photo: Andrew Holt

disabled activities

Throughout this guide you will find details of disabled facilities in the individual listings for each centre, in whatever sport. There are, however, several centres that specialize in opening up the world of outdoor adventure sports to the disabled, and these have been gathered into the following chapter. The sports offered include climbing, canoeing, sailing, riding, water skiing and quad biking.

The subject is too wide for a specialist introduction – disabled people can participate in just about every outdoor sport, but obviously the extent depends on the type and severity of their disability; many disabled people can rise to the top of any given sport while some may only be able to participate in a small way. What can be stated here is that several sports lend themselves particularly well to the physically disabled – notably air sports such as microlighting, parachuting and paragliding, and anyone interested in finding air sport centres open to the disabled should turn to the relevant chapters in the guide and read through the practical sections of the centre listings.

Riding, too, has long been available to the disabled and there is not the space here to list every single centre that offers it. Where relevant, such centres are included in the Riding chapter of the guide. However, if you want to know more about riding for the disabled, or indeed any sport, contact one of the many governing bodies listed opposite.

selected centres

bendrigg trust

Bendrigg Lodge
Old Hutton
Kendal
Cumbria
LA8 ONR
Tel (01539) 723 766
Fax (01539) 722 446

Multi-Activity

The Bendrigg Trust is a charity-run residential activity centre specializing in courses and holidays for special-needs groups. All courses are tailored to suit the requirements of each group that comes, under the supervision of 9 instructors trained to national governing body award standards.

Groups get about 6 hours of tuition per day in rock climbing and abseiling, archery, orienteering, caving, canoeing and dinghy sailing. There are also some pure fun things such as a zip-wire, tube-slide and an adventure course. Courses and holidays run from 2 to 7 days, but activities can also be booked by the day.

The centre is based in a large old whitewashed Victorian farmhouse and has been running since 1978.

Season: Year round.
Accommodation: Twin rooms and dorms available on-site, as well as a self-contained annexe for 20 people. Guests may also camp.
Food: Residential courses include full board.
Children: Minimum age 8; unaccompanied children must be at least 14. Special youth courses available. Game facilities at centre.
Disabled Facilities: All equipment adapted for use by the disabled.
Insurance: Clients should provide personal insurance cover.
Safety: Instructors trained in first aid.
Affiliations: Northern Council for Outdoor Education, Recreation and Training.
Tariffs: Tariffs include instruction, equipment, accommodation and full board (unless otherwise noted). A weekend course costs £93 per person, 3 nights is £130 per person, 4 nights £160 per person, 5 nights £187 per person, 6 nights £210 per person, and 7 nights £230 per person. Please note that the above prices do not include VAT.
Booking: Contact centre for booking details.
Access: Leave the M6 at Junction 37 and turn right to Sedbergh. After half a mile turn right at the signpost for Old Hutton and right again another half-mile later at Killington Reservoir. The centre is signposted from here. Groups arriving by train will be picked up from Oxenholme station and those arriving by bus will be picked up from Kendal station.

british disabled water ski association

Whitworth Water Ski Centre
Tong Lane
Whitworth
Rochdale
Lancashire
OL12 8BE
Tel (01706) 852 534

Water Skiing

Run by a charity, the Whitworth Centre specializes in teaching water skiing to people with any type of disability. This is a non-residential centre, though help can be given in booking local accommodation, and clients will need their own transport to get to and fro. Because the centre covers the whole of the North, bookings are often made months in advance. You can turn up on spec to see if there's a cancellation, but that's taking a chance. Even if you have booked, the centre recommends that you telephone on the morning of your session to check that water conditions are favourable. Whitworth has been running for 5 years.

Season: Open all week April to October, weekends only in the winter.
Accommodation: Groups can camp on grounds, or centre can help arrange local accommodation.
Food: Not available.
Children: Tuition for children available, but must be water-confident.
Disabled Facilities: Centre fully wheelchair-accessible. Equipment designed for various disabilities.
Insurance: Clients should provide personal insurance cover.
Safety: All staff trained in first aid.
Affiliations: British Water Ski Federation.
Tariffs: Prices include tuition and use of equipment. Water skiing instruction session: £10.
Booking: Deposit required. Contact centre for details. Clients may show up same day, but disabled skiers are given priority. Advance booking recommended.
Access: Off the A671 at Whitworth. Trains and buses to Whitworth; pick-ups from stations may be arranged by centre.

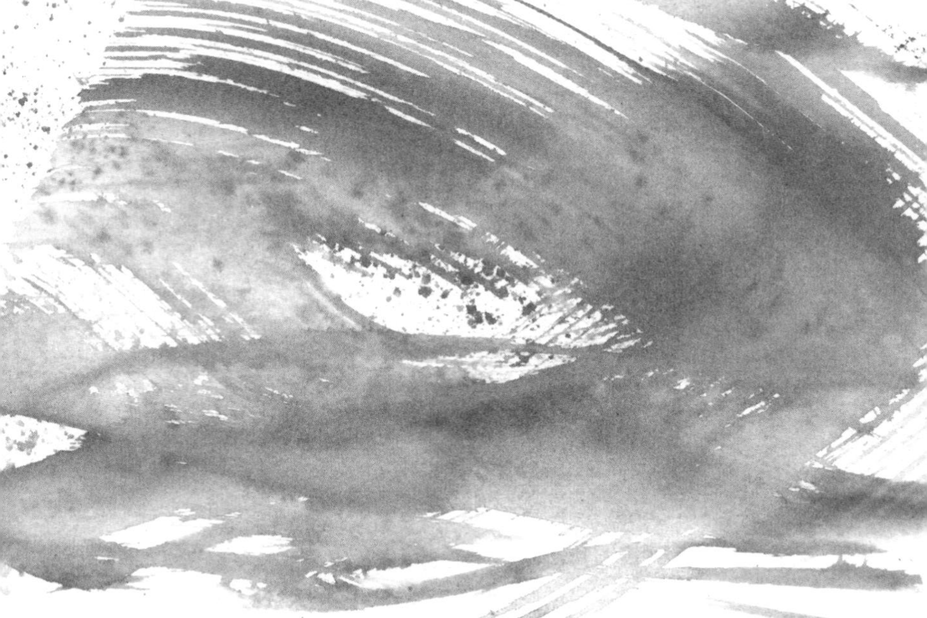

calvert trust

Little Crosthwaite
Under Skiddaw
Keswick
Cumbria
CA12 4QD
Tel (017687) 72254
Fax (017687) 73941

Low Crancleugh
Kielder Water
Felstone
Hexham
Northumberland
NE48 1BS
Tel (01434) 250 232

Multi-Activity, Including Riding

With the lakes, crags and hills of the Lake District and the Northumberland borders right on their doorsteps, the Calvert Trust's 2 centres do the lot: rock climbing and abseiling, canoeing, riding and carriage driving, dinghy sailing, kayaking, mountain biking, orienteering, quad biking, paragliding and windsurfing. There's also a bunch of stuff to do in the evenings, including table tennis, a disco, learning to swim in an indoor pool, and a pool table. Not bad.

Conceived in 1974, the trust's centres can cope with most forms of disability – physical, motor, sensory and mental – and the staff are very experienced – each centre has about 11 outdoor instructors as well as caring and nursing staff. The centres, based in old stone farmhouses, can accommodate up to 40 people in en suite double rooms, single rooms and dorms. There are also separate bunkhouses. Tariffs include instruction, accommodation and full board. Courses can be tailored to individual needs.

Season: Open all year.
Accommodation: Double, single and dorm rooms for up to 40 people available at the centre. Self-catering dormitory accommodation for 16 people arranging their own activities. 2 wheelchair-friendly cottages for families. Heated indoor swimming pool on-site.
Food: Full board included; vegetarian and special diets catered for.
Children: All ages welcome.
Disabled Facilities: Centre has specialist or adapted equipment for all activities. Centre is fully accessible for disabled use, and aids such as bath and mobile hoists are available.
Insurance: Clients are advised to arrange personal holiday insurance, available through centre.
Safety: All staff trained in first aid and disabled safety practices.
Affiliations: British Canoe Union; British Horse Society; National Association of Heads of Outdoor Education Centres; Riding for the Disabled Association; Royal Yachting Association.
Tariffs: Prices include tuition, equipment, transport during course and full-board accommodation. Prices vary according to season. Full week course: £160–280; 6-day course: £140–225; 5-day mid-week course: £99–160; 3-day weekend course: £85. Groups booking 35 places may have 2 additional places free. Discounts for able-bodied guests coming as carers. Bursaries available. Contact centre for more information.
Booking: £25 non-refundable deposit required. Balance due 8 weeks in advance of course. Cancellation charges: if notice received 6–12 weeks in advance: 50%; 1–5 weeks in advance: 80%; less than 1 week: 100%. Bookings must be made at least 1 week in advance.
Access: 3 miles north of Keswick on the A591; trains to Penrith, buses to Penrith or Keswick. Pick-ups can be arranged by centre (£12 from Penrith, free from Keswick).

churchtown outdoor adventure centre

Lanlivery
Bodmin
Cornwall
PL30 5BT
Tel (01208) 872 148
Fax (01208) 873 377

Multi-Activity

With 20 years' experience in providing outdoor education for the disabled, this is a good place at which to begin. While there is no coaching to advanced standard, the centre will find out where your talents lie and offer help in taking it further.

Both mental and physical disabilities can be catered for, though their speciality is teaching people with spasticity. A range of activities is taught: dinghy and keel-boat sailing, canoeing, rock climbing and abseiling, fishing, orienteering and hill walking. Eco-field studies are also included. There are 6 permanent instructors and the centre accepts groups of up to 55.

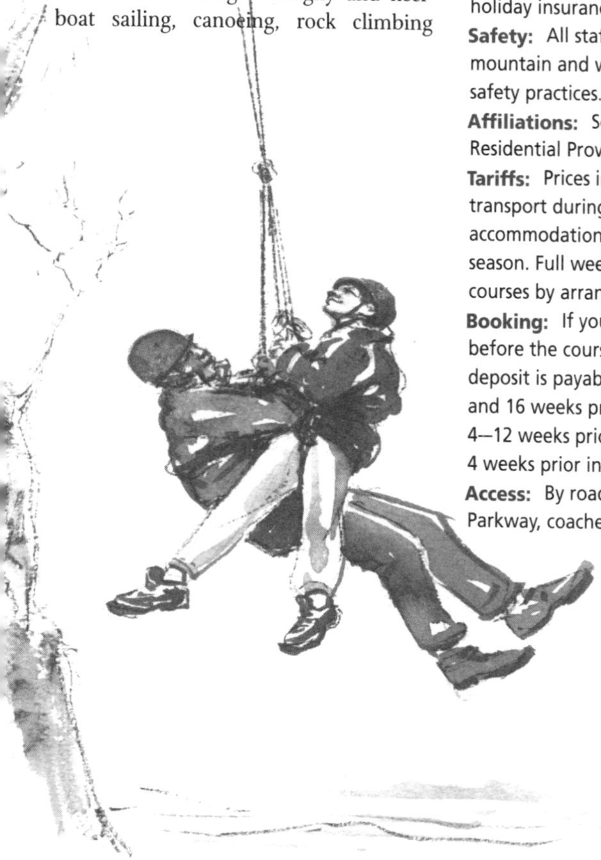

Season: Open all year.
Accommodation: Double, single and dorm rooms for up to 55 people available at the centre.
Food: Full board included; vegetarian and special diets catered for.
Children: All ages welcome.
Disabled Facilities: Centre has specialist equipment for all activities. Centre is designed for disabled use, and aids such as bath and mobile hoists are available.
Insurance: Clients should provide personal holiday insurance.
Safety: All staff trained in first aid, mountain and water rescue and disabled safety practices.
Affiliations: South-West Association of Residential Providers; Adventure for All.
Tariffs: Prices include tuition, equipment, transport during course, and full-board accommodation. Prices vary according to season. Full week course: £165–385; other courses by arrangement: £175–499.
Booking: If you book more than 16 weeks before the course/holiday, only a 25% deposit is payable on booking. Between 12 and 16 weeks prior incurs a 50% deposit, 4–12 weeks prior a 75% deposit. Less than 4 weeks prior incurs full fee payment.
Access: By road off A390. Trains to Bodmin Parkway, coaches to Bodmin coach stop.

jubilee sailing trust

Test Road
Eastern Docks
Southampton
Hampshire
SO14 3GG
Tel (01703) 631 388
Fax (01703) 638 625

Yacht Sailing

This centre offers recreational tall-ship sailing aboard the charity-owned *Lord Nelson* for the physically disabled and able-bodied – they try for a 50/50 mix, not including the 10-man permanent crew. The 2-berth cabins have been adapted for wheelchair use, making it possible for clients to stay on board for voyages of 3–12 days' duration. The ship is straight out of the past, a real piece of romance – 55m long with 3 tall masts. All clients are fully active as crew members. Navigation and chart work are also taught. Once on board everything is included; all you have to do is make arrangements for getting to and from the embarking and debarking ports, which can be one of several around the UK. Some of the voyages visit France and Ireland. Doctors and watch leaders are offered a 50% discount on the cost of the voyage.

Season: April to October.
Accommodation: Clients sleep in berths on board.
Food: Full board provided; vegetarian and special diets catered for upon request.
Children: Must be 16 or older.
Disabled Facilities: Ship designed to accommodate the physically disabled: powered lifts between decks, power-assisted steering for people with restricted movement, speaking compass for the visually impaired.
Insurance: Full insurance cover is included in the berth fee.
Safety: Medical purser on board ship, usually a doctor as well.
Affiliations: None.
Tariffs: Prices include full-board accommodation. Prices vary according to voyage chosen. Some examples are – 7-day voyage from Southampton to Guernsey: £395; 10-day voyage from Bristol to Weymouth: £670; 5-day voyage from London to Southampton: contact centre for details; 7-day voyage from Liverpool to Cardiff: contact centre for details.
Booking: 25% deposit required. If cancellation is within 2 months of voyage, clients are liable for full berth fee if place cannot be resold (if full berth fee paid upon booking, cancellation insurance will be in effect). Cancellation or change of voyage date incurs £15 charge. Bookings are normally made in advance, but late bookings accepted if space available. Access and several Visa cards accepted.
Access: Varies according to voyage chosen. Detailed access instructions will be mailed to clients upon booking.

medina valley centre

Dodnor Lane
Newport
Isle of Wight
PO30 5TE
Tel (01983) 522 195
Fax (01983) 825 962

Dinghy Sailing and Yachting

This is a sailing centre with a difference – a Christian sailing centre. It's very successful, having been open since 1963, and while its requirements for good behaviour might put off would-be buccaneers, it is nonetheless a well-regarded sailing school. Its courses for the disabled are highly recommended, with yachts purpose-designed to enable the physically handicapped to sail independently and on equal terms with the able-bodied crew members. The centre has 2 such purpose-built yachts and several 16ft Seastar dinghies fit for the job. Courses can be designed either by the day or on a residential basis of up to 2 weeks.

Disabled Facilities: Boats designed for use by the disabled.
Tariffs: Prices include instruction, equipment, accommodation and full board (unless otherwise noted). 5-day sailing course: £304 (£237 under-16); 5-day non-residential sailing course (includes lunch): £182 (£152 under-16). Some courses are slightly more expensive in high season, 29 July–26 August.

See Sailing (p. 354) for full details.

outward bound

PO Box 1219
Windsor
Berkshire
SL4 1XR
Tel (01753) 731 005
Fax (01753) 810 666

Multi-Activity

The Welsh, Scottish and Lakeland Outward Bound centres run courses under the umbrella heading of 'John Hawkridge Challenge' which are tailored for disabled groups. These cover, where possible, the full range of activities offered by Outward Bound – hill walking, climbing and abseiling, canoeing and other activities where appropriate. There is no fixed schedule; the courses vary according to the needs and demands of each group. Telephone the main office in Windsor to arrange a John Hawkridge Challenge break.

Tariffs: All prices include tuition, equipment, full-board accommodation and transport during programme. Prices do not include VAT. 7-day access programmes: £500; 12-day access programmes: £850.

See Walking (p. 428) for full details.

the red ridge outdoor centre

Cefn Coch
Welshpool
Powys
Wales
Tel (01938) 810 821
Fax (01938) 810 767

Multi-Activity

Established in 1978, the Red Ridge centre offers rock climbing and abseiling, caving, open Canadian canoeing, kayaking, orienteering and archery for the disabled. Zip-wiring is also offered for those in wheelchairs, as are all-terrain go-karts and mini-tractors. With up to 15 instructors in the summer, this is a large centre that can cater for groups of up to 100, depending on the level of instruction required. The centre occupies a converted farm in Powys. Day visitors are welcome, but the centre specializes in 6-night, 4-night and weekend breaks that give clients long enough to discover where their proficiencies lie.

Season: Open all year except January.
Accommodation: Dorm beds in main guest house, plus camping site.
Food: Full-board or self-catering options available.
Other Activities: Pony trekking by arrangement.
Children: Youth and school groups welcome.
Disabled Facilities: All facilities purpose-built for use by disabled guests; all activities open to disabled participants. Volunteers can be arranged to assist disabled clients throughout their stay.
Insurance: Insurance included in tariff.
Safety: Staff trained in first aid, mountain and water rescue skills.
Affiliations: Adventure for All; Wales Tourist Board.
Tariffs: Prices are for multi-activity holidays and vary according to season. Full-board accommodation packages (dormitories) – weekend: £65–90; mid-week (4 days): £90–139; full week: £216. Prices do not include VAT.
Booking: Non-refundable deposit required, £15–30. Balance due 4 weeks before start date. Late bookings sometimes accepted if space available. Payment by cheque.
Access: Difficult to reach by public transport (though a cab from Welshpool station costs about £10). If coming by car, head from Welshpool to Llanfair Caereinion and look out for the signs to Cefn Coch.

share holiday village

Smiths Strand
Lisnaskea
County Fermanagh
BT92 OEQ
Northern Ireland
Tel (013657) 22122 / 21892
Fax (013657) 21893

Multi-Activity

The Share Holiday Village has been running outdoor adventure courses for the disabled for over 15 years. Set in the Fermanagh lake country of Northern Ireland, the village offers dinghy sailing, canoeing, archery and rowing in a Viking longship (!) for all levels of competence. As well as about 5 hours of outdoor education, guests may use the centre's leisure pool complex, sauna and steam room, and there are indoor and outdoor play areas for children. Choose between full-board and self-catering packages.

Season: Open all year (closed for 2 weeks at Christmas).

Accommodation: 24 dorm beds in main guest house, 15 self-catering chalets, camping and caravan site.
Food: Full-board or self-catering options available.
Other Activities: Cycle Sports (see p. 124); Orienteering (p. 184).
Children: Toddlers' pool, children's play area. Youth and school groups welcome. Must be 21 years old to book holiday.
Disabled Facilities: All facilities purpose-built for use by disabled guests; all activities open to disabled participants. Volunteers can be arranged to assist disabled clients throughout their stay.
Insurance: Clients should provide their own holiday insurance.
Safety: Staff trained in first aid, mountain and water rescue skills.
Affiliations: Celtic Budget Accommodation.
Tariffs: Prices are for multi-activity holidays and vary according to season. Full-board accommodation packages (dormitories) – weekend: £40–60; mid-week (5 days): £75–88; full week: £150. Clients can also stay in self-catering chalets or camp, and pay for activities separately – each 2½-hour activity session (including tuition and equipment): £4.50.
Booking: Non-refundable deposit required, £15–30. Balance due 6 weeks before start date. Clients who cancel less than 6 weeks in advance are liable for total holiday cost if place can't be refilled. Late bookings sometimes accepted if space available.
Access: 3 miles from Lisnaskea. Trains and buses to Maguiresbridge; pick-ups can be arranged by centre.

---

the stackpole centre

Home Farm
Stackpole
Pembroke
Dyfed
SA71 5DQ
Wales
Tel (01646) 661 425
Fax (01646) 661 456

Multi-Activity

One of the longer-running outdoor centres for the disabled, the Stackpole Centre, a charity-run organization, has been operational since 1979. Sited on the beautiful Dyfed coast, the centre has sandy beaches, cliffs and castles all within easy reach, and boasts an indoor and an outdoor sports complex. Activities available include open Canadian canoeing, kayaking, rock climbing and abseiling, orienteering, coasteering, boogy barding (body surfing with the aid of a short, half-length, surfboard), and archery. There is an indoor pool, gym and jacuzzi. Clients can visit by the day or for longer breaks, staying in the centre's cottages, houses or hotel, all very comfortable and attached to the main complex. There is also cheap camping nearby. Clients can also be picked up free of charge from Pembroke BR or coach station. Highly recommended.

Season: Open all year.
Accommodation: Self-catering cottages are available (sleeping 6–8, from £190–480 per week), or there is hotel accommodation at the Patrick House Hotel (£15–25 per day).
Food: Full board available from hotel restaurant; vegetarian options offered.
Children: All ages welcome.
Disabled Facilities: Centre is primarily for the use of disabled clients in the summer. Accommodation is fully wheelchair-accessible.
Insurance: Clients should provide their own holiday insurance.
Safety: All instructors plus on-call night worker trained in first aid.

Affiliations: British Canoe Union; Sports Council for Wales; Wales Tourist Board.
Tariffs: Price includes instruction and use of equipment, and applies to entire group. 2½-hour activity session: £40 (1–6 persons), £60 (7–12 persons).
Booking: 10% deposit required, not refunded if cancellation notice received less than 6 weeks in advance. Bookings normally made in advance. Credit cards accepted.
Access: Off the B4139 near Pembroke. Trains and buses to Pembroke, pick-ups from station will be arranged by centre.

the uphill ski school and training centre

Dell Road
Nethy Bridge
Highland
PH24 3BN
Tel (01497) 821 771
Fax (0171) 636 1989

Downhill Skiing

Despite its name, this charity is not about going up, but rather down. Presumably the 'up' refers to the struggle involved in mastering downhill skiing when not able-bodied. In 1995, the charity built and opened a disabled ski centre in the Cairngorms, catering for just about any form of disability, with the chance to train to competition standard. Both children and adult courses are run, as well as more conventional ski holidays and skiing by the day. Not only are there specially adapted skis and wheelchair skis, but there is also a chair-lift and several runs of different grades of difficulty. Specialist instructor courses for disabled skiing are also offered. The building is fully equipped for wheelchairs and there are trained nursing staff on hand.

Season: November to May.
Accommodation: Not provided at centre, but the club can arrange local accommodation adapted for disabled use.
Food: Lunches available; special diets by arrangement.
Children: All ages welcome.
Disabled Facilities: Centre is primarily for the use of disabled clients. Accommodation is fully wheelchair-accessible.
Insurance: Clients should provide their own holiday insurance.
Safety: All instructors plus nursing staff trained in first aid.
Affiliations: British Association of Ski Instructors; Scottish Tourist Board.
Tariffs: Prices include instruction and use of equipment. An hour's session is £15 per person, 2 hours £25 per person and 4 hours £45.
Booking: 10% deposit required, not refunded if cancellation notice received less than 6 weeks in advance. Bookings normally made in advance. Credit cards accepted.
Access: Just at the foot of the Cairngorm ski area, about 2 miles north of Aviemore. Contact centre for exact details. A specially adapted rail system takes disabled skiers from the main lodge to the pistes.

kitting yourself out

Because disabled sports cover just about every activity included in this book, there isn't space here to go into detail, which would in any case be unhelpfully repetitive. Instead, turn to the kit pages of the relevant chapters.

What is important as a general rule – at least for wheelchair-bound disabled people – is the right chair. With so many on the market, a lot of people find it difficult to choose one that is going to maximize their ability to get around outdoors – especially over rough ground. However, the word among wheelchair-bound sportspeople is that Bromakin Wheelchairs, 12 Prince William Road, Belton Park, Loughborough, Leicestershire, tel (01509) 217 569, are a good bet, as are Gerald Simmons Healthcare Ltd, Unit 9, March Place, Gateway House, Aylesbury, Buckinghamshire HP19 3UG, tel (01296) 436 557, fax (01296) 433 273, and GBL Wheelchairs, Units 1–3, Shield Drive, Brentford, Middlesex TW8 9EX, tel (0181) 569 8955, fax (0181) 560 5380 – the latter have several factories in southern England. Expect to pay between £300 and £700 for a good sports chair – though prices can get much higher.

Second-hand sports chairs are a slightly cheaper option. Classified ads for them can be found in *Red Herring* magazine, which you can order from 14 First Avenue, Dursley, Gloucestershire GL11 4NW, tel (01453) 543 347.

As for adapted equipment, this is generally very expensive as it has to be tailored to individual needs. All outdoor centres specializing in sports for the disabled provide the necessary equipment, although Gerald Simmons Healthcare make specially adapted bikes and water skis, as do the Chevron Factory, Brunswick Business Park, 18 Summers Road, Liverpool L3 4BL, tel (0151) 707 1146, fax (0151) 707 0353.

If you want something very specialized, the best thing is to consult the staff of such a centre to discuss what you need, then to contact one of the regular manufacturers to have it custom-made. Again, the most helpful advice we can give is to recommend that you turn to the relevant equipment pages of the sport you are interested in and, once you have decided what you need, contact the manufacturers listed there to discuss prices.

checklist

✔ *a good chair*

✔ *specially adapted equipment*

representative bodies

English Nature
Northminster House
Northminster Road
Peterborough PE1 1UA
Tel (01733) 340 345
Fax (01733) 68834

Royal Society for the Protection of Birds (RSPB)
The Lodge, Sandy
Bedfordshire SG19 2DL
Tel (01767) 680 551
Fax (01767) 692 365

Scottish Natural Heritage
16–17 Rubislaw Terrace,
Aberdeen AB10 1XE
Tel (01224) 642 863
Fax (01224) 643 347

photo: Acorn Activities

eco-sports

bird-watching
extreme bird-watching
swimming with dolphins
whale-watching
guided wildlife treks
field studies
joining research groups
botanical trips

Few of us ever get really close to wildlife, or even get a chance to explore its habitat. Eco-sports offer a way for the non-woodsman to do this, with knowledgeable guides to bring you in close and show you what to look for. At the same time, because the establishments listed here are very ethically run, you can be sure that your incursion into the wild will leave no more lasting impression than footprints, and all you take away will be photographs.

Eco-sports encompass a range of activities: from guided day walks in country woodlands to week-long treks through the Scottish Highlands in search of deer, otters, wild cats and other elusive creatures. You can watch whales from a boat or actually get into the water and swim with a dolphin – even here, off the coast of Britain. As for bird-watchers or 'twitchers', they can watch red kites (our rarest bird) coming down to feed on a farm high in the Cambrian Mountains. The really serious can visit the remote bird research station on Fair Isle, or go on bird-watching treks with llamas (yes, llamas) in the north of Scotland.

These 'sports' are probably the best way to get out into nature. There is no specialized equipment to worry about, nor are you trying to pit yourself against the landscape. Quite the opposite – you have to try to become a part of the landscape, so that the wild creatures will approach you. For anyone sick of the endless sensory assault of urban life, of continual traffic roar, endless crowds, irritating gadgets and their accompanying electronic noises, there can be few better therapies than to sit in silence, waiting for a glimpse of the living wild.

selected centres

acorn activities

PO Box 120
Hereford
Hereford & Worcester
HR4 8YB
Tel (01432) 830 083
Fax (01432) 830 110

Bird-watching and Guided Wildlife Walks

On the third weekend in May, Acorn run a bird-watching weekend in Powys, in the Welsh Borders. You stay at the 16th-century Maesmawr Hotel at Caersws, about 5 miles west of Newtown, and spend most of the weekend looking for rare birds such as red kite, goldcrest, merganser, coal tit, goldeneye, peregrine and even the occasional merlin. There's a wide variety of habitats, from heather moorland to sessile oak forest, estuarine salt marsh and peat bog.

Acorn run a June wildlife weekend in Dyfed (usually during the third week) which concentrates on seabirds and mammals. Highlights include a visit to the puffin colony at Skomer Island, sightings of razorbills, oyster-catchers, Manx shearwaters, guillemots and fulmars, as well as grey and common seals and, if you are lucky, an occasional otter. Accommodation is in the Old Cross Hotel, St David's.

In August (usually the second week), Acorn run a more general wildlife weekend in the Golden Valley of west Hereford & Worcester. Roe, fallow and muntjac deer are common, as are badgers (though only by night), ravens and herons. You may be lucky and spot a small hobby hawk – this is one of their few breeding areas – and there is extensive walking in ancient woodland of oak, beech and ash. Accommodation is in the Red Lion Hotel, Bredwardine.

Note that Acorn offer some other interesting pursuits among their adventure holiday packages, such as dry-stone walling and building conservation. Contact them to find out more about these activities, and see Walking (p. 416) for a list of the adventure sports offered by this centre that are featured in this guide.

Accommodation: Depending on package chosen, accommodation is provided or can be arranged through centre (from camping to luxury hotels).
Tariffs: Full day of bird-watching with ornithologist in Shropshire or Dyfed: £40; wildlife weekend with experts in Powys, Dyfed or Hereford & Worcester (includes accommodation and full board): £175.

See Walking (p. 416) for full details.

birdwatching in london & s.e. england

PO Box 7229
London
E11 3UD

Bird-watching

This is a one-man band – trips in and around London led by Gary Hewitt, a 'twitcher' of 20 years' standing. Sites as diverse as Paddington Cemetery, Regent's Park, Battersea Park and various reservoirs, parks and riversides around the London fringes reveal a wealth of birdlife – things you'd never expect to find in a city such as short-eared owls, smews, bitterns and water rails (in the Lea Valley), black terns, cuckoos (even in Hackney!), sandpipers, peregrine falcons, Montagu's harrier, even ospreys: all have been seen on Gary Hewitt's trips in and around London. He also runs forays further afield in the south-east, to the North Kent Marshes and Dungeness, the Suffolk and Norfolk Broads and Breckland, and the Wash.

The trips are run over weekends, full days or half-days, with special tours for school groups, youth clubs, pensioners' clubs, etc.

Season: Open all year.
Accommodation: Centre can help arrange local B&B or camping.
Food: Not provided.
Children: Must be 10 years old for regular tours; younger children welcome on designated family tours. Discounts for youths. Special tours offered for schoolchildren.
Disabled Facilities: Disabled clients can be accommodated, and many of the bird-watching sites are wheelchair-accessible.
Insurance: Clients should provide personal insurance cover if desired.
Safety: No specific medical training.
Affiliations: None.
Tariffs: Half-day tour: £8; full-day tour: £15; half-day family tour: £18 per family. Binocular rental: £1 per pair. 50% discount for children aged 10–16. Unemployed persons only pay £1 (if space available).
Booking: Payment due at time of booking, preferably 2 weeks in advance. Refunds only made when tour is cancelled. Late bookings accepted if space available.
Access: All bird-watching sites are accessible by public transport; contact centre for details.

brathay exploration group

Brathay Hall
Ambleside
Cumbria
LA22 OHN
Tel & Fax (01539) 433 942

Field Studies, Botanical Trips

Part eco-centre, part mountaineering school, Brathay is a pretty serious place, organizing wildlife and geographical expeditions into remote parts of Britain and the rest of the world: Nepal, Costa Rica, China, Siberia, New Zealand, Scandinavia, and the Alps. The British trips, which place an emphasis on wildlife and its habitats, run through the summer to the Isle of Mull and Shetland.

The 10-day Mull trip is part of a programme of environmental survey work developed by Warwick University to assess the status of some of the island's unique flora, including Iceland purslane – one of Britain's rarest plants. There are 2 (2-week) trips to Shetland, one to the island of Foula, apparently Britain's most isolated inhabited island and home to a vast colony of puffins, fulmars, gannets and other seabirds, and one to the northern part of mainland Shetland to look at Alpine Arctic plants. All the trips require extensive hill walking, but you don't need any scientific knowledge to take part – just a willingness to take notes and to work under fire from midges.

The Mull trip starts from Oban and the Shetland trips from Aberdeen (you get yourself there). You spend most of the time under canvas (in your own sleeping bag) and the price of the trip includes all food and local transport. (Note: at the time of writing, Brathay's 1997 expedition listings were not available. Check with Brathay for current offerings.)

Season: Expeditions July to September.
Accommodation: Camping equipment provided.
Food: Food supplied; clients cook their own meals.
Other Activities: Mountain Skills (see p. 275); Skiing (p. 373–4).
Children: Minimum age 16.
Disabled Facilities: Disabled people will be accepted as expedition members when practicable; contact centre for more information.
Insurance: Insurance cover is included in expedition fee.
Safety: All staff are medically trained, and comprehensive medical kits are taken on all expeditions.
Affiliations: Duke of Edinburgh's Award Scheme; Royal Geographical Society.
Tariffs: Prices include food, travel and accommodation. At time of writing, 1997 prices and expedition offerings were not available. Examples of past expeditions are – 10-day Isle of Mull expedition: £225; 2-week Shetland expedition: £395; 16-day Isle of Foula expedition: £366.
Booking: Non-refundable deposit required. Balance due 10 weeks before start date. No refunds in case of cancellation. Bookings must be made well in advance.
Access: Depends on site chosen; contact centre for more details.

dolphin ecosse

Bank House
High Street
Cromarty
Highland
IV11 8UZ
Scotland
Tel & Fax (01381) 600 323

Whale-watching

Dolphin Ecosse run short excursion trips to view the pods of bottlenose dolphins that swim in the Cromarty and Moray Firths, as well as occasional minke whale and harbour porpoise. There are also plentiful common and grey seals and superb birdlife – puffins, gannets, razorbills, guillemots, fulmars, terns, swans, kittiwakes, skuas, eider and scoter ducks and even peregrine falcons along the cliffs.

The bottlenose dolphins of the firths are the only known resident group in the whole North Sea, and the colony is large – over 100 dolphins are regularly sighted. Trips into the firths vary between 2 hours (to see the dolphins only) and 4 hours (to get out into the more open water to look for minke whales). Groups on the boat are limited to a maximum of 12 people.

Please note that this is not a centre with accommodation, though the owners are happy to arrange it for you if you want to stay in the area.

Season: Open all year.

Accommodation: Operator will provide help in arranging local accommodation.
Food: Light refreshments on board boat. Coffee available at centre.
Children: All ages welcome.
Disabled Facilities: Activity is suitable for some disabled clients; contact centre for details.
Insurance: Clients should obtain personal insurance cover if required.
Safety: Staff trained in first aid.
Affiliations: European Cetacean Society; Reseau Cetaces; Whale and Dolphin Conservation Society; RSPB.
Tariffs: 4–5-hour whale-watching boat trips (July, August and September only): £50; $2\frac{1}{2}$-hour dolphin-watching boat trips (all year): £15. No charge for children 3 years and under.
Booking: Book over the phone; no deposit required. Bookings usually made in advance, but late bookings accepted if space available.
Access: From Inverness take the A9, then the A832 to Cromarty. Trains available to Inverness, then buses to Cromarty.

fair isle bird observatory

Fair Isle
Shetland
ZE2 9JU
Scotland
Tel & Fax (01595) 760 258

Bird-watching and Extreme Bird-watching

This is one of Britain's oldest eco-centres, with about 50 years' experience behind it. Fair Isle, set in the Atlantic midway between the Orkneys and Shetland, has a permanent crofting community of about 70 people and a permanent nesting community of many thousands of seabirds, including puffins by the ton, guillemots, razorbills, terns, kittiwakes and gannets. Visitors are encouraged to help during the observatory's early-morning round of checking the traps where birds are caught for ringing and measuring, and to take part in the island's on-going census. Make sure you bring plenty of camera film. Fair Isle has a lodge offering full board from which the bird-watching trips are run.

This is one of the few places in Britain where the editors encountered extreme bird-watching – that is, abseiling off cliffs to look closely at and photograph nesting birds. While this is very risky and only possible for people with their own equipment, there is also controversy as to whether it is lawful. Check with the staff at the field centre.

Season: May to October.
Accommodation: Lodge offers dorm rooms (£25 per night), single rooms (£40 per night), and twin rooms (£35 per person per night).
Food: Full board included; vegetarian and special diets can be catered for.
Children: All ages welcome; child discounts available.
Disabled Facilities: None.
Insurance: Clients should arrange their own holiday insurance.
Safety: Staff trained in first aid.
Affiliations: None.
Tariffs: Use of bird-watching facilities included in accommodation price, £25–£40 per night. Group and return visit discounts available.
Booking: £35 deposit required. Deposit refunded if booking cancelled more than 4 weeks in advance. Early booking recommended for spring and autumn migration periods. Late bookings accepted if space available. Visa and Access cards accepted.
Access: Fair Isle can be reached by air via Shetland or Orkney, or by sea via Shetland.

island underwater safaris

'Nowhere'
Old Town
St Mary's
Isles of Scilly
Cornwall
TR21 ONH
Tel (01720) 422 732

Snorkelling with Seals!

Mark Groves's 'safaris' operate in the warm, clear waters of the Isles of Scilly. You don't need any previous experience to go in with the seals – you are given all the equipment, taken out in a boat to the seals' feeding grounds, and in you go (behind Mark, of course). Once in the water the experience is magical; seals are incredibly graceful, athletic swimmers and these ones, well used to people, carve sweeping arabesques and circles around you as you hover on the surface, delighted.

Mark also leads scuba dives off the reefs to look at the other marine life. Again, you don't need any previous experience – after some basic instruction you are led down for some shallow reef diving. More experienced divers (those holding a British Sub-Aqua Club Sport Diver certificate) can go further afield and may have the opportunity of swimming with dolphins, if they're in the area.

Tariffs: Snorkelling Safari (includes instruction and equipment): £25.

See Sub-Aqua Diving (p. 393) for full details.

---

kindrogan field centre

Enochdhu
By Blairgowrie
Perthshire & Kinross
PH10 7PG
Scotland
Tel (01250) 881 286
Fax (01250) 881 433

Field Studies Courses

Primarily aimed at school and college groups, Kindrogan has been running field courses for about 50 years. Courses last for a week or a weekend with most of the day spent outdoors walking and identifying plants and animals. On some of these practical study holidays – especially the purely botanical courses – the walking involves quite rough terrain. Other courses have a more scientific slant, such as primary and secondary biology and geography courses, or the tertiary biology and geology weeks aimed at university-level natural scientists, with ranger training programmes also included for those wishing to start environmental careers.

Kindrogan occupies a large old Victorian neo-Gothic manor with its own grounds. Comfortable double and single rooms are available and guests can choose whether to stay here or in alternative accommodation outside.

Season: May to October.
Accommodation: Family rooms, twin and single rooms available for up to 90 people.
Food: Full board included; vegetarian and special diets catered for. Coffee room and bar at centre.
Other Activities: Child and Youth Sports (see p. 62); Woodlore (p. 475).
Children: All ages welcome. Special youth courses and family holidays available; see Child and Youth Sports (p. 62).
Disabled Facilities: Some disabled clients can be accommodated; contact centre for details.
Insurance: Clients should arrange their own holiday insurance.
Safety: Staff trained in first aid.
Affiliations: Scottish Field Studies Association.
Tariffs: Prices include tuition, full-board accommodation and transport during course. A variety of botanical and wildlife courses is available; some examples are – Tree Identification and Appreciation (1 week): £265; Mountain Flowers (1 week): £275; Introducing Mosses (3 days): £84; Ferns (3 days): £120; Bird Sounds (3 days): £84; Autumn Birds (1 week): £270; Introduction to Spiders (4 days): £120; Moths (1 week): £270; Spring Surprises Walk (3 days): £84; Walks, Wildlife and Teashops (1 week): £265; Games with Nature (6–10-year-olds, 3 days): £43; Young People's Walks (10–13-year-olds, 3 days): £52.
Booking: £20–50 deposit required, non-refundable. Bookings normally made in advance; late bookings sometimes accepted if space available.
Access: Off the A9, 10 miles north-east of Pitlochry. Trains and buses to Pitlochry; pick-ups from stations can be arranged by centre.

kingspark llama farm

Berriedale
Highland
KW7 6HA
Scotland
Tel (01593) 751 202

Walking, Bird-watching with Llamas

An eccentric one, this, and the editors were a little unsure as to whether it belonged with eco-sports or walking – probably both, so it's going in both. A llama farm up in the far north-east of Scotland, this centre hires its charges out as obliging pack animals for exploring the surrounding coast and mountains, whether as day trips or hikes of several days. A guide and experienced llama-wrangler accompanies you, pointing out things of interest along the way, such as wild flowers, wildlife and historic sites, eventually guiding you to one of several coastal bird-watching hides built by the RSPB. Presumably the guide is also on hand to wrestle down the pack beast should it become intransigent. You can either stay at the farm, taking different walks each day, or arrange for longer treks inland. Contact the farm for details.

Season: Open all year.
Accommodation: 2 single, 2 double and 1 family room available at farm (£14 per night). Camping is possible, but no ablution facilities.
Food: Breakfast included; evening meals can be arranged.
Children: All ages welcome.
Disabled Facilities: Disabled guests can be accommodated.
Insurance: Clients should arrange their own holiday insurance if required.
Safety: No special safety provisions.
Affiliations: None.
Tariffs: £12 per llama (can be shared).
Booking: Deposits required only for large groups, non-refundable. Late bookings accepted if space available.
Access: On the A9 north of Helmsdale. Trains to Helmsdale station, buses to llama farm available. Centre will pick up from train station (£10 return fare).

millfield village of education

Millfield School
Street
Somerset
BA16 0YD
Tel (01458) 445 823
Fax (01458) 840 584

Bird-watching

Led by Steve Payne of the RSPB, Millfield's bird-watching weeks and weekends cover the biological side of ornithology as well as bird-watching in the field. Preliminary classroom sessions deal with bird anatomy and life history and how to locate the parts of the body that are essential for speedy and accurate identification. Bird songs are also covered, along with migration patterns and conservation. After that you are taken to various West Country RSPB reserves and are shown how to identify by physiology and song patterns. Bring your own binoculars.

Millfield School is a co-ed independent boarding school of great beauty set in about 100 acres of grounds. Full board and accommodation are included. You will need your own transport to get there.

Tariffs: Course includes 2 half-day instruction sessions: £73. Full-board accommodation for 1 week: £166 (adult), £136 (under-12). (5% senior discount.)

See Circus Skills (p. 83) for full details.

scottish conservation projects trust

Balallan House
24 Allan Park
Stirling
FK8 2QG
Tel (01786) 479 697

Research Groups, Botanical Trips

A large charity devoted to involving the public in the conservation of Scotland's environment, the SCP organizes over 70 action breaks each year. These last from 1 to 2 weeks, often taking place in some of the remoter parts of Scotland, and are carried out by volunteers under the supervision of experienced leaders. Volunteer projects include such things as path maintenance on old tracks, construction of bothies and shelters and dry-stone walling (or dry-stane dyking as the Scottish call it), as well as wildlife- and botany-oriented activities. There are also over 60 training courses. These are aimed at aspiring countryside rangers or National Park officials as well as the general public, and are recognized as relevant experience on the CVs of anyone trying to get into the conservation profession. Courses usually last from 1 to 2 weeks and cover the whole country, from the Borders to Shetland.

Among the more directly ecologically slanted courses are 10-day ancient woodland management courses in Wester Ross, Glen Orchy, the Isles of Rum and Skye, and in the old Caledonian pine forests of Glen Affric and Badenoch/Strathspey. There is an introduction course on Scottish bats, habitat management for invertebrates, moor and bog management and plant identification, wildlife garden design, silviculture, and the planting of tree and wild flower nurseries.

Other courses involve ancient settlement sites and include working on Roman and Pictish hill-forts in the Scottish Borders. As a volunteer or trainee you are part slave labour, part pupil, but the work is rewarding and the potential for learning unlimited. Write to SCP for a full prospectus.

Season: March to November.
Accommodation: Varies from site to site, from camping to youth hostels and holiday chalets.
Food: Simple but plentiful food included; volunteers are expected to help with the cooking. Vegetarian and special diets can be accommodated if advance notice given.
Children: Minimum age 16 (18 if not UK citizens).
Disabled Facilities: Depends on which site is chosen.
Insurance: Clients are covered by the organization's insurance, except for their personal belongings.
Safety: Staff qualified in first aid.
Affiliations: None.
Tariffs: Required donations for 10-day action breaks (including accommodation and full board): £50 or £40 concessions.
Booking: In order to book an action break you must be a member of the Scottish Conservation Projects Trust or the British Trust for Conservation Volunteers (£15 annual membership, £8 concessions). Full balance must be paid at time of booking. If cancellation notice received more than 28 days in advance, refunds (minus £10 fee) will be given. Visa and Access cards accepted. Bookings normally made in advance, but late bookings sometimes accepted if space available.
Access: Varies according to site chosen, but pick-ups arranged from nearest train station.

sealife surveys

Dervaig
Isle of Mull
Argyll & Bute
PA75 6QL
Scotland
Tel (01688) 400 223
Fax (01688) 400 383

Whale-watching, Research Groups, Bird-watching, Guided Wildlife Treks

The whale grounds around the Inner Hebrides are becoming famous all over Europe for their beautiful island coast-lines, clean waters and frequently sighted pods of minke whale, harbour porpoise, killer whales (orcas), common and Risso's dolphin, and basking shark. Sealife Surveys, based on the Isle of Mull, offer a choice between land-based or sea-based tours – or a combination of the two. The 5- or 7-day combination tours are truly magical, with either 3 or 4 full boat days, 1 land-based wildlife tour, and a free day to 'do' Mull or go across to Iona. On Mull itself you stand a very good chance of seeing otters – the island is a breeding stronghold for the species and along the coasts there are always seals and spectacular birdlife.

You are actually partaking in a scientific survey by booking a course with Sealife Surveys. You record any animal you see along with details of the circumstances, time of day, weather, etc., and the data is supplied to research groups at Oxford, Bristol and Aberdeen Universities as well as the International Whaling Commission. If you want to do more than record, you can join some of the on-site research team in analysing and processing data collected on the boat. Part of the money you spend goes to Sealife's own charity, the Hebridean Whale and Dolphin Trust. This blend of tourism and environmental work earned Sealife the Scottish Tourist Board's top award for Tourism and the Environment in 1994.

Sealife are open to all budgets, with choices of full board and hotel-standard accommodation, camping with meals in the lodge, or camping and cooking for yourself. There is a washing machine and a drying room for all guests. When out in the boat you have the comfort of being on a 40ft trawler yacht with a roomy viewing platform and indoor cabins for rough weather. The land days are split between a Land Rover and walking.

In addition to the regular 5- and 7-day packages, there are cheaper 3-day 'mini-packages', as well as special trips such as Wild Water in April, which includes high seas, puffin, guillemot and razorbill colonies and the first whales of the season, or Autumn Babies, viewing the minke whale, porpoise and Risso's dolphin calves, grey seal pups, and migratory wildfowl and waders.

Season: April to October.
Accommodation: Lodge with 5 double rooms; camping facilities.
Food: Meals available; vegetarian and special diets catered for.
Children: Education tours and games for children.
Disabled Facilities: Lodge has special facilities for the disabled.
Insurance: Clients should arrange their own holiday insurance.
Safety: Staff trained in first aid.
Affiliations: Hebridean Whale and Dolphin Trust; Holiday Mull; International Fund for Animal Welfare; Scottish Activity Holiday Association; Scottish Tourist Board; West Highland and Island Area Tourist Board.
Tariffs: 7-day package includes 4 boat days and 1 land tour (prices vary according to

level of accommodation and board desired): £470–665 per person; 5-day package includes 3 boat days and 1-day land tour: £397–545. (Seasonal discounts available.) Mini-packages (including 1 boat day, 2 nights' accommodation and full board: £107.

Booking: £100 non-refundable deposit required, balance due 6 weeks in advance. Credit cards accepted. Bookings normally made in advance, but late bookings sometimes accepted if space available.

Access: Take the A85 to Oban, then take ferry to Isle of Mull. Trains and buses also available from Glasgow to Oban. Clients will be picked up at port by centre.

---

uist outdoor centre

Cearn Dusgaidh
Lochmaddy
Isle of North Uist
Western Isles
PA82 5AE
Scotland
Tel (01876) 500 480

Guided Wildlife Treks, Bird-watching, Whale-watching

North Uist and its surrounding Hebridean islands are rich in wildlife, both land-based and marine. Large herds of red deer inhabit the central moorlands, while otter frequent the streams and sea lochs, sharing the latter with common and grey seals.

In the open waters around the islands swim dolphins, porpoises and sometimes pods of orca (killer whale), while the combination of Arctic and Gulf Stream currents attracts fish and marine invertebrate species of an astonishing range – including sunfish, mako shark, warm-water sea slugs, anemones and soft corals. The birdlife is no less intense: expect to see a great variety of waders and seabirds including curlews, sanderlings, greenshanks, puffins, storm petrels, fulmars, guillemots and razorbills, Manx shearwaters, greylag goose, barnacle goose, bar-tailed godwit, purple sandpiper and (pause for breath) twite. Inland, the island is one of the last European strongholds of the endangered corncrake and there are black and red-throated divers on the lochs, while various ducks, mute swans, shelduck, gadwall and shoveller, widgeon and garganey also pass through. Raptors include merlin, hen harrier, golden eagle, peregrine falcon, long-eared owl, buzzard and, occasionally, white-tailed eagle.

The centre offers wildlife holidays ranging from day trips to 5- and 7-day packages taking in the land and sea species, all guided by local naturalists and with support from local RSPB wardens – though if you wish you can set off alone. You are asked to record your sightings.

Accommodation is either in the centre's own bunkhouse or can be arranged locally to suit your budget, with a free pick-up (if nearby) for your day's walking or sea-hopping.

Tariffs: Prices include guided tours/talks and accommodation. 1-week holiday (wildlife viewing and/or field studies only or combined with other centre activities): £220 (self-catering), £270 (with full board). Day visitors: £25.

See Sub-Aqua Diving (p. 397) for full details.

viewbank guest house

Golf Course Road
Whiting Bay
Isle of Arran
North Ayrshire
KA27 8QT
Scotland
Tel (01770) 700 326

Bird-watching

John Rhead, an experienced local ornithologist, guides these intensive bird-watching weeks on the Isle of Arran. The package includes full board in a comfortable old stone house, the guide and around 6 hours of bird-watching per day. Arran has some very good birdlife, including nightjar – a difficult bird to spot in the UK – ptarmigan and golden eagle. Along the rugged coast, there is a host of migratory and resident seabird species, as well as plentiful seals and the chance of spotting whales, dolphins or porpoises. The inland trips feature regular sightings of deer, fox, hare and occasional feral goat. Groups are limited to a maximum of 14 people.

Season: Open all year.
Accommodation: Viewbank Guest House has 6 double rooms and 1 single room; en suite facilities available.
Food: Full board available. Vegetarian and special diets are catered for.
Children: All ages welcome.
Disabled Facilities: None.
Insurance: Clients should arrange their own holiday insurance.
Safety: Staff not specially trained for emergencies.
Affiliations: Scottish Tourist Board.
Tariffs: Prices include guided bird-watching and accommodation. Daily rate £16.50–19 per night (including breakfast); weekly rate £187–226 (including full board).
Booking: 20% non-refundable deposit required. Bookings are normally made at least 1 week in advance, although late bookings may be accepted if space available.
Access: From Ardrossan on the mainland of Scotland, take the ferry to Brodick on the Isle of Arran, then take the A841 (by car or bus) to Whiting Bay.

appendix: swimming with dolphins

At present, no centre organizes trips to swim with dolphins in the UK, though several companies have started doing it abroad – its therapeutic value is well known. However, please be aware that dolphins can be as mischievous as people. Several swimmers have found, after tiring of playing with dolphins, that the dolphins had not tired of playing with them. The result was near-drowning through exhaustion. Talk to locals before going down to swim.

Known sites for swimming with dolphins are: Church Bay, Anglesey, and Dingle Bay, off the west coast of Ireland.

If you want to organise a trip to swim with a dolphin, ring International Dolphin Watch at Parklands, North Ferriby, **Humberside**, HU14 3ET Tel (01482) 84468, Fax (01482) 634914. They can put you in touch with local groups who have the dolphins' trust and who can make sure the swim is conducted as safely as possible.

kitting yourself out

A good pair of pocket-sized binoculars is essential – pocket-sized and lightweight (under 650g) so as not to encumber you as you creep through the undergrowth, but powerful enough to let you remain outside an animal's field of vision and scent. You can get a decent pair of powerful lightweights for under £100. Try a pair of Viking 8 x 22s or 8 x 24s – these retail at about £70 and £100 respectively. Pentax offer the DCF HR 8 x 42 for about £90 and the Nikon 8 x 23s are just over £100. Bausch and Lomb supply the Natureview 8 x 42, recommended by *Birdwatching* magazine, for about £130. Further up the range, the Minolta Compact Weathermatic 8 x 23 is a mountaineer's favourite for its ability to stand up to extreme cold and costs about £175. The Zeiss 10 x 25 BTP costs about £360. Above these are Swarovski and Leica, who produce the world's best compact binoculars , but for about £500–600 a pair.

Then you'll need a camera. There are so many on the market that it would be impossible to go into proper detail here. Many photographers recommend that beginners start their wildlife photography with one of the Canon EOS range of cameras, which start at about £320, to which you'll have to add a 200mm long lens (at least another £100). However, many people cannot afford these prices and a good camera shop should be able to advise you on cheaper gear, or where to find good second-hand cameras. Just remember that for photographing wildlife in the field or from a hide an automatic wind-on is a must, despite the slight noise it makes. Use a Fuji film, and preferably Velvia slides, to capture natural colour.

checklist

- ✔ *a good chair*
- ✔ *binoculars*
- ✔ *identification handbooks for birds, mammals, reptiles, insects and flora*
- ✔ *camera*

further reading

The Collins Guide to European Mammals is a useful handbook to carry in the field, as is the RSPB's *Birdwatcher's Pocket Guide*. If you are going to look at whales, dolphins and porpoises, pick up *On the Trail of the Whale* by Mark Cowardine (published by Thunder Bay Books).

governing body

British Falconers Club (BFC)
Home Farm, Hints, Nr Tamworth
Staffordshire B78 3DW
Tel & Fax (01543) 481 737

falconry

The only field sport, after fishing, to have crossed the boundary between élitist and general appeal, falconry, or hawking, is an ancient art that fires even the dullest imagination. Something about the ferocity of the birds, their inherent wildness (captive-bred birds can usually be returned to the wild with no problems), their physical beauty, their soaring aerial acrobatic ability and their lack of dependence on man make them fatally attractive for many people. And to become a falconer, or austringer, you must expect to spend years in training.

Falconry has recently undergone something of a resurgence in popularity in Britain and new centres are opening all the time. Although many of the birds used represent endangered species in the wild (such as peregrines, merlins and goshawks), all the birds used for falconry in Britain are captive-bred, being raised from eggs in incubators. The rising demand for trained birds of prey has therefore helped to augment the gene pool in this country – particularly as many birds are returned to the wild after a few years' service, where they find mates and raise young.

To take up falconry is to re-enter the medieval world. Many words in common use today derive from falconry; for example booze comes from the name for a falcon's drinking bowl; a mews was originally the narrow alley in a castle where the falcons were kept; a lure was originally a falconer's term for the mock prey bird (two wings stitched to a leather bag) which the falconer twirls around his head on the end of a string, to teach a young bird how to catch its prey on the wing. However, most other terms are unique to the art: you hold your falcon or hawk by a pair of jesses, leather straps attached to its legs with bells on them, so that you can locate the bird by its jingling if it flies into a tree for a sulk; you can attach the jesses to a creance, or a long string, when flying the young bird in its early training – though this tends to get snagged round thistles and saplings; or you can lamely attempt to calm your bird if it bates, or throws a tantrum when on your wrist, hanging upside down from its jesses, screaming and tearing at any exposed flesh it can see. The only key falconer's words readily understandable to the layman are the glove (for your protection) and the hood (to keep the bird calm when travelling).

There are two types of raptor, or birds of prey: longwings – which comprise falcons; and shortwings – which comprise hawks and eagles. The longwings take their prey at high speed, whether through a stoop – dive-bombing another bird from high above – or grabbing it after an aerial chase. Shortwings tend to catch their prey on the ground, dropping on it from a hovering position atop a thermal, or from a tree branch or rock ledge. The kestrel is the only longwing falcon that hovers, but it uses an intense wing-flap to maintain its position, and cannot rise on a thermal.

Falconry courses first introduce you to the different types of birds, letting you fly ready-trained species known for their even temper – such as Harris hawks, buzzards and kestrels. You learn about their keep (very complicated), their training (fantastically complicated), and the nuances of flying them (akin to nuclear physics). After such an introductory course (usually a week long), you can progress through further training until the school deems you fit to own your own bird. Allow at least a year to get from complete novice to owner/falconer.

selected centres

the british school of falconry at gleneagles

Gleneagles Hotel
Auchterarder
Perthshire & Kinross
PH3 1NF
Scotland
Tel (01764) 662 231
Fax (01764) 664 345

Stephen and Emma Ford were pioneers of falconry when the sport was being revived in Britain back in the late 1970s. For a relatively young couple they have a wealth of experience behind them and have to be among the UK's best falconers. They offer a wide range of falconry and hawking options: days after walked-up game with Harris hawks, days after grouse with peregrines, weekend introductory courses, week-long basic courses or a 2-year diploma. You can also tailor a course to your own requirements if you are already an experienced falconer and want to improve or learn specialized skills. Stephen and Emma are happy to help their students get their own birds and will help out with any problems that may subsequently occur.

Season: Year round.
Accommodation: Course packages include accommodation at the world-renowned Gleneagles Hotel.
Food: Available at the Gleneagles Hotel – meals included in the beginners' course packages.
Children: Suitable for 5-year-olds and upwards.
Disabled Facilities: The school is wheelchair-accessible. Lessons and hawking are adapted to accommodate disabled clients.
Insurance: Clients should arrange their own holiday insurance.
Safety: Staff trained in first aid.
Affiliations: British Falconers Club (BFC); British Field Sports Society (BFSS); Scottish Tourist Board (STB).
Tariffs: Introductory lesson (45 minutes): £47; half-day hawking (2½ hours): £115; full day hawking (6 hours): £175; group session (minimum of 6, 1½ hours): £49 per person; beginners' course (4 days): £1,376.
Booking: A 30% non-refundable deposit required for courses only. Access, Visa or American Express accepted.
Access: The centre is in the grounds of the Gleneagles Hotel in southern Perthshire & Kinross.

the cotswold falconry centre

Batsford Park
Moreton-in-Marsh
Gloucestershire
GL56 9QB
Tel (01386) 701 143

Set in a valley between two ridges of the Cotswolds, this is very beautiful country in which to learn falconry. The centre offers both 'walked-up' hawking days – hunting with Harris hawks after rabbit and pheasant – and more intensive courses for the would-be serious falconer. Introductory weekend courses or 5-day basic falconry weeks can be followed up with more specialized tuition on care and management, building your aviary and court, training problems, feeding, and minor veterinary skills. The centre can also assist pupils to get their own bird once they are deemed ready, and operates a back-up advice service should any problems occur with the bird.

Season: Year round, but some courses subject to seasonal variations.
Accommodation: Not provided, but centre will help with arranging local B&B.
Food: Not provided.
Children: Over-16s only.
Disabled Facilities: None.
Insurance: Clients should arrange their own holiday insurance.
Safety: Staff trained in first aid.
Affiliations: BFC; BFSS; The Hawk Board.
Tariffs: Prices include instruction and equipment only – a 2-day course is £165, a 5-day course £480, while a hawking or peregrine day costs £80.
Booking: 70% non-refundable deposit required. Bookings for courses are normally made 3 weeks in advance, but late bookings up to 48 hours in advance can be taken if space available. Payment by cash, cheque or Access/Visa card.
Access: The centre is signposted off the A44 west of Moreton-in-Marsh. Clients arriving by train at Moreton can sometimes be picked up. Ring centre for details.

country pursuit

Moonrakers
Allington
Salisbury
Wiltshire
SP4 OBX
Tel & Fax (01980) 610 594

You are in good hands here – Country Pursuit's school of falconry is run by Jim Chick (appropriately named), the chairman of the Hawk Board. Jim teaches falconry and takes people hunting with Harris hawks on the wide acres of Salisbury Plain. He uses ferrets to flush rabbits from their burrows, which are then (if all goes as planned) jumped on by the hawks hovering above and made ready for the pot. Jim also uses pointers to flush game for the birds. Anyone may sign up for a hunting day, but only the serious should sign up for tuition on one of Country Pursuit's falconry courses. These are not structured in the same way as those of the other, larger falconry schools, but are arranged individually each time. Jim is a hard taskmaster, but if you learn under him, you are assured of becoming a good falconer. Ring him up to arrange a day's hunting or a course.

Season: Year round, but some courses subject to seasonal variations.
Accommodation: Not provided, but centre will help with arranging local B&B.

Food: Not provided.
Children: Over-16s only.
Disabled Facilities: None.
Insurance: Clients should arrange their own holiday insurance.
Safety: Staff trained in first aid.
Affiliations: BFC; BFSS; The Hawk Board.
Tariffs: A hawking day usually costs about £50 per person. Course tariffs by arrangement.
Booking: Hunting days usually booked at least 7 days in advance, but late booking welcome if space allows. Courses booked by private arrangement. Payment by cash or cheque.
Access: The centre is in Allington, a few miles from Salisbury. Clients can sometimes be picked up from the train station in town. Ring Jim Chick for full details.

---

grampian hawks and falcons

Bramble Cottage
Broom of Hoy
Forres
Moray
IV36 0SR
Tel (01309) 675 788

The coastal barrens and the inland moors of the Vale of St Andrew provide the flying grounds for this centre, which offers days with Harris hawks after rabbit and pheasant and days with peregrine falcons after grouse or crows, using pointers and spaniels to flush the game. Courses can also be arranged, and the centre will assist you in getting and training your own bird, if you learn to a sufficient level.

Season: Year round.
Accommodation: Not provided, but centre will help with arranging local B&B.
Food: Not provided.
Children: Over-16s only.
Disabled Facilities: None.
Insurance: Clients should arrange their own holiday insurance.
Safety: Staff trained in first aid.
Affiliations: BFC; BFSS; The Hawk Board; STB.
Tariffs: A hawking day usually costs about £50 per person with Harris hawks and £80 per person with peregrines. Course tariffs by arrangement.
Booking: Hunting days usually booked at least 7 days in advance, but late booking welcome if space allows. Courses booked by private arrangement. Payment by cash or cheque.
Access: The centre is just outside Forres on the road to Elgin. Clients arriving by public transport can be picked up from Forres by prior arrangement.

the hawk conservancy

Andover
Hampshire
SP11 8DY
Tel (01264) 773 850

The wide chalk country around Andover is good falconing – not too much cover for the birds to get lost in and good views of their flights. The Hawk Conservancy run courses at all levels of falconry, plus 'taster' days for beginners to fly birds under supervision. Walked-up hunting days using Harris hawks on pheasant and rabbit, or flying peregrines after partridge, are also offered.

For would-be full-time falconers, the conservancy runs 2-day introductory courses which sort out how far you want to take the sport. If you get hooked, further courses can be arranged individually until the centre feels you are ready to own a bird. They can then help with obtaining one, and supervise your training of it.

Season: Year round, but some courses subject to seasonal variations.

Accommodation: Not provided, but centre will help with arranging local B&B.
Food: Food provided on courses.
Children: Over-16s only.
Disabled Facilities: Disabled clients can sometimes be accommodated; contact centre for details.
Insurance: Clients should arrange their own holiday insurance.
Safety: Staff trained in first aid.
Affiliations: BFC; BFSS; Southern Tourist Board.
Tariffs: Prices include instruction and equipment only – a half-day course is £35, while a hawking or peregrine day costs £65.
Booking: Full payment required at time of booking, non-refundable. Bookings normally made 3 weeks in advance, but late bookings up to 48 hours in advance can be taken if space available. Payment by cash, cheque or Access/Visa card.
Access: The centre is signposted off the A303 west of Andover. Clients arriving by train at Andover can sometimes be picked up. Ring centre for details.

the national birds of prey centre

Newent
Gloucestershire
GL18 1JJ
Tel (01531) 820 286

This large centre operates as both a falconry school and a tourist attraction, with displays for the public and a private collection of exotic and indigenous raptors. The courses, though non-residential, are intensive: they reckon that you could start owning your first bird (under supervision) after taking their 5-day course. The 2-year diploma is definitely worth doing if you really want to learn the art, or if you are thinking of taking up a career in falconry. Should you decide to get a bird, the centre will help you build a court and aviary and be on hand to advise on any problems you and your bird might have together.

Season: Year round, but some courses subject to seasonal variations.
Accommodation: Not provided, but centre will help with arranging local B&B.
Food: Lunch provided for those taking courses. Special diets by arrangement.
Children: Over-16s only.
Disabled Facilities: None.
Insurance: Clients should arrange their own holiday insurance.
Safety: Staff trained in first aid.
Affiliations: BFC; BFSS; English Tourist Board.
Tariffs: Prices include instruction and equipment only – a day course is £100, a 5-day course £395 and a 2-year diploma course about £1,500.
Booking: 70% non-refundable deposit required. Bookings normally made 3 weeks in advance, but late bookings up to 48 hours in advance can be taken if space available. Payment by cash, cheque or Access/Visa card.
Access: The centre is signposted from the B4215 between Huntley and Newent about 10 miles west of Gloucester.

scottish academy of falconry

Bonchester Bridge
Hawick
Borders
TD9 9TB
Scotland
Tel & Fax (01450) 860 666

The open Teviots are perfect flying country – high moors with few woodlands but plenty of game. The Scottish Academy of Falconry has been established 10 years and offers residential courses and holidays for both serious falconers and recreational hawkers at any level of competence. They will also assist clients in buying and training their own birds, once the client has gained sufficient experience. A speciality is falconry from horseback – open only to clients with some riding experience – which involves flying peregrine and saker falcons after carrion crows and other corvids, and galloping beneath the aerial combats so as to be in the right spot when the birds come down – an incredible insight into an aspect of the medieval world.

Season: April to November.
Accommodation: Double rooms in modern country house.
Food: Full board provided; vegetarian and special diets catered for upon request.
Children: All ages welcome; instruction tailored to age of child.
Disabled Facilities: None.
Insurance: Clients should arrange their own holiday insurance.
Safety: Staff trained in first aid.
Affiliations: BFC; BFSS; STB.
Tariffs: Prices include instruction, equipment and full-board accommodation. 1-week course: from £310.
Booking: £50 non-refundable deposit required. Bookings normally made 3 weeks in advance, but late bookings up to 48 hours in advance can be taken if space available.
Access: Off the B6357 south of Bonchester Bridge. Buses to Jedburgh or Hawick. Pick-ups can be arranged by centre (£5 charge).

kitting yourself out

A beginner's bird, like a red-tailed buzzard or Harris hawk, will set you back about £350, while a falcon or goshawk (only for the very experienced) goes for £500 and up. A telemeter, which tracks the bird when it has flown out of sight, costs around £150.

You can buy the whole kit – jesses, hoods, aviary and court – for about £2,000 if you do the woodwork yourself, following the instructions laid down in *Training Birds of Prey*, by Jemima Parry-Jones. Jesses, blocks, boozes (drinking bowls), creances and other accessories can be bought through Martin Jones Falconry Furniture, The Parsonage, Llanrothal, Monmouth, Gwent NP5 3PQ, tel (01600) 750 300.

further reading

Training Birds of Prey, Jemima Parry-Jones, David & Charles, 1994.

checklist

- ✔ *hawk (for beginners), falcon (for more the experienced)*
- ✔ *jesses*
- ✔ *creance*
- ✔ *block*
- ✔ *booze*
- ✔ *hoods*
- ✔ *aviary and court*
- ✔ *telemeter*

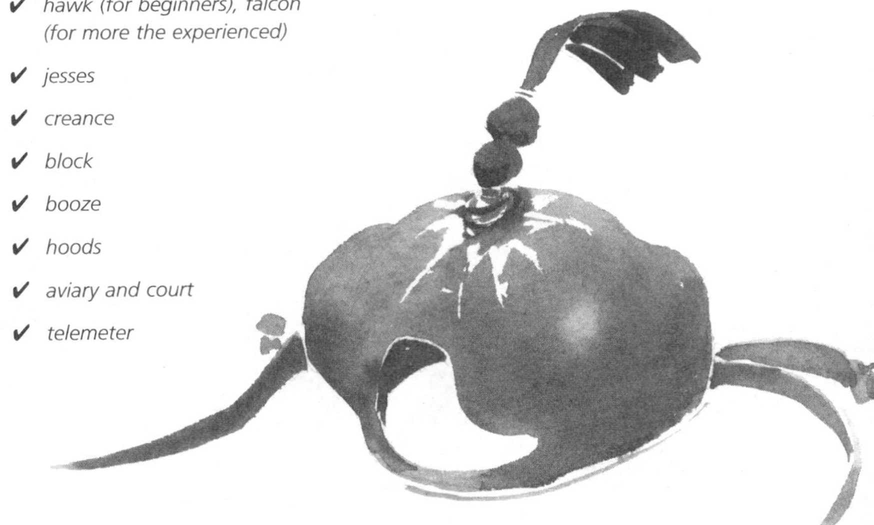

photo: Acorn Activities

governing body

British Gliding Association (BGA)
Kimberley House, Vaughan Way
Leicester LE1 4SE
Tel (0116) 253 1051

gliding

Towed up by a plane and set adrift in the endless expanses of the sky – you are flying a light aircraft but without the noise and bother of an engine. It is not unusual for glider pilots to cover more than 200 miles in a day, and there is a whole world of competition and aerobatic flying as spectacular as anything you can do in a small plane.

You make your first flights in a dual-control glider with an instructor – whether you're on a day's pleasure flight or beginning your pilot's training. After about 50 flights or so, including take-offs and landings, you can move on to solo flying. And here's the real beauty of it – with gliding you do not need to obtain a licence, and you can be as young as 16 to fly solo. The British Gliding Association (BGA) requires you to make a solo flight before giving you your first certificate, and that you pass its Bronze Certificate before making cross-country flights. During the Bronze test you'll have to make two soaring flights (like a buzzard rising on the thermals) and be tested on air law, weather systems and flight theory. After your Bronze Certificate there are, of course, Silver, Gold and Diamond badges to gain. But after these you can soar to heights that require oxygen equipment, and can either buy your own glider or (much more affordable) buy a share in a syndicate-owned glider.

Gliders are surprisingly small things – getting into the cockpit feels a bit like climbing into a canoe – but with a wingspan of 15–22m and a top speed of 150mph, there is no feeling of being under-powered. In fact, because you are so much a part of the air currents, gliding offers more than enough excitement for most people.

You can either take your first BGA certificates during the summer on a 1-week or 2-week course, or you can accumulate hours gradually over the course of a few months or more. Sign up for a 'taster' flight to see if you like it first. And ask your instructor to show you a few stunts. Looping the loop in a glider is unforgettable.

selected centres

bristol & gloucestershire gliding club

Nympsfield
Nr Stonehouse
Gloucestershire
GL10 3TX
Tel (01453) 860 342
Fax (01453) 860 060

Offering flying over the Cotswolds and Mendips, this large gliding club (over 30 instructors) has been going since 1956. It offers residential or non-residential courses, beginning with a half-hour trial flight, progressing through 2–3-day introductory courses to the 5–7-day Club Pilot certificate and on to the more advanced Cross-Country certificate. These longer courses include accommodation and an evening meal – a package that the club calls a 'holiday in the sky'.

Ridge flights of 300km and more are not unusual here, even in the winter (though courses don't run in this season due to occasional high winds). The school has a fleet of Schleicher Kal-13s and single-seaters from the Ka-8 to the ASW19 which provide a good training base and a suitable progression for learning to fly solo. Once you feel ready, the school can offer intensive one-to-one full-day flight training, or special improver courses over 5 days.

Season: Open all year, courses April to September.

Accommodation: Double, single and bunk rooms at centre. (Clients may camp for free if they don't choose residential packages.)

Food: Breakfast and dinner included (in residential packages), vegetarian selections available.

Children: Must be 16 or older; consent of parent or guardian required.

Disabled Facilities: Disabled clients can often be accommodated; contact centre for details.

Insurance: Clients should arrange personal insurance cover.

Safety: Staff trained in first aid.

Affiliations: BGA.

Tariffs: Basic winch trial lesson: £16; standard aerotow trial lesson: £33; advanced trial lesson: £55. Residential courses (R) include tuition, flights, accommodation and breakfast/dinner, non-residential courses (NR) include tuition and flights only. There is also a choice of intensive courses (2 pupils per instructor) or standard (4 pupils).
5-day intensive course: £305 (R) / £210 (NR);
5-day standard course: £245 (R) / £150 (NR);
4-day intensive course: £250 (R) / £190 (NR);
4-day standard course: £205 (R) / £126 (NR).
Private instruction: £100 per day.

Booking: £50 non-refundable deposit required. Late bookings accepted if space available.

Access: 5 miles south-west of Stroud on the B4066. Trains to Stroud, buses from Stroud to centre. (Cabs from Stroud around £5).

deeside gliding club

Aboyne Airfield
Dinnet
Aboyne
Aberdeenshire
AB34 5LB
Scotland
Tel & Fax (03398) 85339

Easily reached by bus from Aberdeen, this 32-year-old gliding school offers soaring over the hills of Royal Deeside in some of the least restricted airspace in Europe. Climbs to 20,000ft and above are commonplace here, and the school's club pilots regularly complete flights in excess of 300km.

Introductory and Club Pilot courses are offered here, either residential (2–7 days) or broken up over sessions to suit your availability; 1-hour 'taster' flights are also offered. If you opt for a residential course, you can stay either in the airfield's own bunkhouse or arrange alternative accommodation outside – though for that you'll need your own car. If you are already an experienced pilot, you can hire gliders and plot your own cross-country routes.

Season: Open all year.
Accommodation: 2 double and 2 single rooms (£4 per night) available for visitors to the area. Camping available on-site (£1 per night). Centre will also provide help in arranging local accommodation.
Food: Self-catering kitchen. Bar at centre.
Children: All ages welcome.
Disabled Facilities: Toilets wheelchair-accessible. Disabled clients can be accommodated depending on type of disability. Contact centre for details.
Insurance: Clients should arrange personal insurance cover if desired.
Safety: Staff trained in first aid.
Affiliations: BGA; Scottish Sports Council.
Tariffs: Trial lesson: £33. Course prices include tuition, unlimited soaring, and 1 month's club membership. 2-day course (8 aerotows): £156; 1-week course (10 aerotows): £195. Students can take additional lessons to obtain solo pilot certificate; contact centre for details. Group discounts available.
Booking: £50 non-refundable deposit required for courses. Advance bookings must be made for courses, otherwise late bookings accepted if space available.
Access: Off the A93 near Aboyne village. Trains to Aberdeen, buses from Aberdeen to site.

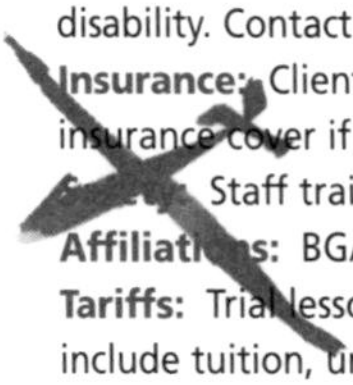

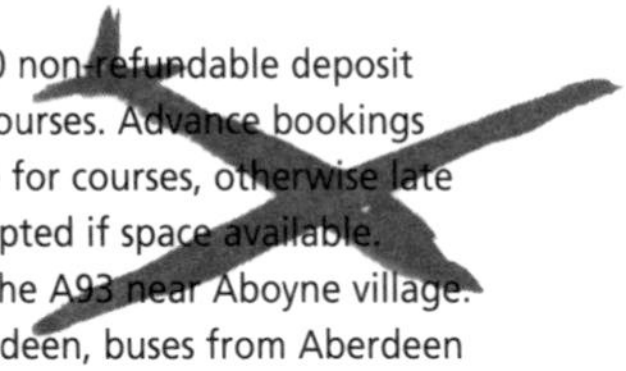

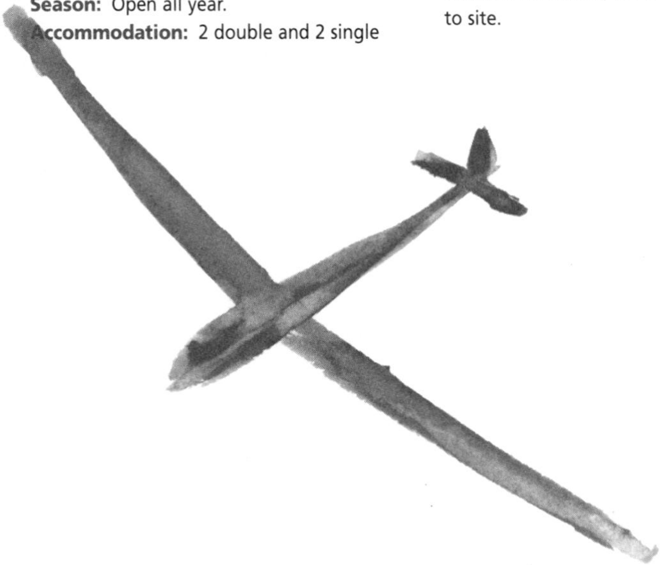

devon & somerset gliding club

North Hill Airfield
Broadhembury
Nr Honiton
Devon
EX14 0LP
Tel (01404) 841 386

One of Britain's larger gliding clubs, with 26 instructors and a large fleet of twin-seater aircraft for training and single-seaters for solo flying – you don't get to go solo until you've been up for at least 100 flights or 'launches'.

If you want to try out gliding, go for a short Air Experience Flight. If you decide you want more, you'll have to become a club member, which enables you to take advantage of the 5-day Club Pilot courses (which can be intensive, held over separate daily sessions or a series of week-ends). If you take an intensive course – i.e. every day over consecutive days – the club can help you to find a local B&B, but you'll need a car to get to and fro.

Season: Open all year (Wednesdays, Thursdays, Saturdays and Sundays).
Accommodation: Tent pitches and 1 caravan available. Otherwise centre can help arrange local accommodation.
Food: Midday meals available, bar and self-catering kitchen on-site.
Children: Minimum age about 13, depending on height and ability to use all controls.
Disabled Facilities: Some disabled clients can be accommodated (must be able to climb into glider and use controls); contact centre for details.
Insurance: Clients should arrange personal insurance cover.
Safety: Club members trained in first aid.
Affiliations: BGA.
Tariffs: Trial flight, winch launch: £16; trial flight, aerotow: £24; 5-day gliding course: £195. Club membership available at £95 per year (plus initial joining fee).
Booking: Deposit required for courses; contact centre for details. Late bookings accepted if space available.
Access: Exit 28 on M5, take A373 to Broadhembury, between Cullompton and Honiton. Trains and buses to Cullompton or Honiton. Cabs to centre available (approximately £5–7).

enstone eagles

Old Control Tower
Enstone Airfield
Enstone
Oxfordshire
OX7 4NP
Tel (01608) 677 461; for course bookings ring (01865) 300 518

About 15 miles north-west of Oxford, Enstone Eagles is a small club that wel-comes beginners. The club has dual-seat gliders and a single-seater for post-solo pilots. Single and syndicate ownership of gliders can be organized through the club, which also offers full hangarage and maintenance services. 'Taster' flights to see if you like the sport are offered along-side more structured 3-day, 5-day and 3-month courses, which should take you successfully through your pilot's licence assessment. The club has 8 instructors and has been open 30 years.

Season: Open all year (5-day courses April to September).
Accommodation: Free camping or caravanning, otherwise local B&B accommodation can be easily arranged.

Food: Not provided.
Children: Must be 16 or older; consent of parent or guardian required.
Disabled Facilities: Disabled clients can often be accommodated; contact club for details.
Insurance: Clients should arrange personal insurance cover if desired.
Safety: No specific medical training.
Affiliations: BGA.
Tariffs: Basic winch trial lesson: £20; mini-course (3 flights): £45; 5-day course: £215-285.
Booking: £50 non-refundable deposit required. Late bookings accepted if space available. Payment by cheque or cash.
Access: 15 miles north-west of Oxford, signposted from the B4030, off the A44 between Woodstock and Chipping Norton.

---

highland gliding club

Roselea
Drum Road
Keith
Moray
AB55 3ER
Tel (01542) 887 585

Open since 1972, Highland Gliding is based at Easterton Airfield near Elgin, flying most weekends throughout the year and mid-week evenings in summer.

You can take a trial flight, but if you want to go further you must become a club member. The advantage of this is that all tuition is then covered in the price of membership, with very minimal charges for the flight time and the winch launches. Should you want to train for a full licence and/or buy a glider, this can be arranged, along with hangarage and maintenance.

Offering flying to the south over the Grampians, this has to be one of the most spectacular soaring sites in Britain. The club has 6 instructors.

Season: Open all year, courses April to September.
Accommodation: Not provided.
Food: Not provided.
Children: Must be 16 years or older; consent of parent or guardian required.
Disabled Facilities: Disabled clients can often be accommodated; contact centre for details.
Insurance: Clients covered by club's insurance.
Safety: Staff trained in first aid.
Affiliations: BGA.
Tariffs: Basic winch trial lesson: £15; membership thereafter costs £90 per year plus a £6 joining fee. All tuition included in the membership fee, but launch costs and flight time extra.
Booking: £50 non-refundable deposit required. Late bookings accepted if space available. Payment by cheque, cash or Visa/Mastercard.
Access: From Elgin take the A941 towards Rothes. About 2.3 miles after leaving New Elgin turn right at the junction marked 'Birnie' and follow the road for 1.5 miles to a T-junction at the Birnie Inn. Turn left for half a mile and look out for the Easterton Farm buildings. The entrance to the gliding site is on the left of the road just after the farmhouse. Own transport a necessity.

london gliding club

Tring Road
Dunstable
Bedfordshire
LU6 2JP
Tel (01582) 663 419

British gliding started here in 1930, not in fact in London at all, but about 40 miles to the north in Bedfordshire. Still, the club is quite easy to reach by car from the big city, and offers flying over the wide rolling ploughlands of southern East Anglia and the wooded Chilterns. Long cross-country flights are made from this club – the longest being 750km. Flights of 7 hours and more are not uncommon and the club also organizes expeditions to Wales and Scotland. Long winter flights are also made regularly.

The club has a fleet of single- and twin-seat gliders, most of which can get up to 1,000ft in about 20 seconds. Computerized flight-planning and sophisticated weather forecast equipment provide a good back-up for learners and experienced pilots alike.

Courses offered include the basic 5–7-day Club Pilot certificate (residential or broken up into evening sessions to suit your time schedule), as well as the more advanced Cross-Country qualification. 'Taster' flights of 1 or 2 hours can also be arranged, as can 2-day specialist courses in meteorology, navigation, spot landing and advanced techniques, such as cross-country racing, cloud flying and the use of radio and navigation aids.

Season: Open all year, courses April to September.
Accommodation: Double, single and bunkrooms at centre. (Clients may camp for free if they don't choose residential packages.)
Food: Breakfast and dinner included (in residential packages); vegetarian selections available.
Children: Must be 16 or older; consent of parent or guardian required.
Disabled Facilities: Disabled clients can often be accommodated; contact centre for details.
Insurance: Clients should arrange personal insurance cover.
Safety: Staff trained in first aid.
Affiliations: BGA.
Tariffs: Basic winch trial lesson: £16; standard aerotow trial lesson: £33; advanced trial lesson: £55. Residential courses (R) include tuition, flights, accommodation and breakfast/dinner; non-residential courses (NR) include tuition and flights only. There is also a choice of intensive courses (2 pupils per instructor) or standard (4 pupils).
5-day intensive course: £305 (R) / £210 (NR);
5-day standard course: £245 (R) / £150 (NR);
4-day intensive course: £250 (R) / £190 (NR);
4-day standard course: £205 (R) / £126 (NR).
Private instruction: £100 per day.
Booking: £50 non-refundable deposit required. Late bookings accepted if space available.
Access: Contact centre for details.

north wales gliding club

Bryn Gwyn Bach Farm
Rhualt
St Asaph
Clwyd
LL17 0TH
Tel (01745) 582 268

Established in 1978, this is a large gliding club with 8 instructors and beautiful flying over the Vale of Clwyd, a superb soaring site, with prevailing westerly winds, regular climbs in the lee wave to 10,000ft and above, and plenty of thermals. The club has a small, friendly membership and offers 'taster' flights as well as training from beginner to Bronze standard. More specialist advanced courses are also organized for club members to improve their skills. If you come for a course you must have your own transport if you are not prepared to camp at the club's airfield.

Season: Open all year, courses from May to September.

Accommodation: Camping or caravan £2 per night. Other accommodation can be arranged locally.

Food: Restaurant on site.

Children: Minimum age 16. Under-18s must have parental consent.

Disabled Facilities: Disabled clients can sometimes be accommodated; contact centre for details.

Insurance: Clients should arrange their own holiday insurance.

Safety: Staff trained in first aid.

Affiliations: BGA.

Tariffs: It costs £15 for a trial lesson or £185 for a 5-day course. Prices do not include accommodation. To join the club costs £96 as a flying member.

Booking: Non-refundable £50 deposit required. Balance due 28 days in advance. Bookings normally made in advance but late bookings accepted if space available. Cash or cheques only.

Access: On the A55 west towards Conway, take the first exit after the Traveller's Inn. The centre is then a short distance down on the right.

stratford-upon-avon gliding club

Snitterfield Airfield
Bearly Road
Snitterfield
Stratford-upon-Avon
Warwickshire
CV37 OEX
Tel (01789) 731 095
Fax (01926) 429 676

Open 17 years, this club flies every day through the summer and at weekends the rest of the year, offering trial lessons for beginners followed by summer courses – short-term or up to full pilot. The latter course requires you to join the club. Groups of up to 20 can be catered for in trial flights – the club has 18 instructors. The soaring southwards over the Cotswolds and the Vale of Evesham is particularly beautiful.

Season: Open all year, holiday courses from May to September.
Accommodation: Camping or caravanning free. Other accommodation can be arranged locally.
Food: Cooked breakfast, buffet lunches and snacks available.
Children: Minimum age 14. Under-18s must have parental consent.
Disabled Facilities: Disabled clients can sometimes be accommodated; contact centre for details.
Insurance: Club members should take out personal insurance cover.
Safety: Some members trained in first aid.
Affiliations: BGA.
Tariffs: It costs £20 for a trial lesson or £215 for a 5-day course. Prices do not include accommodation. To join the club costs £130 as a flying member.
Booking: Non-refundable £25 deposit required for holiday courses. Balance due 28 days in advance. Bookings normally made in advance but late bookings accepted if space available. Cash and cheques only.
Access: From Stratford take the A34 towards Birmingham, turn right at Golden Cross through Bearly and look out for the club on the right under the radio mast. From the M40 take Junction 15 and the A46 towards Stratford, turn right through Snitterfield towards Bearly. Public transport not available.

kitting yourself out

After the last war, Germany was prohibited under international law from building powered aircraft. Instead they turned their attention to gliders and, today, the Germans have cornered the market. The two most widely recommended makes are Schleicher and Schempp-Hirten. Prices start at about £5,000 for an older second-hand model (not including instruments), while the most expensive new ones retail at around £75,000. There is no need to buy a new aircraft, however, as gliders have to pass an inspection of airworthiness every year, and any worn parts are then replaced. For this reason, and owing to the simplicity of their structure and design, even the oldest wooden models can be kept in service for decades.

A set of instruments is much more expensive. Cambridge are probably the most popular makers, and a barograph (which records where you've been and how high – like the black box in an aeroplane), radio, oxygen set and global positioning system will set you back around £13,000.

As for parachutes, not all glider pilots carry them, as most accidents occur during take-off or landing. Once in the air a glider is pretty safe and can be brought down just about anywhere. However, pilots who fly up to very high altitudes and spend a lot of time in cloud do rely on parachutes for extra safety. Once again, these are not cheap – see Parachuting (p. 305) to get some idea of manufacturers and prices.

checklist

- ✔ *global positioning system*
- ✔ *glider*
- ✔ *oxygen mask and cylinders*
- ✔ *radio (for flying at very high altitudes only)*
- ✔ *barograph*
- ✔ *parachute*

photo: Andrew Holt
governing body
British Orienteering Federation
Riversdale, Dale Road North
Darley Dale, Matlock
Derbyshire DE4 2HX
Tel (01629) 734 042
Fax (01629) 733 769

gorge walking coasteering orienteering

At its most intense, gorge walking requires even more nerve than bungee jumping. On a really hard-core gorge walk you follow the course of a young river, going where the water goes. This means that when you encounter a waterfall with a deep enough pool, you jump. Some jumps get up to 20m high, though there are more moderate forms of gorge walking that do without the jumps. And then, of course, you have to climb back out of the gorge at the end of the day, this time up the waterfalls. The Brecon Beacons is the main gorge walking area of Britain, but centres are beginning to spring up elsewhere. It's always worth calling up centres in the upland area you want to visit to see if anyone has started gorge walking trips.

Coasteering is another strange pursuit, but quite fun. You climb down a cliff, sometimes using abseiling equipment, to the sea below. Then, using a buoyancy aid, you bob across the bay and climb the cliff on the other side. Dyfed is a good location for this activity, but as with gorge walking, the sport is growing and it is worth ringing up centres in other cliff areas to see if they are offering it.

Orienteering involves getting muddy, wet and knackered by running around the hills with a map, compass and a set of clues to questions that have to be answered on your return. There are many forms of orienteering – at its mildest, it's a pleasant country walk enhanced by a few easy mental problems. But people quickly get the bug. There is a strong national competition scene (even an international one) where solving the problems is really tough – perhaps involving climbing a tree to find something hidden, or burrowing down a hole. At a competitive level, speed is everything, so the tough, usually hilly courses have to be completed at the double. And then you have to map-read the whole time – often on a compass bearing – so as not to get lost. The centres listed in this chapter encompass the full range of orienteering levels from gentle to full assault, but many of them are happy to make it tougher for you if you want . . .

selected centres

acorn activities

PO Box 120
Hereford
Hereford & Worcester
HR4 8YB
Tel (01432) 830 083
Fax (01432) 830 110

Gorge Walking and Coasteering

Acorn offer gorge walking trips in Snowdonia and coasteering off the Dyfed coast. This is a good company to go with if you'd like a gentle introduction to these sports rather than a full-scale scare: there is little jumping involved, but plenty of abseiling. They offer the sports at a number of locations throughout North Wales and Dyfed, and include B&B, guides, wet suits and some local transport in the general tariff.

Note that Acorn offer a variety of sports among their adventure holidays which may be of interest to gorge walkers, including abseiling, climbing and caving. Contact them to find out more about these activities, and see Walking (p. 414) for a list of the adventure sports offered by Acorn that are featured in this guide.

Children: No unaccompanied children.
Tariffs: Include accommodation, guide, lunch and all equipment. A full day costs £40.

See Walking (p. 414) for full details.

black mountain activities

PO Box 5
Hay-on-Wye
Hereford & Worcester
HR3 5YB
Tel (01497) 847 897

Gorge Walking

Black Mountain call their gorge walking days adventure walking. These guided day trips take place in the waterfalls area of the Brecon Beacons National Park and can be tailored to adults or children, but always including a range of leaps, swings, slides and scrambles with some swimming thrown in. The really adventurous can opt for a route that includes leaping off a waterfall more than 20ft high. The guides tend to be cagey about exactly where you will go and what you will encounter on any given day, however, and like to save a few surprises for the end. Black Mountain usually require you to find your own way to the starting points, but they will take you there by minibus from a central pick-up point; either way you'll need your own car. They will also book local accommodation at a budget to suit you.

Season: All year.
Tariffs: A full day's gorge walking costs £35 per person.
See White-water Rafting and Coracles (p. 446) for full details.

croft-na-caber

Kenmore
Loch Tay
Perthshire & Kinross
PH15 2HW
Tel (01887) 830 588
Fax (01887) 830 649

Gorge Walking

The hills around Loch Tay have some excellent routes for gorge walking. As long as you're over 14, you can sign up for a full or half-day's wet, exhausting splashing up and down the waterfalls of the local forests. Croft-na-Caber's guided gorge walks include plunging from waterfalls, abseiling down into the less accessible reaches of the gorges, scrambling up ridges and riding down water chutes on your butt – great fun! All safety equipment is provided.

Season: Year round.
Tariffs: Gorge walking is £29 per person.

See White-water Rafting and Coracles (p. 447) for full details.

dartmoor expedition centre

Rowden
Widecombe
Newton Abbot
Devon
TQ13 7TX
Tel (01364) 621 249

Orienteering

Dartmoor Expedition Centre occupies an old stone farm and outbuildings at the foot of the wild moor. At 25 years old and still running, it's one of Britain's most established centres and mostly caters for groups, though individuals can fill free slots in existing bookings.

Unless you want to put together a tailor-made orienteering weekend or week, the sport is offered only as part of a more general multi-activity programme, where it is taught at an introductory level only. However, should you want to make up your own orienteering package, the level of tuition can be raised to competition level. Ring the centre and tell them your requirements.

Accommodation is in a bunkhouse or your own tent. If you want to stay in a local B&B the centre will arrange it and can ferry you to and fro at a cost of 30p per mile.

Tariffs: Prices include tuition, equipment and full-board accommodation. Orienteering instructors' course (6 days): £200. Orienteering is included in the multi-activity package offered by centre: £200 per week. An instructor for group orienteering trips can be hired for £90 per day.

See Walking (p. 418) for full details.

edale yha activity centre

Rowland Cote
Nether Booth
Edale
Sheffield
S30 2ZH
Tel (01433) 670 302
Fax (01433) 670 234

Orienteering

Newcomers to orienteering would do well to attend Edale's 2-day weekend in the Derbyshire Peak District, which provides a thorough introduction to the 'thought sport', from basic map and compass work through to more advanced orienteering techniques such as route-finding, pacing over rough terrain, building up fitness and working as a team. The practical training is supplemented by evening lectures and culminates in your entering an event on the Sunday.

Season: Year round.
Children: Minimum age 16.
Tariffs: Price includes equipment, instruction and full-board accommodation – 2-day course: £82. Orienteering is also one of the sports offered in the centre's multi-activity package deals: approximately £42 per day in high season (April–August), £32 in low season (November–February).

See Caving (p. 45) for full details.

fairburn activity centre

Marybank
Muir of Ord
Highland
IV6 7UT
Scotland
Tel (01997) 433 397
Fax (01997) 433 328

Orienteering

Fairburn offers orienteering as one of several action sports packages, which include archery and canoeing (at very basic levels), mountain biking and walking. Their courses are introductory, designed to teach you the basics of the sport – such as map-reading and figuring out clues. The routes are laid out in the surrounding woodland – very beautiful – and are not overly demanding.

The centre is a converted stone stable on the old Fairburn estate. The loose boxes are still there in the dining room, where they make alcoves for tables for two. Accommodation is in general a little more comfortable than is usual at outdoor centres, and this is reflected in the prices.

Season: Open all year.
Accommodation: Double and twin rooms in converted estate stables (jacuzzi baths in all the bathrooms!).
Food: Full board included.
Children: Activities for children over 10.
Disabled Facilities: Disabled clients can be accommodated; contact centre for details.
Insurance: Clients should arrange personal insurance if desired; can be arranged through centre.
Safety: Staff trained in emergency first aid.
Affiliations: None.
Tariffs: Prices include tuition, equipment and full-board accommodation. Half-day session: £8; full day session: £15. Orienteering is also included in the centre's multi-activity packages (prices vary according to season). 1-week holiday: £205–274; 1-week children's holiday (10–17-year-olds): £154–210.
Booking: £60 non-refundable deposit required. Late bookings accepted if space available.
Access: Off the A832 near Muir of Ord. From Inverness take train or bus to Muir of Ord, then taxi to centre (approximately £4).

free spirits

5 Ballinlaggan
Acharn
Aberfeldy
Perthshire & Kinross
PH15 2HT
Tel (01887) 830 633

Gorge Walking

Like its neighbour (and competitor) Croft-na-Caber, Free Spirits organize gorge walking trips into the Perthshire hills. These generally last about 3 hours and may include abseiling, leaping into pulls and even a 'zip wire' or aerial ropeway over a 60ft gorge, which you hang on to by means of a pulley with wheels while descending frighteningly fast. However, the adrenalin level of the gorge walks can be tailored to any group's or individual's needs, so you don't have to do the alarming stuff if you don't want to.

Unlike Croft-na-Caber, Free Spirits do not provide accommodation, but the owners will book it for you locally at a budget to suit you.

Season: Year round.
Tariffs: 3-hour gorge walk: £20 per person.

See White-water Rafting and Coracles (p. 448) for full details.

green rock

20 Castle Hill
Duffield
Belper
Derbyshire
DE56 4EA
Tel (01332) 840 712

Orienteering

A relatively new school – at the time of writing it had been open just a year – Green Rock offers a good introduction to orienteering, with helpful instruction for those wishing to take the sport up seriously. Beyond beginner level, Green Rock can coach both teams and individuals, providing solid back-up for the would-be competitor. The steep Derbyshire hills will also do their bit to prepare you for the tough up-and-down courses of the British competition circuit.

Although no residential courses are offered, Green Rock will help you book accommodation locally and will help out if you don't have your own transport.

Season: Open all year.
Accommodation: Organization will provide help in obtaining local accommodation.
Food: Not provided.
Other Activities: Climbing and Abseiling (see p. 98).
Children: No age restrictions.
Disabled Facilities: None.
Insurance: Clients must provide their own insurance.
Safety: Staff trained in first aid.
Affiliations: None.
Tariffs: Instruction is £12 per group per hour (any number of people up to 12 maximum). 25% discount for students, registered unemployed or clients who come alone.
Booking: Deposit of £20 per group per day. Cancellation notices received more than 7 days in advance will be charged 50% of deposit, less than 7 days 100% of deposit.
Access: Clients must arrange to meet instructor at specified sites in the Peak District of Derbyshire. Contact organization for directions and possible help with transport.

high trek snowdonia

Tal y Waen
Deiniolen
Gwynedd
LL55 3NA
Wales
Tel & Fax (01286) 871 232

Gorge Walking and Coasteering

High Trek Snowdonia have been bitten by the gorge walking and coasteering bug. Their gorge walking involves abseiling down into some of Snowdonia's deepest gorges, scrambling up foaming waterfalls and coasteering round Anglesey's rugged coast – alternately scrambling, climbing and bobbing on the waves. These 3-day trips are run over various long weekends through the summer. They are residential and include all food, equipment and local transport. High Trek will also pick you up from Bangor station if you have no private transport.

Tariffs: 3-day gorge walking and coasteering course (includes accommodation, full board, equipment and instruction): £189.

See Walking (p. 421) for full details.

mill on the brue activity centre

Trendle Farm
Bruton
Somerset
BA10 0BA
Tel (01749) 812 307
Fax (01749) 812 706

Orienteering

You can choose either a general introduction to orienteering during a residential multi-activity break at this Somerset centre, or take a non-residential 2-day course with a British Orienteering Federation (BOF) award at the end of it, which is a good preparation for going on to competition level. This a friendly, family-run centre known for its good food. Established in 1982 and employing up to 16 instructors during high summer, Mill on the Brue offers a high standard of tuition.

Tariffs: Orienteering is one of the sports offered in the centre's adult multi-activity days (tuition and equipment only): £25 per day. 2-day course for BOF award (includes tuition, equipment and meals): £54. Residential packages can also be arranged; contact centre for details.

See Child and Youth Sports (p. 63–4) for full details.

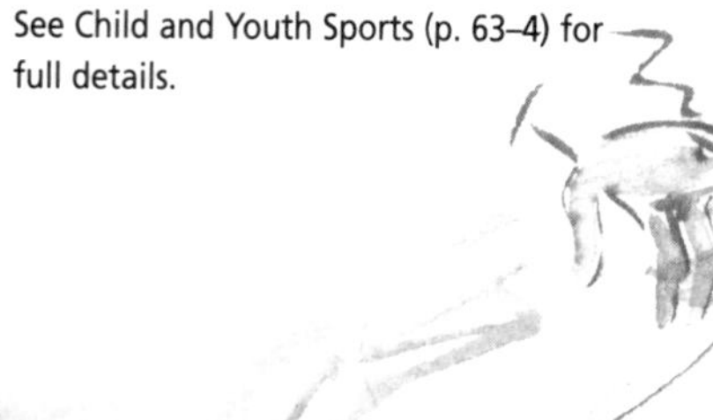

outward bound

PO Box 1219
Windsor
Berkshire
SL4 1XR
Tel (01753) 731 005
Fax (01753) 810 666
Outward Bound Scotland, Loch Eil
Tel (01397) 772 866
Outward Bound Wales, Aberdovey
Tel (01654) 767 464
Outward Bound Ullswater, Penrith
Tel (017684) 86 347

Orienteering

Outward Bound's 3 centres offer orienteering as a component of their week-long multi-activity breaks, which are divided into age groups of 11–14, 14–15, 16–17, 18–24, 25+ or 50+, as well as a 7-day women-only multi-activity course. Orienteering is usually introduced on the fifth day of the holiday, with a full day spent on the hills, camping overnight in forest. This is a good introduction to orienteering, with supervised tuition and advice on route-finding, use of a compass, interpretation of contours, and pacing yourself to measure distance.

Affiliations: Mountain Leaders Training Board.
Tariffs: All prices include tuition, equipment, full-board accommodation and transport during programme. Prices do not include VAT. Orienteering is included as part of the multi-activity holidays offered by centres (for 14–24-year-olds unless otherwise stated). 7-day multi-activity programme (Scotland, Wales, Ullswater): £249; 12-day multi-activity programme (Wales, Ullswater): £399; Outward Bound Classic (Scotland, Wales, Ullswater, 19 days): £499–599; weekend breaks (Wales, Ullswater, 25+): £130; 7-day programme (Scotland, Wales, Ullswater, 25+, 50+): £325; 12-day programme (Wales, Ullswater, 25+): £470.

See Walking (p. 426) for full details.

plas y brenin

The National Mountain Centre
Capel Curig
Gwynedd
LL24 0ET
Wales
Tel (01690) 720 280 / 720 363
Fax (01690) 720 394

Orienteering

Plas y Brenin offers an intensive but accessible introduction to orienteering, with a weekend course covering rough and fine navigation, setting the map, contour interpretation, pacing to estimate distance, choosing and using 'attack points', and rough and accurate use of the compass. By the time the course is over, the centre confidently expects you to be ready to go in for novice-level competitions.

A second weekend is aimed at experienced orienteers, teaching you to introduce others to the sport – a recommended course for teachers, youth leaders and instructors who may not be committed orienteers themselves, but who have to lead trips and take youngsters for the sport.

Affiliations: British Mountaineering Council; BOF; Mountain Leaders Training Board; United Kingdom Mountain Training Board.

Tariffs: All courses include instruction, equipment, accommodation and full board. Orienteering weekend: £130; BOF instructor training weekend: £130.

See Mountain Skills (p. 286) for full details.

preseli venture

Parcynole Fach
Mathry
Haverfordwest
Dyfed
SA62 5HN
Wales
Tel (01348) 837 709
Fax (01348) 837 656

Coasteering

This small, friendly, family-run centre located in a National Park invented coasteering, which can be done either as part of their general multi-activity breaks (which include sea kayaking, mountain biking, walking and orienteering) or on its own.

The centre is in fact a cosy Welsh cottage (sleeping a maximum of 16 people) and is known for its good food. There are 4 instructors and the centre has been running for 8 years. Their safety record is exemplary.

Tariffs: Coasteering is included as part of the centre's multi-activity packages – 2-day holiday: £129; 3-day holiday: £189; 5-day holiday: £285.

See Cycle Sports (p. 121) for full details.

r&l adventures

The Byre
Knotts Farm
Patterdale Road
Windermere
Cumbria
LA23 1NL
Tel (015394) 45104

Orienteering

Although R&L are not affiliated to any governing body, the staff are fully qualified and the centre has been running for over 15 years. Instruction is by the day only – this is not a residential centre. There are no set courses; everything is tailored to your experience (or lack of it). Choose between active days on the hill and more theoretical training with map and compass, or tuition at basic or competitive level, or put together a competition using the centre's staff as guides. Tuition is of a very high standard, and while groups can be catered for, this is a very good place to come for intensive, one-on-one teaching.

Tariffs: Prices include instruction and use of equipment. Half-day of orienteering: £50 for 1 or 2 people, £60 for group of 3–5 people, £10 each for group of 6–8 people.

See Canoeing (p. 33) for full details.

shropshire outdoor education centre

Arthog
Gwynedd
LL39 1BX
Wales
Tel & Fax (01341) 250 455

Gorge Walking

Among a range of other activities, the Arthog centre runs gorge walking trips into Snowdonia. It mostly caters for Shropshire school and college groups, but gorge walking is open to single adults too. With 35 years of experience behind it the centre provides a high standard of tuition and safety, offering 8 hours of instruction per day from 6 full-time outdoor instructors, all of whom have first aid and rescue qualifications. You can come for a day, a weekend, 5 days or 7 days, and (by arrangement) combine gorge walking with other activities – rock climbing and abseiling, caving, canoeing and kayaking, mountain biking and hill walking – either at recreational or course level, with assessment for the relevant certificates if desired.

Tariffs: These vary with the season and include dormitory accommodation plus all instruction, equipment and food. For peak season (May–July) rates are £66 per weekend and £165 for 5 days. For high season (August–October and March– May) rates are £64 per weekend and £160 for 5 days. For low season (November– February) rates are £60 per weekend and £150 for 5 days.

See Child and Youth Sports (p. 72) for full details.

share holiday village

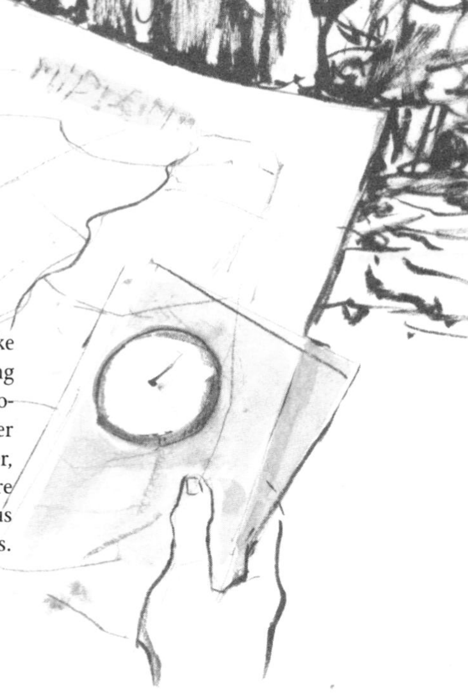

Smiths Strand
Lisnaskea
County Fermanagh
BT92 OEQ
Northern Ireland
Tel (013657) 22122 / 21892
Fax (013657) 21893

Orienteering

The hills and forests of Fermanagh's lake country make for good orienteering ground. The centre mostly offers introductory orienteering as part of a wider multi-activity sports package. However, if orienteering is your thing, the centre will be happy to arrange more serious stuff, particularly for group bookings. Ring them up to discuss your needs.

Tariffs: Orienteering is one of the sports included in the multi-activity holidays offered by centre. Prices vary according to season. Full-board accommodation packages (dormitories) – weekend: £40–60; mid-week (5 days): £75–88; full week: £150. Guests can also stay in self-catering chalets or camp, and pay for activities separately – each 2½-hour activity session (including tuition and equipment): £4.50.

See Disabled Activities (p. 136) for full details.

summitreks adventure services

4 Yewdale Road
Coniston
Cumbria
LA21 8DU
Tel (015394) 41212
Fax (015394) 41055

Gorge walking

Gorge walking and scrambling through the upper ghylls and fellsides of the Lake District National Park can be done on its own through Summmitreks, or combined with a range of other activities, including rock climbing and abseiling, aquaseiling (abseiling into water) and mountain biking. Summitreks base their weekend courses and days out in several Lake District youth hostels, and they are aimed at people on a middle to low budget. This does not detract from the standard of leadership and instruction, however.

Season: March to October.

Tariffs: A weekend of gorge scrambling and other activities costs £110 fully inclusive of accommodation, food, equipment, etc. A gorge scrambling day costs £30 including transport and a packed lunch.

See Mountain Skills (p. 288) for full details.

kitting yourself out

Gorge Walking and Coasteering

As with white-water rafting, even if you own your own wet suit, helmet and buoyancy aid (the kayakers among you probably will), it is unwise to risk them gorge walking or coasteering, as they are very likely to get damaged. Wet suits get torn on rocks, helmets have to be chucked away after any serious ding, and even buoyancy aids can get messed up in the hurly-burly of shooting rapids feet first or scrambling up waterfalls and cliffs.

checklist

- ✔ *helmet*
- ✔ *wet suit*
- ✔ *buoyancy aid (for coasteering)*

The centres listed in this chapter provide all the gear you will need and regard its damage as a risk of the game. Let them replace it – that's what you're paying for. If you want to gorge walk or coasteer independently it's worth buying second-hand gear through the classified sections of kayaking magazines. However, please be aware that unless you really know a route well, it's incredibly risky to undertake these sports without supervision or back-up, and this book cannot recommend that you try it.

Orienteering

To avoid repetition we will not go into any detail here as regards the outdoor gear needed for orienteering – it is discussed in full later in the book. Suffice to say here that you should invest in a decent Gore-Tex jacket (or equivalent) that keeps out the weather but lets you breathe – for you will be sweating. Equally important is that your boots should not be overly heavy, as you may be running, but they should have strong grip and ankle support.

checklist

- ✔ *weatherproof jacket*
- ✔ *hiking boots*
- ✔ *compass*

Clothing as for Walking (see p. 434).

Compass as for Mountain Skills (p. 290).

further reading

Orienteering, Carol MacNeill, Crowood Press, 1989.

governing body

British Hang Gliding and Paragliding Association (BHPA)
Old Schoolroom, Loughborough Road
Leicester LE4 5PJ
Tel (0116) 261 1322
Fax (0116) 261 1323

photo: Andrew Holt

hang-gliding

Opinions vary as to whether hang-gliding or paragliding is the closest a human can get to flying. Certainly, hang-gliding was developed first. Successful hang-gliders were being flown at the end of the last century, as part of the general research into flight that was going on at the time. However, with the advent of powered aircraft, with their commercial and military potential, hang-gliders fell by the wayside until the 1960s, when flying enthusiasts began to experiment with them once more. Within a decade the sport had taken off in North America and Europe and it has remained popular ever since – there is even a thriving international competition scene.

Hang-gliding is not a cheap sport, and, in contrast to paragliding, the gear is not easy to learn your way around – the glider and all its related equipment are highly specialized and difficult to transport – but the rewards are great: practitioners describe the feeling as akin to soaring like a giant bird of prey.

If you want to get going, only consider learning at a school that is affiliated to the British Hang Gliding and Paragliding Association (BHPA). You will need to book in for a 4–6-day Elementary Pilot course, which teaches you the basics and gets you airborne. After that comes the Club Pilot qualification, which can take up to 2 weeks, unless you get perfect weather, in which case it will take about 8 days. You can go on from Club Pilot to take Pilot and finally Advanced Pilot qualifications, but you should allow a couple of years to get there.

selected centres

cairnwell mountain sports ltd

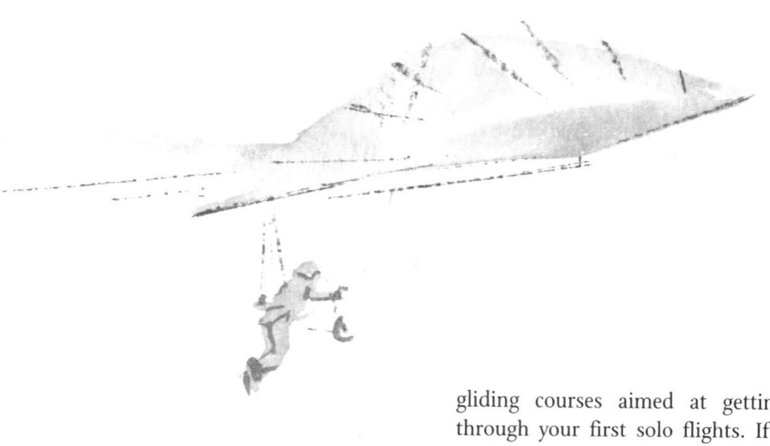

Gulabin Lodge
Glenshee
By Blairgowrie
Perthshire & Kinross
PH10 7QQ
Scotland
Tel (01250) 885 238, winter (013397) 41331
Fax (01250) 885 238

Flying from the Spittal of Glenshee, one of the highest mountain sites in Britain, this summer school offers weekend introductory courses taking you from complete beginner to tethered flights and short hops, and 4-day mid-week basic hang-gliding courses aimed at getting you through your first solo flights. If you're really serious, then you can take the Club Pilot course, which lasts from Monday to Sunday; an additional 3 days are necessary to get through the exam.

Those who already hold a licence can take the 3-day advanced course which includes ridge soaring, spot landings, 180- and 360-degree turns, and thermal and mountain flying. The school has 21 years of experience, and offers all its courses on a full-board basis.

Children: Those under 18 need consent of parent or guardian.
Insurance: Clients must obtain third-party insurance by joining BHPA. Membership can be obtained for varying periods – 2 days: £8; 3 months: £29; 1 year: £59; and 1 year concessionary membership: £40.
Affiliations: BHPA.
Tariffs: 2-day introductory course: £90; 4-day Elementary Pilot course: £170; Club Pilot course (1 week plus 3 days as needed to obtain certificate): £365; 3-day advanced course: £120.

See Skiing (p. 374) for full details.

fly high sky sports

101 Heath Road
Barming
Maidstone
Kent
ME16 9JT
Tel (01622) 728 230 /
(0860) 351 130 (mobile)

With 22 instructors and courses in hang gliding, paragliding, parascending and powered paragliding (or powerchuting), this is probably Britain's biggest non-aircraft sky sports centre. The hang-gliding courses are aimed at beginner- and improver-level flyers: you can opt for a 'taster' day or a 5-day Elementary Pilot course, which gives you your first hang-gliding qualification and sets you on your way towards cross-country flying.

The courses can be residential or not as you wish; the centre has a comfortable bunkhouse or it will book you into a local B&B nearby and ferry you to and from the flight sites at no extra cost.

Affiliations: BHPA; Fédération Aéronautique Internationale; Royal Aero Club.
Tariffs: All prices include tuition, accommodation and use of equipment. 1-day hang gliding course: £59; Elementary Pilot course: £240.

See Paragliding and Parascending (p. 312) for full details.

green dragons

Paragliding and Hang-gliding Centre
Warren Barn Farm
Slines Oak Road
Woldingham
Surrey
CR3 7HN
Tel (01883) 652 666
Fax (01883) 652 600

Set in the North Downs of Surrey, Green Dragons is a handy school to reach from London. They offer hill-launch and tow-launch hang-gliding and have 12 instructors. Unfortunately it's a club, not a residential centre (though you can camp), and you need your own car to get to the flight sites. However, it is a good place to learn, with courses varying from introductory days through the full range of pilot certificate courses to 6 days of learning advanced cross-country techniques. Green Dragons also lead trips abroad for advanced flyers,to Spain and Turkey. Green Dragons was one of Britain's first hang-gliding schools – it's been running since 1974 – and now employs 11 instructors.

If you take one of their UK courses, ring on the morning of each course day to check that weather conditions are right for flying, and to find out which of the club's several flying sites is to be used. You then have to arrive by 9.30 a.m. Any lost flight days are made up as soon as the weather permits.

Tariffs: Prices include tuition and use of equipment. 1-day introductory course: £69; Elementary Pilot course: £270; Club Pilot course: £270.

See Paragliding and Parascending (p. 313-314) for full details.

high adventure

Yarborough House
Nettlecombe Lane
Whitwell
Isle of Wight
PO38 2QA
Tel (01983) 730 075
Fax (01983) 731 441

This Isle of Wight centre offers 5-day residential Elementary Pilot courses every week, starting on Mondays at eleven o'clock in the morning. Practical training begins with tethered flights – where the instructor flies you like a kite – and progresses through gentle flights from low down the hill to higher flights, learning to turn, flight planning and hillside landings, and finally soaring. If you just want to try it out, there are 1- and 2-day introductory courses. Those who already hold an Elementary Pilot certificate should take the 5-day Club Pilot course.

Season: Open all year.
Accommodation: B&B for 8 people at £17–20 per night.
Food: Meals available.
Other Activities: Paragliding (p. 314).
Children: Minimum age 14; anyone under 18 requires consent of parent or guardian.
Disabled Facilities: None.
Insurance: Clients must obtain third-party insurance by joining BHPA. Membership can be obtained for varying periods – 2 days: £8; 3 months: £29; 1 year: £59; and 1 year concessionary membership: £40.
Safety: All instructors trained in first aid.
Affiliations: BHPA.
Tariffs: 1-day introductory course: £69; 2-day introductory course: £100; 5-day Elementary Pilot course: £260; 5-day Club Pilot course: £260.
Booking: £50 non-refundable deposit required. Balance due upon arrival. 10% fee for cancellations. Late bookings accepted if space available. Visa, Mastercard and Switch cards accepted.
Access: Take ferry to Isle of Wight from Portsmouth, Southampton or Lymington. Centre picks up from port.

peak hang-gliding school

York House
Ladderedge
Leek
Staffordshire
ST13 7AQ
Tel (01538) 382 520

The Peak Hang-gliding School flies, not surprisingly, over the Peak District National Park in Derbyshire and South Yorkshire. At 18 years old it's also Britain's oldest operative hang-gliding school and takes people from complete beginners right through their Elementary, Club, Cross-Country and Advanced Pilot certificates, as well as offering the usual 'taster' days and weekends. They also practise 'tethered soaring', where students catch an up-draught at the top of a slope while being restrained with ropes. It's a useful way of learning how to cope with the 3-dimensional aspect of hang-gliding while at the same time being able to hear your tutor's instructions. The centre supplies all equipment, though experienced flyers seeking instruction may bring their own (there are 6 instructors here). They also have a shop selling the full range of gear.

Accommodation is at your discretion and budget – the centre will book it and then pick you up each morning for flying (weather permitting).

Season: Open all year.
Accommodation: Hostel accommodation only. Local B&B can be booked through the centre.
Food: Not provided.
Children: Minimum age 16; those under 18 must have consent of parent or guardian.
Disabled Facilities: None.
Insurance: Clients must obtain third-party insurance by joining BHPA. Membership can be obtained for varying periods – 2 days: £8; 3 months: £29; 1 year: £59; and 1 year concessionary membership: £40.
Safety: All instructors qualified in first aid.
Affiliations: BHPA.
Tariffs: 1-day introductory course: £55; weekend introductory course: £90; 4–7-day Elementary Pilot course: £225; 4–7-day Club Pilot course: £245. (Discounts for groups or for those using their own equipment.)
Booking: Deposit required – 1-day course: £5; weekend course: £10; Pilot courses: £25. Balance due at start of course. No charge for cancellations. Although booking is usually made in advance, late bookings are accepted if space available.
Access: Centre is off the A53 between Buxton and Stoke-on-Trent. Take the train to Buxton or Stoke-on-Trent stations; the centre can arrange pick-ups. Or take the bus to Leek; station is only 5 minutes away from centre.

peak school of hang-gliding

The Elms
Wetton
Ashbourne
Derbyshire
DE6 2AF
Tel & Fax (01335) 310 257

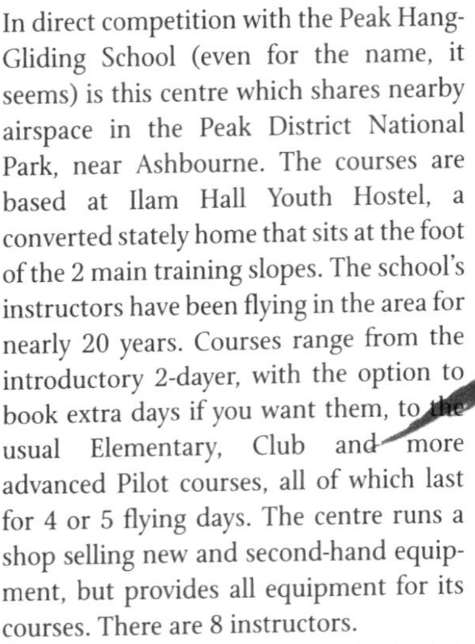

In direct competition with the Peak Hang-Gliding School (even for the name, it seems) is this centre which shares nearby airspace in the Peak District National Park, near Ashbourne. The courses are based at Ilam Hall Youth Hostel, a converted stately home that sits at the foot of the 2 main training slopes. The school's instructors have been flying in the area for nearly 20 years. Courses range from the introductory 2-dayer, with the option to book extra days if you want them, to the usual Elementary, Club and more advanced Pilot courses, all of which last for 4 or 5 flying days. The centre runs a shop selling new and second-hand equipment, but provides all equipment for its courses. There are 8 instructors.

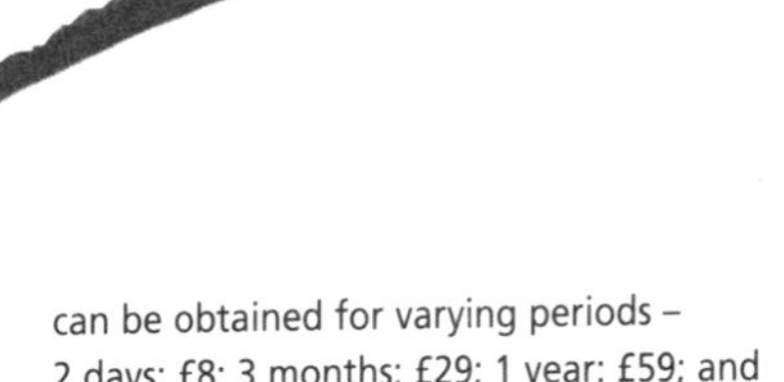

If you don't want to stay at the hostel, there's a variety of other accommodation in the area, which the centre is happy to book for you, but you'll need your own vehicle to get to the flying sites each morning.

Season: Open all year.

Accommodation: No on-site accommodation. Centre will provide help in obtaining local accommodation.

Food: Not provided.

Children: Minimum age 16; those under 18 must have consent of parent or guardian.

Disabled Facilities: None.

Insurance: Clients must obtain third-party insurance by joining BHPA. Membership can be obtained for varying periods – 2 days: £8; 3 months: £29; 1 year: £59; and 1 year concessionary membership: £40.

Safety: All instructors are trained in first aid and are BHPA-registered.

Affiliations: BHPA.

Tariffs: 2-day introductory course: £85 (can be extended in order to obtain the Elementary Pilot certificate for £40 each extra day); 5-day Elementary Pilot course: £190; 4-day Club Pilot course: £50 per day.

Booking: £20 deposit required, non-refundable. Balance payable on or before start of course. Refunds not normally given, but if training cancelled due to bad weather it will be rebooked.

Access: Off the A515 near Ashbourne. Trains available to Buxton, buses to Ashbourne. Pick-ups from stations can be arranged by centre.

sheffield hang-gliding and paragliding centre

Cliffside
Church Street
Tideswell
Derbyshire
SK17 8PE
Tel & Fax (01298) 872 313

Stephen Hudson, the chief flying instructor at the Sheffield centre, has been hang-gliding for about 12 years and has competed for Britain. He offers the standard hang-gliding 'taster' weekend and suggests that total beginners try this before signing up for the 5-day Elementary Pilot certificate. All equipment is included in the courses.

The Sheffield centre flies over the Peak District National Park – one of 3 hang-gliding and paragliding outfits in the area. Courses are offered at all levels, including cross-country. There are no residential courses – you stay in local B&Bs and are picked up by minibus each morning for the 5-mile drive to the training slopes. If you don't have transport, Stephen will pick you up from the train station at Hope, on the Manchester–Sheffield line.

The Sheffield centre also sells the full range of equipment – new and second-hand – as well as operating a repair and overhauling service.

Season: Open all year.
Accommodation: Centre will help arrange local accommodation.
Food: Not provided.
Other Activities: Paragliding (see p. 318).
Children: Must be 16 or over; anyone under 18 requires consent of parent or guardian.
Disabled Facilities: None.
Insurance: Clients must obtain third-party insurance by joining BHPA. Membership can be obtained for varying periods – 2 days: £8; 3 months: £29; 1 year: £59; and 1 year concessionary membership: £40. Personal insurance can also be arranged; contact centre for details.
Safety: All instructors trained in first aid.
Affiliations: BHPA.
Tariffs: 2-day taster courses and 5-day Elementary Pilot courses available. Tuition is £45 per day, including use of equipment. Group discounts available.
Booking: £25 deposit required. Cancellation charges – if less than 1 month in advance: £10; if less than 1 week in advance: £25.
Access: Take the A625 from Sheffield, or the A623 from Manchester. Trains to Hope station on Sheffield–Manchester line. Buses from Sheffield to Bradwell. Pick-ups from stations can be arranged.

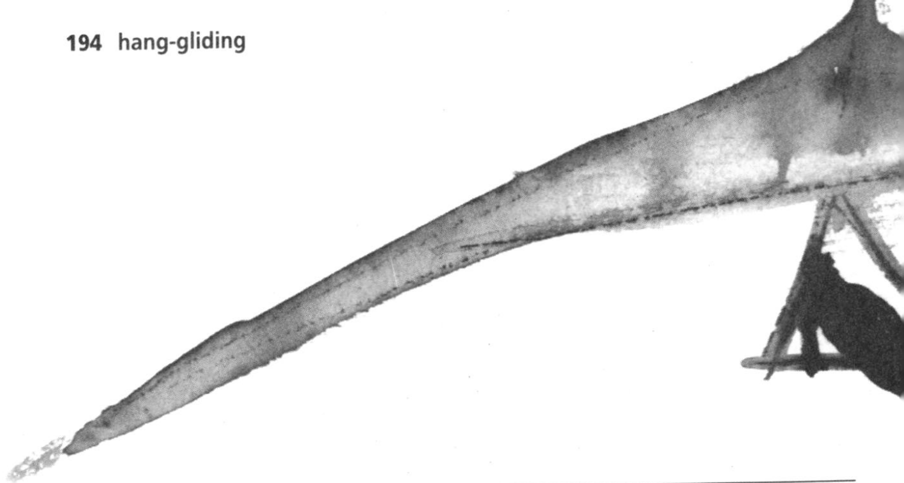

skysports international hang-gliding school

104 Dan-y-Deri
Abergavenny
Gwent
NP7 6PN
Wales
Tel (01873) 850 157 / 856 112,
(0421) 372 896

Flying over the Black Mountains and Brecon Beacons, Skysports offers tuition for the Elementary Pilot (over 5–6 days) and Club Pilot certificates (over 6–7 days). Beginners are welcome and all equipment is provided (there's also no charge if you do any minor damage to it). There are also 1- and 2-day introductory courses. The school is lucky in that it has a plethora of flying sites to choose from and both free and tethered flight tuition is offered. Groups run to a maximum of 6 people and the school aims at 'letting you learn at your own pace, without pressure or competition in an informal atmosphere'. As Neal Philips, who runs the school and is its only instructor, says, 'The sky's the limit. Can you reach it? Do you want to?'

Skysports cannot provide accommodation but will organize it for you at whatever budget. You will need your own transport to get to the flying sites.

Season: Open all year.
Accommodation: No on-site accommodation. Centre will provide help in obtaining local accommodation.
Food: Not provided.
Children: Minimum age 16; those under 18 must have consent of parent or guardian.
Disabled Facilities: None.
Insurance: Clients must obtain third-party insurance by joining BHPA. Membership can be obtained for varying periods – 2 days: £8; 3 months: £29; 1 year: £59; and 1 year concessionary membership: £40.
Safety: Instructor has advanced training in first aid.
Affiliations: BHPA.
Tariffs: 1-day introductory course: £50; 2-day introductory course: £90; 6-day Elementary Pilot course: £210; Club Pilot training: £50 per day (£40 with own equipment).
Booking: £25 non-refundable deposit required. Balance due 14 days before course starts. Cancellation charges if notice received 2–12 days in advance: 50% of total cost; 1 day in advance: 100% of total cost.
Access: At Abergavenny off the A40. Trains and buses available to Abergavenny.

sussex hang-gliding and paragliding ltd

16 Scarborough Road
Brighton
Sussex
BN1 5NR
Tel (01273) 888 443
Fax (01273) 880 572

A handy place to reach from London and the south-east, this school on the South Downs offers beginner, recreational and BHPA pilot certificate courses up to Club Pilot level. With a clubhouse and office in Brighton, this is a fairly large school, employing between 10 and 12 instructors, depending on the season. You get about 6 hours of tuition per day. They claim that from the first morning of a course 'you will be harnessed into a glider and you will achieve your first tethered flights', i.e. catch an up-draught off a slope but stay in one place, held there by ropes while your teacher shouts instructions.

There are weekend and 3-day introductory courses, 5-day Elementary and Club Pilot courses. The school will help you find accommodation in Brighton, and will drive you out to the training slopes each morning from the clubhouse on Crescent Road.

Season: Open all year.
Accommodation: Centre will provide help in arranging local accommodation.
Food: Not provided.
Other Activities: Paragliding (see p. 319).
Children: Must be 16 or over; anyone under 18 requires consent of parent or guardian.
Disabled Facilities: Disabled clients can sometimes be accommodated. Contact centre for more details.
Insurance: Clients must obtain third-party insurance by joining BHPA. Membership can be obtained for varying periods – 2 days: £8; 3 months: £29; 1 year: £59; and 1 year concessionary membership: £40. Clients should arrange personal insurance if desired.
Safety: All instructors trained in first aid and BHPA-registered.
Affiliations: BHPA.
Tariffs: Fees include instruction and use of equipment. 1-day taster: £70 (includes insurance); 2-day taster course: £110; 5-day Elementary Pilot or Club Pilot certificate (weekdays): £275 / £260.
Booking: Full payment in advance is required. Mastercard, Visa and Switch cards accepted. Bookings usually made 2 weeks in advance for weekends, 2 days in advance for weekdays. Late bookings sometimes accepted if space available.
Access: Off the A23 near Brighton, at Preston Park. Trains and buses available to Preston Park station; quick walk to centre from station.

welsh hang-gliding centre

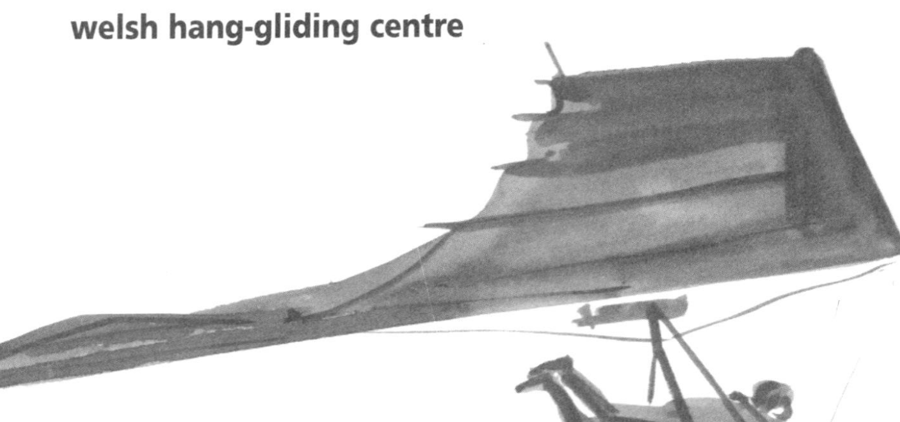

Parc Bryn-Bach Visitor Centre
Tredegar
Gwent
NP2 3AY
Tel (01873) 832 100

Established in 1975, this centre in South Wales is still going strong. Its courses are mostly designed for beginner to intermediate hang-gliders. The courses are non-residential, but accommodation to suit all budgets can be booked locally through the centre. However, you will need your own transport to get to and from the flight sites. Training begins on low slopes, with 3 tether ropes for safety. There are 3 full-time instructors.

Season: Open all year.

Accommodation: No on-site accommodation. Centre will provide help in obtaining local accommodation.

Food: Not provided.

Children: Minimum age 14; those under 18 must have consent of parent or guardian. 14–16-year-olds must be accompanied by an adult. There is no lower age limit for tandem flights, but child must be mature enough to understand flight briefings.

Disabled Facilities: Certain disabilities can be catered for; contact centre for details.

Insurance: Clients must obtain third-party insurance by joining BHPA (included in the course fee). The centre recommends that clients take out their own personal accident policy.

Safety: Instructors have St John's first-aid training. Hospitals are 5 miles away and injured clients will be driven there straight away.

Affiliations: BHPA; Wales Tourist Board.

Tariffs: 2-day introductory course: £100; 5-day Elementary Pilot course: £230; Club Pilot course: £45 per day.

Booking: £50 deposit required, non-refundable. Balance due 28 days in advance of start date, or at time of booking if made less than 28 days in advance. In the event of cancellation, deposits and final balances are not refundable. Bookings are normally made in advance, but late bookings are sometimes accepted if space available. Cheques only.

Access: The centre is 40 minutes from Cardiff. Take the A470 to Merthyr Tydfil, then the A465 towards Abergavenny. Turn off at the Tredegar roundabout and continue for about 2 minutes, following the signs to Bryn Bach. The nearest railway station is Rhymney (walking distance from the centre) which is accessed via Newport or Cardiff.

wiltshire hang-gliding and paragliding centre

The Old Barn
Rhyls Lane
Lockeridge
Marlborough
Wiltshire
SN8 4EE
Tel (01672) 861 555

Another handy school for those living in the south of England. Dave Bullard's Wiltshire school flies over the beautiful Marlborough Downs. Like the Sussex school, this is more for beginner hang-gliders, with courses ranging from introductory up to Club Pilot level. If you have already gone beyond Club Pilot level and want to fly, you should make private arrangements with the school. The courses run from Monday to Saturday, with 4 flying days within that time (weather permitting).

Although there is no accommodation on-site, the school will help arrange it for you and pick you up and take you to the flying sites free of charge, as long as you are staying in Marlborough itself – or along the route from there to the training slopes. Otherwise you'll need your own transport. Accommodation can be arranged at any budget.

The Wiltshire school offers special vouchers so that you can buy someone a 'taster day' or even a 4-day course as a present, letting the recipient arrange the date.

Season: Open all year.
Accommodation: No on-site accommodation. Centre will provide help in obtaining local accommodation.
Food: Not provided.
Other Activities: Paragliding (see p. 319).
Children: Minimum age 16; those under 18 must have consent of parent or guardian.
Disabled Facilities: None.
Insurance: Clients must obtain third-party insurance by joining BHPA. Membership can be obtained for varying periods – 2 days: £8; 3 months: £29; 1 year: £59; and 1 year concessionary membership: £40.
Safety: All instructors St John's-certified and BHPA-registered.
Affiliations: Association of Free-Flight Professionals; BHPA.
Tariffs: 1-day introductory course: £65 (£55 on weekdays); 2-day introductory course: £120 (£100 weekdays); Elementary Pilot course: £220 over 2 weekends, £190 over 4 weekdays; advanced courses for Club Pilot certificate: £45 per day (£55 at weekends).
Booking: Deposit required: £20 per day. Balance must be paid 7 days in advance if paying by cheque, and on first day of instruction if paying by cash, PO or cheque with banker's card. Cancellation charges: 50% of deposit if 2+ weeks in advance, 90% if 7–14 days in advance, 100% if less than 7 days; no refunds. If flights cancelled due to bad weather, no refunds given but credit applied to later booking. Bookings are normally made in advance, but late bookings are sometimes accepted if space available.
Access: Nearest town is Marlborough, off the A4. Trains can be taken to Pewsey or buses to Marlborough, and pick-ups can be arranged by centre.

checklist

- ✔ *buoyancy aid*
- ✔ *glider and harness*
- ✔ *helmet*
- ✔ *flying suit*
- ✔ *boots*

further reading

A Beginner's Guide to Airsports, Keith Carey, A & C Black, 1994; *Hang Gliding Training Manual* and *Performance Flying* both by Dennis Pagen, published by Sporting Aviation Press, 1993.

kitting yourself out

Airwave are a very good British manufacturer of hang-gliders – in fact, the largest in Europe, having grown in about 5 years from a back-yard affair run by enthusiasts to their current imperial status, with test centres around the country and a full maintenance service for anyone buying a new glider. Rapidly catching up are Avian, Solar Wing and Discovery. From any of these manufacturers, expect to pay around £2,500 for a new glider and harness. For this price you can get a glider that will last you from beginner to cross-country level. A second-hand glider aimed at the same level of competence will cost you about £800 in good condition. Cruise the classifieds in *Sports in the Sky* magazine or ask your club instructor.

Getting the right flying suit is important. What you're looking for is warmth, as even in summer it can be very cold up at cloud base. Many instructors swear by the Skywear (German) and Skysystems (British) suits. An unlined suit costs around £100, while a fully lined one will set you back about £250. With the suit you will need a helmet. The main choice here is between open-face or full-face, and a good design is anything in the Fly range (Italian). An open-face helmet costs around £60, while a full-face is £100–150.

It is definitely safer, though not compulsory, to carry a reserve parachute. This is particularly useful if flying abroad in higher mountain ranges where the thermals are stronger and the air currents more turbulent. There is a very broad range of reserve parachutes to choose from, so it is best to ask your instructor for his or her particular recommendation. Expect to pay £350+. You should have the reserve parachute inspected once a year at a good school.

Although first-timers can get away with good hiking boots, if you're planning to fly seriously, it's best to buy proper hang-gliding boots, which have extra ankle support and are waterproof. Salomon, who also manufacture ski boots, offer good flying boots for around £110 a pair.

Finally, if you are intending to try for any records, or if you simply want to know how high you have been, you can buy an electronic altimeter. The best of these have audio and visual indications and come with a barograph, which will produce an on-screen graph for you after your flight, showing exactly how high and how far you have been. Altimeters cost about £200+ for a basic model, and around £600 with the barograph. Again, get your instructor to recommend a particular brand, as there are several good ones on the market.

principal governing body

British Horse Society (BHS)

British Equestrian Centre,
Stoneleigh Park, Kenilworth
Warwickshire CV8 2LR
Tel (01203) 696 697
Fax (01203) 692 351

horse sports

trail riding
pony trekking
cross-country
show jumping
dressage
carriage driving
western riding

It may come as a surprise to the uninitiated, but riding a horse is probably the most dangerous action/adventure sport you can try, though more so for experienced riders than for beginners. The injury (and, unfortunately, fatality) rates for riders among the various disciplines of horse riding are extremely high, but most of these occur at competition level, usually in cross-country or show jumping classes, and are not dangers likely to be faced by a beginner on a quiet pony. But because of this slight *frisson* of danger that always accompanies horse riding, and the necessity of getting to know your horse's personality (they aren't machines, after all), it is probably one of the most rewarding sports to learn, on both a physical and emotional level.

It would be impossible to list every single riding school in Britain here. For practicality's sake we can only list those establishments offering residential courses of 2 or more days. Some centres have suitable options for beginners, but most of the listings are for more experienced riders, and are divided into disciplines: trail riding (guided long-distance trails) holidays, and places offering courses in cross-country jumping, show jumping and dressage (the art of teaching the horse to perform advanced movements). You can also find out where to learn Western riding – the cowboy style, evolved from medieval Spanish riding techniques – carriage driving, polo and horseball.

selected centres

acorn activities

PO Box 120
Hereford
Hereford & Worcester
HR4 8YB
Tel (01432) 830 083
Fax (01432) 830 110

Trail Riding, Cross-country, Pony Trekking, Carriage Driving, Beginners' Courses

Acorn arrange trail riding in Wales for experienced riders only, using Welsh cobs. You can take a 2-day weekend break in mid-Wales, a 3-day ride in the Brecon Beacons National Park, a 6-day ride through the Black Mountains (April–October only), or even a trans-Wales ride (May–October only) covering 110 miles of moor and mountain over 7 days. There's also a slightly less serious Real Ale Trail, which runs for 7 days from pub to pub through the mid-Wales hills. Accommodation is in various farmhouses and B&Bs.

If you are not an experienced rider, Acorn run pony trekking breaks of 2–3 days in the Black Mountains, staying in farmhouses. These breaks are offered from April to November.

For those wanting to try carriage driving, Acorn offer an introductory day to try your hand at it, using a small Surrey or Governess cart, pulled either by horses or ponies. You get a fully qualified instructor with whom you can arrange to take longer courses if you get the carriage-driving bug.

Total beginners should go for the Learn to Ride beginners' courses, which run over 2 or 5 days. You get qualified instruction in the basics of rising, and also learn tacking-up, grooming, some stable management, and general horse care. Unlike the trail riding or pony trekking, these courses run at any time of year.

Accommodation: Local accommodation provided in farmhouses and B&Bs.
Children: Over-16s only.
Tariffs: Prices include accommodation, meals and guide. Black Mountains trail (6 days): £425; Trans-Wales trail (7 days): £645; Brecon Beacons National Park trail (3 days): £295; Real Ale trail (7 days): £535; pony trekking (2 days): £140; Learning to Ride course: £100 (2 days), £250 (5 days). 2-hour carriage driving instruction session also available (instruction only): £60.

See Walking (p. 414) for full details.

albion rides

Duck Row
Cawston
Norwich
Norfolk
NR10 4EZ
Tel (01603) 871 725

Trail Riding, Learning to Ride, Carriage Driving

North Norfolk is a little-visited, but surprisingly beautiful, corner of rural England. A quiet countryside of rolling wolds, large tracts of ancient woods and modern plantations, and open heaths. At this centre the rides are broken up into small groups of 5 or 6 people and are taken at varying paces over about 4 hours. The horses are good, strong cobs and hunter crosses, offering a keen ride for an experienced rider.

If you are not experienced, try one of Albion's Learner Breaks, which include instruction on the flat, stable management and long supervised hacks. Jumping lessons can also be arranged, as can lessons in carriage driving. Unless staying at the centre for one of the accommodation-inclusive holidays, you will need your own transport to get to the stables each morning.

Season: All year.

Accommodation: For the 2½-day breaks, accommodation in comfortable twin rooms is included in the tariff. Otherwise accommodation can be booked for you locally – from £7 camping to £30 per person per night in nearby hotels.

Food: Vegetarian catering by prior arrangement.

Children: Adults only.

Disabled Facilities: None.

Insurance: Clients should arrange their own personal accident policy.

Safety: Clients taken to hospital if necessary.

Affiliations: Ponies Association UK.

Tariffs: Weekly riding holidays (not including accommodation) cost £240 in summer, £193 in winter; 2½-day breaks (including accommodation) cost £200 in summer and £184 in winter. Day rides cost £40–60 depending on the season.

Booking: £70 deposit required with booking. Balance payable 6 weeks prior to holiday.

Access: Cawston is 3 miles west of the A140, about 10 miles north of Norwich.

appaloosa holidays

Ardfern Riding Centre
Craobh Haven
Lochgilphead
Argyll & Bute
PA31 8QR
Scotland
Tel (01852) 500 632

Western Riding, Dressage

Founded in 1972, this Western riding centre has a herd of well-schooled American quarter-horses and Appaloosas. The owners are qualified Western instructors, as well as British Horse Society (BHS)-qualified instructors. Tuition can be given in all aspects of Western riding, from sliding stops and barrel racing to roping. The centre can take people from complete novice to show level. English riding is also available, with dressage, jumping and hacking on the centre's own estate. Riding is non-residential, but the centre will help you to book somewhere nearby at whatever budget. You will need your own transport to get to and from the centre.

Season: All year.
Accommodation: Not provided. Local accommodation can be booked through the centre.
Food: Not provided.
Children: Accompanied children from 9 upwards are welcome.
Disabled Facilities: Riding for the Disabled (RDA)-affiliated.
Insurance: Clients should arrange their own personal accident policy.
Safety: Air rescue if necessary. On-site first-aid-trained staff.
Affiliations: BHS; RDA.
Tariffs: 2-day breaks including 5 hours' trail riding, 3 hours' Western tuition and 1 picnic trail cost £95.
Booking: Full payment at least 1 week in advance.
Access: The centre is just outside Lochgilphead on the A83, which runs down the western shore of Loch Fyne.

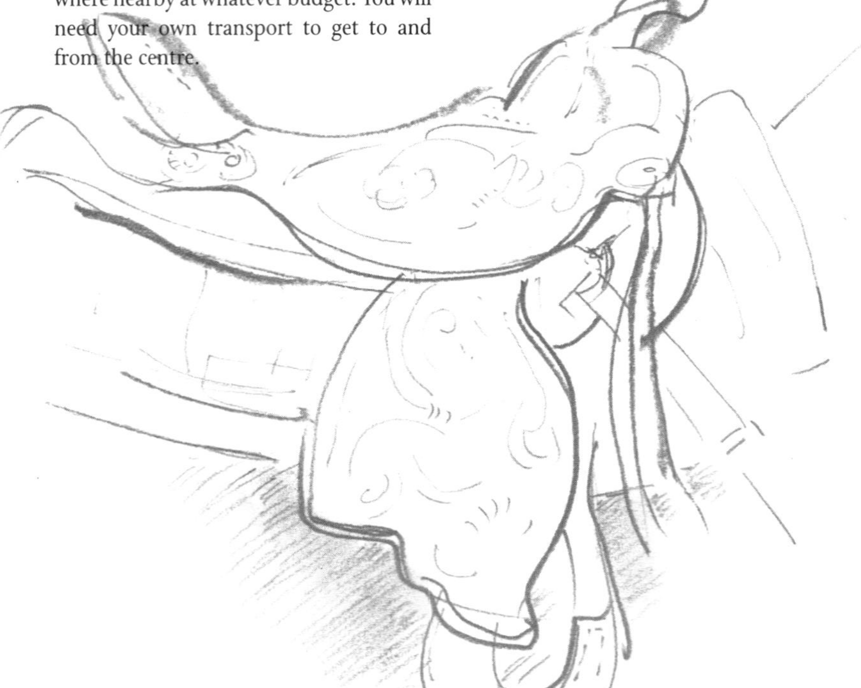

black mountain holidays

Capel-y-Ffin Youth Hostel
Abergavenny
Gwent
NP7 7NP
Wales
Tel (01873) 890 650

Trail Riding, Pony Trekking, Beginners' Riding Courses

One of several trail riding centres in the Black Mountains, this centre offers residential trail riding holidays lasting from 2 to 6 days, or post-trail rides from 2 to 7 days with nights spent at different youth hostels in the Brecon Beacons National Park, with your baggage taken on for you by car. The centre can cater for novice and experienced riders alike. Whatever the type of ride you choose, lunch is always taken at a country pub along the route. If you take a learn-to-ride course, you will be taken on shorter trail rides in between lessons in the school, and be taught basic horse care such as tacking-up, grooming, feeding, mucking out, etc. At the end of a learn-to-ride course the centre holds a gymkhana where you can put some of your newly learned skills into practice in a friendly competition.

The groups consist of no more than 7 riders and you can choose between Western and English riding. If you take a learn-to-ride course using the Western style, the centre will put on a rodeo at the end of the course: no bucking broncs, though, but mounted rodeo games such as pole-bending and flag races.

Season: March to October.
Accommodation: 40 dormitory beds.
Food: Breakfast and dinner provided at hostel, lunches provided at pubs and cafés on the trail. Vegetarian and special diets catered for upon request.
Children: Minimum age 11.
Disabled Facilities: None.
Insurance: Clients should arrange their own holiday insurance. Inexpensive packages available through the YHA.
Safety: Staff have no first-aid training.
Affiliations: Wales Tourist Board (WTB); Wales Trekking & Riding Association.
Tariffs: Prices include tuition, use of horses and full-board accommodation. 2-day / 2-night Brecon Beacons trail ride: £120; 2-day / 2-night Black Mountains riding course: £100; 4-day / 5-night Black Mountains riding course: £235; 6-day / 7-night Black Mountains riding course: £300.
Booking: Non-refundable deposit required: £25 (2-day holidays), £50 (3+-day holidays). Balance due 2 months before start date. Cancellation charge is 30% of total cost if notice received 29–56 days in advance; 45% if 15–28 days; 80% if 1–14 days; 100% same day or later. Visa and Access cards accepted. Although bookings are normally made in advance, late bookings are sometimes accepted if space available.
Access: Near Abergavenny off the A465 at Llanfihangel Crucorney and Hay-on-Wye off the A438. Trains and buses available to Abergavenny. Taxis must be taken to hostel, approximately £16.

brenfield activity centre

Argyll Trail Riding
Castle Riding Centre
Brenfield Farm
Ardrishaig
Argyll & Bute
PA30 8ER
Scotland
Tel (01546) 603 274
Fax (01546) 603 225

Trail Riding

Along with Highland Horseback's trans-Scotland ride, Brenfield's Wild Boar trail is probably the most fun trail ride available in Britain. Aimed at experienced riders, it travels at a fair pace through the mountains of Argyll to Loch Awe and Inverary, visiting several castles, Iron Age sites and villages deserted during the Highland Clearances. In some places you jump low stone walls and ditches, take fast gallops along the loch shores and, if the tide is high, swim with your horse as well. For those with less time, the centre runs 'Taste of Trail' shortened sections of the Wild Boar route.

If you don't feel up to this, the centre also runs a clinic week for improving your riding, with hacks, lessons on the flat and cross-country schooling. Or try some of the other activities on offer at Brenfield, such as cycling, golf, shooting, fishing, canoeing and walking. In addition to these options, Brenfield run a 5-day 'economy' holiday, with half-days of riding and the rest of the time exploring the area on your own. Weekend breaks at any of these levels are also available.

Season: March to September.

Accommodation: Stay in castles, hotels, farmhouses and B&Bs on trail rides, or in centre's own twin rooms or dorms for centre-based holidays. Accommodation prices included in general tariffs, charged on a sliding scale depending on the level of comfort required.

Food: Vegetarian catering by arrangement.

Children: Accompanied and experienced only. Age 10 minimum.

Disabled Facilities: None.

Insurance: Clients need their own personal accident cover.

Safety: Mountain and air rescue in hills, otherwise clients driven to hospital if necessary.

Affiliations: Association of British Riding Schools (ABRS); BHS; Trekking and Riding Society of Scotland.

Tariffs: Prices given in general ranges, according to the level of accommodation required. 7-day trails – Wild Boar trail: £695–850; clinic: £400–680; economy (5 days): £310–590. Weekend breaks: £80–120. Children (5 days): £240–340.

Booking: Deposit of £100 required with booking. Balance payable 6 weeks prior to holiday.

Access: The Castle Riding Centre is on the hills above Ardrishaig on the A83, which runs down the western shore of Loch Fyne. The nearest town is Lochgilphead, also on the A83, about 4 miles to the north of Ardrishaig.

cae iago

Ffarmers
Llanwrda
Dyfed
SA19 8LZ
Wales
Tel (01558) 650 303

Trail Riding

This was one of the first centres to start trail rides in the UK, and it now has over 30 years' experience behind it. Routes climb up into the Cambrian Mountains along old Roman roads and medieval drovers' tracks. You can choose between centre-based day trails or overnighting at pubs and youth hostels further afield. Week-long rides, mid-week breaks of 2–5 days and weekend trail rides are offered on good Welsh cobs and cob crosses. Full board is thrown in with the tariff. All you need to bring is your toothbrush, towel and some money for a pint. The centre can arrange for transport to and from Llandovery station for those without cars.

Season: All year.
Accommodation: B&Bs along the routes; prices included in general tariff.
Food: Vegetarians and vegans welcome by prior arrangement.
Children: Adults only.
Disabled Facilities: None.
Insurance: Clients should have personal accident policies.
Safety: Mountain rescue can be called if needed, otherwise clients will be taken to hospital if necessary.
Affiliations: WTB; BHS; Wales Trekking and Riding Association.
Tariffs: A full week costs £223–240 depending on the routes followed. A 3-day break costs £156, 2 days costs £100 mid-week and £86 for a weekend. All riding, hats, food and accommodation are included.
Booking: A deposit of £30 is required with booking, the balance payable 30 days prior to the holiday's start date. Payment by cheque or cash.
Access: Cae Iago is 2 miles off the A482 between Llandovery and Lampeter.

cwmfforest riding centre

Talgarth
Brecon
Powys
LD3 OEU
Wales
Tel (01874) 711 398
Fax (01874) 711 122

Trail Riding

Cwmfforest is the oldest of the Black Mountains riding and trekking centres, and was the first company to pioneer the trans-Wales ride. The centre offers active trail rides on fit, well-schooled Welsh cobs and cob crosses, lasting from 2 to 7 nights. Riders can also bring their own horses, but the horse must be fit, sociable and well shod. Groups average between 4 and 9 riders. The Trans-Wales Trail is quite challenging and comes highly recommended, covering about 20 tough mountain miles per day with long stops for pub lunches. Ride your horse into the sea at the end of the trail.

Season: All year.
Accommodation: In farmhouses and B&Bs along the trails.
Food: Good, hearty farmhouse food. Vegetarians can be catered for by prior arrangement.
Children: Adults only. Teenagers 15+ if accompanied by a parent.
Disabled Facilities: None.
Insurance: Clients need their own personal accident policy.
Safety: Mountain rescue if needed, otherwise clients driven to hospital if necessary.
Affiliations: BHS; WTB.
Tariffs: The 6-day trails cost: £420 for the Black Mountain trail, £525 for the Historic Inns trail and £645 for the Trans-Wales trail. The 3-day trail costs £315 and the 2-day trail £135. Prices include riding, board, accommodation and luggage transfers. (Prices current at time of writing; check with centre for updated prices.)
Booking: Deposits for 6-day trails are £140–215 depending on the route. 3-day deposit is £105, 2-day deposit £45. Deposits must be paid at time of booking. Balance due 40 days prior to start of ride.
Access: Cwmfforest is just off the A479 between Talgarth and Crickhowell.

ellesmere trail riding

Llangorse
Brecon
Powys
LD3 7UN
Wales
Tel (01874) 658 252 / 658 429

Trail Riding

This centre comes highly recommended – Ellesmere put together very small groups of experienced riders to trail through the Black Mountains and Brecon Beacons for up to 5 days on good Welsh cobs. Myfanwy, who leads the rides, is as Welsh as they come – flaming red hair *et al* – and knows a good deal about the local folklore, as well as the ways through the mountains. One of her 2-day rides takes you up over a steep pass to a track cut through the mountains as a carriage road in the last century so that the local lord could reach his mistress, whom he had installed in a stone house in a narrow valley hidden from the world. You pass the ruins of the house, then ride through forest to a 12th-century priory, where you stay the night. The pub-lunch stops have been chosen as much for the real ale on offer as the good food.

Season: March to October.
Accommodation: In comfortable B&Bs, local hotels and farmhouse inns along the route.
Food: Good farm cooking. Vegetarian catering by arrangement.
Children: Over-16s only.
Disabled Facilities: None.
Insurance: Clients should arrange personal insurance cover.
Safety: Mountain rescue on call.
Affiliations: None.
Tariffs: 2-day ride: from £160 per person all inclusive. Longer rides cost roughly £80 per person per day.
Booking: A deposit of £75 is required for all courses. Balance payable 8 weeks prior to course start date. Payment by cheque or cash.
Access: Contact centre for details.

equi-study

Moreton Hall
Moreton Morrell
Warwickshire
CU35 9BL
Tel (01926) 651 085
Fax (01926) 651 190

BHS Instructor Courses Only

Equi-Study is the equestrian wing of Warwickshire Agricultural College. It offers competitively priced courses for would-be professionals to attain Assistant Instructor level (BHSAI) and Intermediate Instructor level (BHSII). You can bring your own horse or work with those at the college. The courses are designed to be as affordable as possible, with the instruction averaging out at a cost of only £2 per hour – very good value. Courses are non-residential and students will be expected to arrange their own accommodation and transport.

Season: All year.
Accommodation: Not provided.
Food: Not provided.
Children: Over-16s only.
Disabled Facilities: None.
Insurance: Students require their own personal accident policies.
Safety: First-aid-trained staff on-site. Students will be taken to hospital if necessary.
Affiliations: BHS; Warwickshire College.
Tariffs: Each BHS stage course costs £375, except those for Intermediate Instructor which cost £425.
Booking: A deposit of £75 is required for all courses. Balance payable 8 weeks prior to course start date. Payment by cheque, Visa, Access, Mastercard, Amex or Switch.
Access: Contact centre for details.

exmoor riding holidays

North Wheddon Farm
Wheddon Cross
Nr Minehead
Somerset
TA24 7EX
Tel (01643) 841 224 / 841 159
Fax (01643) 841 159

Trail Riding

Exmoor is superb riding country. North Wheddon Farm offers experienced riders a choice between centre-based explorations of the Exmoor National Park and post-trail rides between different points each day, with the baggage taken on by car. They have been running the 7-day trips since 1972 and offer horses from 14.2–17.2 hands (or you can bring your own). They also make it very easy for you to get there, picking people up from Heathrow Airport every Saturday, if they have no transport to get to Exmoor themselves, and delivering them back again the following Saturday.

Look out for the famous herds of red deer as you ride, and the harder-to-spot foxes and badgers that frequent the area. The week's ride goes through varied terrain – open moorland, wooded ravines, forestry and farmland. Particularly beautiful times of year to go are early September, when the heather is in bloom, and the wild-flower season of May and June.

Season: 29 March to late November.
Accommodation: Guests stay at North Wheddon Farm or the Rest and Be Thankful pub for centre-based holidays, and move between local farmhouses for riding tours. Single-room supplement required.
Food: Breakfast provided for centre holidays, full board provided for tours.
Children: No special facilities for children.
Disabled Facilities: None.
Insurance: Guests must provide their own holiday insurance.
Safety: Staff trained in first aid.
Affiliations: ABRS; BHS.
Tariffs: Centre-based riding holiday includes riding and B&B; guests must care for horses themselves (or pay £30 supplemental charge). 6-night holiday: £330–390 (depending on accommodation desired). Touring holidays include full-board accommodation, riding and care of horses – 6-night Rider's Paradise tour: £870; 6-night Horse Lover's Utopia tour: £570. Weekend centre-based riding includes 2 days' riding and 2 nights' B&B: £125-142 (depending on accommodation desired).
Booking: Deposit of £100 required (£40 for weekends). Balance due 6 weeks before start. No refunds made in case of cancellation. Late bookings accepted if space available.
Access: Few miles off the M5 near Wheddon Cross. Buses and trains available to Taunton; cab from Taunton to Wheddon Cross costs £24.

ferniehurst mill riding centre

Jedburgh
Borders
TD8 6PQ
Scotland
Tel (01835) 863 279

Trail Riding, Pony Trekking

The Teviot Hills of the Borders are criss-crossed by a network of old turf tracks – Roman military roads and medieval drovers' and pack-horse roads where riders and walkers still have full rights of access. You can canter for miles and miles. Ferniehurst offers centre-based trail rides on good, fit horses for experienced riders only, riding in small groups of 4 to 6 people. Some of the routes follow those of the old reivers – Scotland's border-country cattle-raiders who made their living from slaughter and pillage but who were sanitized and romanticized in Walter Scott's Waverley novels. Still, it's a pretty romantic area and you'd have to be made of stone not to react emotionally to the wild landscape. Ferniehurst offers about 5 hours of riding per day.

Season: May to October.
Accommodation: 9 comfortable twin and double rooms with en suite bathrooms. Accommodation and board included in general tariff.
Food: Vegetarians by prior arrangement.
Children: Adults only.
Disabled Facilities: None.
Insurance: Clients must arrange their own personal accident cover.
Safety: Clients taken to hospital if necessary.
Affiliations: ABRS; Trekking & Riding Society of Scotland.
Tariffs: A week's residential holiday is £350 including full board. A half-day's ride is £30.
Booking: Deposit of £50 required with booking. Balance payable 4 weeks prior to holiday.
Access: Off the A68, 2½ miles south of Jedburgh and 8½ miles north of the Scottish border at Carter Bar.

free rein riders

The Coach House
Clyro
Hay-on-Wye
Hereford & Worcester
HR3 5LE
Tel (01497) 821 356

Unaccompanied Trail Riding

The hills of the Welsh Borders have a network of 'green roads' – old drovers' tracks left over from the Middle Ages which you can ride at will. They snake through the hills forever – you could ride for a couple of weeks and still not exhaust them. You come down from the hills to villages where you can stick the horse in a field and put up for the night in the local pub or B&B. While up on the hills you will seldom see anyone and hardly ever cross a road.

Free Rein is unusual in that it allows its clients to go off into the hills unaccompanied, having marked their route on a map and made the necessary bookings. You must sign a statement to the effect that you are experienced both in riding and horse handling before setting off. But to make sure that people don't get into trouble, the centre only uses slow, cobby horses that cope admirably with the hills but are not particularly keen.

Season: May to October.
Accommodation: In comfortable farmhouses and B&Bs along the route. Please note that accommodation costs are not included in Free Rein's general tariff.
Food: Vegetarians by prior arrangement.
Children: Under-16s must be accompanied by 2 adults. 16–18-year-olds must have parent or guardian's written consent.
Disabled Facilities: None.
Insurance: Clients need personal accident cover.
Safety: There is a vehicle back-up. In emergencies clients must phone for a pick-up.
Affiliations: None.
Tariffs: Free Rein charges £55 per day for the horse, maps and bookings. Clients pay for accommodation by the night at the place of accommodation.
Booking: A deposit of 10% required on booking. Balance due 42 days before holiday begins. Payment by cheque.
Access: Clyro is about 2 miles west of Hay and sits on the A438 between Lowes and Whitney.

highland horseback

Auchinhandoch
Glass
Huntly
Aberdeenshire
Scotland
AB54 4YJ
Tel & Fax (01466) 700 277

Trail Riding

This is probably the toughest trail ride currently running in Britain, a 9-day trans-Scotland ride from the centre's hill farm in Glass, Aberdeenshire, across the Grampians, Cairngorms and into the western Highlands, riding through to the Atlantic via the high emptiness of the Forest of Kintail. If you haven't the time to do the full ride, you can opt for half of it, either the western or eastern sections, ridden over 4 days. The standard of horses is high – good, fit cobs and hunters between 15.2 and 16.2 hands.

You stay in comfortable hotels en route, with your luggage taken on by car. Experienced riders only should tackle this one.

Season: May to October.
Accommodation: In country hotels along the route – cost included in general fee.
Food: A good standard of cuisine. Special diets by prior arrangement.
Children: Over-16s only.
Disabled Facilities: None.
Insurance: Clients should arrange their own personal accident insurance.
Safety: Ride leader contacts mountain and air rescue if necessary.
Affiliations: None.
Tariffs: 8-day trans-Scotland ride costs £925 per person. 4-day halfway ride costs £465.
Booking: Deposit of £100 with booking. Balance due 6 weeks prior to ride. Payment by cheque.
Access: Huntly lies at the junction of the A97 and the A920 in Aberdeenshire. For directions to Glass, ring centre. The nearest railway is at Huntly, which can be reached from Aberdeen or Inverness.

---

kidlandlee

Harbottle
Morpeth
Northumberland
NE65 7DA
Tel (01670) 650 254

Trail Riding

Angus Davidson's trail riding holidays are limited to groups of 6 people and are aimed at advanced adult riders only. The guided trail-rides up into the wide uplands of Northumberland and south Scotland have been running since 1974. Each ride lasts for 5 days (6 nights) with accommodation at a different spot each night – your baggage is taken on for you by car. You cover about 85 miles during the ride, over some very testing terrain, using old military saddles and good, corn-fed horses. Shorter trail riding weekends and 3-day trips are now being offered too, as well as an option to bring your own horse. If you have no transport, the centre will pick you up from Harbottle, which can be reached by bus from Newcastle or Morpeth.

Season: 1 May to 1 October.
Accommodation: Double, single and 3-bedded rooms in a private farmhouse.
Food: Full board included. Vegetarian and special diets are catered for upon request.
Children: Holiday designed for those aged 16 and up.
Disabled Facilities: None.
Insurance: Clients need their own holiday insurance.
Safety: Staff trained in basic first aid.
Affiliations: None.
Tariffs: Prices include full-board accommodation, guide, horse and luggage transport. 5-day / 6-night post trail: £385; 3-day / 4-night post trail: £240; 2-day / 3-night post trail: £175.
Booking: Deposit of £35–65 required. Full cost of holiday forfeited if cancellation made within 30 days of start date. Late bookings accepted if space available.
Access: Off the A1 at Morpeth. Contact centre for public transport details; pick-ups from nearby stations can be arranged by centre.

llangorse riding centre

Gilfach Farm
Llangorse
Nr Brecon
Powys
LD3 7UH
Wales
Tel (01874) 658 272
Fax (01874) 658 280

Trail Riding, Pony Trekking

The Black Mountains of southern mid-Wales provide the backdrop for Llangorse's trail riding and pony trekking breaks. There are approximately 26 miles of private bridleways running around the farm, which connect with several public bridleways up into the mountains – many of them ancient drovers' roads with sound old turf for galloping on. The trail rides and treks go out from and return to Llangorse each day, with a lunchtime stop at a pub. The centre is open to riders at all levels of experience, and you can put together a package of as many days as you like.

There is no on-site accommodation, but the riding centre does own a farmhouse B&B nearby, or you can arrange your own accommodation. If you choose the latter option, however, you will need your own transport to get to and from the stables each day. Llangorse have been operating for 35 years and know the mountains very well. Should you wish to take a day out of your trail riding or trekking for some riding lessons, this too can be arranged as the stables has its own manège. For a further change of pace, take advantage of Llangorse's indoor climbing and abseiling facilities.

Season: Open all year.
Accommodation: The family that runs the centre also runs a nearby B&B guest house: en suite rooms available, £18 per night. Bunkhouse accommodation for groups.
Food: Guest house serves hot meals, breakfast included in accommodation tariff.
Children: Instruction and rides out for children available, but not specific children's holidays.
Disabled Facilities: Ramps and mounting blocks available.
Insurance: Guests should take out their own holiday insurance.
Safety: Staff trained and certified in first aid.
Affiliations: BHS; Riding for the Disabled Association; WTB Accredited Activity Centre; Wales Trekking and Riding Association.
Tariffs: Prices include tuition and hire of horses. Trekking: £7 for 1 hour, £11 for 2 hours, £18 for full day. Riding: £14 for 2 hours, £22 for full day. Hacking: £17 for 2 hours, £28 for full day. Private tuition also available by arrangement.
Booking: Deposit required; contact centre for details. Late bookings accepted if space available.
Access: From Brecon take the A40 to Bwlch, then the B4560 to Llangorse. Trains available to Abergavenny station. Taxi must be taken to farm, 15 miles.

loch ness riding centre

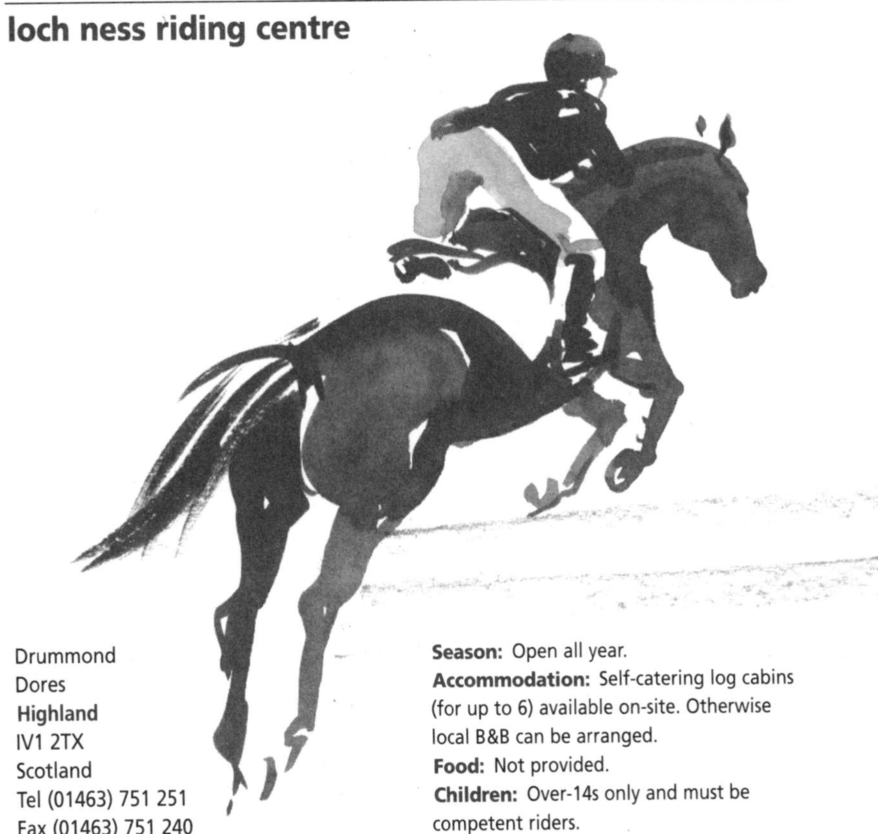

Drummond
Dores
Highland
IV1 2TX
Scotland
Tel (01463) 751 251
Fax (01463) 751 240

Day Rides, Dressage, Cross-country, Show Jumping

For open access and freedom there is nothing to beat the Scottish hills. The trail riding here is breath-taking and virtually limitless. The Loch Ness Riding Centre offers day rides of 4 to 5 hours a day for competent adult riders, either on the centre's horses or on your own (but riding out with a guide). You can vary the schedule to include schooling sessions in dressage, cross-country and show jumping and can stay either on-site in the self-catering bungalows or in nearby B&Bs (though you'll need your own transport for the latter).

Season: Open all year.
Accommodation: Self-catering log cabins (for up to 6) available on-site. Otherwise local B&B can be arranged.
Food: Not provided.
Children: Over-14s only and must be competent riders.
Disabled Facilities: Toilets wheelchair-accessible.
Insurance: Clients should provide personal insurance cover.
Safety: Staff trained in first aid.
Affiliations: Inverness Tourist Organization; South Loch Ness Tourist Group; Trail Riding Society of Scotland.
Tariffs: Accompanied hacks: £15 (1 hour), £20 (1½ hours), £25 (2 hours), £35 (3 hours); instruction (horse hire included): £20 for 45 minutes or £25 for 2 people for 1 hour; guide hire: £10 per hour; livery: £5 per day.
Booking: No deposit required. At least 24 hours' advance notice required.
Access: Off the B862 near Dores. Trains and buses to Inverness; pick-ups from Dores can be arranged by centre.

lydford house riding stables

Lydford House Hotel
Lydford
Okehampton
Devon
EX20 4AU
Tel (01822) 820 347
Fax (01822) 820 442

Trail Riding, Learning to Ride

Riding out across the open hills of Dartmoor on good horses, returning to luxurious, 4-crown accommodation by night (pink 4-posters and all) is what Lydford House offers. Riding holidays last from 2 days to 1 week, whether for experienced riders or complete beginners (their 2-day 'Introduction to the Horse' is particularly recommended). It's not cheap, though, with rates as for a hotel rather than for an outdoor centre or B&B.

Despite the rugged nature of the country you ride over, these are not demanding trail rides, with only 2 to 3 hours in the saddle per day, or 18 hours over the course of a week. The centre's great strength is that it can cater for whole families, even ones whose members have varied riding experience.

Season: Open all year.
Accommodation: Guests stay in the Lydford House Hotel; single, double, twin and family rooms available (all with en suite facilities).
Food: Breakfast provided, dinner options available. Vegetarian and special diets catered for upon request.
Children: Must be 5 or older. Children on residential holidays must be accompanied by adults. Discounts on hotel rates for children.
Disabled Facilities: None.
Insurance: Clients should arrange their own holiday insurance; can be arranged through centre.
Safety: Staff trained in first aid.
Affiliations: BHS.
Tariffs: 1-week holiday (includes B&B accommodation and 18 hours of riding): from £308 (October–May), from £326 (June–September and bank holidays), add £75 for dinner option; 2-night holiday (includes B&B accommodation and 2-hour hack): £92; 2-night holiday (includes B&B accommodation, 45-minute lesson and 1-hour hack): £100. Hourly rates are as follows – riding: £8; class lesson: £9; private lesson: £15 (45 minutes). Livery from £11 daily, £70 weekly.
Booking: £20 non-refundable deposit required. Cancellation charge: up to two-thirds of total cost if place not refilled. Bookings normally made in advance, but late bookings accepted if space available.
Access: Off the A386 at Lydford. Public transport to hotel can be awkward; contact centre for details.

lyncombe lodge

Churchill
Nr Bristol
Avon
BS19 5PQ
Tel (01934) 852 335
Fax (01934) 853 314

Trail Riding, Dressage, Cross-country and Show Jumping, Learning to Ride

With beautiful riding over the wild Mendip Hills of Somerset and Avon, Lyncombe Lodge can be recommended for the scenery alone. It also offers very good tuition – for adult or children's groups, as well as trail rides for both novice and experienced riders. The riding holidays either last from Sunday to the following Saturday, or run as weekend courses. You are given a horse for the week, which you catch, tack up and feed yourself. The more experienced riders can take overnight riding trips away from the centre – otherwise all rides go out from and return to the centre each day. The children's riding holidays have a gymkhana at the end of the week. Lyncombe Lodge has 2 outdoor manèges, a cross-country course and immediate riding access to the open hills.

Season: Open all year.

Accommodation: 5 twin rooms, 2 single rooms and 3 dormitory rooms.

Food: Breakfast and dinner included, bar lunches available. Vegetarian and special diets catered for upon request.

Other Activities: Archery (see p. 6); Child and Youth Sports (p. 63); Skiing (p. 379).

Children: Special children's courses available at reduced rates.

Disabled Facilities: None.

Insurance: Clients should arrange their own holiday insurance; may be arranged through centre.

Safety: Staff trained in first aid.

Affiliations: BHS.

Tariffs: Prices include accommodation, half-board, horses and instruction. 6-day course: £245-285 (according to season) +VAT; 2-day course: £110 + VAT. Riding is also one of the sports offered in the centre's multi-activity package deals. 6-day holiday: £275-315 (according to season) + VAT; 2-day holiday: £110 + VAT. Discounts available for children under 16.

Booking: £30–40 non-refundable deposit required. Balance due 4 weeks before start date. Charges for cancellation depend on when notice is received. Late bookings accepted if space available.

Access: A368 to Churchill. Trains to Yatton, buses to Churchill. Taxi ride from station arranged by centre.

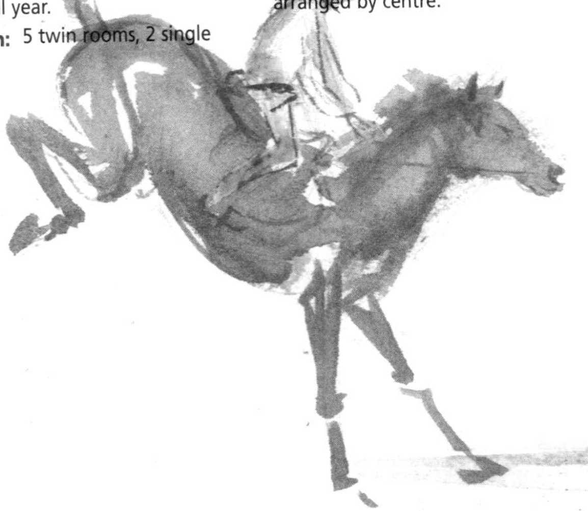

millfield village of education

Millfield School
Street
Somerset
BA16 0YD
Tel (01458) 445 823
Fax (01458) 840 584

Learning to Ride, Show Jumping, Dressage, Cross-country

Millfield has 47 horses and ponies, an outdoor and an indoor school, and a cross-country course. The school offers 2 courses, both over a week in the summer, under the instruction of well-qualified teachers. There is a beginners' course – Riding for Recreation – which introduces the basic riding skills and develops confidence in handling horses and ponies, teaches basic stable management and grooming, as well as hacking out into the countryside and introductory jumping for those with some experience.

The more advanced course – Advanced Riding – is aimed at riders with some years of experience who preferably have owned their own horse. The programme includes an introduction to basic dressage, i.e. flat work, cross-country and indoor jumping with an emphasis on improving the rider's effectiveness and position. Practical sessions are supported by theory of riding lectures and the use of video – including replay of lessons.

Tariffs: Riding for Recreation course includes horse hire and 6 half-day instruction sessions: £99; Advanced Riding course includes horse hire and 3 half-day instruction sessions: £112. Full-board accommodation for 1 week: £166 (adult), £136 (under-12). (5% senior discount.)

See Circus Skills (p. 83) for full details.

moyfield riding school

South Littleton
Evesham
Hereford & Worcester
WR11 5TP
Tel (01386) 830 207

Dressage, Cross-country, Show Jumping

Week-long courses on the full range of riding skills are offered at Moyfield, with facilities for everyone from the beginner to the regularly competing rider. You get a minimum of 3 hours' riding per day (quite a lot when this is mostly intensive tuition in the manège), and there are 5 full-time instructors. If you stay for a week, they guarantee at least 22 hours of riding. Except in very quiet weeks, there is no on-site accommodation besides camping, and you have to stay in local B&Bs. If you don't have your own transport, the riding school can take you to and from the stables, but there is an extra charge for this, which varies according to the distance.

Moyfield have 41 years of experience behind them, and stable an impressive 100 horses and ponies. There are 300 acres of private hacking available, as well as riding along the River Avon and into the north Cotswolds, and arrangements can be made for you to compete at local shows. Children's groups and adults are equally welcome.

Season: Open all year.
Accommodation: A few guests can be accommodated at centre (£24 per day with full board). Centre will also provide help in obtaining local farmhouse accommodation.
Food: Full board available for guests.

Children: All ages welcome. Special children's holidays available.
Disabled Facilities: Lessons and rides for the disabled.
Insurance: Guests should arrange their own holiday insurance.
Safety: Staff trained in first aid.
Affiliations: ABRS; BHS.
Tariffs: Hourly tuition: £12.
Booking: Deposit requested. Late bookings accepted if space available.
Access: Near Evesham off the A44. Trains to Evesham or Honeybourn. Buses to South Littleton.

northumbria horse holidays

East Castle
Annfield Plain
Stanley
Durham
DH9 8PH
Tel (01207) 235 354 / 230 555

Trail Riding

The high fells and moorlands of Northumberland's Pennine uplands provide some of the best – and least explored – riding country in Britain. Northumbria Horse Holidays take you up into the hills for anything from a weekend to 2 weeks, sleeping at different hotels each night, with your baggage taken on by car for you.

There are 3 kinds of riding holiday here: the Learn to Ride package for total beginners and/or nervous riders; the Improve Your Riding package for people with some experience, where you work on ironing out bad habits and making progress; and the Post Trail Riding holidays for experienced riders who are comfortable at all speeds, on fit, corn-fed horses, riding over all types of terrain. Northumbria Horse Holidays were one of the first centres to open up trail riding in Britain and their popularity has soared – so book as far ahead as you can, especially if you want to go as a group.

Season: 31 March to 2 November.
Accommodation: Accommodation provided at the Dale Hotel in Allendale, mostly double rooms.
Food: Full board provided. Vegetarian and special diets catered for upon request.
Children: 10% discount for children under 16 sharing room with adults. All ages welcome.
Disabled Facilities: None.
Insurance: Guests must provide their own holiday insurance; can be arranged through centre.
Safety: All staff trained in first aid.
Affiliations: British Appaloosa Horse Association (BAHA).
Tariffs: Prices include instruction, horses and full-board accommodation. Prices vary according to season. 5-day / 4-night Learn to Ride or Improve Your Riding holiday: £233–329; 6-day / 7-night Post Trail holiday: £339–459; riding weekend: £149–187; Romany caravan hire (self-catering caravan): £245–410 per week. (Tariffs current at time of writing; contact centre for updated prices).
Booking: £45 non-refundable deposit required. Cancellation charges: if more than 42 days in advance: deposit;
29–42 days in advance: 50% of total;
15–28 days in advance: 60% of total;
1–15 days in advance: 90% of total;
same day: 100% of total.
Access: The Dale Hotel is on the B6295. Trains available to Hexham station. Buses available to Newcastle (then train must be taken to Hexham). Pick-ups from Hexham station can be arranged by centre.

parc-le-breos riding & holiday centre

Parc-Le-Breos House
Parkmill
Gower
West Glamorgan
SA3 2HA
Wales
Tel (01792) 371 636

Pony Trekking, Learning to Ride

This is a classic trekking centre, offering complete beginners the chance to take to the countryside (steadily) on horseback. Parc-Le-Breos has been open for 35 years and is still going strong – one of the more popular and reliable trekking centres in the UK. For those who get the bug, the centre also offers instructional courses on basic riding, enabling you to get more out of your pony, both in the saddle and in the stable.

The house is baronial – a manor that has stood in various forms on the site since the 1300s, its present incarnation having been built in the 1840s. The surrounding area is very beautiful – the Gower Peninsula has views out over the ocean and is dotted with nature reserves and ancient sites, all on the itinerary for the rides.

Season: Open all year.
Accommodation: Double and family rooms available in large estate house.
Food: Full board included; vegetarian and special diets catered for upon request.
Children: Must be 10 or older if unaccompanied by adults.
Disabled Facilities: None.
Insurance: Clients should arrange their own holiday insurance, available through centre.
Safety: Staff trained in first aid.
Affiliations: BHS; WTB.
Tariffs: Prices include tuition, horses and full-board accommodation. Prices vary between low and high season. 1- week holiday (includes 5 full day rides): £199–209; weekend holiday (includes 2 full day rides): £74. Discounts available for groups and children.
Booking: Deposit required, not refundable in cases of late cancellation. Bookings normally made in advance, but late bookings accepted if space available.
Access: Off the A4067 at Swansea. Trains and buses to Swansea, bus station within walking distance of centre.

porlock vale house

Porlock Weir
Somerset
TA24 8NY
Tel (01643) 862 338

Dressage, Show Jumping and Cross-country, Side-saddle

Porlock Vale has been running brush-up-your-riding courses for competent riders for over 30 years. They specialize in getting people going before the hunting season, after a summer out of the saddle. The house itself is very handsome and bedrooms are large and comfortable. Training is given on the flat and over cross-country fences, with time off spent hacking in the local woods and bridleways. Porlock Vale is relaxed but very professional – you will learn as much about horse care as about riding. Side-saddle lessons are also available.

Season: All year.
Accommodation: Comfortable B&B on site, included in general tariff.
Food: Special diets by arrangement.

Children: 15 and over.
Disabled Facilities: None.
Insurance: Clients should arrange their own personal accident policy.
Safety: Clients taken to hospital if necessary.
Affiliations: BHS.
Tariffs: 7-day holiday: £265; 3-night mid-week break: £114; 2-night break: £89. Tariffs include riding, instruction and B&B.
Booking: Deposit of £50 required with booking. Balance payable 7 days prior to start of holiday. Payment by cheque or cash.
Access: Porlock Weir is on the coast about 2 miles from Porlock village, which lies on the A39 5 miles west of Minehead.

---

raygill riding centre

Lartington
Barnard Castle
Durham
DL12 9DG
Tel (01833) 690 118

Trekking, Learning to Ride

Teesdale is an underpopulated, beautiful stretch of Pennine England. Based in an old stone farm, Raygill offers day trekking and learn-to-ride courses on the moors, with instruction in a manège. A speciality of the centre is its small herd of Dales ponies, perfect mounts for scrambling up and down the ghylls and fells – they are very strong and go forever. The holidays and courses last either for a weekend, 4 days (mid-week) or a full week, and cater to all ages and abilities. People are also welcome to bring their own horses.

Season: Open all year, though winter trekking can be limited by bad weather.
Accommodation: Single and double rooms for adults. Shared dorms for children.
Food: Good farmhouse cooking. Special diets by request.
Children: Unaccompanied children over 10 welcome.
Disabled Facilities: None.
Insurance: Clients should have their own holiday cover (riding covered by centre).
Safety: Staff first-aid-trained.
Affiliations: BHS; ABRS.
Tariffs: Subject to seasonal variations. All-inclusive weekend breaks: £85–100 per adult, £70–80 per child; mid-week breaks: £45 per night per adult, £35 per night per child; weekly holidays: £230–250 per adult, £180–195 per child. Special rates for B&B only.
Booking: Send large SAE for details.
Access: Raygill Farm is signposted south of the B6277 from Barnard Castle to Lartington. Own transport necessary.

rhiwian riding centre

Llanfairfechan
Gwynedd
LL33 OEH
Wales
Tel (01248) 680 094
Fax (01248) 681 143

Dressage, Cross-country, Show Jumping

Rhiwian offer general riding holidays aimed at improving rider skills in the arena, in between more relaxing rides along the coast and in the woods and mountains behind the centre. All levels of rider are welcome, with horses to suit. Weekly holidays include about 20 hours of riding and several more learning stable management.

Those arriving by public transport can be met at Bangor. A small charge for the petrol will be levied for this.

Season: All year.
Accommodation: Comfortable guest house with singles, twins and dorms.
Food: Special diets by arrangement.
Children: Unaccompanied children welcome in school holidays.
Disabled Facilities: None.
Insurance: Clients must arrange their own personal accident insurance.
Safety: Staff trained in first aid.
Affiliations: WTB; BHS; Trail Riding Society of Wales.
Tariffs: Prices include riding, instruction and full board. 1-week riding holiday: £245 adult, £225 child (18 and under); weekend breaks: £90 adult, £80 child; 3 days: £142 adult, £124 child; 4 days: £179 adult, £156 child; 2-week holiday: £450 adult, £410 child.
Booking: 25% deposit required with booking. Balance payable on arrival. No credit cards.
Access: From A55, southbound, take second turn-off (northbound, first turn-off) signed Llanfairfechan; follow the brown touring sign to the right on Gwyllt Road – about 1 mile.

rookin house farm riding & activity centre

Rookin House Farm
Troutbeck
Penrith
Cumbria
CA11 0SS
Tel (017684) 83561
Fax (017684) 83276

Trail Riding, Carriage Driving, Learning to Ride

At the foot of the Lakeland fells, Rookin House is a traditional hill farm that has 'diversified' into outdoor adventure sports. In addition to riding, several other activities are on offer, such as go-karts, quad bike treks, archery, clay pigeon shooting and argo-cats (all-terrain six-wheeled vehicles). You can choose between accompanied trail riding and lessons for beginners, or even take lessons in carriage driving, staying in the farm's self-catering converted barn and cottage. This is a particularly good place for children's groups – less so for a long-stay riding holiday. However, a day visit or a weekend riding break here is good value if you're already an experienced rider and can take advantage of the open country to which the farm has access.

Those with no private transport can be picked up from the bus stop at Troutbeck.

Season: Open all year.
Accommodation: Double rooms and bunk beds for 20 available in converted 18th-century barn and cottage.

Food: Café on site serves meals; vegetarian selections available.
Other Activities: Human Bowling (see Related Activities, p. 334).
Children: Half and full multi-activity days available for children (minimum age 8). Lead rein for children 8 and under.
Disabled Facilities: Sports can be adapted for disabled clients; contact centre for details.
Insurance: Clients should arrange their own holiday insurance.
Safety: Staff trained in first aid.
Affiliations: ABRS.
Tariffs: Prices are for accompanied rides. 1 hour: £8; 2 hours: £15; 3 hours: £21; full day: £36; horse driving: £15; lead rein (half-hour): £4. Multi-activity group rates are available; contact centre for details.
Booking: Non-refundable deposit of 25% required. Balance must be paid 5 weeks in advance of holiday. Late bookings accepted if space available.
Access: From Penrith take the A66 to the A5091. Trains to Penrith, buses to Troutbeck. (Cabs from Penrith approximately £10).

---

somerby riding school

Newbold Lane
Somerby
Leicestershire
LE14 2PP
Tel (01664) 454 838

Dressage, Show Jumping and Cross-country, Learning to Ride

This is a small riding school set in some of England's best-known riding country – made famous by the Quorn, Cottesmore and other big hunts of the area. It is a good place to learn jumping, and despite its small size has some very versatile horses and an indoor school. Holiday courses are largely instructional – catering for any standard of rider – the lessons interspersed with a chance to relax by hacking on the local bridleways. Eastern Leicestershire, though well off any tourist map, is a beautiful corner of rural Britain – classic hedge and ditch country with long hills and carefully maintained small woodlands. Despite being only a couple of hours from London or Birmingham, there are no big towns or roads – the feel of the place is deeply rural.

Season: All year.
Accommodation: Not provided – but centre will help to arrange local B&B.
Food: Not provided.
Children: All ages welcome, but children should be accompanied.
Disabled Facilities: None.
Insurance: Clients should have their own personal accident policies.
Safety: Clients taken to hospital if necessary.
Affiliations: BHS.
Tariffs: A weekend break, with 7½ hours of tuition, costs £60. A week's holiday with 15 hours of riding costs £120.
Booking: £10 required, late bookings accepted if space available.
Access: Somerby is situated midway between Melton Mowbray and Oakham. Clients must provide their own transport.

tregoyd mountain riding holidays

Tregoyd
Three Cocks
Brecon
Powys
LD3 0SP
Wales
Tel (01497) 847 351
Fax (01497) 847 680

Trail Riding, Pony Trekking

Tregoyd are past winners of the Riding and Welsh Pony Trekking Centre of the Year Award. They offer 5-day trail riding and pony trekking in the Brecon Beacons on horses to suit total beginners as well as experienced riders wanting to try more testing country. With 10 instructors, there's plenty of scope for tuition along the way, and if you are out to improve your skills a trail riding holiday here will consolidate and extend your effectiveness over rough and steep ground.

There is a wide variety of accommodation available, from hotels and guest-houses to the centre's own bunkhouse (recommended for children's groups). Those staying in outside accommodation can arrange for transport to and from the stables for each day's ride.

Season: March to October.
Accommodation: Centre will arrange accommodation in a variety of local hotels, B&Bs or campsites.
Food: Not provided by centre.
Children: Ponies available for small children.
Disabled Facilities: None.
Insurance: Guests must provide their own holiday insurance.
Safety: All staff trained in first aid.
Affiliations: BHS; WTB; Wales Trekking and Riding Association.
Tariffs: Prices include tuition and use of horses. Half-day ride: from £11.50; full day ride: from £18.50; 5-day ride: from £87.50 (prices vary according to season).
Booking: A non-refundable deposit is required (contact centre for details). Balance due 8 weeks before start date. Cancellation charges: 5–8 weeks in advance: 30% of total; 2–4 weeks: 45% of total; less than 2 weeks; 60% of total. Access, Visa, Eurocard and Mastercard accepted. Late bookings accepted if space available.
Access: At Three Cocks off the A4079 near Hay-on-Wye. Trains available to Abergavenny or Hereford. Buses available to Three Cocks.

wellington riding

Heckfield
Hampshire
RG27 0LJ
Tel (01734) 326 308
Fax (01734) 326 661

Dressage, Cross-country and Show Jumping, Training Courses for Instructors

Wellington is one of the more prestigious British training centres. If you are a serious rider wanting to work on a specific technique, or just want to brush up on general skills before the competition season, these non-residential courses are worth taking, with 3 hours of mounted instruction per day plus lectures and stable management sessions. Wellington has superb facilities – 1 indoor and 2 outdoor manèges, cross-country courses at various levels, and specialized dressage training up to Grand Prix level. Guests need their own transport to get to and from the centre.

If you are thinking of beginning the long process of BHS exams necessary for starting a career with horses, Wellington is known as a reliable training centre. Its 12-, 24- and 52-week courses can be tailored around an existing work schedule or taken intensively, with students staying on the premises.

Season: All year.
Accommodation: Not included; must be booked locally.
Food: None.
Children: 8–17-year-olds can book lessons by prior arrangement.
Disabled Facilities: RDA member. Disabled riding by arrangement.
Insurance: Clients need their own personal accident cover.
Safety: Clients taken to hospital if necessary.
Affiliations: BHS; RDA.
Tariffs: 5-day course: £295; 1-day course: £79. Professional training course prices by application. Tariffs include all tuition and the horse.
Booking: A £50 deposit is required for bookings made over 30 days before course begins; full course fee required on booking if under 30 days before course begins. Payment by cheque, Visa or Mastercard.
Access: Wellington Riding is off the A33 south of Junction 11 of the M4. The centre is signposted from the A33 just north of the Wellington Monument.

---

wheal buller riding school

Buller Hill
Redruth
Cornwall
TR16 6ST

Tel & Fax (01209) 211 852
Cross-country, Dressage, Show Jumping

This is a good school if you want to improve existing riding skills rather than enjoying a trail riding holiday. The 6-day courses can be tailored to whatever is your speciality – or would-be speciality – whether cross-country, dressage or show jumping, interspersed with relaxing hacks in the surrounding countryside and along the local beaches. The school also offers endurance and side-saddle coaching.

The courses are divided into 2 types: for children's groups during school holidays and for adults during term-time. There is an indoor school, cross-country course and an outside manège. All accommodation is on-site, and the school will arrange to pick you up from Redruth train or bus station.

Season: Open all year.
Accommodation: Farmhouse accommodation with sea views.
Food: Full board provided; vegetarian diets catered for upon request.
Children: Unaccompanied children's holidays (7 and over) available during school breaks. Complete package offered including trips out.
Disabled Facilities: None.
Insurance: Guests need their own holiday insurance.
Safety: Staff trained in first aid.
Affiliations: ABRS; BHS.
Tariffs: 6-day course (includes tuition, use of horse and full-board accommodation): £300. (Group and child discounts available.)
Booking: 20% non-refundable deposit required. Access and Visa cards accepted. Late bookings sometimes accepted if space available.
Access: At Redruth on the B3297 to Helston. Trains and buses to Redruth, pick-ups provided by centre. Collection from Gatwick and Heathrow also available: £100 return.

the wyke of shifnal

The Wyke
Shifnal
Shropshire
TF11 9PP
Tel (01952) 460 560
Fax (01952) 462 981

Dressage, Cross-country, Show Jumping

The Wyke specializes in training riders with some experience to be more effective on the flat, i.e. elementary dressage with a view to training them on to further dressage or establishing a really deep seat for jumping. Their residential riding holidays are hard work, but worthwhile. Groups are kept very small and most of the instruction takes place in the indoor school. This is a place at which to improve your techniques and really work at your riding, and you will be expected to do your share of stable duties. As the centre has only very limited accommodation, local transport can be arranged for those staying outside, and only a very small fee is charged to cover petrol. The Wyke has been running for 25 years. Most of their horses compete, from the most basic novice level up to national standard.

Season: Open all year.
Accommodation: 3 double rooms, 1 single room and camping available at centre. Rates vary according to length of stay; contact centre for details.
Food: Full board available.
Children: All ages welcome.
Disabled Facilities: This is a Riding for the Disabled centre.
Insurance: Clients should arrange personal holiday insurance.
Safety: Staff trained in first aid.
Affiliations: ABRS; British Equestrian Trade Association; BHS.
Tariffs: Prices include instruction and use of horses. Adult group hour lesson: £11.75; junior group hour lesson (under-16): £9.50; private hour lesson: £22; half-hour private lesson (on lunge): £12.25; half-hour private lesson (off lunge): £14.75; tots' group half-hour lesson (under-7): £6.50. Discount for multiple bookings paid in advance.
Booking: 10% deposit required. Cancellation fee of £5 if lesson not cancelled at least 1 day in advance. Bookings normally made in advance, but late bookings accepted if space available.
Access: Off the A4192 near Shifnal. Trains and buses to Shifnal, then walking distance to centre (or centre will pick up by arrangement).

yorkshire riding centre

Markington Hall
Harrogate
North Yorkshire
HG3 3PE
Tel (01765) 677 207
Fax (01765) 677 065

Dressage, Cross-country, Show Jumping

Markington Hall is a beautiful old Queen Anne house with a surrounding estate set in the western part of the Vale of York, where it starts to roll up towards the Dales. The large-scale equestrian complex, the Yorkshire Riding Centre, which is attached to the hall, is the home of Christopher Bartle and Jane Bartle-Wilson, two of Britain's most successful international dressage riders. For instructional courses and holidays, particularly for already-competent riders wishing to progress, there can be few better places. Courses are residential and can be tailored to suit your requirements, using either your own horse or ones from the centre.

Obviously, dressage is the speciality, as are career training courses preparing and assessing students taking the BHS instructor exams. Clients wanting to bring their own horses can be transported to competitions for an extra charge.

Season: All year.
Accommodation: There are 2 levels of accommodation – in twin rooms in the main house (expensive), or in the student hostel (fairly cheap).
Food: Vegetarians and special diets catered for by prior arrangement.
Children: Summer riding camps for children aged 8 and upwards. Contact centre for details.
Disabled Facilities: None.
Insurance: Clients should have their own personal accident policies.
Safety: First-aid-trained staff. Clients will be driven to hospital if necessary.
Affiliations: BHS.
Tariffs: Prices include all tuition, board and accommodation. Resident in main house: £748 per person per week; resident in student hostel: £488 per week.
Booking: A deposit of £40 must be submitted with the application form. Balance due 4 weeks in advance of course date. Payment by cheque or cash.
Access: Markington Hall is about 2 miles west of Wormald Green, signposted from the A1. From Harrogate, take the A61 north via Ripley and look out for signs to the right. Clients arriving by rail at Harrogate can be collected by prior arrangement. A small charge to cover petrol costs will be made.

appendix i: polo clubs

It is now possible to learn polo affordably, playing on club ponies and receiving tuition from club instructors. Many of them are near London. Contact the British Horse Society (see p. 200) for your nearest one. A day's tuition, with pony and all equipment, costs around £40–50.

selected polo clubs for beginners' days

Ascot Polo Club, tel (01344) 21312, fax 20399 – Berkshire
Ashfields Polo Club, tel (01371) 872 380, fax 872 492 – Essex
Cambridge & Newmarket Polo Club, tel (01223) 337 659, fax 337 610 – Cambridgeshire
Cheshire Polo Club, tel (01829) 760 206 – Cheshire
Dundee and Perth Polo Club, tel (0131) 538 8682 – Scotland
Edinburgh Polo Club, tel (0131) 449 6696 – Scotland
Epsom Polo Club, tel (01372) 748 200, fax 747 631 – Surrey
Kirtlington Polo Club, tel (01869) 350 138, fax 350 777 – Oxfordshire
New Forest Polo Club, tel (01425) 473 359 – Hampshire
Rutland Polo Club, tel (01476) 860 146, fax 860 451 – Rutland
Stoneleigh Polo Club, tel (01926) 851 989, fax 851 997 – Warwickshire
Taunton Vale Polo Club, tel (01278) 782 266, fax 792 123 – Somerset
Tidworth Polo Club, tel (01980) 841 513, fax 842 558 – Wiltshire
Toulston Polo Club, tel (01398) 323 174 – Yorkshire
West Somerset Polo Club, tel (01398) 323 174 – Somerset

appendix ii: horseball

This is a growing sport, also played at club level. You need to be a very athletic, capable rider as the ball, which is picked up by leather straps, often hits the ground and you have to lean down to grab it. You also need light hands so as not to saw the horse's mouth during the quick stopping and starting. For information on clubs near you contact The British Horseball Association, 67 Clifford Road, New Barnet, Hertfordshire EN5 5NZ, tel (0181) 441 1799.

appendix iii: mad horse things

If you are a really good cross-country rider and more than a little suicidal, there is an annual midnight steeplechase at Tenbury Wells, Hereford & Worcester. The big brush chase fences are lit by torches, but it's still mad and you're likely to hurt yourself. Call any riding school in the area to find out how to enter.

Another mad horse thing is jousting: riding towards another rider with a lance – albeit blunted – and trying to knock him or her off. In fact, most jousting these days is done by display teams who stage shows for festivals, and country fairs, tourist board events and film work. As a result, most of the falls are staged – but falling off a galloping horses is no mean feat, even when it is deliberate. You have to be a good enough equestrian to control the horse while making sure you don't knock your opponent's head off or trip up your own horse. You also have to be good enough at handling the lance to perform the other displays. These include tilting at a ring suspended from a string some feet above your head – you have to place the point of the lance through the ring at a gallop and carry it away.

Then there is the saracen – a rotating straw dummy of a human torso and arms that holds a ball and chain or flail in one 'hand' and a shield in the other. You have to gallop at the thing, hit it on the shield with the point of your lance and gallop past, ducking as it swings round and tries to whack you across the back with the flail.

There are several jousting teams up and down the country, mostly based at riding schools and equestrian centres. If you'd like to join one, contact Sam Humphreys at the Nottingham Jousting Association, Bunnyhill Top, Costock, Leistershire LE12 6XE, tel (01509) 852 366, and he can tell you what's currently in your area.

kitting yourself out

Before going for your first lesson, you must get adequate footwear. This means that your shoes or boots must have a small heel that will stop your foot slipping through the stirrup if and when you fall off – if your foot slips through there's a danger of being dragged. Therefore it's really best to purchase a pair of short riding boots, or jodhpur boots, in which to learn. A cheap pair will cost you about £30. If you are going to stick with it, you could then get a pair of long rubber riding boots. These will keep your legs warmer and you can wash off the inevitable mud and dung without fuss. Pay no more than about £40 for a good pair. Of course, long leather boots are stronger and more elegant, but they cost hundreds of pounds and are only worth getting if you are going to take up riding more or less full time.

Now you need a crash hat – riding is too damn risky without one. It doesn't matter what type you buy provided it has a British Kite mark on the inside of the crown. This means that it has been tested for strength and quality. A good hat costs about £45–60.

You can ride in jeans, or tight trousers, but these are seldom quite tight enough and often rub painfully at the knee. Jodhpurs (which come all the way down to the ankle) or breeches (which only come down to the calf, and are designed for wearing with long boots) are designed for the job and won't rub. Expect to pay between £30 and £70 depending on the quality of material. Stretch corduroy is the most practical for warmth and comfort and looks good too.

Another option is to buy a pair of suede chaps, which zip over jeans or jodhpurs. These are especially good for trail riding, as they are thorn-proof, warm and semi-waterproof. Chaps are expensive – from £50 – but they last forever. And again, you can show off in them.

Once you've been riding for a year or more, you might decide to buy your own horse. Your first horse is a major step in life and you should take no chances. Always go with a friend who really knows horses, and beware of falling in love with the first one you see. If possible, ask to have the horse on trial for a fortnight and make sure that you get it vetted before any money changes hands. No matter how much you may want to get into competition riding or other specialist disciplines, there is a world of difference between riding at a school and forming a private partnership with a horse. Look for one that has done a variety of jobs and which will be able to teach you during your transition from part-time passenger to fully active rider. A horse of

10 years and more has usually overcome its neuroses. You should also set yourself a ceiling price – no more than £3,000 for your first horse. If possible, always buy privately, rather than from a dealer. Get your riding teacher to advise and accompany you when you go to try a horse – they will have a better idea than you as to whether you and the animal are likely to get along. Allow as long as it takes to find the right one – it will come along eventually and you won't regret waiting once you've found each other.

Now you'll have to buy your own 'tack' – principally a saddle and bridle. Measure your horse's back from the wither to the loins, then measure his head and work on meeting those measurements. Always buy tack that has been made from strong dark leather, preferably English. Never buy the more reddish and cheaper Indian leather. If a strap breaks at the wrong moment it can mean disaster. A good new bridle with a snaffle bit costs around £50. A new general-purpose saddle of decent quality will be around £350–400. However, you can always buy good tack second-hand for much less. Again, get your riding teacher to take you round a few tack auctions and second-hand shops, and then make sure that the tack fits properly.

Once you've bought your saddle and bridle, there's a whole universe of other equipment you'll need: numnahs or saddlecloths to put under the saddle; a head collar or halter for the horse to wear in the field so you can catch him; leading ropes and a grooming kit of brushes and hoof-pick; tendon boots to stop the horse from laming itself with a blow from one of its own hooves while exercising; a martingale to stop the horse from throwing its head up and bopping your nose; rugs for the stable and for the field – the list is endless and the amount of gear you will eventually acquire is enormous. Here too your riding teacher should be able to advise you on what you need as you go along. But full-time riding is more a way of life than a sport, so if you've got far enough to need these accessories, you will have long ago come to terms with the black hole of expenses – and again, much of this stuff can be bought second-hand.

checklist

beginner

- ✔ *boots – long or short*
- ✔ *jodhpurs or breeches*
- ✔ *hard hat*
- ✔ *chaps*

experienced rider

- ✔ *horse*
- ✔ *saddle*
- ✔ *bridle*
- ✔ *horse box*
- ✔ *sundries – tendon boots, numnahs, rugs, travelling boots, etc.*

further reading

The Handbook of Riding, Mary Gordon-Watson, Pelham, 1982; *Basic Riding*, Carol Foster, Crowood Press, 1991; *Start to Ride*, Heck and Greiner, J.A. Allen, 1991

photo: BFSLYC / Arthur Sidey

representative body

British Federation of Sand and Land Yacht Clubs (BFSLYC)

23 Piper Drive, Long Whatton
Leicestershire LE12 5DJ
Tel (01509) 842 292

land yachting

Land yachting (also known as sand yachting) is a relatively new sport. Although it has hundreds of private adherents there are as yet very few places where the sport is on offer to the general public. However, if you do track down one of the centres in this chapter, you're in for an interesting ride. Land yachting is high-speed sailing without the water. You have an aerodynamic 'yacht' – a seat mounted on a kind of long platform, a tall sail and 3 wheels. The back two are angled to aid turning while the front wheel is extended on the end of a long bar. Land yachts are purpose-built and expensive to buy but the centres listed in this chapter will supply all equipment.

Most land/sand yachting is done on beaches, preferably at low tide. This allows for plenty of space in which, with the help of strong sea winds, the practised can perform a variety of stunts, all expressed in terms known only to the initiated; a flying gybe into moon country is one such rite, as are manoeuvres in the orange zone (both these strange terms were culled by the author from the British Federation of Sand and Land Yacht Clubs' newsletter). There are regular racing events up and down the country, as well as international events.

Land yachting is also open to children. Although the average age of a sand yachter is, again according to the Federation newsletter, 45, there are plenty of competent pilots under 15. It's worth considering as a safer alternative to waterborne sailing for the young.

Finally, land yachting also has its own weird sub-disciplines – parakarting (speeding along pulled by a small parasailing canopy) and speedsailing (standing on a kind of skateboard and sailing with a windsurfing rig). Parakarting is still in its experimental stages, but speed records are creeping up all the time. Speedsailing can be as fast as regular land yachting (speeds of up to 70mph at club level), but requires considerable niceties of sailing technique. Ask your instructor to put you in touch with parakarters or speedsailors if you're interested in trying these sports.

selected centres

borth youth hostel and field study centre

Morlais
Borth
Dyfed
SY24 5JS
Wales
Tel (01970) 871 498
Fax (01970) 871 827

With a beach right outside its doors, this residential land yachting school (and accredited youth hostel) offers courses on the west Wales coast. The courses run over weekends through the summer and are aimed primarily at beginners and would-be recreational land yachters rather than aspiring competitors or instructors. Tuition is given in groups, varying from 6 to 20 in size, with about 6 hours of sailing per day.

You can stay either in the centre's own bunkhouse accommodation or at local B&Bs within easy walking distance of the beach. The centre will help to arrange for B&Bs if you wish.

Season: March to October (open in winter for groups).
Accommodation: 68 beds, including 12 family rooms.
Food: Vegetarian choices available.
Children: Cots and games provided.
Disabled Facilities: None.
Insurance: Clients should take out personal insurance cover if desired; can be arranged through centre.
Safety: Transportation to a hospital provided if necessary.
Affiliations: Youth Hostels Association; International Federation of Youth Hostels.
Tariffs: Sand yachting tuition: £25 per day. Accommodation: £8.50 per night. Meals: £2.80 for breakfast, £3.10 for lunch, and £4.15 for dinner. Weekend packages including instruction, use of equipment, accommodation and full board: £99 per person (15 December weekend £105, including full Christmas dinner).
Booking: Payment for package weekends must be made 2 months in advance. Clients can be taken at short notice if space is available. Cheques, Access or Visa cards accepted.
Access: Centre is 2½ hours from the M4. Take the A44 from Llangurig to Aberystwyth, then the B4353 to Borth. Trains go from Birmingham to Aberystwyth. Buses available from Aberystwyth to hostel.

brean land yacht club

c/o Adrian Gage
15 Thatcham Court
Yeovil
Somerset
TA21 3DT
Tel (01935) 472 583

With 5 qualified instructors and a selection of different craft, including 2-seaters with dual control, the Brean club aims at taking people from beginner to competition-standard sailing. Club members regularly enter club races, national regattas and the European Championships.

Because it is a club, not a residential centre, learning to land-yacht at Brean is only convenient for locals, or people on holiday in the area – which is famous for its long sandy beaches. If you just want to try it out, the club won't charge for tuition, but will ask you to buy an inexpensive day membership. If you are taken with the sport, they then offer an introductory course of 4 2½-hour sessions, the last session of which includes a test for your pilot's licence.

Season: September to June.
Accommodation: Centre can provide help in obtaining local accommodation.
Food: Refreshments available.
Children: Should be 10 or older.
Disabled Facilities: 2-seater yachts with dual controls available for disabled clients.
Insurance: Participants are covered by centre's insurance.
Safety: Instructors trained in first aid.
Affiliations: BFSLYC.
Tariffs: Prices include tuition and use of yacht. 1-day introductory course: £15; 3-day introductory course: £30.
Booking: No deposit required. Late bookings accepted if space available.
Access: 10 miles off the M5 at Brean. Public transport difficult; contact centre for details.

iris activity breaks

29 Alandale Drive
Pinner
Middlesex
HA5 3UP
Tel (0181) 866 3002

Iris organize land yachting weekend breaks for beginners, taking them through the Royal Yachting Association (RYA) Level 1 course, which teaches all the basics – starting and stopping, tacking and jibbing – with about 6 hours of instruction per day under the tutelage of Chris Moore, British Landspeed Sail Association Grand Prix champion for 1991.

The package includes 2 nights' B&B at the Royal Hotel in Weston-super-Mare and all equipment and local transport to and from the beach.

Accommodation: B&B at the Royal Hotel in Weston-super-Mare.
Tariffs: Weekend includes 6-hour course and 2 nights' B&B: approximately £120.

See Ballooning (p. 13) for full details.

west coast outdoor adventure

63 Swanswood Gardens
Westward Ho!
Devon
EX39 1HR
Tel (01237) 477 637

West Coast's activities are aimed primarily at children and teenagers, but open to all comers. The centre does not offer true land yachting, but a derivation of the sport known as 'speedsailing', which is like windsurfing on a skateboard, but with the potential for far greater speeds. Tuition is mostly at beginner and improver level, though arrangements can be made for more experienced speed-sailors. The centre is fully residential and all holidays and courses include full board.

Tariffs: Prices include tuition, equipment and full-board accommodation. Prices vary according to season, and do not include VAT. Land yachting is one of the activities offered in centre's multi-activity packages – weekend holiday: £49–69; 4-day / night holiday: £79–141; 5-day / night holiday: £99–164.

See Child and Youth Sports (p. 74) for full details.

windsport international ltd

Mylor Yacht Harbour
Falmouth
Cornwall
TR11 5UF
Tel (01326) 376 191
Fax (01326) 376 192
Falmouth Centre, Cornwall
Tel (01326) 376 191
Grafham Centre, Cambridgeshire
Tel (01480) 812 288

Windsport run 3 centres in Britain, 2 of which offer land yachting – at Falmouth and at Grafham Water. Land yachting is taught as part of a multi-activity package. The other sports include catamaran and dinghy sailing, powerboating and water skiing. Multi-activity packages are run either as 'fun days' or, more usefully, over 5 days, where there is really time to learn. Bookings are divided between various types of group: individuals may sign up for a general adults' course, while others are run specifically for families, unaccompanied children and corporate groups. However, if you decide that you want to concentrate on land yachting only, private tuition on student-to-instructor ratios of 1:1 and 2:1 is offered.

Courses can be residential or non-residential – whatever suits you. There is also a variety of accommodation available, and fees are charged on a sliding scale reflecting the level of comfort you choose.

Affiliations: BFSLYC.
Tariffs: Land yachting is one of the activities offered in the centre's multi-activity packages. 5-day adult course: £125; 1-day adult course: £48. Residential packages are also available (including tuition, equipment and accommodation; prices vary according to level of accommodation chosen: hotel, guest-house or farmhouse. 5-day course (6 nights' accommodation): £365–545; weekend course (2 nights' accommodation): £220–280. Group discounts available.

See Sailing (p. 366) for full details.

kitting yourself out

Being a relatively young sport, land yachting is not yet overloaded with different types of kit. There are two basic boards available in this country – the Dragonfly, aimed at beginners, and the Yorker, aimed at racers. Either will cost between £900 and £1,500 new, but can be obtained for far less second-hand. Most clubs will supply boards to beginner members and will help with finding second-hand boards. For those interested in speedsailing, there is a craft called the Speedsail, produced by the British Land Speedsail Association, which uses windsurfing masts and sails. For prices and information on models, call the Speedsail Association on (01736) 762 950. Land yachts also use windsurf rigs, especially at beginner level. Ask a shop manager for advice on what kind of windsailing rig goes well with a land yacht board. Neil Pryde are generally reliable as manufacturers of rigs that cross the line between land and water boards. Expect to pay between £150 and £350 new for the sail and mast.

Helmets are the same as for white-water kayaking. For a choice of makes and prices, see the kit page for the Canoeing chapter (p. 39).

That's about it, except that all schools and clubs recommend that you wear good thick overalls and gardening gloves for protection when you fall off.

checklist

- ✔ *yacht*
- ✔ *helmet*
- ✔ *sail and mast*
- ✔ *thick gloves*

governing body

British Microlight Aircraft Association (BMAA)
Bullring, Deddington, Banbury
Oxfordshire OX15 OTT
Tel (01869) 338 888

photo: Acorn Activities

microlighting

After paragliding and hang-gliding, microlighting is about the closest you can get to pure flying. But with microlighting you do not have to drift with the wind, but can go from A to B at will. Microlights do not require the same pilot training as light aircraft – meaning that it is an affordable sport – although some types of machine have enclosed cockpits and resemble small aeroplanes (the others resemble hang-gliders with engines). When flying an enclosed machine – officially called a 'fixed wing' or 'three-axis type' – you have to use controls that closely resemble those of a light aircraft, and this puts off some people who do not want to use such complicated instruments. By contrast, the hang-glider type of machine – known as a 'flex wing' or 'trike' – is controlled by moving the whole wing canopy and appeals to those wanting simplicity. Some flex wings can be assembled and ready to fly in under 30 minutes and can be stored in a garage. Most microlight models can be towed behind a car in a small trailer.

Microlights can cover great distances – one British flyer has completed a London–Cape Town journey (though not in one go) and Channel crossings are commonly made. If you want to learn, the British Microlight Aircraft Association (BMAA) and Civil Aviation Authority (CAA) recognize several schools in the UK where you can take the necessary courses to gain a Private Pilot's Licence (Microlight). Most of them also offer 'taster' flights for interested people who want to experience microlight flight, but don't want to invest the time and money necessary for taking up the sport full-time. The courses are spread out over at least a month as there are several sets of exams to pass, as well as 25 hours of flying time (including 10 hours solo and cross-country). If you take up flying seriously, most of the schools encourage you to buy your own aircraft – it saves money in the long run and means that you will always have an aircraft available, which makes the process of passing pilots' courses that much faster. Several of the schools listed in this chapter act as dealers for new and second-hand microlights and have differing sets of tariffs for tuition in school-owned and privately owned aircraft.

Anyone between 17 and 80 years old can obtain a microlighting pilot's licence, and the sport is accessible to disabled people.

selected centres

aerolite ltd

Long Marston Airfield
Stratford-upon-Avon
Warwickshire
CV37 8RT
Tel (01789) 299 229 /
(0608) 202 675 (mobile)
Fax (01789) 292 006

Aerolite proudly proclaims that it can take anyone – from beginners to world champions. Both flex-wing and fixed-wing aircraft are available for 'taster' flights or a series of 8-hour courses culminating, after some weeks (and all being well), in your PPL – private pilot's licence.

Long Marston Airfield has plenty of hangarage space for those wanting to buy their own aircraft – which can be done through Aerolite, thus bringing down the cost of a PPL course. There is no accommodation for humans, however, except for camping, but Aerolite make up for this by arranging accommodation for you if you're outside the area and even pick you up from Stratford train station free of charge.

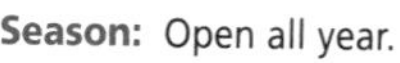

Season: Open all year.

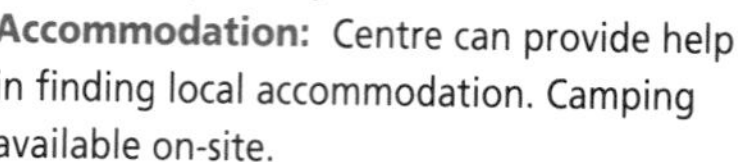

Accommodation: Centre can provide help in finding local accommodation. Camping available on-site.

Food: Not provided.

Children: Minimum age for pilots is 17. Those under 17 may fly as passengers with an adult.

Disabled Facilities: None.

Insurance: Clients need personal insurance cover.

Safety: Contact centre for details.

Affiliations: BMAA.

Tariffs: Prices include tuition and use of aircraft. 30-minute trial flight: £35; dual instruction: £62 per hour; ground school: £12 per hour; solo supervision: £18 per hour; 8-hour course (flex wing): £452; 8-hour course (fixed wing): £494.

Booking: No deposit required. No charge for cancelled bookings. Late bookings accepted up to 48 hours in advance if space available.

Access: On the B4632 near Stratford. Trains and buses to Stratford; pick-ups from station can be arranged by centre.

airbourne aviations

Popham Air Centre
Winchester
Hampshire
SO21 3BD
Tel (01202) 822 486 /
(0831) 306 939 (mobile)
Fax (01202) 822 486

This school has been going for 17 years, flying over the Hampshire countryside. They offer a variety of courses, from 1-hour and 8-hour introductory courses to full training for the PPL, taken over several weeks, with 2 to 3 lessons per week. You can take out a share in one of the school aircraft to defray long-term costs and to ensure that there is always one at your disposal. You can also give introductory courses as presents to timid friends, so as to blackmail them into the air. These range from 20-minute 'taster' flights to a 4-day course in which flight hours count towards a pilot's licence should the recipient decide to take up microlighting full-time.

Although you can camp by the airfield and use the school's toilet and shower, if you don't already live locally the school will arrange local B&B for you.

Season: Open all year.
Accommodation: Camping on-site. Centre will provide help in arranging local B&B accommodation.
Food: Restaurant at centre; vegetarian selections available.
Children: Can receive instruction at any age, but must be 17 to fly solo.
Disabled Facilities: Disabled clients are welcome; contact centre for details.
Insurance: Clients should arrange personal insurance cover.
Safety: Trained medic on staff.
Affiliations: BMAA; British Paramotor Association; CAA; Popular Flying Association.
Tariffs: Prices include instruction and use of microlight. 20-minute trial lesson: £30; 40-minute trial lesson: £57; 1-hour trial lesson: £77; 4-day course: £462.
Booking: No deposit required. Same-day bookings accepted if space available. Visa and Mastercard accepted.
Access: Between Basingstoke and Winchester on the A303. Trains from Waterloo to Mitcheldever, short walk to airfield. Pick-ups can be arranged from nearby stations; contact centre for details.

baxby airsports club

Baxby Manor
Husthwaite
North Yorkshire
YO6 3SW
Tel (01347) 868 572 / 868 443
Fax (01347) 868 572

This is one of the few microlight schools that can offer residential courses – there is self-catering accommodation on the airfield, as well as camping, and B&B a quarter-mile walk away. If you stay a little further afield, one of the club's 2 instructors will pick you up free of charge. Baxby is a small, friendly club occupying a private 110-acre farm at the edge of the North Yorkshire Moors. Complete beginners can sign up for their PPL course while those already holding licences for other kinds of flying can take conversion courses. There are also trial or 'taster' flights to introduce you to the sport, as well as a 1½-hour introductory lesson. If you decide to go on, this time counts towards your PPL, gaining which can be spread over several residential 2–5-day courses.

Baxby also operates as a dealership and can help you to get kitted out, which works out cheaper in the long run, as you pay only for instruction.

Season: Open all year.
Accommodation: Self-catering cottage and camping on-site.
Food: Meals available at centre, including vegetarian selections.
Children: Minimum age 16.
Disabled Facilities: Disabled clients can be accommodated; contact centre for details.
Insurance: Clients should arrange personal insurance cover.
Safety: First-aid kit on site.
Affiliations: BMAA.
Tariffs: Prices include instruction and use of aircraft. 15-minute trial lesson: £27; 1½-hour trial lesson: £58; basic PPL course (15 hours' flying): £775; weekend residential course (includes 2 nights' B&B): £270: 5-day mid-week residential course (includes 4 nights' B&B): £525.
Booking: £25 deposit required. No charge for cancellations. Late bookings accepted if space available. Visa, Mastercard, Access and Eurocard accepted.
Access: Off the A19 north of York, at Husthwaite. Trains and buses to York; pick-ups from stations can be arranged by centre.

cambridgeshire microlight club

114 High Street
Sutton
Ely
Cambridgeshire
CB6 2NW
Tel (01353) 778 446

The wide, flat fenlands around Ely make for great freedom of flying – you can take off and land just about anywhere. This school offers the classic range of microlighting activities: 'taster' flights, lessons by the hour, and an intensive pilot's course of 25 hours, spread out over several weeks. The school has been operational for 15 years.

At 17 miles north of Cambridge, the school is handy for people at the university – indeed, microlighting is just about the only form of flying within the range of a student's (or, these days, even an academic's) budget.

There is no accommodation other than camping, and you will need a car to get to and from the airfield at Sutton Meadows, Staunton Gault, about 7 miles from Ely.

Season: Open all year.
Accommodation: Camping and caravanning sites available (£2 per night).
Food: Not provided.
Children: Minimum age for pilots is 17. Those under 17 may fly as passengers with an adult.
Disabled Facilities: Training for disabled people can be arranged; contact centre for more details.
Insurance: Clients need personal insurance cover.
Safety: Staff trained in first aid.
Affiliations: BMAA.
Tariffs: Prices include instruction and use of aircraft. A variety of courses is available; some sample tariffs are – 45-minute introductory flight: £55; dual instruction: £64 per hour; 5-day course: £560; full course for unrestricted licence (25 flight hours and 15 hours of ground instruction): £1,750.
Booking: No deposit required. No charge if bookings are cancelled. Late bookings accepted if space available.
Access: Off the A10 at Ely. Trains and buses available to Ely; cabs can be taken to centre

---

david clarke microlight aircraft

Unit 2
The Hangar
Worthing
East Dereham
Norfolk
NR20 5HR
Tel (01362) 637 405 /
(0831) 222 172 (mobile)

This is a small flying school with just 2 instructors who offer full flight training programmes and 'taster' flights for individuals and groups (up to 15 people). They also operate as a dealership, and if you buy a microlight through them the PPL training is included in the purchase price – the exams and solo supervision as well as the more regular flight training, which is charged at only £8 per hour to cover the cost of the fuel. Although the school has no accommodation beyond camping, local B&B can be arranged, but you will need your own transport to get to and from the airfield. The school has been running since 1987.

Season: Open all year.
Accommodation: Centre can help arrange local accommodation in a B&B (£25–30 per night) or campsite.
Food: Not provided.
Children: Can receive instruction at any age, but must be 17 to fly solo.
Disabled Facilities: Dual flights available for disabled clients.
Insurance: Clients should arrange personal insurance cover.
Safety: Medic on airfield.
Affiliations: BMAA; CAA.
Tariffs: Prices include instruction and use of aircraft. Trial flight: £20; hourly instruction: £58; 10 hours' pre-paid instruction: £522. If student buys aircraft from centre, instruction for PPL is free.
Booking: No deposit required. Same-day bookings accepted if space available.
Access: Off the B1145 near Worthing. Contact centre for public transport details.

flylight airsports

Sywell Aerodrome
Sywell
Northamptonshire
NN6 OBT
Tel (01604) 494 459

Based just outside Northampton, Flylight offer full training from beginner to instructor level on both flex-wing and fixed-wing microlights. They require a declaration of fitness from your GP. They also offer 30-minute or 1-hour trial lessons to see if you want to take up the sport. If you decide to, then the time spent on the trial lesson will count towards your total flying time. Flylight deal in new and second-hand microlights and offer reduced rates for tuition in your own aircraft, particularly if you buy that aircraft through them. Maintenance and aircraft servicing can be undertaken on-site.

Flylight are quite a popular school, so if you are thinking of taking a course, book as far ahead as you can. Also, each morning before you are due to fly, ring in to check that the weather is right, and that aircraft will be going up that day.

Season: Open all year.
Accommodation: Hotel on-site.
Food: Restaurant and bar on-site.
Children: Can receive instruction at any age, but must be 17 to fly solo.
Disabled Facilities: Disabled persons can sometimes be accommodated; contact centre for details.
Insurance: Clients should arrange personal insurance cover.
Safety: First-aiders on stand-by at airfield.
Affiliations: BMAA.
Tariffs: Prices include tuition and use of school aircraft. Trial lesson (half-hour): £35; trial lesson (1 hour): £65; tuition (1 hour flying, 1 hour ground time): £60; solo pilot's licence course: £1,600. Discounts for own aircraft.
Booking: No deposit required. No cancellation charges if notice given in advance. Late bookings accepted if space available.
Access: Off the A43 at Sywell Aerodrome. Trains to Northampton station. Pick-ups can be arranged by centre; contact them for details.

invicta airsports

Rose Cottage
Watery Lane
Petham
Canterbury
Kent
CT4 5QR
Tel (01227) 750 441 / (0421) 013 668
Fax (01227) 750 441

The purely curious or the aspiring instructor are equally welcome at this small flying school in Kent. In the 8 years since they opened, Invicta have taught all kinds of people to fly, including the disabled – with several blind pilots gaining their licences through Invicta's 2 full-time instructors.

This is not a residential school, and you need to have your own transport to get to and from the airfield – either that or be charged for a pick-up. Consequently, it is mostly locals who take their PPLs here, but if you are passing through the area for a while and want some tuition, Invicta will help to book local accommodation. All tuition is undertaken in club-owned aircraft. Since Invicta is not a dealership they can advise on purchase, but cannot sell you a microlight.

Season: Open all year.
Accommodation: Camping on-site, or centre will provide help in finding local accommodation.
Food: Not available.
Children: Must be 14 or older; consent of parent or guardian required.
Disabled Facilities: Some disabled clients can be accommodated; contact centre for details.
Insurance: Clients should arrange personal insurance cover.
Safety: Ambulance called in case of emergency.
Affiliations: BMAA.
Tariffs: 30-minute trial flight: £30; 1-hour trial flight: £60; PPL course (15 hours' flying): £795.
Booking: Deposit negotiable. Full fees liable if client fails to give cancellation notice, otherwise given voucher valid for 1 year. Late bookings accepted if space available.
Access: 15 minutes from Ashford. Trains and buses to Ashford; pick-ups from stations can sometimes be arranged.

light flight

38 Wallett Avenue
Beeston
Nottinghamshire
NG9 2QR
Tel (0115) 922 2807
Fax (0115) 925 9900

A one-man show run by Chief Flying Instructor Dr Andy Buchan, this small microlighting school caters mostly for locals from the surrounding central Midlands. The flight courses and training sessions are non-residential, but Light Flight will arrange local accommodation. You will need your own transport to get to and from the airfield. Training is given from complete beginner to PPL level and the school can help with aircraft purchase and maintenance.

Season: Open all year.
Accommodation: Farmhouse B&B on-site.
Food: Not provided.
Children: Minimum age for solo pilots is 17. Those under 17 may undergo dual tuition.
Disabled Facilities: Some disabilities can be catered for. Contact the centre for full details.
Insurance: Clients should arrange personal insurance cover if desired.
Safety: Instructor is trained in first aid. Mobile phone carried at all times.
Affiliations: BMAA.
Tariffs: £60 per hour dual tuition in school aircraft. Includes briefing and debriefing.
Booking: No deposit required. No charge for cancelled bookings. Late booking accepted on day of flight if space available. Cheques or cash only.
Access: The airfield is on private land about 5 miles north of Southwell. Directions for reaching the site only given once a booking has been confirmed.

moorland flying club

Davidstow Moor Aerodrome
Camelford
Cornwall
PL32 9YE
Tel (01840) 261 517 / 213 844

Based at Davidstow Aerodrome on Bodmin Moor, with the sea a few miles to the north, this school has access to some really fine flying country. Instruction is in both three-axis and fixed-wing aircraft and caters for anyone, from beginner to instructor standard. All training is given in club-owned aircraft, which are also available to licence-holders who do not have their own microlight. However, if you do buy your own aircraft – and you can do this through the club – the costs of training are considerably less.

In addition to microlighting, the Moorland Flying Club offers powered paragliding, a really exhilarating way of getting into the air. Although powered paragliding has recently been deregulated by the CAA, the club has evolved a structured training syllabus ending with a flying test and the issue of a certificate of competence.

The club is non-residential, but because the area gets so many holidaymakers, it is used to taking people from outside the area and will help in arranging local accommodation at whatever budget. You will, however, need your own transport.

Season: Open all year.
Accommodation: Club will provide help in finding local accommodation.
Food: Not provided.
Other Activities: Paragliding (see p. 315).
Children: Minimum age for pilots is 17. Those under 17 may fly as passengers with an adult.
Disabled Facilities: None.
Insurance: Clients must arrange personal insurance cover.
Safety: Centre uses air ambulance transport in case of emergencies.
Affiliations: BMAA; CAA.
Tariffs: Prices include tuition and use of aircraft. Club offers a variety of courses; some sample tariffs are – 30-minute trial flight: £35; ground instruction: £21 per hour; 15-hour course: £930; Assistant Flying Instructor course: £1,800. Hourly and course instruction are only available to members of the Moorland Flying Club; membership: £40 per year. (Discounts available on courses if clients use own aircraft.)
Booking: Deposits not required. No charge if bookings are cancelled. Late bookings accepted if space available.
Access: Off the A39 at Camelford. Trains to Otterham station, buses to Camelford. Taxi to centre approximately £3.

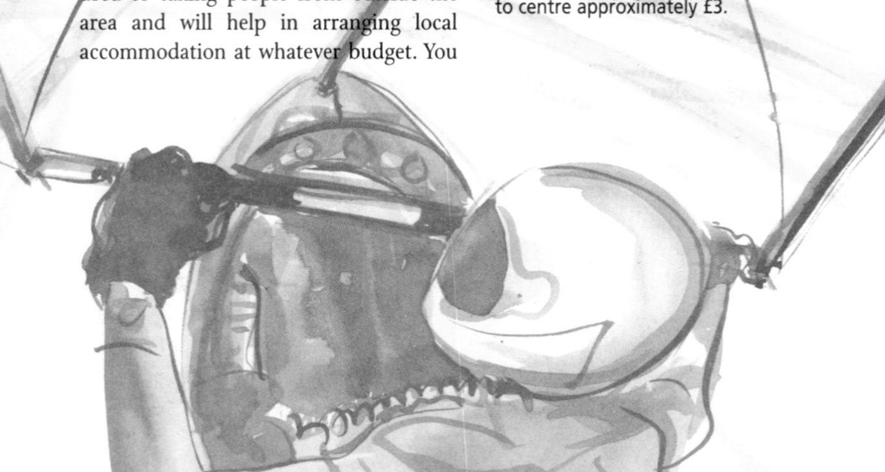

northern microlight school

2 Ashlea Cottage
St Michaels Road
Bilsborrow
Preston
Lancashire
PR3 ORT
Tel (01995) 641 058

This is a small school, with just 1 instructor, but it nonetheless caters for beginners and experienced pilots, and has been successful enough still to be in business after 14 years. The Northern Microlight School also operates as a licensed dealer in microlights and accessories and can help you to get kitted out once you have the 25 hours needed to qualify for a PPL. 'Taster' flights are on offer if you just want to find out what it feels like to be up there, with flights out to the Lake District, which isn't far by air.

There is no accommodation; the school mainly caters to a local clientele. However, if you want to stay in the area long enough to complete a few hours of flight, the school is happy to book B&B for you locally. You will need your own transport to get to and from the private 40-acre airfield.

Season: Open all year.
Accommodation: Local B&B can be arranged.
Food: Not provided.
Children: Minimum age for pilots is 17. Those under 17 may fly as passengers with an adult.
Disabled Facilities: None.
Insurance: Clients only require their own insurance once they start solo flights.
Safety: Staff trained in first aid.
Affiliations: BMAA; North West Microlight Club.
Tariffs: Prices include instruction and use of aircraft. 20-minute trial flight: £27; course instruction: £60 per hour.
Booking: No deposit required. No charge if bookings cancelled. Late bookings accepted if space available.
Access: Off the A6 near Preston. Trains and buses available to Preston.

old sarum flying club

Hangar 3
Portway
Salisbury
Wiltshire
SP4 5BJ
Tel (01722) 322 525
Fax (01722) 323 702

Flying over the Wiltshire Downs is great fun – the ancient Ridgeway track, Stonehenge, the Uffington White Horse and other ancient sites can be clearly seen from the air, and the wide spaces of this area of unenclosed southern England afford easier landings than is usual for lowland England. Old Sarum, just 2 miles outside Salisbury, offers half-hour 'taster' flights in a flex-wing microlight as well as full training for a pilot's licence and then on to instructor level. As is usual with flying clubs, there are no residential courses on offer, but camping and B&B can be arranged close by. You will need your own transport to get to and from the airfield.

In addition to microlighting, Old Sarum offers trial flights and pilot tuition for helicopters and light aircraft.

Season: Open all year.
Accommodation: Centre will help arrange local accommodation from camping to B&B.
Food: Fully licensed bar and restaurant on-site providing home-cooked meals; vegetarian selections available.
Children: Children may fly as passengers or receive instruction if capable; must be 17 to go solo.
Disabled Facilities: Disabled access and toilets.
Insurance: Clients covered by club insurance when they complete the day membership form provided.
Safety: Staff trained in first aid and fire-fighting.
Affiliations: BMAA; CAA; Aircraft Owners and Pilots Association; Popular Flying Association.
Tariffs: 30-minute trial flight: £37.50. Instruction for PPL is available; contact centre for rate details. Group discounts available.
Booking: No deposit required. £25 fee for bookings cancelled less than 24 hours in advance. Late bookings accepted if space available. Visa, Mastercard accepted.
Access: Off the A345 between Amesbury and Salisbury. Trains and buses to Salisbury. Cab from train station around £5, bus station within walking distance of airfield.

sabre air sports

Shobdon Airfield
Shobdon
Nr Leominster
Hereford & Worcester
HR6 9NR
Tel (01568) 708 168
Fax (01568) 708 553

Sabre Air Sports offer stunning flying over the extensive hill ranges of the mid-Welsh Borders. Trial flights of half an hour or trial lessons of 1 hour lead on to 4-day courses (you usually need 2 or 3 of these to make up the necessary hours for a PPL), aimed at getting you fully qualified.

If you are already some way towards getting your PPL, it is worth coming on one of the 4-day courses here to make up the hours and enjoy the superb countryside. There are on-site camping and caravanning facilities, and really good B&Bs nearby. You will need your own car to get to and from the airfield.

The school has been operating for 5 years now, and doubles as a dealership in microlight aircraft, both new and second-hand. It is worth negotiating with them for discounted flight training if you decide to buy an aircraft through them.

Season: Open all year.
Accommodation: Camping available on-site (£3 per night) or else local B&B can be arranged (from £15 per night).
Food: Bar and café on-site; vegetarian selections available.
Children: Minimum age 16; under-18s require consent of parent or guardian.
Disabled Facilities: None.
Insurance: Clients should arrange personal insurance cover.
Safety: First-aid officers on site.
Affiliations: BMAA; Herefordshire Aero Club.
Tariffs: Prices include instruction and use of aircraft. 30-minute trial lesson: £30; 1-hour trial lesson: £60; 4-day flex-wing course (10 hours flying): £550; 4-day three-axis course (10 hours flying): £680. Group discounts available.
Booking: Non-returnable deposit of £250 required for courses. Late bookings accepted if space available.
Access: On the B4362 at Shobdon. Trains to Leominster. Cabs may be taken to airfield, around £6.

ultraflight microlights ltd

Roddige Lane
Fradley
Lichfield
Staffordshire
WS13 8QS
Tel (01283) 791 917
Fax (01283) 792 927

The woods and fields of south Staffordshire and Leicestershire provide the 'underdrop' for these microlight flights from an airfield near Lichfield. There is no accommodation, so the flight school is really only convenient if you're local. However, they can pick you up from Lichfield, Burton upon Trent or Tamworth if you don't have your own transport.

The school has been open for 4 years now and offers the usual 'taster' flights to see if you like the sport, followed by instruction to private pilot or instructor level. There are 4 instructors, and the school operates on a more informal, friendly level than some of the larger flight schools, where the atmosphere can be a little intimidating for the beginner.

Season: Open all year.
Accommodation: Not available.
Food: Not available.
Children: Play area on-site for use under parental supervision. Children can receive instruction at any age but cannot officially record it in logbooks until aged 14. Must be 17 to solo.
Disabled Facilities: Disabled clients can be accommodated; contact centre for details.
Insurance: Clients should arrange personal insurance cover.
Safety: Staff trained in first aid.
Affiliations: BMAA; CAA.
Tariffs: 30-minute trial lesson: £30; 1-hour trial lesson: £60; PPL course: £1,500–2,000 (depending on how much instruction is needed; cheaper if in own aircraft).
Booking: 25% deposit required. No cancellation charges. Late bookings accepted if space available.
Access: Off the A38 north of Lichfield. Trains and buses to Lichfield or Burton upon Trent. Pick-ups from stations can be arranged by centre.

kitting yourself out

The lighter models of microlight (flex wings) cost about £7,000–15,000 new; it's £12,000–20,000 for the three-axis models. But there is a big second-hand market: flex-wings can be picked up from around £3,000 and three-axes from about £6,000. If you join a syndicate and share an aircraft (most clubs can arrange this) the costs are cut still further. Also, if you buy a craft through a club or school and train in it, the cost of tuition goes down considerably. If you do this (with a flex wing), the outlay from purchase of the aircraft to obtaining your pilot's licence, including tuition, will be something near £4,000. As for knowing which of the many models of microlight to buy, consult your instructor.

Helmets are quite specialized. The Lynx 'Micro-System' helmet, which includes a headset, costs around £100. Flying suits are in much the same price range. An electronic navigator by Skytec costs anything between £150 and £300 depending on how sophisticated a model you require. Radios, also by Skytec, are between £250 and £400.

further reading

A Beginner's Guide to Airsports, Keith Carey, A & C Black, 1994

checklist

- ✔ *flying suit*
- ✔ *microlight*
- ✔ *electronic navigator*
- ✔ *helmet*
- ✔ *radio*

governing body

Royal Automobile Club Motor Sports Association (RAC MSA)
Motor Sports House, Riverside Park
Colnbrook, Slough
Buckinghamshire SL3 0HG
Tel (01753) 681 736
Fax (01753) 682 938

motor sport

racing circuits off roading
hill climbing quad bikes
rally driving motorcycles

Michael Schumacher is into the straight and now he's all over the back of Damon Hill's car. They approach the corner, Schumacher ducks out of the slipstream and tries the inside line . . . but no, Damon's shut the door and Michael must back off. This is great stuff.

Formula 1 motor racing, with its own peculiar language and the endearing hysterics of TV's Murray Walker, is undeniably a glamorous and exciting sport. Mix in a little danger, and it's easy to see why Grand Prix racing is so popular worldwide. For most of us, F1 racing will only ever be a spectator sport. But don't worry: there's much more excitement to be had at a far more modest level. If you've got a driving licence, just do it yourself.

It is easier than you think to get behind the wheel of a pukka race car – and there's nothing quite like the experience of driving a single-seater or stiffly sprung racing saloon around a closed circuit, knowing you can go as fast as you like without having to worry about speed cameras, radar traps and flashing blue lights. (Or, for that matter, anything coming the other way.)

Most visitors to race schools up and down the country go just to taste the excitement. They might spend a day or so honing their driving skills under the watchful eye of a qualified instructor – usually a professional racing driver – or try their hand at a different discipline such as rally driving, karting or even off-road driving. Some schools even allow you to drive your own car on the track to see what it can do.

But of course, if you do harbour serious aspirations to be the next Damon Hill, a racing school is the best, indeed only, place to start. No one can race in the UK without a licence from the sport's governing body, the Royal Automobile Club (RAC) Motor Sports Association (RAC MSA). And the RAC MSA won't give anyone a competition licence unless they've undertaken a course at a recognized school, a member of the Association of Racing Drivers Schools (ARDS).

The best way to start is to send an SAE to the RAC MSA (address opposite), asking for their free booklet, *Starting Motor Sport*. This includes application forms for the RAC MSA's 'Go Motor Racing' starter pack (£35) which outlines all you need to know about the sport. For a National 'B' competition car racing licence to be issued, applicants must be 17 and hold a driving licence, or be 16 with at least one year's karting experience behind them. They must have bought the starter pack, taken (and passed) a medical and taken (and passed) a 1-day introductory course at an ARDS school – the set fee for the latter is £135.

There are parallel schemes for aspirant karters and rally drivers – when looking at rally schools, opt for a member of the British Association of Rally Schools (BARS). After that the traditional and proven route to the top goes through junior single-seater formulae like Formula Ford, Renault or Vauxhall, before moving into F3, International F3000 and then F1.

Of course, if it's just a bit of fun you're after, the sky's the limit. You could try one-make saloons, like the Ford Fiesta series. If you like old cars, there is any number of series for classics, including those run by one-make owners' clubs. Or you could add some vital bits of safety equipment, like a fire extinguisher and fuel cut-off switch, to your road car and go racing.

Whatever route you choose, there's nothing quite like the satisfaction of putting in the perfect lap . . . or the frustration of getting one corner wrong lap after lap.

There's even a branch of the sport aimed at kids – you can start cadet karting from as young as 8. Indeed, if you do want to get to the top these days, you virtually have to start at 8. Just ask Michael Schumacher . . .

selected centres

racing circuits, hill-climbing

aintree racing drivers school

1 Fairoak Court
Whitehouse
Runcorn
Cheshire
WA7 3DX
Tel (01928) 712 877
Fax (01928) 790 086

Operating at the Three Sisters race circuit near Wigan, the Aintree school offers half- and full-day courses in single-seater Formula Fords and racing saloons. The centre also offers karting, off-road driving and skid training as well as a Drive Early scheme for youngsters, run in conjunction with the British School of Motoring. They can supply a list of local B&B and hotel accommodation.

Season: Open all year, but the school only operates on certain dates. Call for details.
Accommodation: List of local options available.
Food: Café on site. Vegetarian menus on request.
Children: Karting lessons for 8-year-olds and above; children must have consent of parent or guardian. Young driver's course for children under 17, but must be more than 1.47m tall.
Disabled Facilities: None.
Insurance: Clients are covered by centre's public liability insurance, though indemnities must be signed.
Safety: All instructors trained in first aid. Hospital is 5 minutes away!
Affiliations: ARDS.
Tariffs: Introductory race car trial: £89; advanced saloon car instruction: £89; super race car trial: £119; 1-day intensive race training programme: £359; 2-day intensive course: £699; Drive Early 2.5-hour session: £40.
Booking: Full payment in advance required, to include £25 non-refundable deposit against cancellation. Bookings are normally made in advance, but late bookings are sometimes accepted if space available.
Access: By car, Junction 25 from the M6, then follow signs to Three Sisters, on the outskirts of Bryn near Wigan. Train and bus services to Wigan.

brands hatch leisure

Brands Hatch
Fawkham
Longfield
Kent
DA3 8NG
Tel (01474) 872 367
Fax (01474) 874 766

Racing, Off-road, Karting, Motorcycles

Brands Hatch was the scene of Nigel Mansell's first-ever Grand Prix win (for Williams in the 1985 European Grand Prix) so it is fitting that the circuit's racing school has Mansell's name emblazoned all over it. Just don't expect tuition from Britain's former world champion – he'll be on a golf course somewhere. The Brands Group embraces Oulton Park in Cheshire, Snetterton in Norfolk and Cadwell Park in Lincolnshire as well as the Kent track, and each circuit offers driving opportunities. The Nigel Mansell Racing School operates at Brands Hatch, Oulton and Snetterton, while the group also operates the Yamaha motorcycle racing school at Donington in Derby (see the Jim Russell School, p. 258, for geographical details). Brands also offers 4x4 tuition, rally driving, skid training, while early drive and karting are available to youngsters over 1.47m tall.

Brands Hatch also offers superb motorcycle race training, as part of the Yamaha Racing School programme. The 1–2 day non-residential courses are conducted on the centre's own bikes and are run at beginner and advanced level, with a certificate at the end of each. Instructors are successful race riders in their own right.

Season: Open all year, but school operates only on certain dates. Call for details.
Accommodation: None, but centre will assist with local bookings.
Food: Café on-site. Vegetarian menus on request.
Children: Karting lessons for 8-year-olds and above; children must have consent of parent or guardian. Young driver's course for children under 17, but must be more than 1.47m tall.
Disabled Facilities: None.
Insurance: Clients are covered by centre's public liability insurance; personal accident cover available.
Safety: All instructors trained in first aid. Medics on-site during test days.
Affiliations: ARDS.
Tariffs: Nigel Mansell Racing School – initial trial: from £85 (weekday), £105 (weekend), (Snetterton from £80). Yamaha Race School, Cadwell Park – introductory trial: from £85. Brands Hatch – advanced course: from £165 (Donington from £185); off-road school: from £75; rally school: from £105; early drive: from £45; karting: from £25; skid training: from £59. Beginner's Motorcycle Race Course £105, Advanced Motorcycle Course £165–£201 depending on length of course.
Booking: Full payment in advance required. Cancellation fee 30 per cent of total cost if made less than 14 days before course commences. Bookings normally made in advance, but late bookings sometimes accepted if space available.
Access: Brands Hatch is on the A20 and linked to the M20 and M25 motorways.
It is a 10-mile taxi ride from Swanley train station.

castle combe skid pan and kart track

Castle Combe Circuit
Chippenham
Wiltshire
SN14 7EX
Tel (01249) 782 101
Fax (01249) 782 161

Skid Training, Karting

Skid pan instruction is carried out by a senior police driving instructor, and courses are available on virtually every Saturday and some Sundays. Kart tuition is available to 10-year-olds and above. Castle Combe Racing School – (01249) 782 417 – organizes single-seater and racing saloon tuition.

Season: Open all year. Call for details.
Accommodation: None, but centre will assist with local bookings.
Food: No food available on-site.
Children: Karting lessons for 10-year-olds and above; children must have consent of parent or guardian.
Disabled Facilities: None.
Insurance: Clients are covered by centre's public liability insurance.
Safety: All instructors trained in first aid.
Affiliations: Association of Racing Kart Schools (ARKS).
Tariffs: Karting: racing from £29.50, practice from £15; tuition: £20 per session; skid pan: £49.50 per 3-hour course.
Booking: Full payment in advance required. Cancellation fee varies. Bookings normally made in advance, but late bookings sometimes accepted if space available.
Access: Castle Combe is near Chippenham, not far from Junctions 17 and 18 on the M4.

everyman driving centre

Mallory Park Circuit
Kirkby Mallory
Leicestershire
LE9 7QE
Tel (01455) 842 931
Fax (01455) 848 289

Racing, Off-road, Tanks

Although offering conventional circuit racing school activities, such as karts and single-seaters, the Everyman school goes a few steps beyond, offering a Tank Commando course. Stretch your imagination by driving an Abbot tank, a 6-wheel-drive Stalwart and forward-control Land Rovers. Everyman also has a Junior Drive course for 14–17-year-olds based at the Mallory Park circuit, while a rally course is based at the nearby Prestwold Hall rally stage, near Loughborough. The centre can supply an accommodation list from which to book B&B or local hotels.

Season: Open all year, but Driving Centre days limited by other track activity. Call for availability of dates.
Accommodation: List of local options available.
Food: Café on-site. Vegetarian menus available.
Children: Karting lessons for 8-year-olds and above; children must have consent of parent or guardian. Young driver's course for children under 17.
Disabled Facilities: None.
Insurance: Clients are covered by centre's public liability insurance, though indemnities must be signed.
Safety: All instructors trained in first aid. Safety marshals and on-site medics also on hand.
Affiliations: ARDS; RAC MSA.

Tariffs: Golf GTi and single-seater trial (3–4 hours): £105; Super Day course (6–7 hours): £165. Tank driving from £85, rally driving from £125. Junior Drive starter course: £55.
Booking: Full payment in advance required, to include non-refundable £30 deposit. If booking is cancelled within 14 days of course full fee is forfeited. Bookings normally made in advance, but late bookings sometimes accepted if space available.
Access: Situated between Leicester and Hinckley, between the M1 and M6 motorways. Circuit is well signed off the A47. Nearest station Hinckley.

jim russell racing drivers school uk ltd

Donington Park
Castle Donington
Derbyshire
DE74 2RP
Tel (01332) 811 430
Fax (01332) 811 422

Racing, Off-road, Quad Bikes, Motorbike Racing

Donington is one of Britain's most historic race tracks, and was the home of the British Grand Prix before the Second World War – the sight and sound of the crack German racers from Auto Union and Mercedes-Benz howling round the Derbyshire track must have been really something. The circuit was reborn in the 1970s after local businessman Tom Wheatcroft ploughed millions into creating a state of the art facility including an excellent museum crammed with historic racing cars, well worth a look. Today the track ranks among the most demanding in the country – especially the extremely fast drop down through the Craner Curves – and hosts the British Motor Cycle Grand Prix. It has also hosted the European Grand Prix for cars in the past. As well a bike racing school – see Yamaha Race School – Donington has its own car racing school, run by one of the most respected names in the business, Jim Russell. The school counts the likes of former World and Indycar champion Emerson Fittipaldi and current GP star Jacques Villeneuve among past pupils. The popular and slickly run school is closely linked with Vauxhall, and the school's fleet of single-seater and saloon cars carry the Vauxhall Griffin logo. Qualified instructors offer everything from race track experience to full intensive racing instruction. Novel Track and Country course mixes off-road-tuition in Land Rovers and quad bikes with track time in single seaters. There's also a chance to try your hand driving blindfold in a Vauxhall Astra saloon! The centre can supply an accommodation list from which to book B&B or local hotels.

The Jim Russell motorcycle school (part of the Yamaha Racing School) also uses the Donington racetrack. The 1–2 day non-residential courses are conducted on the centre's own bikes and are run at beginner and advanced level, with a certificate at the end of each. Instructors are successful race riders in their own right.

Season: Open all year, but school days limited by other track activity. Call for availability of dates.
Food: Café on site. Vegetarian menus available.
Disabled Facilities: None.
Insurance: Clients are covered by centre's public liability insurance, though indemnities must be signed.
Emergencies: All instructors are trained in first aid. Safety marshals and on-site medics also on hand.
Affiliations: ARDS, BARS, RAC MSA recognised.
Tariffs: Introductory trial in one of the

following disciplines – single seaters, racing saloons, £99. Supertrial (two disciplines) £199. Track and country, £235. Beginner's Motorcycle Racing Course £85 weekday and £105 at weekends, Advanced Motorcycle Course £185–£221 depending on length of course.

Booking: Full payment in advance required. No refund on cancellation within 28 days of start of course. Centre also offers cancellation indemnity. Bookings are normally made in advance, but late bookings are sometimes accepted if space available.

Access: By car, from North leave M1 at junction 24 (you cannot exit at J23A) taking A453 and following signs to Castle Donington. From South, leave M1 at junction 23A and take A453 to Castle Donington. East Midlands airport is 2 miles away.

the ian taylor motor racing school

Thruxton Circuit
Andover
Hampshire
SP11 8PW
Tel (01264) 773 511
Fax (01264) 773 441

Racing, Off-road, Karting

Britain's fastest race track, the 2.4-mile-long Thruxton is a difficult circuit with a number of tricky corners – the Campbell / Cobb / Segrave 'complex' for starters – as well as a daunting fast sweep from Church corner into a tight chicane. The Ian Taylor school has operated from the airfield site for 15 years, though founder Ian Taylor, a driver of exceptional talent, was tragically killed in a freak racing accident a few years ago, underlining the dangerous nature of the sport. The school caters for both the one-off thrill-seeker and the driver with serious racing aspirations. As well as tuition in saloon cars and single-seaters, the school offers 4x4 and skid training, karting and, for a bit of fun, a reverse-steer car (turn the wheel left and the car goes right). There's also the opportunity to drive a trials car, a purpose-built 2-seater designed to climb slopes you can walk up, with individual brakes for the left and right wheels, enabling it to negotiate slalom-style gates. Other activities at Thruxton include a flying school and clay pigeon shooting.

Season: Open all year, but days can be restricted by other track activity or weather. Call for availability of dates.

Accommodation: None, but centre will assist with local bookings.

Food: Café on site. Vegetarian menus available.

Children: Karting lessons for 8-year-olds and above; children must have consent of parent or guardian.

Disabled Facilities: None.

Insurance: Clients are covered by centre's public liability insurance.

Safety: Safety marshals and on-site medics on hand. Other staff have basic first-aid training.

Affiliations: ARDS; RAC MSA.

Tariffs: Courses tailor-made to suit individual; trials start from £95.

Booking: Deposit required in advance. Cancellation charges vary. Bookings normally made in advance, but late bookings accepted if space available.

Access: Thruxton is on the A303, 5 miles from Andover. Nearest train station is Andover, with express links to Waterloo and the south-west.

knockhill racing circuit

By Dunfermline
Fife
KY12 9TF
Scotland
Tel (01383) 622 090
Fax (01383) 620 167

Racing, Rallying, Performance Driving, Karting

Knockhill calls itself Scotland's national motor sport centre. Although the tight and twisting track is only 1.3 miles long, it packs in all manner of tricks ready to catch out the unwary. Enthusiasts can sample the 'Knockhill Experience' with a number of half-day trial lessons and courses designed to give a flavour of the sport, or take a full Association of Racing Drivers Schools (ARDS) Novice Racing Drivers course to qualify for a National Racing Licence. Courses include the Racing Drivers Trial in which, after learning driving techniques in the classroom, participants are allowed 5 laps of one-to-one tuition in a racing saloon with a qualified instructor, followed by 5 thrilling laps in a single-seater. Knockhill also offers a Tarmac Rally Stage Trial which follows much the same format, but uses a rally-prepared Toyota in which to teach the very different skills needed for driving a rally car quickly. The full-day Master Drivers Super Trial combines both racing and rally driving, while a Performance Driving course, using either your own car or the centre's Ford Sierra Cosworth, allows you to hone your road driving skills within the safe confines of a race track. A small kart track is also open to children above 8 years old.

As with most racing schools, there is no accommodation on-site, but the centre supplies all clients booking courses with an accommodation list from which they can book for themselves, whether camping, B&B or local hotels.

Season: Open all year; racing season March to October.
Accommodation: No on-site accommodation, but list of locally available options supplied.
Food: Restaurant and café on site. Vegetarian menus available.
Children: Karting lessons for 8-year-olds and above; children must have consent of parent or guardian.
Disabled Facilities: None.
Insurance: Clients are covered by centre's public liability insurance.
Safety: All instructors trained in first aid.
Affiliations: ARDS.
Tariffs: Racing drivers trial: £89 (open), £69 (mid-week). Rally stage trial drive: £99 (open). Master drivers super trial £159 (mid-week). Performance driving: own car £69; Cosworth £129 (mid-week).
Booking: Full payment in advance required. No cancellation charge. Bookings are normally made in advance, but late bookings are sometimes accepted if space available.
Access: By car, leave the M90 at Junction 4 and follow signs. Knockhill is on the A823, 5 miles north of Dunfermline. Trains and buses available to Dunfermline. Centre can arrange pick-ups from Dunfermline; contact them for more details.

oulton park

Little Budworth
Tarporley
Cheshire
CW6 9BW
Tel (01829) 760 381
Fax (01829) 760 378

For course details, see Brands Hatch (p. 256).

Access: Oulton Park lies 2 miles from the A54 south of Winsford and close to M6 Junction 19 (north) or Junction 18 (south).

prescott hillclimb drivers school

c/o Bugatti Owners Club Ltd
Prescott Hill
Gotherington
Cheltenham
Gloucestershire
GL52 4RD
Tel (01242) 673 136
Fax (01242) 677 001

Hill-climbing

And now for something completely different. Unlike circuit racing, where you can go round and round to your heart's content, hill-climbing is over much quicker. But it's no less demanding threading your car up the tight and twisting hill that is Prescott. Steeped in history – the climb today is essentially the same as it was pre-war – Prescott is the home of the Bugatti Owners Club. It has a certain class!

Tuition in the art of speed hill-climbing is available at Prescott on 10 occasions during the year. Each session runs for 6 hours for a maximum of 25 students per course. Two instructors, both hill-climb champions, are on hand to reveal their secrets. You use your own car, which can be modern or classic but must be properly silenced, taxed and with legal on-road tyres. You are also required to bring a current driver's licence, a crash helmet – though they are available on loan – as well as an umbrella (!) and a long-sleeved shirt (!). Curious bunch, these Bugatti Owners . . .

Season: Open on 10 occasions during the year. Call for details.
Accommodation: None, but centre will assist with local bookings.
Food: Food, including vegetarian menus, available on-site.
Children: No specific facilities available.
Disabled Facilities: None, though disabled drivers have attended the course and are welcome.
Insurance: Clients are covered by centre's public liability insurance, but are advised to check their own insurance for speed hill-climbing cover.
Safety: Instructors and marshals are trained in first aid. Paramedics on-site.
Affiliations: None.
Tariffs: £96 per course.
Booking: Full payment in advance required. Cancellation fee usually 50 per cent of course fee. Bookings normally made in advance, but late bookings sometimes accepted if space available.
Access: Prescott is 5 miles from Junction 9 on the M5. Follow the A438 to Weston, then go south on the A435 for 2 miles until crossroads with signpost to Gotherington. Prescott is 1 mile along this road.

the silverstone driving centre

Silverstone
Nr Towcester
Northamptonshire
NN12 8TN
Tel (01327) 857 177
Fax (01327) 858 268

Racing, Karting, Off-road, Performance

Home of the British Grand Prix, Silverstone is the UK's premier race circuit and the facilities are among the best anywhere in the world. The Driving Centre, which has 110 qualified instructors, offers everything from a single-seater experience to full intensive racing instruction. The centre also has a kart track, an off-road driving area and a rally school. This is a very popular school and you will find it slickly run, whether just opting for the introductory trial or going for the full Track Open Day, which takes in 6 events – single-seaters, saloon cars, passenger rides, kart racing, skid cars and an autotest, which is a series of against-the-clock tests driving around cones. The school also caters for youngsters, whether they want to try karting or drive a real car. Any child over 1.47m can take a young driver's course, which provides an introduction to the car, plus practical driving experience with a qualified instructor.

There is camping on-site, and the centre can supply an accommodation list from which to book B&B or local hotels.

Season: Open all year, but Driving Centre days limited by other track activity. Call for availability of dates.
Accommodation: Camping on-site; list of off-site options available.
Food: Café on-site. Vegetarian menus available.
Children: Karting lessons for 8-year-olds and above; children must have consent of parent or guardian. Young driver's course for children under 17, but must be more than 1.47m tall.
Disabled Facilities: None.
Insurance: Clients are covered by centre's public liability insurance, though indemnities must be signed.
Safety: All instructors trained in first aid. Safety marshals and on-site medics also on hand.
Affiliations: ARDS; ARKS; BARS; RAC MSA.
Tariffs: Introductory trial in one of the following disciplines – single-seaters, racing saloons, rally driving, 4x4, road skills: £99. Supertrial (2 disciplines): £175. Track open day: £290.
Booking: Full payment in advance required. No refund on cancellation, though one alternative date will be accepted. Centre also offers cancellation indemnity. Bookings normally made in advance, but late bookings sometimes accepted if space available.
Access: By car, leave the M1 at Junction 15A, or the M40 at Junction 11, and follow signs. Silverstone is near the village of Towcester in Northamptonshire. Nearest train stations are Milton Keynes and Northampton; buses go to Silverstone village.

Snetterton

Norwich
Norfolk
NR16 2JU
Tel (01953) 887 303
Fax (01953) 888 220

For course details, see Brands Hatch (p. 256).

Access: Snetterton is 10 miles north-east of Thetford on the A11 London–Norwich road.

rally and off-road driving

bill gwynne rally school

Turweston Aerodrome
Westbury
Brackley
Northamptonshire
NN13 5YD
Tel (01280) 705 570
Fax (01280) 701 691

Rallying

Headed by a rally professional passing on his skills, Bill Gywnne's school is based in Brackley, but he also runs courses in Wales for Acorn Activities (see p. 414) on a special stage used in the RAC Rally. Groups are small – a maximum of 6 clients per course – although private one-to-one tuition is also available. As a memento of the day, a personal video of your efforts can be arranged (£17.50), while guests are also welcome, though a £10 per head charge for refreshments is made. The centre can supply an accommodation list from which to book local B&B or hotels.

Season: Open all year depending on weather.
Accommodation: List of local options available.
Food: No food available on-site. Lunch is taken at a nearby pub where vegetarian meals are available.
Children: No facilities.
Disabled Facilities: None.
Insurance: Clients are covered by centre's public liability insurance.
Safety: Staff trained in first aid.
Affiliations: BARS.
Tariffs: Standard 1-day course: £195 (deposit £85); standard half-day course: £110 (deposit £60). Private tuition – full day: £595 (deposit £100); half-day: £350 (deposit £100).
Booking: Bookings must be made in advance, though late bookings can occasionally be taken.
Access: Close to M40, Junction 10. 15 miles from Banbury. Nearest train and bus stations: Banbury.

david mitchell's landcraft

Plas-Yn-Dre
23 High Street
Bala
Gwynedd
LL23 7LU
Wales
Tel (01678) 520 820
Fax (01678) 258 864

Off-road

Concentrating solely on off-road driving, Landcraft courses will take you places you never thought it possible to get to on 4 wheels. The course follows a set format, starting with familiarization with the vehicle and an explanation of the difference between 2- and 4-wheel-drive machines. Practical lessons include the use of engine compression to descend hills and how to cope with ditches, gullies, water, mud, soft ground, and so on. Safety is stressed at all times. The course lasts a full day (9 a.m. to 5 p.m.). Advanced courses are also available, teaching winching, recovery, use of specialist equipment, etc. Landcraft's main centre is a 200-acre site in the Bala and Lake Vyrnwy area of North Wales, but the company also operates from 5 other sites in Wales and the West Country. Contact the school for full details.

The basic course can be undertaken in your own 4x4 or, for an extra £75, in one of Landcraft's vehicles – a fleet that includes Range Rovers, Fronteras and Land Rover Defenders.

The centre can advise on good local accommodation ranging from B&Bs to hotels.

Season: Open all year.
Accommodation: Centre will advise on local options.
Food: Not available on site, but quality catering including vegetarian meals available at Landcraft's HQ.
Children: No facilities.
Disabled Facilities: None.
Insurance: Clients are covered by centre's public liability insurance, but must insure their own vehicles.
Safety: Staff trained in first aid; paramedics available on club days.
Affiliations: The Off-Road Training Association (TORTA).
Tariffs: First-day basic course, for a group of 4 using own vehicle: £95 per head. One-to-one tuition available at £175. Non-driving passengers welcome for a nominal £10 to cover lunch costs.
Booking: Contact centre for details.
Access: By car to Bala, Gwynedd. Train and bus service not suitable.

---

drive-it-all ltd

The Rally and Off-Road Driving Centre
Church Enstone
Chipping Norton
Oxfordshire
OX7 4NP
Tel (01608) 678 339
Fax (01608) 678 639

Rally, Quad Bikes, Off-road

Concentrating on the off-road side of the sport, Drive-it-all has its HQ in Oxfordshire, together with a 3-mile-long loose-surface rally stage, although it can also arrange trials and events at any one of 120 centres countrywide, from Scotland to Cornwall. As well as 140bhp rally-prepared cars, Drive-it-all has a selection of quad bikes and 4x4s to complement the rally experience. In addition to the thrill of driving on a loose surface, you'll learn such techniques as opposite lock control, power slides and handbrake turns. The centre can supply an accommodation list from which to book local B&B or hotels, or arrange events at other locations.

Season: Open all year depending on weather.
Accommodation: List of local options available.
Food: Café on-site. Vegetarian menus available.
Children: No facilities.
Disabled Facilities: Some disabilities can be catered for by prior arrangement.
Insurance: Clients are covered by centre's public liability and personal accident insurance.
Safety: Staff trained in first aid; paramedics on-site at events with 30 or more clients.
Affiliations: BARS.
Tariffs: Full-day rally tuition course: £109–225.
Booking: Deposit required in advance. Cancellation charges vary but a late cancellation (within 30 days of the booking) means that the full fee must be paid. Bookings must be made 3–6 weeks in advance, though late bookings can occasionally be taken.
Access: Drive-it-all is on the B4030 just to the east of Church Enstone, near Chipping Norton, approximately 14 miles north of Oxford. Nearest train station is Charlgrove (5 miles away), but bus service is very infrequent. Taxis can be arranged by the centre.

the forest experience rally school

Cambian House
Carno
Powys
SY17 5LO
Wales
Tel (01686) 420 201
Fax (01686) 420 670

Rallying, Quad Bikes, Off-road

Run by factory-supported rally drivers Mark and David Higgins, and held on a real loose-surface rally stage, the 2-mile Forest Experience – complete with trees and (short) drops – is as close to the real thing as it is possible to get. As well as pukka rally cars – both front- and rear-wheel drive – the Experience offers quad bikes, 4x4s and clay pigeon shooting. In addition to half- and whole-day courses, a 2-day residential course is also available.

Season: Open all year depending on weather.

Accommodation: B&B accommodation included with residential packages.
Food: Available on-site, including vegetarian meals.
Children: No facilities.
Disabled Facilities: None.
Insurance: Clients are covered by centre's public liability insurance.
Safety: Staff trained in first aid.
Affiliations: BARS.
Tariffs: Half-day rally driving: £115; 1-day rally driving: £235; 2-day residential course, including 2 nights' accommodation: £555, or £445 per head for groups of 5 or more.
Booking: Bookings must be made in advance, and a £50 deposit is required. Cancellations more than 30 days before course starts subject to a £10 charge; full forfeit of fee under 30 days unless place can be resold.
Access: Carno is around 90 miles west of Birmingham, located on the A470 between Newtown and Dolgellau. Own transport is the only practical way to get to the school.

pentti airikkala's rally driving experience

Airikkala Technique Ltd
17 Grange Close
Goring
Reading
Berkshire
RG8 9DY
Tel/Fax (01491) 875 445

Rallying

Pentti Airikkala is a world-class rally driver – and former winner of the RAC Rally – who concentrates on honing rally driving skills. It helps if you have had some experience if you are to get the most from Pentti's advanced techniques. Using 280bhp 4-wheel-drive Ford Sierra Cosworths and 150bhp Escort RS2000s, Pentti and his instructors teach the art of left-foot braking, handbrake turns, starting and stopping (not as easy as it sounds), how to minimize turbo lag and how to plot the fastest line through a corner. The day finishes with an exhilarating demonstration run strapped alongside Airikkala in a rally-prepared car – this is described as optional and not for the faint-hearted. Rather than having one base, the Airikkala Experience moves around the country, operating at one of 8 special stages from Brooklands in the south-east to Kirknewton in Scotland and Nutts Corner near Belfast.

Season: Open all year depending on weather.
Accommodation: None, but centre will assist with local bookings.
Food: Available on-site, including vegetarian meals.
Children: No facilities.
Disabled Facilities: None.
Insurance: Clients are covered by centre's public liability insurance.
Safety: Staff trained in first aid.
Affiliations: None.
Tariffs: Standard fee: £246.75.
Booking: Bookings must be made 3–4 weeks in advance, but no deposit is required, nor is there a cancellation fee.
Access: Various centres. Contact school for directions.

phil price rally school

Coed Harbour
Llangunllo
Knighton
Powys
LD7 1TD
Wales
Tel/Fax (01547) 550 300

Rallying

Run by professional rally driver Phil Price, this school is based on a large loose-surface area in the middle of the Welsh forest (take warm clothing), a perfect location for learning all about car control. Groups are small (maximum 10 people), ensuring personal tuition at all times. The school operates day courses and a weekend experience which starts at noon on Saturday, running through to 4.30 p.m., and resumes on Sunday from 9.30 a.m. to 1.30 p.m. The weekend course includes quality overnight accommodation, an evening meal on Saturday and buffet lunch on Sunday.

Season: Open all year depending on weather.
Accommodation: Included in weekend course. B&B accommodation available locally from £17 per person per night.
Food: Available on-site, including vegetarian menus.

Children: No facilities.
Disabled Facilities: None.
Insurance: Clients are covered by centre's public liability insurance.
Safety: Staff trained in first aid.
Affiliations: BARS.
Tariffs: Half-day: £110; full day: £185; weekend: £250.
Booking: 50 per cent deposit required in advance. Bookings must be made in advance, though late bookings can occasionally be taken.
Access: From Knighton take the A488 for about 5 miles, then turn right to Llangunllo. After 1.4 miles turn right to Cefnsuran Farm, following signs to rally school. (Caution: very narrow 2-way road.)

motor cycle sport

yamaha race school

Cadwell Park
Old Manor House
Cadwell Park
Louth
Lincolnshire
LN11 9SE
Tel (01507) 343 555
Fax (01507) 343 519

Motorbike Racing

The Yamaha Race School is the country's leading motorcycle racing school and operates from three centres. As well as Cadwell park, courses are run at Brands Hatch and the home of the British Motor Cycle Grand Prix, Donington. Cadwell is an extremely daunting circuit, dubbed the 'mini Nürburgring' after the famous German circuit in reference to its high number of twists and turns. Expert tuition is given by some of Britain's best bike racers with a pupil to instructor ratio of two to one and the school uses Yahama FZR600R machines. All safety equipment including helmets is supplied, but you can use your own protective clothing; if you do, leathers must be one-piece suits. Introductory trials are held at Cadwell with advanced courses run at Brands and Donington.

The Yamaha Race School also operates courses from Cadwell. The 1–2–day non-residential courses are conducted on the centre's own bikes and are run at beginner and advanced level, with a certificate at the end of each. Instructors are successful race riders in their own right.

Season: Open all year, but school only operates on certain dates. Call for exact details.
Disabled Facilities: None.
Insurance: Clients are covered by centre's public liability insurance, personal accident cover available from the circuit.
Emergencies: All instructors are trained in first aid. Medics on site during test days.
Affiliations: ARDS.
Tariffs: Cadwell Park - introductory trial: from £85. Brands Hatch - advanced course: from £165; Donington - advanced: from £185. Beginner's Motorcycle Racing Course £85 weekday and £105 at weekends, Advanced Motorcycle Course £165–201 depending on length of course.
Access: Cadwell Park is on the A153 near Louth and links the A158 and A16.
For Donington access details see Jim Russell Racing Drivers School (p. 258).
For Brands Hatch details see p. 256.

kitting yourself out

If going along to a circuit or driving school just to get a taste of motor sport action, you need no special kit other than a pair of comfortable thin-soled gym shoes – not all trainers are suitable, as many have soles that are too wide and too thick. Jeans or other casual clothes are perfect for driving – above all, you need to feel comfortable behind the wheel, so don't turn up in a suit (it has happened!). All schools supply a full range of crash helmets, both open- and full-face, in sizes to fit all.

If you are considering taking up the sport at a more serious level, then it does make sense to consider buying your own kit, in particular a well-fitting crash helmet that conforms to all the RAC MSA safety requirements – don't think that the helmet you wear to ride your Honda moped is necessarily good enough for serious motor sport. There is a number of specialist suppliers of racewear and safety kit, all of whom are perfectly placed to give excellent advice. Some, like Demon Tweeks (01978 664 466), Grand Prix Racewear (0181 993 7555), Road and Stage Motorsport (01524 844 066), and Road and Racing Accessories (0171 736 2881), also supply by mail order, though it is advisable to buy a helmet in person to ensure the best possible fit. Helmet brands to go for include Simpson, Bell, Arai, Shoei and Top Tek. Prices range from £70 for a simple open-faced helmet to £600-plus for a high-tech full-face helmet ready plumbed for its own oxygen supply.

Fire is probably the biggest threat facing drivers, and serious enthusiasts will appreciate the need for flameproof Nomex underwear. Top brands include OMP and Sparco. A pair of Nomex socks will cost around £7, while balaclavas range from £10 to £20, and a full set of Nomex underwear will set you back £75.

On top of this you'll need a race suit, preferably Nomex-protected. Prices range from a simple clubman's suit at £50 to suits approved by the International Automobile Association (FIA) (motor sport's governing body) at anything up to £500. The outfit is finished off with a set of race boots (£50–100) and a pair of gloves (£20–50).

So now you're all dressed up, but with nowhere to go. You need a car. And that's where the expenses really start to mount up. The choices are either to buy and run your own machine or to rent a seat in a team. How much you spend is entirely up to you, but in motor racing even shoestrings are expensive – a budget season in a club saloon series won't give you much change from £20,000 once you've bought a race car and trailer to get to and from the circuits, tyres, petrol, overnight accommodation, spares, repairs . . . The list goes on. Still tempted? Check the classified adverts in the weekly magazines (see below) for starter bargains. Of course, if you're any good, after a while the top teams will come to you . . . Next stop Monte Carlo.

checklist

- ✔ *buoyancy aid*
- ✔ *race suit*
- ✔ *crash helmet*
- ✔ *race boots*
- ✔ *flameproof underwear*
- ✔ *gloves*

further reading

Serious enthusiasts get their motor sport fix every week from *Motoring News* (£1, published Wednesday) and the glossy *Autosport* (£2.10, every Thursday). Both are full of news, race and rally reports, previews and reviews from F1 to the most humble club events. *Autosport* also publishes *The Autosport Guide*, an A5 loose-leaf guide to all the circuits and hill-climb courses in Britain, full of detailed spectator and competitor advice . . . everything from the best line through the corners to where to stay overnight. This is available at £29.99 from Dent Publications Ltd, Newbarn Court, Ditchley Park, Oxfordshire OX7 4EX. Finally, *How to Start Motor Racing* and its sister *How to Start Rallying*, both published by Haynes but now out of print, provide vital insights for beginners. Try Mill House Books, The Mill House, Eastville, Boston, Lincolnshire (01295 270 377) for copies.

governing bodies

British Mountaineering Council (BMC)

172–179 Burton Road,
West Didsbury
Manchester M20 2BB
Tel (0161) 445 4747

Mountain Leaders Training Board (MLTB)

Plas y Brenin, Capel Curig
Gwynedd LL24 0ET
Wales
Tel (01690) 720 280 / 363
Fax (01690) 720 394

mountain skills

first aid
navigation
scrambling
winter skills

This chapter deals with centres that offer the more specialized mountain knowledge you need to be really safe in the hills: navigation, winter skills, such as digging snow-holes, avoiding avalanches and use of ice axe and crampons, mountain first aid and scrambling – safely negotiating steep rocky slopes, sometimes with the use of ropes. There is a number of centres offering courses in these skills, mostly to existing or would-be outdoor instructors and wilderness leaders. In fact, anyone interested in taking up a career in outdoor recreation must take the Mountain Leaders Training Board (MLTB) courses in mountain leadership. Schools offering these courses are listed below. If you are planning any long treks into unpopulated mountain areas in the UK or abroad, it is also worth taking a course – often schools and centres offering mountain skills will tailor their tuition to suit people about to embark on expeditions in such areas, simulating as far as possible the conditions they will find there. Mountain rescue is often a feature of the courses, and it'll stand you in good stead to learn it. However, it's not just for professionals. Many experienced hillwalkers enjoy taking courses in mountain skills, or going on holidays that introduce the skills on a recreational basis. It makes your foray into the uplands that much more challenging, and it also means that you will, eventually, really know what you are doing, especially on steep or exposed ground in bad weather or in fog, when all you have is a map and compass.

selected centres

alan kimber professional mountaineering services

Heathercroft
Fort William
Highland
PH33 6RE
Scotland
Tel (01397) 700 451
Fax (01397) 700 489

Scrambling, Winter Skills

Alan Kimber is a fully qualified instructor and international mountain guide who has written a guidebook on climbing in the western Highlands. His courses are aimed at everybody – from the beginner to the already qualified professional. Course lengths vary from a day or weekend to 2 weeks. Some are for groups, others involve private guiding. Alan Kimber can supply equipment such as boots, helmets, harness, crampons and ice axes, but you have to specify what you need on the booking form. You can stay in Alan's own bunkhouse on the edge of Fort William, or arrange your own accommodation – or get him to do it for you.

The centre specializes in winter skills, offering 7 courses in this field, from a 2-day pre-winter training session or a basic winter skills weekend to courses at all BMC levels, right up to Grade V. There is also a specialist course in climbing steep ice, and experienced winter mountaineers can hire Alan as a guide for £110 per day.

Summer courses run from April to October and include weekends and weeks scrambling along the classic ridge routes of Ben Nevis and Glen Coe. There are also guided weeks on Skye, scrambling in the steep Cuillin range, as well as more expensive guided trips to the Italian Apennines, the French and Swiss Alps, and even to Mount Kenya.

Season: Open all year.
Accommodation: Self-catering flat (6 beds) or 2 apartments (8 beds each) cost around £8 per person per night, or full-board accommodation costs from £30 per person per night.
Food: Self-catering or full board available; vegetarian or special diets catered for if requested in advance.
Other Activities: Climbing and Abseiling (see p. 91).
Children: Baby-sitting can be arranged for an extra charge.
Disabled Facilities: None.
Insurance: Personal insurance included in fees.
Safety: All instructors are trained in mountain first aid.
Affiliations: Association of Mountaineering Instructors; British Mountain Guides Association.
Tariffs: Pre-winter training courses (includes self-catering accommodation): £90; Introductory Winter Mountaineering week: £220; Scrambling and Mountaineering week: £240; Basic Winter Skills weekend: £95; Scrambling Week on the Isle of Skye (includes self-catering accommodation): £315. Fees include instruction and equipment (except boots).
Booking: 50% non-refundable deposit required. Balance due on arrival. If cancellations made within 4 weeks of start date, entire fee is forfeited (but covered by holiday insurance, which is included in fees). Late bookings sometimes accepted if space available.
Access: A82 to Fort William. Trains and buses available to Fort William; pick-ups can be arranged by centre.

alba walking holidays

24 Lundavra Road
Fort William
Highland
PH33 6LA
Tel (01397) 704 964

Scrambling, Navigation, Winter Skills

Alba run some excellent summer trips aimed at helping hillwalkers develop into mountaineers. Groups of up to 8 people are led on week-long scrambling expeditions with a maximum student-to-instructor ratio of 4:1. The Aonach Eagach ridge in Glen Coe and the main ridge of the Cuillins are tackled.

Winter courses are also worthwhile, with a guided Winter Munro week involving the use of ice axe and crampons, navigation and route-planning, snow and avalanche awareness, learned during ascents of Ben Nevis, Glen Coe, the Mamore and the Grey Corries. One step up from this is the more hard-core Winter Mountaincraft week, which includes all the above skills, but with the addition of ropework and belaying, moving over some very, very steep and exposed ground, also in the Ben Nevis and Glencoe area.

Tariffs: All packages are 1 week long and include 5 days' guiding services, equipment and transport. Guests have the option of arranging own accommodation, or 7 nights' B&B. Winter mountain skills week: £240 / £365; summer scrambling weeks: £230 / £340. (Group discounts available).

See Walking (p. 415) for full details.

andy sherriff specialist first aid training

73 Goronwy Street
Gerlan
Bethesda
Gwynedd
LL57 3TU
Wales
Tel & Fax (01248) 601 975

First Aid

These courses are aimed at those with experience who want to learn specific mountain rescue, emergency and first-aid techniques. The non-residential courses usually last for 2 days and run nationwide at various venues – it is not a centre. The most regular venue for the courses is the Tyn y Coed Hotel, Capel Curig, Gwynedd in North Wales, which usually hosts one course in the second or third week of each month. The prime areas covered are: accident and emergency procedures, infections and illness, emergency life support, patient diagnosis, guidance on first-aid kits, some outdoor exercises/ scenarios, thermal illnesses and injuries, shock and shock management, treatment of major and minor injuries, patient management and care.

Andy Sherriff's courses satisfy the requirements of most of the bodies governing mountain sports, as well as the Ski Council for Ski Instructors. Training is open to individuals or groups, but prospective students must arrange their own accommodation. Call Andy Sherriff to book it according to your budget.

Season: Open all year.
Accommodation: Courses are run nationwide at regional venues, often at hotels. Contact Andy Sherriff for accommodation details.
Food: Refreshments provided.
Children: Courses not designed for children.

Disabled Facilities: None.
Insurance: Not necessary.
Safety: Instructor is a trained medical professional.
Affiliations: The British Association for Immediate Care.
Tariffs: 2-day First Aid for Mountaineers & Instructors course (includes materials, certificate, refreshments): £125. Specialist rescue courses also available; contact Andy Sherriff for more details.
Booking: 50% deposit required. Late bookings sometimes accepted if space available.
Access: Contact Andy Sherriff for venue details.

black dragon outdoor experiences

7 Ethelbert Drive
Charlton
Andover
Hampshire
SP10 4EP
Tel (01264) 357 313

Scrambling, Navigation

Most of Black Dragon's day, weekend and 3-day mountain skills courses take place in the mountains of the Brecon Beacons National Park and in Snowdonia. Scrambling, rope techniques and navigation are the specialities (though they also offer guided hillwalking and climbing) and all courses are run from a local inn or hotel. If you have no transport, they will pick you up from the nearest train or bus station, at no extra charge.

Black Dragon caters for beginners and the slightly experienced, rather than for high-level mountaineers, and their courses offer a sound grounding in the basics of all mountaineering skills, with no more than 4 students to 1 instructor. If you are thinking of taking up the sport seriously, but have had little or no prior experience, Black Dragon makes a very good starting point. They also run an introduction to winter skills in Scotland, and a few guided mountain trips abroad to the Austrian Alps.

Season: Open all year.
Accommodation: Accommodation provided in local inn (South Wales), or local hotel (North Wales).
Food: Breakfast, packed lunch and dinner included; all diets catered for.
Other Activities: Climbing and Abseiling (see p. 93); Walking (p. 417).
Children: Clients under 18 must be accompanied by a parent or guardian.
Disabled Facilities: None.
Insurance: Clients should arrange personal insurance cover if desired.
Safety: All staff trained in first aid and mountain rescue; medic on staff.
Affiliations: National Navigation Award Scheme; National Association for Outdoor Education.
Tariffs: Day courses include instruction and equipment; weekend courses also include accommodation and full board. Mountain Navigation day course: £28; Scrambling day course: £33; Brecon Beacons Mountain Navigation weekend: £137; Snowdonia Mountain Navigation weekend: £147; Snowdonia Classic Mountaineering weekend: £157.
Booking: 20% deposit required, non-refundable. Balance due 4 weeks prior to start date. Cancellation fees: 3–4 weeks: 40% of total; 2–3 weeks: 60% of total; 0–2 weeks: 100% of total. Late bookings accepted up to 48 hours in advance if space available.
Access: Meeting point at accommodation; pick-up from stations can be arranged.

brathay exploration group

Brathay Hall
Ambleside
Cumbria
LA22 OHN
Tel & Fax (01539) 433 942

First Aid, Scrambling, Winter Skills

Brathay run mountaineering and eco-research expeditions in northern Britain and some remoter mountain areas of the world. Their Mountain Skills courses are run in the Cairngorms and are aimed at young people (aged 18–25) with differing levels of experience, but who have a good hillwalking background. The summer leadership courses, run during the second week of September, require no specific mountaineering training, but the 2 7-day Winter Skills courses, run in March and April, require at least a knowledge of how to use a compass and walk on a bearing. Brathay also organize a 3-day Mountain First Aid course at their Ambleside centre in May, open only to holders of a basic First Aid Certificate.

All the mountain trips include accommodation in chalets, food and local transport. Write to the centre to find out about collection points.

Season: April to September.
Accommodation: In chalets adjacent to home of instructors.
Food: Food supplied to make up breakfast and packed lunches, evening meal provided.
Tariffs: Prices include full-board accommodation, instruction and equipment. 1-week summer leadership course: £198; 1-week Winter Skills introductory course: £212; 1-week winter leadership course: £212; 4-day Mountain First Aid course (dormitory accommodation): £94.

See Eco-Sports (p. 144) for full details.

cobalt total mountain experiences

25 Royal Park Terrace
Edinburgh
EH8 8JB
Scotland
Tel (0131) 652 1794

Winter Skills

Cobalt specialize in winter skills – guided day trips up onto the varying Munro locations from December through March. The trips are divided into 4 grades: Grade I involves easy walking on snow with little or no exposed sections and no previous winter experience required; Grade II involves a few short exposed sections and basic knowledge of ice axe and crampons; Grade III tackles steeper slopes with more exposed areas and a working knowledge of ice axe and crampon use is essential, as is a reasonable level of fitness; Grade IV walks are run over continuous steep ground, with sustained exposed sections; some experience of scrambling and use of ice axe and crampons should be combined with good aerobic fitness.

If you want more than a day on the hills, Cobalt offer a variety of 2-day courses run along the same grading system, which cover snow-holing, winter belays and emergency bivvy techniques. Real enthusiasts who have achieved at least a Grade III level can undertake the 5-day Winter Mountaincraft course which promises that 'by the end you will have the skills with which to tackle any of the Scottish hills and confidently in winter conditions.'

Season: Open all year.
Accommodation: Centre provides help in arranging a variety of local accommodation, from bunkhouses to hotels, dependent on course and location.
Food: Not provided by centre.
Other Activities: Climbing and Abseiling (see p. 94).
Children: Anyone under 18 must have consent of parents or legal guardian.
Disabled Facilities: None.
Insurance: Clients need personal insurance.
Safety: All staff trained in first aid.
Affiliations: Association of Mountaineering Instructors.
Tariffs: Fees cover tuition, in-course transport and use of equipment. Exact course offerings and prices vary, but some past examples are – Winter Munro days: £15; 2-day Winter Skills course: £85; 2-day Winter Mountaineering course: £105; 5-day Winter Mountaincraft course: £235.
Booking: Non-refundable deposit of £50 required. Balance payable 4 weeks in advance. Charge for cancellation notices received less than 4 weeks in advance: 80% of total fee. Bookings can be accepted up to 24 hours in advance if space available.
Access: Course locations vary; contact centre for details.

edale yha activity centre

Rowland Cote
Nether Booth
Edale
Sheffield
S30 2ZH
Tel (01433) 670 302
Fax (01433) 670 234

Navigation, First Aid, Scrambling

The northern section of the Peak District National Park sees fairly serious conditions year round on the high tops: it's a good place to train for hillwalking and mountaineering in other parts of Britain and/or the world. Edale offers 2 courses in mountain skills: the Map and Compass weekend (at either beginner or improver level), which provides an excellent grounding in the art of finding your way over rough wild country in bad weather, and a Duke of Edinburgh's Award supervisor training course of 4 days, aimed at preparing those involved in the supervision and training of young people in skills relevant to leading expeditions in hill country.

Season: Open all year.
Children: Over-16s only for the Map and Compass courses; over-18s only for the Duke of Edinburgh Award supervisor course.
Tariffs: Prices include equipment, instruction and full-board accommodation – 2-day beginners' or improvers' course: £82; 4-day supervisor training course: £148. Navigation is also one of the sports offered in the centre's multi-activity package deals: approximately £42 per day in high season (April–August), £32 in low season (November–February).

See Caving (p. 45) for full details.

---

go higher

High Dyonside
Distington
Cumbria
CA14 4QQ
Tel & Fax (01946) 830 476

Scrambling, Navigation, Winter Skills

Go Higher offer only guided mountaineering day trips into the Cumbrian mountains, rather than trips or courses, although you can put together more than one day if you want, either at the centre or in a local B&B. Camping is also offered, with use of kitchen and bathroom facilities. The instruction is aimed at all levels of competence, from beginners to the aspiring professional. Scrambling, navigation and winter skills are all offered, as well as private guiding for individuals or groups. Go Higher will pick you up for free if you get to Workington or Distington, but charge a tenner to get you to or from Penrith, the nearest large town.

Longer winter trips can also be arranged into Scotland, as well as to the mountains of Majorca in February. Go Higher have 18 years of experience behind them and are especially recommended for nervous beginners because of their low-key, non-intimidating approach.

Season: Open all year.
Accommodation: B&B can be arranged: £14 per day. Hostel accommodation or camping also available.
Food: B&B includes breakfast and packed lunch.
Other Activities: Climbing and Abseiling (see p. 98).
Children: Instruction for children available.
Disabled Facilities: None.
Insurance: Clients need their own holiday insurance; can be arranged through centre.
Safety: Staff trained in first aid.
Affiliations: BMC; Mountaineering Instructors Association.
Tariffs: Prices are for equipment, guiding and instruction. Winter mountaineering: £40 per day; scrambling: £36 per day.
Booking: £40 non-refundable deposit required. Balance due 30 days before start date. If cancellation notice received less than 27 days in advance, 50% of total is forfeited unless place is refilled. Late bookings accepted if space available.
Access: A66 to Cockermouth and A595 to Distington. Trains available to Workington, buses to Distington. Pick-ups can be arranged by centre.

hadrian mountaineering

19B Carnoch
Glencoe
Argyll & Bute
PA39 4HS
Scotland
Tel (01855) 811 472

Navigation, Scrambling, Winter Skills

Guided scrambles and navigational trips (summer and winter mountaineering) into the Black Cuillins of Skye, Glen Coe, Lochaber and the Mamores are Hadrian's speciality, with about 8 hours of tuition per day. Most of the weekend and 5-day trips are aimed at people with at least good hillwalking experience and you should be relatively fit before signing up. Groups are kept as small as possible, with an instructor-to-student ratio of no more than 1:3.

Winter skills, such as use of the ice axe and crampons and navigation in white-out, are particularly well taught here, as are the courses for would-be instructors in single-pitch climbing.

The courses are non-residential, but Hadrian Mountaineering will organize local accommodation at any budget, picking you up for the day's activities in the mountains, or taking you in for several nights under canvas.

Season: Open all year.
Accommodation: Option of arranging own accommodation or full-board accommodation arranged at local B&B.
Food: Included in full-board option.
Other Activities: Climbing and Abseiling (see p. 98); Walking (p. 420).
Children: Courses not designed for children.
Disabled Facilities: None.
Insurance: Clients need personal insurance; may be arranged through centre.
Safety: Staff trained in first aid.
Affiliations: Association of Mountaineering Instructors.
Tariffs: Fees include instruction, equipment and in-course transport, self-arranged accommodation or full-board options available. A range of courses is available; some examples are:
5-day (6-night) Skye Scrambling course: £239 / £419; 2-day (2-night) Classic Scrambles and Ridges course: £79 / £129; 5-day (6-night) Mountaincraft & Navigation course: £189 / £339; 4-day (5-night) Winter Mountaineering course: £159 / £279.
Booking: Contact centre for booking details.
Access: Take the A82 to Glencoe. Trains available to Fort William, buses to Glencoe. Pick-ups can be arranged by centre (£5 charge).

high trek snowdonia

Tal y Waen
Deiniolen
Gwynedd
LL55 3NA
Wales
Tel & Fax (01286) 871 232

Winter Skills, Scrambling, Navigation

High Trek Snowdonia offer several mountain skills courses. Probably the best introduction for the hill walker who wants to progress is the 'Scrambling Is Fun' 3-day course, which introduces ridge techniques and basic ropework and navigation. Those with a bit more experience in scrambling should try the Learning to Lead course – also 3 days – which teaches more sophisticated ropework, belays and compass readings, with the aim of preparing you to take to the ridges on your own.

In June, there is often a 6-day Mountain Skills course, which teaches ropework and navigation, but also includes night exercises, looking at weather, first aid, access and conservation.

If you don't want to be part of a group, private guiding and tuition are always available.

As for winter skills, High Trek run a series of long weekends through the winter which introduce you to the ice axe and crampons and concentrate on winter navigation and survival, ropework and reading snow conditions.

Tariffs: 3-day scrambling courses for beginners or intermediates (including accommodation, full board, equipment and instruction): £189. Check with centre for details about other mountain skills courses.

See Walking (p. 421) for full details.

highlander mountaineering

Highlea
Auchnarrow
Tomintoul
Aberdeenshire
AB37 9JN
Scotland
Tel (01807) 590 250

Winter Skills, Navigation, Scrambling

Pete Hill's Highlander mountaineering school has been going for 7 years, offering technical instruction in most mountain skills, with a consistently low student-to-instructor ratio. All courses and accommodation are based in Tomintoul, Moray, and trips are led into the Cairngorms, Lochnagar, the Cromdale Hills and the cliffs of the Spey Valley and Moray Firth. There are introductory weeks and weekends of winter hillwalking for those who want to progress from hillwalker to mountaineer, with the first use of ice axe and crampons and simple ropework. Special snow-holing weekends are also available. Summer courses include an excellent week learning how to scramble the high ridges, with ropework and navigation thrown in.

Tariffs: Courses include guide, equipment, accommodation and meals (either B&B or full board). 1-week summer scrambling/navigation course: £295 (B&B) / £365 (full board); 1-week winter skills course: £295 (B&B) / £365 (full board); 2-day winter skills course: £95 (B&B) / £120 (full board); 2-day snow-holing course: £55.

See Walking (p. 422) for full details.

howtown outdoor centre ltd

Ullswater
Penrith
Cumbria
CA10 2ND
Tel (01768) 486 508
Fax (01768) 486 875

Mountain Leader Training Courses

This centre on the eastern shore of Ullswater offers courses for would-be instructors who want to sit the MLTB certificates. For this reason, courses are open only to experienced mountaineers who have already acquired basic rope-work and navigation skills, and weather awareness. However, you do not have to be an aspiring instructor to take an MLTB qualification – it is also a very good way of consolidating the skills you already have and putting them into a more regulated framework – something that cannot fail to benefit you in the hills. Contact the centre for full details. The courses are residential, with students staying in shared rooms overlooking the lake.

Affiliations: MLTB.
Tariffs: Prices include tuition, equipment and full-board accommodation. VAT is not included. 1-week mountain leader course (training or assessment): £260; mountain first-aid course (3-day weekend): £110. Hill-walking is also one of the sports offered in the centre's youth multi-activity holiday weeks: £195. Group and unemployed discounts available.

See Child and Youth Sports (p. 61) for full details.

john white mountain school

Garden Cottage
High Close
Langdale
Ambleside
Cumbria
LA22 9HH
Tel (015394) 37387

Scrambling, Navigation, Winter Skills

A mountain skills centre aimed more at introducing beginners to the hills than at serious mountaineers, John White's school is a great place at which to learn winter skills. The weekend or week-long introductory courses teach you how to use the ice axe, for moving on steep ground and for stopping yourself when sliding, use of crampons, avalanche awareness and prediction, snow-holing, and navigation. If you are more experienced, the Winter Mountaineering course combines climbing techniques with basic rope skills and belaying, ridge scrambling, and more navigation. Winter skills courses are run from January to March – and during this season, John White also organizes 6-day trips into the Sierra Nevada in Andalucia in Spain.

Summer courses in scrambling and general mountaineering are also offered. John White's school is small and friendly – ideal if you want to bring kids along, as long as they're over 8 years old. Accommodation varies between dormitory and family rooms. You can arrange for alternative accommodation if you wish – from camping to hotels from which you'll be picked up every day for a small charge. With easy access from Ambleside (John White will collect from the bus or train station), this is a feasible place for a weekend break if you're coming up from the south.

Season: Open all year.
Accommodation: YHA or B&B accommodation provided.
Food: Breakfast included.
Other Activities: Climbing and Abseiling (see p. 101).
Children: Minimum age 8; special discounts for youths.
Disabled Facilities: None.
Insurance: Clients need their own holiday insurance.
Safety: Staff trained in first aid and mountain rescue.
Affiliations: Adventure Activities Licensing Authority; BMC.
Tariffs: Day courses include instruction and equipment; weekend or longer courses also include accommodation and breakfast. Gorge Scrambling day course: £16.50; Bad Weather Navigation Techniques day course: £16.50; Winter Mountaineering weekend: £120; 6-day Winter Mountaineering course: £295; Navigation and Hill Walking Skills weekend: £90; 5-day Navigation and Hill Walking Skills course: £225.
Booking: 10% deposit required, non-refundable. Balance due 2 weeks before start date. Late bookings accepted if space available.
Access: Ambleside is off the A591. Trains available to within 7 miles, buses within 1 mile (contact centre for details); pick-ups arranged by centre.

---

kevin walker mountain activities

74 Beacons Park
Brecon
Powys
LD3 9BQ
Wales
Tel & Fax (01874) 625 111

Navigation, First Aid, Scrambling, Winter Skills

With over 15 years of guiding and instructing behind him, Kevin Walker runs some very fine courses for both summer and winter mountaineering. These are tailored for novice and experienced mountaineers and there is quite a choice: 2-day mountain navigation, steep ground, wild country camping and mountain survival, and search and rescue courses; 5-day scrambling and general mountaincraft courses. There is never a higher student-to-instructor ratio than 4:1.

The centre also runs specialist instructor training courses: the MLTB Mountainwalking Leader (Summer) course, lasting 6 days, is really worth taking, as is the Outdoor First Aid award. These courses have a student-to-instructor ratio of 6:1. Experienced mountaineers can hire the centre's instructors for private guiding.

All courses include bunkhouse accommodation or camping, full board and equipment hire.

Season: All year.
Tariffs: A large range of courses is available, all of which include tuition and equipment. Some examples are – 1-day mountain navigation course: £50; 2-day mountain survival course: £119; 5-day scrambling course: £295; 5-day mountaincraft course: £235.

See Walking (p. 423) for full details.

mountain craft

Glenfinnan
Fort William
Highland
PH37 4LT
Tel (01397) 722 213
Fax (01397) 722 300

Scrambling, Navigation, Winter Skills

Simon Powell has been running Mountain Craft for over 10 years now and his 'Mountaincraft' course is a recognized classic for experienced hillwalkers who want to take their skills further. The programme involves ridges and scrambles, and mountain ascents using more difficult route-finding and navigation, with an introduction to ropework and some simple rock climbing. Groups are kept small, with no more than 5 students to 1 instructor. The Skye summer scrambling week in the Cuillins is also to be recommended. Winter mountaineering, including ridge walks and gullies with a night in a snow-hole, and specialist climbing courses are also offered. Private instruction and guiding can also be arranged. It should be noted that Mountain Craft is for the fit and experienced; beginners may find themselves struggling, and anyone considering a course at Mountain Craft should expect to be challenged, though not pushed.

Courses are either weekend or week-long, though the weekend courses are limited to a few dates per summer or winter season. Ring Simon to find out when they run. The courses are not cheap. The tariffs include instruction, equipment and local transport, but not accommodation and food – Mountain Craft will book accommodation for you if required, at whatever budget. What you are paying for is the high-level tuition.

Season: Open all year.
Accommodation: Local accommodation can be arranged through centre, from hostels to hotels.
Food: Not provided.
Other Activities: Climbing and Abseiling (see p. 104)
Children: Minimum age 16; those under 18 must be accompanied by parent or guardian.
Disabled Facilities: None.
Insurance: Clients may wish to provide their own holiday insurance, or cover may be arranged through centre.
Safety: All staff trained in mountain first aid.
Affiliations: Association of Mountaineering Instructors; BMC; Scottish Sports Council.
Tariffs: Rates include instruction, equipment and local transport. Winter Mountaincraft week: £225; Advanced Winter Mountaincraft week: £265; Winter Mountaincraft weekend: £98; Summer Ridges and Scrambles week: £225; Skye Cuillins and Scrambles week: £235. Private instruction available; contact centre for more details.
Booking: £50 non-refundable deposit required. Balance due 4 weeks before start date. Once paid, balance is not refundable. Credit cards accepted (3% surcharge).
Access: Depends on site of chosen course; details supplied after booking. Pick-ups from nearest bus or train station can be arranged by centre.

ossian guides

Sanna
Newtonmore
Highland
PH20 1DG
Scotland
Tel & Fax (01540) 673 402

Winter Skills, Scrambling

Guided summer wilderness trekking and learning winter skills combined with mountaineering are Ossian's specialities. All their trips are week-long and all equipment is supplied with the exception of sleeping bags. For winter skills, their Snow Hole Introduction course is hard to beat, with 2 nights spent in holes dug by yourself, the rest in a warm guest house. There is also guided winter Munro-bagging and mountaineering aimed at teaching you to read snow and sleet conditions – in the sky and on the ground. Two of these trips are up Ben Nevis and wild Ben Alder, as well as through the high wildernesses around the northern edge of Rannoch Moor, round beautiful Loch Ossian and Corrour – a particularly deer-rich area. There is also a specialist course in Snow and Ice Photography and a desperate March climb up onto the ridges of the Cairngorms. All the winter trips demand a reasonable level of fitness, though some are open to beginners.

The same areas are covered in Ossian Guides' summer trips, with the addition of the wild Knoydart Forest, and the moors of Lochaber and Badenoch. By contrast with the winter trips, not all the summer ones require you to be super-fit, but for their Classic Ridges trek, along Lancet Edge, Curved Ridge, Aonach Eagach, the Forcan and Devil's Ridge (all legendary names among Scottish mountaineers), you should be fit and have a good head for heights.

Season: 13 January to 20 October.
Accommodation: 8 twin rooms and 2 singles at centre.
Food: Tariffs Include full board provided by a nearby hotel.
Other Activities: Walking (see p. 426).
Children: No special facilities for children.
Disabled Facilities: None.
Insurance: Clients are covered by centre's insurance.
Safety: Staff trained in mountain rescue and first aid.
Affiliations: Euro Mountain Leader Association; Scottish Activity Holiday Association.
Tariffs: All courses include 6 days' guiding and equipment, 7 nights' accommodation and full board. Snow Hole Introduction: £359; Winter Skills and Munros: £379; Snow and Ice Photography: £399; Loch Ossian Expedition: £349; Ben Alder Expedition: £379; Weekend Winter Skills (2 days' instruction and 2 nights' accommodation): £165.
Booking: £50 non-refundable deposit required. Cancellation charges: 4+ weeks in advance: deposit only; 2–4 weeks: 40% of total; within 2 weeks: 100% of total. Late bookings sometimes accepted if space available.
Access: Newtonmore is off the A9, 45 miles south of Inverness. Trains to Kingussie station, buses to Newtonmore stop. Pick-ups arranged by centre.

outward bound

PO Box 1219
Windsor
Berkshire
SL4 1XR
Tel (01753) 731 005
Fax (01753) 810 666
Outward Bound Scotland, Loch Eil
Tel (01397) 772 866
Outward Bound Ullswater, Penrith
Tel (017684) 86347

Scrambling, Navigation, First Aid, Winter Skills

Outward Bound's Lakeland and Scottish centres both offer specialist mountain skills courses, open to anyone over the age of 14. The Ullswater centre runs a 7-day mountaineering course for people who know hillwalking but want to go further. The course takes in some of the classic passages, scrambles and peaks of the area and covers basic navigation, security on steep ground, and campcraft.

The Scottish courses are a bit more hard-core, with a 7-day Winter Hill Walking course open to people over 16 only. Again, the course is aimed at hill-walkers who want to progress and takes place on Ben Nevis, Glen Coe and Lochaber, covering navigation, winter survival, weather awareness, movement on steep ground, river crossings and basic ropework. You are encouraged to make decisions, under supervision, and lead where possible. If you already have some mountain skills experience, try the Scottish Winter Mountaincraft (also 7 days), which teaches the use of an ice axe and crampons, basic ropework, understanding snow conditions, avalanche awareness, and emergency survival. If you're really fit and experienced, there is a third week-long Scottish course: Rock Ice and Ridges, which combines scrambling on the high, snowbound ridges of Glen Coe and Ben Nevis with evening lectures on the theory of winter skills. This is a good course to take if you are considering a career in mountain leadership.

Affiliations: MLTB.
Tariffs: All prices include tuition, equipment, full-board accommodation and transport during programme. Prices do not include VAT.
Summer or Winter Mountaincraft (Scotland, 7 days, 18+): £275;
Lakeland Mountaineering (Ullswater, 7 days): £275;
Navigation Skills (Ullswater, 3 days): £130;
Rock and Ice Ridges (Scotland, 7 days): £395;
Mountain First Aid (Ullswater, 4 days): £175.

See Walking (p. 426) for full details.

pinnacle ridge mountain guiding

Croft 12
Portnalong
Isle of Skye
Highland
IV47 8SL
Tel (01478) 640 330

Winter Skills, Scrambling

The Black Cuillins of the southern Isle of Skye are one of Britain's best mountaineering playgrounds, full of steep ridges, screes and arduous rock-faces. Pinnacle Ridge operate from a croft at the foot of the Cuillin range. Most of their courses are run there, with a few across on the mainland in Glen Shiel, Torridon and Applecross. As usual with mountain skills centres, the programme is divided between winter walking, mountaineering and climbing, and summer scrambling and ridge traversing, all individually guided by Colin Threlfall, a qualified instructor. Both the summer and winter courses offer an introductory 5 days for beginners, but after that Pinnacle really only cater for the fit and experienced serious mountaineer – especially as regards the scrambles along Cuillin Main Ridge and Clach Glas, Bla Bhein, Coire Lagan, Coire Ghreadaidh and Pinnacle Ridge itself, after which the guiding centre is named.

There is no accommodation included in Pinnacle Ridge's trips, but Colin will pick up from anywhere in Glen Brittle, Carbost, Portnalong or Sligachan. He can book the accommodation for you at whatever budget, whether camping or in the local youth hostel, in cheap bunkhouses or B&Bs and hotels.

Season: Open all year.
Accommodation: Help will be provided in finding local accommodation.
Food: Not provided.
Other Activities: Climbing and Abseiling (see p. 105-6); Walking (p. 428).
Children: Courses designed for adults.
Disabled Facilities: None.
Insurance: Clients need their own insurance; inexpensive cover can be arranged through Pinnacle Ridge.
Safety: Staff trained in first aid.
Affiliations: None.
Tariffs: Prices are for guiding services only – 5-day Winter Mountaineering course: £180; 4-day Scrambling course: £145. Private guiding is available; contact centre for more information.
Booking: £40 deposit required; no refunds given for cancellations within 3 weeks of start date. Balance due 3 weeks in advance. Access, Visa and Mastercard accepted. Late bookings accepted if space available.
Access: Cross to the Isle of Skye by bridge or ferry, take the A850 to Sligachan. Trains not available, buses available to Sligachan. Pick-ups from bus station can be arranged by organization.

plas y brenin

The National Mountain Centre
Capel Curig
Gwynedd
LL24 0ET
Wales
Tel (01690) 720 214
Fax (01690) 720 394

Navigation, Scrambling, First Aid, Winter Skills

Famous in the world of outdoor sports as Britain's leading instructor training centre, Plas y Brenin is certainly the place to go if you are planning to start a career in this field, or want to hone your skills to professional level. You should bear this in mind before signing up for a course here, as some people find that the serious atmosphere is not for them.

Plas y Brenin is in the mountains of North Wales and has access to some very rugged, challenging country. Mountain skills courses on offer include, for summer, a 5-day introductory course for beginners' i.e. hillwalkers who want to head off into the trackless mountains, a Map and Compass Familiarization weekend, longer navigation courses held over several days, a weekend course in summer scrambling, a weekend on Avalanche Awareness, Search and Rescue, and a more intensive 5-day Mountain Rescue course. For winter there are 5-day snow walking and ice climbing courses, some of them taking place in Scotland. On top of all this, there are over 10 courses (from 2 to 5 days) aimed at preparing would-be professional guides for the BMC exams, and about as many taking those already qualified for refresher courses and higher-level exams, covering specialist areas such as ropework, single-pitch rock climbing, mountain first aid and emergency life-saving.

Unless otherwise stated in their official literature, Plas y Brenin's courses are all residential, and tariffs include full board.

Season: Open all year.
Accommodation: 65 beds in single, double and triple rooms (some en suite rooms available).
Food: Bar and dining room on-site, meals provided.
Other Activities: Canoeing (see p. 29); Climbing and Abseiling (p. 106); Orienteering (p. 182).
Children: Special courses for 13–16-year-olds.
Disabled Facilities: Wheelchair-accessible rooms, special equipment available.
Insurance: Personal cover is included in all UK residential course fees.
Safety: Staff qualified in mountain first aid.
Affiliations: British Canoe Union; BMC; British Orienteering Federation; MLTB; United Kingdom Mountain Training Board.
Tariffs: All courses include instruction, equipment, accommodation and full board. A wide range of mountain skills courses is available, including 5-day Mountaineering Skills: £325; Map & Compass weekend: £135; 2-day Scrambling: £140; 5-day Scottish Snow & Ice Climbing: £435; 5-day Mountain Rescue: £425; 5-day Mountain Instructor certificate: £340; Mountain First Aid Training weekend: £145.
Booking: Non-refundable deposit of £50–100 required. Balance due 8 weeks in advance of course. Cancellation charges: if 3–8 weeks in advance, 80% of total cost; 0–14 days in advance, 100% of total. Visa and Access cards accepted. Late bookings sometimes accepted if space available.
Access: A5 to Capel Curig. Trains available to Llandudno station (buses not convenient). Cab fare to Capel Curig costs approximately £18.

r&l adventures

The Byre
Knotts Farm
Patterdale Road
Windermere
Cumbria
LA23 1NL
Tel (015394) 45104

Scrambling, Navigation, Winter Skills

Although this centre is not affiliated to any governing body, the staff are fully qualified and the centre has been running for over 15 years. Instruction is by the day only – this is not a residential centre. There are no set courses; everything is tailored to your experience, or lack of it. Choose between active days on the hill (summer and winter) and more theoretical training with map and compass, or ghyll scrambling (including ropework and some abseiling – yikes!), or put together a ridge and steep ground trip using the centre's staff as guides. Tuition is of a very high standard, and while groups can be catered for, this is a very good place to come for intensive, one-on-one teaching.

Tariffs: Prices include instruction and use of equipment. Half-day of mountain walks or scrambling: £50 for 1 or 2 people, £60 for group of 3–4 people, £10 each for group of 6–10 people.

See Canoeing (p. 32) for full details.

the rock climbing and caving centre

Chudleigh
South Devon
TQ13 0EE
Tel & Fax (01626) 852 717

Mountain First Aid and Rescue

Although this Devon centre doesn't offer courses out on the hill, its Mountain First Aid Training course is worth attending if you plan to lead groups into the hills or make a trip as part of a small, independent group. The course is run on a continuous assessment basis – there is no test to take – and is accepted by the MLTB, British Association of Ski Instructors (BASI). The certificate is valid for 3 years. The course has a strong practical element, so bring warm, waterproof clothes.

You can stay in the centre's bunkhouse, camp on-site, or book a B&B nearby. If you do choose off-site accommodation, you can arrange to be picked up by the centre for the price of the fuel. The Rock Climbing and Caving Centre has been running for 17 years and employs 15 full-time instructors.

Tariffs: 2-day Mountain First Aid course: £50 (board £2.50 per night for a dorm bed).

See Caving (p. 47) for full details.

summitreks adventure services

4 Yewdale Road
Coniston
Cumbria
LA21 8DU
Tel (015394) 41212
Fax (015394) 41055

Scrambling, Navigation, Winter Skills

Based on several youth hostels in the Lakes, Summitreks' mountain courses are aimed at all levels of experience – from hillwalkers who want to progress, to would-be mountain leaders. Summer scrambling weekends and 5-day breaks run from April through to October, as do the 'Adrenalin Activity Courses', which include scrambling, abseiling (into water in some cases), basic climbing and mountain biking. From January to March, a bunch of winter courses are run – including basic winter walking weekends and 5-day breaks, during which you are introduced to ice axe and crampons, basic navigation and route-planning and some survival techniques. If you already have some experience with winter skills, try the Improvers' course, which tackles more exposed and steeper ground and involves much greater use of ice axe and crampons. The Improvers' course can be taken over a 5-day break or, in a shortened form, over a weekend. You could also try the weekend or 5-day Winter Navigation and Survival course, which includes overnighting on the hill. Finally there is a basic winter climbing weekend, introducing winter belays and ropework.

Season: Open all year.
Accommodation: Youth hostel accommodation in Derwentwater, Coniston or Grasmere.
Food: Full board included; vegetarian and special diets catered for upon request.
Other Activities: Gorge Walking (p. 184) Walking (p. 430).
Children: Courses geared for those over 16 (over 18 for winter courses).
Disabled Facilities: None.
Insurance: Clients should arrange personal insurance cover; can be arranged through centre.
Safety: All staff trained in first aid.
Affiliations: Association of Mountaineering Instructors; BMC; YHA.
Tariffs: Prices include instruction, equipment and full-board accommodation. Winter Mountaineering weekends: £95; Winter Mountaineering (5 days): £220; Winter Mountaineering Intermediate (3 days, must bring own equipment): £135; Winter Navigation and Survival weekend: £95; Winter Navigation and Survival (5 days): £220.
Booking: 25% deposit required, non-refundable (unless cancellation notice received more than 4 weeks in advance, then only £5 fee). Late bookings accepted if space available. Visa, American Express, Access and Switch cards accepted.
Access: Off the A953 south of Ambleside. Trains to Ambleside, buses to Coniston. Easy walk to centre.

snowgoose activities

The Old Smiddy
Station Road
Corpach
Fort William
Highland
PH33 7LS
Scotland
Tel & Fax (01397) 772 467

Scrambling and Winter Skills

Snowgoose run mountaineering courses and expeditions into the mountains of the western Highlands – day trips, 2-day and 3–5-day courses, targeted at people with some hillwalking experience. Their courses are quite demanding, with a maximum instructor-to-student ratio of 1:6 at the more novice levels, down to 1:2 for the more specialized courses. You should be reasonably fit and start with a summer scrambling programme that teaches the basics of ropework, as well as navigation and walking on steep ground. After that, you are prepared for one of the winter courses, which teach the use of ice axe and crampons and snow-holing (weather permitting). All the mountaineering courses can be tailored to suit more advanced levels and the school offers a guiding service as well, both for groups and individuals. Expect to spend about 7 hours a day on the hill.

All the courses are residential. Choose between self-catering apartments and a bunkhouse. Groups that opt to stay in their own accommodation can be picked up each day for a charge of 50p per mile.

Affiliations: Association of Mountaineering Instructors.
Tariffs: All prices include instruction and use of equipment. A wide range of mountaineering courses is available; some samples are – Navigation: £25 per day; Winter Warmer course (2 days): £70; Winter Mountain Navigation (2 days): £70; Winter Skills & Mountain Safety (3 days): £120; Winter Mountain Craft (5 days): £200; Introduction to Snow & Ice (3 days): £150. Mountaineering is also offered as part of the centre's multi-activity courses (2–5 days): £30 per day. Individual tuition in mountaineering is available: £85–105 per day. Group discounts available.

See Canoeing (p. 33) for full details.

tollymore mountain centre

Bryansford
Newcastle
County Down
BT33 OPT
Northern Ireland
Tel (013967) 22158
Fax (013967) 26155

Scrambling, Winter Skills, Navigation, First Aid and Rescue

Northern Ireland's best outdoor centre offers a variety of courses and holidays relating to mountain skills, from introductory to instructor level. Once you've attended the introductory weekend course (there is a women-only version of this for those put off by mountaineering's overly male image), try the 5-day Kerry Ridges scrambling holiday, which includes a chance to scale Ireland's highest peak, and introduces basic ropework and working over steep and exposed ground. If you want to concentrate on the more technical aspects of mountaineering, Tollymore run 3 weekend proficiency courses – on navigation, scrambling and hazards.

Over the winter, the focus shifts across the water to Scotland: there's a weekend preparation course for winter mountaineering at Tollymore followed by 2 5-day expeditions to Glencoe and Ben Nevis – the fees for which include the price of the ferry. Tollymore also run a preparation weekend for Alpine mountaineering which covers more advanced ropework than is usual for British mountaineering, including short-roping and direct belays. This weekend qualifies you to go on one of Tollymore's 3-week-long Alpine mountaineering trips to the French Alps.

Finally, would-be instructors should sign up for Tollymore's Mountain Leader courses, a series of weekend assessments testing you on steep ground and emergency ropework, navigation and rescue, which prepares you for the Mountain Leader exam – a 5-day test that qualifies you to work as a mountaineering leader and instructor.

Tariffs: Prices vary according to specific course, and whether or not catering is provided. Instruction, equipment and accommodation is included. A wide range of courses is available; some sample tariffs are: 4-day Introduction to Mountaineering course: £120 (catered); 3-day Mountain Leader course: £64 (catered); 4-day Youth Mountaineering course: £32 (self-catered).

See Canoeing (p. 35) for full details.

kitting yourself out

Please turn to Walking (p. 434) for a full breakdown of the gear you need to keep warm and dry on the hills. Specific to Mountain Skills are your navigational aids. It really is worth getting a top-of-the-range compass, for which you should be prepared to spend around £20 and upwards. Silva and Suunto are always good brands: Silva's 4NL is an ideal basic (£22) as is the Suunto m-5/Mils/MA at £26. Top of the range is the Suunto KB14/360/R/T, which has a built-in trintium lamp. It can be used at sea, can be dropped on rocks without breaking, and is accurate to 0.5 of a degree. You'll have to shell out over £120 for this.

Boots are also worth a specific mention: leather or lightweight fabric (Gore-Tex are best) hiking boots are fine for anything up to scrambling, but for winter climbing choose rigid leather or plastic boots, suitable for attaching crampons. There are many good makes of winter boot – visit a mountain store to discuss your needs, and be prepared to pay at least £120 for a reliable pair.

A survival kit can be bought at any good outdoor store and should include a basic first aid kit, a bivvy bag, a whistle, basic provisions for 48 hours, and flares. A good-quality survival kit should come in a small, self-contained lightweight pack and costs around £30. To get you up and down the mountains, an adjustable trekking pole is also a good idea. Two very good brands are Leki and Kohla. Expect to pay between £25 and £35 for a good stick. Trekking poles both reduce the strain on knees when descending and help maintain balance while ascending, especially on difficult terrain.

If you are aiming for winter survival, or are going to be scrambling over ridges as part of your trip, you may want to invest in some basic climbing equipment, such as an ice axe, hammer, 11mm rope, belay devices, karabiners, helmet and harness – prices and reliable brands are detailed in the Climbing chapter on p. 110. Foot crampons are also a good idea. These cost between £70 and £90, and good brands are Grivel, Stubai and Camp. Crampons come in two basic types – strap-on or step-in. Strap-ons can be used with leather boots, while step-ins are designed for plastic or very rigid leather boots. Seek advice at a mountain store before making a choice. More specialist items are 'dead men' and ice screws, for attaching ropes and belaying equipment in snow and ice, and an ice hammer with which to bang in the protection. To kit yourself out with these items, allow at least another £70.

It should be mentioned here that it is only worth buying such specialist stuff if you intend taking to the winter hills under your own steam – and you should not even attempt this without having first taken one or several winter skills courses such as those provided by the centres listed in this chapter.

checklist

- ✔ *buoyancy aid*
- ✔ *clothing and camping gear*
- ✔ *ice axe, ropes and 'friends'*
- ✔ *trekking pole*
- ✔ *compass*
- ✔ *survival kit*

further reading

Land Navigation, published by Ordnance Survey, is what the Duke of Edinburgh Award people use. *Mountaincraft and Leadership* by Eric Langmuir is also superb, detailing navigation techniques at beginner and advanced level. It's the official handbook for the MLTB courses and is published by them.

governing body

British Parachute Association (BPA)
5 Wharf Way, Glen Parva
Leicester LE2 9TF
Tel (0116) 278 5271
Fax (0116) 277 662

parachuting

One of the world's great tests of courage, parachuting has an understandable appeal. Those who do it only once come back flushed with pride and elation – especially as they will almost certainly have spent hours or even days waiting on the ground for the weather conditions to be right, screwing up their courage and battling with their bladders and bowels.

There are 2 basic types of parachuting: static-line jumping and free-falling. Almost everybody starts with static line – this is where, after about 6 hours of training, you jump out of a plane at about 2,000–3,000ft with a parachute that opens automatically. Free-falling, you jump from much, much higher and open the parachute yourself. If you want to bypass the usual route of making a few static-line jumps and then taking a free-fall course, you can take an accelerated free-fall course, which gets you jumping out of a plane at around 12,000ft after only 8 hours of training, spread over one or two days, or, if time is a problem, over a week. You jump with an experienced team who make sure you do everything right, and are then talked through your landing by radio.

If you aren't sure of your nerve but think you might like to try free-fall, a tandem jump, in which you are strapped to your instructor's torso, is a good way to go – and also allows you to jump if you are disabled. The instructor deals with all the technical stuff, while you get the exhilaration combined with the moral support of being more or less umbilically supported.

Few parachute courses of any kind are residential.

You must be over 16 to sign up for a course, and few people over 50 are accepted for novice training. You should also not be overweight for your age, sex and size. Most centres like you to bring a doctor's certificate and a declaration of fitness before they sign you up.

selected centres

NB: All the centres listed here require a medical certificate of fitness for any prospective novice pupils aged between 40 and 50. Also, all encourage charity jumps, in which the participants may parachute for free in return for fund-raising. Contact the manager of your nearest centre for details of charity jumps.

---

black knights parachute centre

Pattys Farm
Hilliam Lane
Cockerham
Lancaster
Lancashire
LA2 ODY
Tel (01524) 791 820

Black Knights have 7 instructors who devote 12 hours per day to making you into a parachutist. The school is one of Britain's oldest – 36 years old in 1995 – and they have a superb safety record. First-jump student courses are held every weekend, beginning at 9 a.m. on Saturday. Your first actual jump will be on the Sunday (weather permitting). You can choose between a Static Line Round course, which involves a jump from about 2,500ft, and a Static Line Square, which involves a jump from about 3,500ft. Free-fall courses are by arrangement only, when the school is convinced that you have made enough jumps to progress.

Season: Open all year.
Accommodation: 16 bunk beds (bring your own sleeping bag) for £2 per night. Camping and caravan sites plus shower facilities available free of charge. Centre will also provide help in obtaining off-site B&B accommodation.
Food: On-site canteen offers light meals and snacks.
Children: Minimum age 16; those under 18 require consent of parent or guardian.
Disabled Facilities: None.
Insurance: Third-party insurance included with membership of the British Parachute Association (BPA); contact centre for more details.
Safety: Staff trained in first aid.
Affiliations: BPA.
Tariffs: Static Line Round course (training and 1 jump): £100 (additional jumps £20 each); Static Line Square course (training and 1 jump): £150 (additional jumps £28 each).
Booking: £20 non-refundable deposit required. Bookings normally made in advance, but late bookings sometimes accepted if space available.
Access: Off the A6 between Preston and Lancaster. Trains and buses available to Lancaster. Clients must take cab to centre (approximately £7).

border parachute centre

Brunton Airfield
Chathill
Northumberland
NE67 5ER
Tel (01665) 589 000

Border specialize in introducing beginners to parachuting. Static-line square canopy courses, static-line round canopy courses, tandem free-falls and accelerated free-fall courses (involving 8 jumps with instructors, the first jump being from 12,000ft and giving 45 seconds of free-fall) are all offered by Border. If you're going on a tandem jump, you can purchase photos or videos of you going down, the footage taken by a free-fall cameraman. Border also issue gift certificates whereby you can give a friend a jump course as a present – which may be the end of the friendship! There are also discounts available for groups of 10 or more. Border have 6 instructors and have been running their parachute school for 18 years. The weight limit for clients is 14 stone.

Season: Open all year.
Accommodation: No on-site accommodation, but bunkhouse accommodation available at the nearby Smugglers Inn (with special rates for parachutists), and there is also a campsite nearby.
Food: Meals are available at centre; vegetarian selections available.
Children: Must be over 16. Anyone under 18 requires consent of parent or guardian.
Disabled Facilities: Disabled clients can take tandem jumps with approval of a doctor.
Insurance: Clients should arrange personal insurance cover.
Safety: Air ambulance called in case of emergencies. Staff trained in first aid.
Affiliations: BPA.
Tariffs: Prices include instruction and use of equipment. Tandem jump: £200; Static Line Round course (includes 1 jump): £99; Static Line Square course (includes 1 jump): £135. An Accelerated Free-fall course (includes 8 jumps) is also available, prices on request. Discounts for groups of 10 or more, also for courses taken mid-week.
Booking: £50 non-refundable deposit required. Bookings normally made 3 weeks in advance, but late bookings accepted if space available. Visa cards accepted.
Access: Off the A1 north of Alnwick. Contact centre for details on bus and train access. Pick-ups from nearest station can be arranged by centre.

british parachute schools

The Control Tower
Langar Airfield
Langar
Nottinghamshire
NG13 9HY
Tel & Fax (01949) 860 878

Langar is open every day of the year except Christmas and has been going since 1977. They offer a wide range of courses: 1-day tandem jumps involving 30 seconds of free-fall, learning to jump with a modern square parachute (static line) or an old-fashioned round canopy (also static line), free-fall courses – you're only allowed on these after a minimum of 6 static-line jumps. Langar also offer a special 6-jump square canopy course to speed you on towards free-falling, as well as a much more expensive accelerated free-fall course that includes 8 jumps, your first skydive coming on the first day with 2 instructors holding on to you. Anyone paying for this course in advance gets a tailor-made jump suit for free.

If you plan to take the round canopy course, Langar's cheapest, you should weigh no more than 14 stone fully clothed. Tandem jumps have a weight limit of 15 stone and square canopy jumps 16 stone. The static-line courses are 2-day, others generally 6-day, weather permitting. On tandem jumps you have the option of having a free-fall photographer or video cameraman accompanying you.

Courses are run both at weekends and mid-week.

Apart from the bunkhouse, the centre also has a canteen, bar and campsite.

Season: Open all year.
Accommodation: 26 bunk beds (bring your own sleeping bag), camping and caravanning sites, and shower facilities available (£1 per night). Centre will also provide help in obtaining off-site B&B accommodation.
Food: Canteen serving hot food at weekends, sandwiches and drinks on weekdays.
Children: Must be over 16; those under 18 must have consent of parent or guardian.
Disabled Facilities: Disabled clients may be able to make a tandem skydive – check with centre to discuss.
Insurance: Clients must obtain third-party insurance with a Student Provisional membership of the BPA: £10.
Safety: All instructors are trained in first aid.
Affiliations: BPA.
Tariffs: Tandem jump: £150; Static Line Round course (training and 1 jump): £115 (additional jumps £20 each); Static Line Square course (training and 1 jump): £165 (additional jumps £30 each); Static Line Square course (training and 6 jumps): £270; Accelerated Free-fall course (training and 8 skydives): £1,350.
Booking: £25 non-refundable deposit required. Balance due on first day of course. Switch, Access, Mastercard, Visa and American Express cards accepted. Bookings normally made in advance, but late bookings sometimes accepted if space available.
Access: Off the A46 near Leicester, or the A52 near Bingham. Trains to Bingham; pick-up can be arranged by centre. Buses can be taken from Nottingham to Langar village (1-mile walk to airfield).

british skysports

East Leys Farm
Grindale
Bridlington
Humberside
YO16 4YB
Tel (01262) 677 367 /
(01836) 276 188 (mobile)
Fax (01262) 401 871

Operational since 1972, this is a small school, with 3 instructors and groups limited to 16. This makes parachuting here a more friendly experience than at some of the larger, more impersonal schools, where you may feel insignificant. You can try tandem jumps or take a static-line course with a square canopy from 3,500ft. Experienced parachutists can sky-dive here, but you will have to learn by private arrangement with the school, as there are no formal skydiving courses.

Although there is no accommodation (apart from camping), the centre will book you into a local B&B, but you'll have to take a taxi to the farm each day – a cost of about £3. The school will, however, pick you up or take you back to Bridlington bus station free of charge.

Season: Open all year.
Accommodation: On-site camping (£2.50 per night).
Food: Food available at centre.
Children: Must be over 16. Anyone under 18 requires consent of parent or guardian.
Disabled Facilities: Tandem skydives available for disabled clients.
Insurance: Clients should arrange personal insurance cover.
Safety: Medic on-site, staff trained in first aid.
Affiliations: BPA.
Tariffs: Tandem jump: £140; Static Line Square course (training and 1 jump): £159. Group discounts available.
Booking: £45–50 non-refundable deposit required. Bookings must be made at least 48 hours in advance (4 weeks advisable in summer).
Access: Take the A165 from Bridlington. Trains and buses to Bridlington; pick-ups from stations can be arranged by centre.

devon & somerset parachute school

30 Tower Way
Dunkeswell
Devon
EX14 0XR
Tel (01404) 891 690 /
(0850) 032 767 mobile

This West Country parachuting centre has 8 instructors and offers 1–2-day square canopy static-line courses from 3,500ft, 1-day tandem free-fall jumps, and an accelerated free-fall course that runs over several days. Free charity jumps are also offered, with the money raised going towards the upkeep of Devon's only helicopter ambulance service.

The courses are not residential – the school has no accommodation – and you will need your own transport to get to and from the airfield.

Season: January to November.
Accommodation: No on-site accommodation, but centre will help to arrange local accommodation from camping to hotels.
Food: Refreshments available on airfield.
Children: Must be over 16.
Disabled Facilities: Tandem jumps available for disabled clients.
Insurance: Clients should arrange personal insurance cover.
Safety: Instructors trained in first aid. Air ambulance on call.

Affiliations: BPA.
Tariffs: Tandem jump: £145; Static Line Square course (training and 1 jump): £135. Courses in accelerated free-fall: contact centre for details. Group discounts available.
Booking: £50 deposit required. Deposit forfeited if cancellation made less than 28 days in advance. Late bookings accepted if space available. Credit cards accepted.
Access: Take the M5 to Junction 26; from there 17 minutes cross-country to Dunkeswell Airfield. Trains and buses to Honiton. Taxis from Honiton to centre cost around £7.

---

eaglescott parachute centre

Eaglescott Airfield
Ashreigney
Chulmleigh
Devon
EX18 7PH
Tel (01769) 560 726 (mid-week) /
520 552 (weekends)

This West Country parachuting school is aimed at all levels, from first-time jumpers to very experienced free-fallers. With 5 instructors and 8–10 hours of tuition per day, the school is open all year. Two-day static-line courses on square canopy parachutes run every weekend. You can then add on extra jumps until, after 6, you qualify for free-fall tuition. If you are really serious about getting to free-fall level, it is worth signing up for the Beginners' Paraweek course, which offers one-on-one instructor-to-student ratios and takes you from the first static-line jump at 3,500ft to your first free-fall at 12,000ft.

The school, which has been going for 12 years, has no on-site accommodation, but will arrange it for you nearby at a price to suit your budget. You need your own transport to get to the centre every morning – lessons start at 8.30 a.m. sharp. The maximum weight for clients is 15 stone.

Season: Open all year.
Accommodation: Centre will provide help in arranging local accommodation.
Food: Refreshments available on airfield.
Children: Must be 16 or over; anyone under 18 requires consent of parent or legal guardian.
Disabled Facilities: None.
Insurance: Clients should arrange personal insurance cover.
Safety: Air ambulance called in case of emergencies. Staff trained in first aid.
Affiliations: BPA; Fédération Aéronautique Internationale.
Tariffs: Static Line Square course (training and 1 jump): £145 (additional jumps £23). Discounts on weekdays and for group bookings.
Booking: £50 non-refundable deposit required. Bookings normally made in advance, but late bookings sometimes accepted if space available.
Access: Off the A377 at Chulmleigh. Contact centre for public transport details.

headcorn parachute centre

Headcorn Airfield
Headcorn
Kent
TN27 9HX
Tel (01622) 890 862
Fax (01622) 890 641

Headcorn is an even bigger affair than Langar (British Parachute Schools) with 15 instructors and a school that has been going for 16 years. There is the usual choice of courses: tandem day jumps, 2-day static-line round and square canopy courses, and longer accelerated free-fall courses. The school organizes jumps every day, weather permitting. The weight/height/sex restrictions are the same for each course – with a maximum of 14 stone 7lbs for men and 12 stone 4lbs for women. There is an option for photography and video recording of your jumps.

This is a handy school to get to if you live in London or the south-east, being only a few miles off the M20 near Maidstone, and there is a direct train service to Headcorn from London's Charing Cross, London Bridge and Waterloo East stations. You can either stay in their bunkhouse or arrange your own B&B.

Season: Open all year.
Accommodation: 24 bunk beds (bring a sleeping bag), campsites and shower facilities provided – all free of charge. Centre will also provide help in obtaining off-site B&B accommodation.
Food: Full-time canteen serving hot food.
Children: Must be over 16; those under 18 must have consent of parent or guardian.
Disabled Facilities: Tandem skydives available for disabled people. Accommodation and briefing rooms are wheelchair-accessible.
Insurance: Clients are covered by centre's third-party insurance; should arrange personal cover if desired.
Safety: All instructors are trained in first aid.
Affiliations: BPA.
Tariffs: Tandem jump: £160; Static Line Round course (training and 1 jump): £120; Static Line Square course (training and 1 jump): £195; Free-fall Square course (training and 8 skydives): £1,250. (Discounts available for groups.)
Booking: Deposit required, non-refundable – Round Parachute course: £50; Square Parachute course: £100; Free-fall course: £300; tandem jump: £50. Balance due on training day, personal cheques require 14 days' advance clearance time. Mastercard and Visa accepted. Bookings normally made in advance, but late bookings sometimes accepted if space available.
Access: Off the A274 near Sutton Valence. Trains available to Headcorn, pick-ups can be arranged by centre.

merlin parachute club

Thornbury Barracks
Pudsey
Leeds
West Yorkshire
LS28 8HH
Tel (01904) 664 529

The bread and butter for this parachute club is static-line square canopy parachuting, with 6 hours' prior training, and the first jump made from about 3,200ft. If you fancy free-fall skydiving but have no experience, try the tandem skydive (open to the disabled) in which you jump out of a plane strapped to an instructor's belly at 2 miles high – and after only half an hour's tuition. You fall at about 120mph to about 5,500ft when the instructor pulls the cord. If you get hooked, Merlin offer an intensive accelerated free-fall course with a first descent made from 12,000ft with 2 instructors and you finish, several jump days later, with your first solo skydive.

The club is non-residential and you will need your own transport to get to and from the barracks. The weight restriction is 14 stone for men, 12 stone for women.

Season: Open all year.
Accommodation: No accommodation on-site, but regulars usually stay at local pub which offers inexpensive B&B (and free camping).
Food: Canteen on-site.
Children: Minimum age 16; anyone under 18 requires parental consent.
Disabled Facilities: Tandem jumps available for disabled clients.
Insurance: Clients should arrange personal insurance cover; can be arranged through centre.
Safety: Staff trained in first aid.
Affiliations: Army Parachute Association; BPA.
Tariffs: Prices include instruction and plane flight (kit hire is £10 per jump). Tandem jump: £145; Static-line square parachute: £135; accelerated free-fall programme: £1,250. Discounts available for groups and military personnel.
Booking: £50 non-refundable deposit required. Late bookings accepted if space available.
Access: Instructions on how to reach centre will be mailed to clients after booking.

peterlee parachute centre

The Airfield
Shotton Colliery
Durham
DH6 2ND
Tel (0191) 517 1234
Fax (0191) 386 5315

Peterlee offer weekend static-line courses starting at 9.30 a.m. every Saturday. Most of these involve jumps with round canopies. If you want to arrange for one with square canopies, which let you jump on a static line from about 3,500ft instead of a round canopy's 2,500ft, you must arrange this in advance. Square canopy courses are also 2-day but involve more training and so are more expensive.

You can also opt for a tandem skydive with only a half-hour of briefing before making the jump, from around 8,000ft or above – firmly attached to your instructor. He or she will allow you to control the parachute during the descent, once it has opened.

The weight limit for Peterlee's courses is 14 stone.

Season: Open all year.
Accommodation: Camping and dormitory accommodation available.

Food: Meals available at centre, including vegetarian selections on request.
Children: Must be over 16. Anyone under 18 requires consent of parent or guardian.
Disabled Facilities: Disabled clients can take tandem jumps with approval of a doctor.
Insurance: Clients should arrange personal insurance cover.
Safety: Staff trained in first aid.
Affiliations: BPA.
Tariffs: Prices include instruction and use of equipment. Tandem jump: £135; Static Line Round course (includes 1 jump): £90, £16 each additional jump; Static Line Square course (includes 1 jump): £120, £25 each additional jump.
Booking: Deposit required, non-refundable. Late bookings sometimes accepted if space available. Guarantee card required if payment is by cheque on day of course.
Access: Off the A19, half-mile west of Peterlee. Trains to Durham, buses to Peterlee. Bus stops at airfield.

---

skydive strathallan

Strathallan Airfield
Nr Auchterarder
Perthshire & Kinross
PH3 1LA
Scotland
Tel (01764) 662 572 (weekends) /
(0374) 686 161 (mobile)

The stunning scenery of Perthshire & Kinross seen from so far above might just help to quell your fear as you leap – but probably not. However, beautiful the scenery certainly is up here and you do appreciate it when drifting gently down, the 'chute having opened as planned. The 35-year-old school's square canopy static-line courses (from 3,500ft) usually last a full day or 2 days and go right through the week. Tandem free-fall jumps run on Fridays and at weekends. Skydiving can be arranged for experienced parachutists, and accelerated free-fall courses, held over several days, are also available.

Strathallan can arrange local accommodation at discounted rates.

Season: Open all year.
Accommodation: Centre will arrange off-site accommodation.
Food: Canteen at airfield offers meals; vegetarian selections available.
Children: Must be 16 or over; under-18s require consent of parent or guardian.
Disabled Facilities: None.
Insurance: Third-party insurance included in course fees; clients should arrange personal insurance cover if desired.
Safety: Instructors trained in first aid.
Affiliations: BPA.
Tariffs: Prices include instruction, equipment, insurance, BPA, club membership and 1 jump. Tandem jump: £150; Static Line Round course: £79–99 (depending on day of week); Static Line Square course: £130. Accelerated free-fall courses available; contact centre for details. Group discounts available.
Booking: £50 deposit required. Deposit is non-refundable, but may be transferred to another date. Late bookings accepted if space available. Visa and Mastercards accepted.
Access: Off the A9 between Perth and Stirling. Trains to Gleneagles, bus to Auchterarder, taxi to airfield.

stirling parachute centre

Thornhill
Stirling
FK8 3QT
Scotland
Tel (01786) 870 788
Fax (01786) 870 748

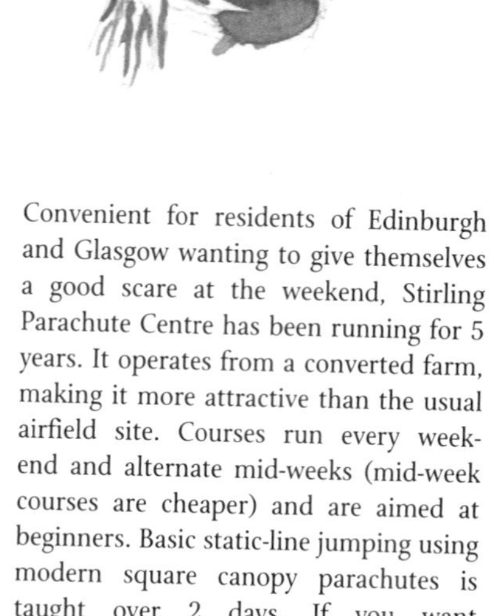

Convenient for residents of Edinburgh and Glasgow wanting to give themselves a good scare at the weekend, Stirling Parachute Centre has been running for 5 years. It operates from a converted farm, making it more attractive than the usual airfield site. Courses run every weekend and alternate mid-weeks (mid-week courses are cheaper) and are aimed at beginners. Basic static-line jumping using modern square canopy parachutes is taught over 2 days. If you want to get into free-falling you have to become a club member, with most of the cost of each jump, including the instruction, being included in the membership fee.

There are 4 instructors, and the weight limit for clients is 14 stone. Stirling Parachute Centre has no on-site accommodation, but is happy to book you into local places at whatever budget, from camping to hotels. You will need your own transport.

Season: Open all year.
Accommodation: Centre will provide help in obtaining local accommodation, from camping to hotels.
Food: Light refreshments available.
Children: Must be over 16; anyone under 18 must have consent of parent or guardian.
Disabled Facilities: None.
Insurance: Clients should arrange personal insurance cover.
Safety: All staff are trained by the BPA.
Affiliations: BPA.
Tariffs: Static Line Round Canopy course (training and 1 jump): £105 weekends, £85 weekdays (additional jumps £17). Group discounts available.
Booking: £55 non-refundable deposit. Late bookings accepted if space available.
Access: Off the B822 between Thornhill and Kippen villages. Buses and trains available to Stirling. Cabs to centre approximately £12.

wild geese parachute club

Movenis Airfield
116 Carrowreagh Road
Garvagh
Coleraine
County Londonderry
BP51 4BB
Northern Ireland
Tel (012665) 58609
Fax (012665) 57050

Northern Ireland's only parachute school offers courses that teach you to jump in one day (weather permitting). The basic courses on offer are: static line with a round canopy, static line with a square canopy, tandem skydives, and a 6-jump square canopy course to prepare you for free-fall.

All courses begin at 7.30 a.m. and for this reason the centre suggests you stay in the bunkhouse or camp to be sure of making it on time. Courses run on any day given sufficient demand, but usually over weekends.

As a bonus, if you're staying on-site, the school has a separate health club. Massage sauna will help you unwind after the demands of the day's intensive tuition and the adrenalin rush of the jump itself. There are also 4 gyms and a full-time beautician! Prices for all this are reduced for visiting jumpers.

Season: Open all year.
Accommodation: 36 bunk beds (bring your own sleeping bag) for £5 per night, including breakfast. Free camping and caravanning sites. Shower facilities provided.
Food: Breakfast included for those staying in bunk beds.
Children: Must be over 16; those under 18 must have consent of parent or guardian.
Disabled Facilities: Tandem skydiving can be arranged for disabled people.
Insurance: Clients must obtain third-party insurance through the BPA: £20.50.
Safety: All instructors are qualified in first aid.
Affiliations: BPA.
Tariffs: Tandem skydive: £115; Static Line Round Canopy course (training and 1 jump): £80; Static Line Square course (training and 1 jump): £120; Extended Square course (training and 6 jumps): £200.
Booking: Deposit required: £10. Balance due 10 days in advance of start date. Courses must normally be booked 2 weeks in advance, but late bookings can sometimes be accepted if space available.
Access: Call centre for directions by car. Buses can be taken to Garvagh; centre will arrange pick-up from station.

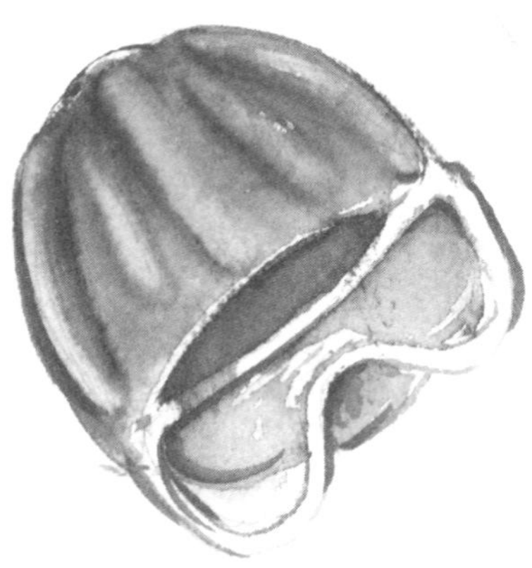

checklist

- ✔ *helmet*
- ✔ *parachute, harness, reserve and container*
- ✔ *goggles*
- ✔ *automatic reserve device*
- ✔ *knife*
- ✔ *flying suit*
- ✔ *altimeter*

kitting yourself out

The editor would like to state at the outset that, because of the extreme dangers involved in parachuting, you cannot think of kitting yourself out and going solo after only a short course. Fortunately, the fact that you have to go up in a plane, and therefore almost always have to go through a club or parachute school, prevents people from just heading out and killing themselves. When buying any kit, do it under supervision – and if it's second-hand, have it vetted thoroughly by your instructor. In fact, you never have to own your own kit if you don't want to – it can be hired from a club or school for every jump.

So much for warnings. If you have set your heart on owning kit, you are looking at somewhere between £1,500 and £2,200 for a main parachute and harness, plus round canopy reserve 'chute and container. If you want to have an automatic activating device for the reserve, this costs around £800–1,000 more. Good manufacturers of harnesses and packs are Sun Path and Relative Workshop, while Parachute de France and GQ and PD are good for canopies. Second-hand kits can be bought for much less, but this is very risky and should only be undertaken with the advice of an instructor.

A customized jump suit (and you should have one – a snug fit is safer) from Symbiosis Suits costs about £150, while a Pro Tech helmet is about £45–50. Frapp-Hat leather helmets for more advanced free-fallers can cost between £100 and £200. Goggles from Pro Tech will set you back around £10. In case you need to cut yourself free, a good knife, bought through your school or club, is also around £10.

Finally, an altimeter (aneroid barometer) with a jewel mechanism – which means it can be mended if it breaks – costs about £150 for a strong model that will survive a few knocks. Audible Altimeters are reliable manufacturers.

further reading

A Beginner's Guide to Airsports, Keith Carey, A & C Black, 1994.

governing body

The British Hang Gliding and Paragliding Association (BHPA)

Old Schoolroom, Loughborough Road
Leicester LE4 5PJ
Tel (0116) 261 1322
Fax (0116) 261 1323

paragliding parascending

Imagine yourself hang-gliding, but supported by an elliptically shaped, rather than kite-shaped, expanse of nylon or silk. You sit in a kind of chair, similar to a baby seat in a car, which is moulded to your lower body and allows full movement of the legs – necessary for making your running take-off from the edge of the cliff. After that, as journalist James Bedding wrote, reporting on a paragliding course for the *Daily Telegraph*, 'I felt . . . as if the gods were thinking me through the sky.'

Paragliding has been around since the early 1980s, developing from specialized beginnings into a mass-appeal sport. It is more accessible than hang-gliding because both the training courses and equipment are cheaper and the gear is lighter – folding up to a total weight of about 20lbs. Most beginners find the first steps frustrating – there's a definite knack to getting the thing airborne. But having flown once, almost everyone who tries it comes back for more. There is no need for great physical strength, and the net result of a flight is quiet euphoria rather than sweat. Yet you can cover great distances.

Beginners' courses (Elementary Pilot Certificate) are usually held over 4 or 5 days for those wanting to gain certificates that qualify them to buy their own equipment and learn advanced flying (Club Pilot, Pilot and Advanced Pilot certificates). As with all air sports, you must expect to be grounded for a certain amount of time if the weather is unfavourable, but don't despair of getting your money's worth, as almost all centres will allow you to come again free of charge if you can't make a flight during your allocated days.

Two things to remember. Firstly, only go to a school that is affiliated to the British Hang Gliding and Paragliding Association (BHPA), otherwise you cannot be assured of the safety standards or the instructors' qualifications. Secondly, this sport isn't for kids, unfortunately. Most centres will not take anyone under 14, and you cannot hold even an Elementary Pilot's licence until you are over 16.

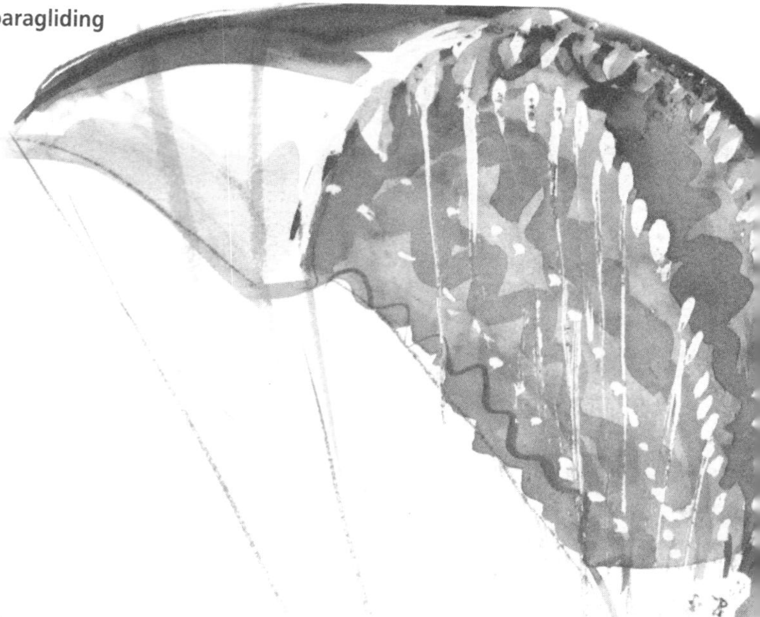

Readers should note that the chapter also includes parascending, which involves being towed in the air behind a car or boat while suspended from a canopy. Although not directly related to paragliding, some paragliding centres offer it as an alternative activity, hence its inclusion here. Unlike paragliding, which involves a system of certificates aimed at enabling you to make solo direct flights, parascending generally relies on a ground team and is designed for recreational flights – except for occasional cross-country flights launched using a winching process, but these are for the very serious only.

selected centres

active edge

Albert Terrace
Glasshouses
Harrogate
North Yorkshire
HG3 5QN
Tel (01423) 711 900
Fax (01423) 712 900

This is one of Britain's leading schools, offering the full range of paragliding courses from 'fun days' through pilots' certificates to glider hire for the already qualified. Courses last between 2 days and a full week, depending on the kind of licence required, with about 8 hours of tuition per day. You fly over some of the grandest scenery in England – the wide moors of the central Pennines – and stay in local accommodation booked by Active Edge to suit your budget. They pick you up and bring you back each day. Active Edge employ 6 instructors and also provide a sales and repairs service for those wanting to buy or already owning their own equipment.

Season: Open all year.
Accommodation: No on-site accommodation. Centre will provide help in obtaining local accommodation.
Food: Not provided.
Children: Over 16 only; anyone under 18 must have consent of parents.
Disabled Facilities: None.
Insurance: Clients are covered by centre's insurance.
Safety: All instructors are trained in first aid.
Affiliations: BHPA.
Tariffs: 1-day introductory course: £60; 2-day introductory course: £100; 4-day Student Pilot course: £195; 1-day Club Pilot course: £50; Advanced course: £50; 7-day full course (from beginner to Club Pilot standard): £295. (Discounts if courses taken on weekdays, or if booked in groups.)
Booking: 50% deposit required, balance payable when course starts. Cancellation charge: £5. Bookings are normally made in advance, but late bookings are sometimes accepted if space is available.
Access: The centre is based at Austwick, located on the main A65 cross-Pennine route between Ingleton and Settle. Trains and buses available to Settle. Centre can arrange pick-up from Settle free of charge. Contact them for more details.

adventure sports

Carnkie Farmhouse
Carnkie
Redruth
Cornwall
TR16 6RZ
Tel (01209) 218 962 / (0589) 427 077

Carnkie's paragliding courses can either be taken as an intensive paragliding-only holiday or as part of a more general multi-activity package. If you choose the latter, your paragliding will be limited to 'taster' flights only. But an intensive paragliding break will get you through your BHPA certificates and get you flying properly. Student Pilot, Club Pilot, Pilot and Advanced Pilot courses are all offered. There is no time limit on these courses – they are kept open-ended until you have gained sufficient hours to get whichever licence you are trying for – which helps if the weather sets in during your course and stops you flying. You can either stay in the centre's various types of accommodation or come in on a daily basis. All courses are self-catering but do not include BHPA membership and exam fees – contact centre for details about these.

Season: March to October.
Accommodation: Double and single rooms (in 'Farmhouse' or 'Chalets'), caravans and camping (with use of showers, WCs and other facilities).
Food: Self-catering.
Other Activities: Climbing and Abseiling (see p. 90); Sailing (p. 339); Surfing (p. 402); Water Skiing (p. 438); Windsurfing (p. 454).

Children: Licensing only available to those over 16.
Disabled Facilities: None.
Insurance: Clients must obtain third-party insurance by joining BHPA. Membership can be obtained for varying periods – 2 days: £8; 3 months: £29; 1 year: £59; and 1 year concessionary membership: £40.
Safety: All instructors are St John's-certified.
Affiliations: BHPA.
Tariffs: 1-day introductory course: £39; weekend introductory course: £69; Student Pilot course: £150; Club Pilot course: £150; Advanced Pilot course: £150. Accommodation offered for £10 per person per night. Paragliding is one of the activities offered in the centre's multi-activity package deals (accommodation included). Prices are variable, depending on season and type of accommodation desired: £44–78 for 2 nights / 2 activities; £110–195 for 5 nights / 5 activities; £154–273 for 7 nights / 7 activities. Group, long-term-stay and previous-customer discounts available. Single persons desiring their own room must pay a 30% surcharge.
Booking: Deposit required of £50, non-refundable. Paragliding course fees non-refundable. For multi-activity bookings, full balance is payable for cancellations received less than 30 days in advance of holiday. Bookings are normally made in advance, but late bookings are sometimes accepted if space available. Access, Mastercard, Visa and Eurocard accepted.
Access: Nearest towns are Redruth, Penzance and Falmouth. Trains and buses available to these towns; pick-ups can be arranged by centre. Contact centre for more details.

eagle quest

Lowgrove Farm
Millbeck
Keswick
Cumbria
CA12 4PS
Tel (017687) 75351
Fax (017687) 75763

Eagle Quest offers flying courses over the mountains of the Lake District – superb flying country. The centre is run from an old stone farmhouse and offers a variety of course prices based on differing types of accommodation. On one of the intensive courses, the centre aims to get you flying up to 800ft on the first day (weather permitting). Courses are divided between Fun Day introductory flights and Student, Club, Pilot and Advanced Pilot courses – these run from 4 to 7 days.

Alternatively, you can try paragliding on a 'taster' basis as part of a multi-activity programme that includes climbing and abseiling, canoeing, raft building, sailing, paintball, scrambling and hillwalking, orienteering, rafting, go-karts and quad bikes (phew!). The multi-activity breaks last from 2 to 7 days and, again, are operated on a sliding scale of fees based on what type of accommodation is required.

On both courses, all local transport is included and the centre can pick up and drop off from the bus station at Keswick, for a small charge.

Season: Open all year.
Accommodation: B&B offered in 18th-century farmhouse (5 double rooms); 42 beds available in bunk rooms, and camping available in stone barn.
Food: B&B available, as are packed lunches.
Other Activities: Canoeing (see p. 22); Climbing & Abseiling (p. 95); Sailing (p. 345).
Children: Paragliding students must be over 14 to take courses (although BHPA only issues pilot licences to over-16s).
Disabled Facilities: None.
Insurance: Clients must obtain third-party insurance by joining BHPA. Membership can be obtained for varying periods – 2 days: £8; 3 months: £29; 1 year: £59; and 1 year concessionary membership: £40. Insurance is included in price of introductory courses.
Safety: All staff are qualified in first aid.
Affiliations: BHPA.
Tariffs: 1-day introductory course: £60; weekend introductory course: £100; 4-day Student Pilot course: £190; 4–6-day Club Pilot course: £200; advanced courses available. (Discounts given for groups.) Package deals are available for instruction and accommodation. Prices vary according to level of accommodation desired (ranging from camping to B&B) – 1-day introductory course / 2 nights' accommodation: £62–89; 2-day introductory course / 2 nights' accommodation: £96–139; Student Pilot course / 4 nights' accommodation: £192–245; combined Student and Club Pilot course / 7 nights' accommodation: £279–385. Paragliding is also one of the activities offered in the centre's multi-activity package deals. Prices vary according to level of accommodation desired (ranging from no accommodation to B&B) – 2 days of activities / 2 nights' accommodation: £60–99; 5 days of activities / 5 nights' accommodation: £160–225; 7 days of activities / 7 nights' accommodation: £200–299.
Booking: 25% deposit required, balance due 6 weeks prior to arrival. Deposit non-refundable. Credit cards accepted. Bookings usually made well in advance, but late bookings possible if space available.
Access: The centre is 19 miles west of Penrith. If coming by car, take the M6 to Penrith, then the A66 to Keswick and the A591 to Carlisle, then turn off north on the Millbeck road. Otherwise, bus or train to Penrith and the centre will arrange a pick-up.

fly high sky sports

101 Heath Road
Barming
Maidstone
Kent
ME16 9JT
Tel (01622) 728 230 /
(0860) 351 130 (mobile)

Paragliding, Powered Paragliding, Parascending

Established in 1970, Fly High are one of Britain's most comprehensive sky sports centres. They offer the full range of paragliding courses, from 'taster' days through basic training weekends and 4-day Student Pilot courses right up to Club and Cross-country Pilot and instructor level. There are also specialist paragliding weekend courses for experienced pilots; for example, they run an Overwater course that involves ditching the harness and canopy and deploying a reserve parachute, with a landing in a lake.

Parascending is also offered here, from purely recreational flights open to anyone, regardless of experience, to advanced courses with untethered flights up to 600ft or higher and incorporating turns, movements in the air, and controlling your own landing.

Finally, the centre also offers powered paragliding – a bit like microlighting but using an adapted paragliding canopy instead of the usual hang-gliding type of wing used by open microlights. The school runs 20-minute trial flights and lessons, 2-day First Solo Flight courses and week-long courses which should gain you a pilot's licence at the end, all being well.

There is on-site accommodation in a comfortable bunkhouse, or you can book into a local B&B. If it's within a few miles, the school will ferry you to and fro at no extra cost.

Season: Open all year.
Accommodation: Free bunkhouse accommodation and camping.
Food: Light refreshments only.
Other Activities: Hang-gliding (see p. 189); Woodlore (p. 475).
Children: Must be 5 years old to fly dual. Anyone under 18 must have consent of parent or guardian. Youth and school groups welcome.
Disabled Facilities: Tandem flights available for disabled clients.
Insurance: Clients must obtain third-party insurance by joining BHPA. Membership can be obtained for varying periods – 2 days: £8; 3 months: £29; 1 year: £59; and 1 year concessionary membership: £40.
Safety: All instructors trained in first aid, several are trained medics.
Affiliations: British Association of Parascending Clubs; BHPA; British Powered Parachute Association; Fédération Aéronautique Internationale; Royal Aero Club.
Tariffs: All prices include tuition, accommodation and use of equipment. Overwater parascending flight: £12; 1-day initial parascending course (round parachute): £40; 2-day advanced parascending course (round parachute): £80; 5-day Overwater Parascending licence course: £299; Overland parascending flight: £18; Overland tandem flight: £25; Tow fun day: £59; 2-day course: £100; Student Pilot course: £140; Club Pilot course: £150.
Booking: 50% deposit required. No cancellation charge, flights can be rebooked for later date. Late bookings accepted if space available.
Access: Off the M20 near Maidstone. Trains to West Malling station, buses to airfield. Pick-ups may be arranged by centre.

great glen school of adventure

South Laggan
Nr Spean Bridge
Highland
PH34 4EA
Scotland
Tel (01809) 501 381
Fax (01809) 501 218

Parascending

The Great Glen school offers 'taster' sessions for parascending, towing you up behind a boat from the waters of Loch Oich. You can take as many flights as you want in a day, with no experience needed. Parascending can also be combined with water sports such as dinghy sailing, windsurfing and canoeing to make up a weekend or full week's holiday, with accommodation in log cabins built on the loch shore.

Season: Open all year, but weather usually only favourable for water sports from April to October.
Accommodation: Luxury 3-bedroom lodges available at the resort, prices vary according to season and lodge chosen (£99–695 per week). Centre can also arrange local B&B off-site.
Food: Bar and restaurant at the resort.
Other Activities: Archery (see p. 5); Circus Skills (p. 83); Sailing (p. 349); Water Skiing (p. 439); Windsurfing (p. 460). Instruction also available in numerous activities such as archery and orienteering.
Children: Baby-sitting available. Kids' Fun Days with games and activities arranged (£7.50 per child).
Disabled Facilities: All lodges wheelchair-accessible.
Insurance: Clients are covered by centre's insurance.
Safety: Staff trained in first aid.
Affiliations: None.
Tariffs: £17.50 per ride.
Booking: 20% deposit required, non-refundable. Access and Visa cards accepted. Late bookings accepted if space available.
Access: Centre at Loch Oich, on the A82 between Fort Augustus and Fort William. Trains and buses available to Fort William; cabs from there to Loch Oich approximately £20.

green dragons

Paragliding and Hang Gliding Centre
Warren Barn Farm
Slines Oak Road
Woldingham
Surrey
CR3 7HN
Tel (01883) 652 666
Fax (01883) 652 600

This Surrey-based school has been going since 1974 and now employs 11 instructors, having started out as a hang-gliding centre and moved into paragliding. It's very convenient for London, by train or car. For complete beginners, there are 'taster' flights – either by yourself or strapped onto a paratandem harness which allows you to soar to about 1,000ft with an instructor. If you get the bug, the 2-day elementary course will give you 10 solo flights and a Student Pilot's licence. A second, 2–3-day course gives you 25 solo flights and, hopefully, a Club Pilot's licence. After that you can join the centre's flying club and begin training towards your Cross-country licence and beyond. Once you've made it to this level, the centre will help you buy your own kit – new or second-hand – as it operates as a paragliding equipment dealership.

The only on-site accommodation is camping, but the centre will help you arrange local accommodation. If you're coming out from London, ring that morning to check that the weather is right for flying.

Season: Open all year.
Accommodation: Camping on-site, or local B&B can be arranged.
Food: Light refreshments available.
Other Activities: Hang-gliding (see p. 189).
Children: Must be 14 or over to fly solo, and 16 or over to fly unsupervised. Anyone under 18 requires consent of parent or guardian.
Disabled Facilities: Tandem flights or tow launches can be arranged for disabled clients.
Insurance: Clients must obtain third-party insurance by joining BHPA. Membership can be obtained for varying periods – 2 days: £8; 3 months: £29; 1 year: £59; and 1 year concessionary membership: £40.
Safety: Instructors trained in first aid.
Affiliations: BHPA; Civil Aviation Authority.
Tariffs: Prices include tuition and use of equipment. Tandem flight: £25; 1-day introductory course (tow launch): £69; Elementary Pilot course (tow launch): £140; Club Pilot course (tow launch): £150; 1-day introductory course (hill launch): £69; Elementary Pilot course (hill launch): £270; Club Pilot course (hill launch): £270. (1 free place given for group booking of 9 or more.)
Booking: Full fees payable at time of booking. Cancellation charges – 14 days in advance: 15%; 7–13 days: 40%; 2–6 days: 80%; less than 48 hours: 100%. Bookings normally made in advance, but late bookings accepted if space available. Visa, Access, Switch cards accepted.
Access: Off the A22 at Woldingham. Trains and buses to Woldingham. Cabs to centre around £2.

high adventure

Yarborough House
Nettlecombe Lane
Whitwell
Isle of Wight
PO38 2QA
Tel (01983) 730 075
Fax (01983) 731 441

High Adventure offers the standard BHPA 3–5-day pilot courses, as well as 1-day introductory courses and 'taster' flights for people thinking of taking up the sport. Since 1990, the centre has taught over 1,000 students through its staff of 6 instructors, and most of these students have made it to at least Club Pilot level.

High Adventure was the first hang gliding school to diversify and put paragliding on its curriculum; many of the current training techniques used in other schools were developed here and are now part of the syllabus laid down by the BHPA.

Affiliations: BHPA.
Tariffs: 1-day introductory course: £59; 2-day introductory course: £100; 3-day Student Pilot course: £195; 3–4-day Club Pilot course: £195; Combined SP and CP course: £350.

See Hang-gliding (p. 190) for full details.

moorland flying club

Davidstow Moor Aerodrome
Camelford
Cornwall
PL32 9YE
Tel (01840) 261 517 / 213 844

Powered Paragliding

This is primarily a microlighting school, but it also offers tuition in the singular sport of powered paragliding – the only place in Britain that we tracked down which teaches such a thing. Tuition consists of a series of day courses, and you do not need to have any previous paragliding experience. First you are shown demonstration flights and given some theory, covering principles of flight, air law, navigation, meteorology and (worryingly) effects of flight on the human body. After that you are taught how to handle the equipment, and then you fly, towed up on a short line for your first powered flight. The Moorland Flying Club state that a paramotor provides an 'extremely safe' means for cross-country flight. One might be sceptical but it has to be tried.

Moorland's flying courses are non-residential and you have to get to and from the airfield, which lies at the foot of Bodmin Moor, by yourself.

Tariffs: Prices include tuition and use of equipment. 1-day introductory course: £150; 1st-stage training: £300; 2nd-stage training: £300; 3rd-stage training: £500; full course: £1,100. (Discounts available on courses if clients use own machine.)

See Microlighting (p. 246) for full details.

northern paragliding

Dunvegan Lodge
Front Street
Barmby Moor
Humberside
YO4 5EB
Tel (01759) 304 404
Fax (01759) 306 747

Though its administration office is based near York, this is another Yorkshire Dales school, operating from the town of Hawes in Wensleydale in the northern Yorkshire Dales. The chief instructors, Ian Currer and Rob Cruikshank, are the authors of *Touching Cloudbase*, one of the best handbooks available on paragliding. It is also one of the few schools to cater for disabled people – unfortunately not BHPA courses, but tandem flights with an instructor. The BHPA courses on offer include a 'Fun Day' taster, a 2-day introductory course, and a 4-day Student Pilot certificate course, as well as others for more experienced flyers and courses abroad.

For those who want to continue, the centre sells both new and second-hand equipment, and will arrange accommodation to suit the budgets of its clients, with a no-charge pick-up to take you to the flying sites.

Season: April to December.
Accommodation: No on-site accommodation. Centre will provide help in obtaining local accommodation.
Food: Not provided.
Children: Over 16 only; anyone under 18 must have consent of parents.
Disabled Facilities: Can provide tandem (2-person) flights for disabled persons.
Insurance: Clients must obtain third-party insurance by joining BHPA. Membership can be obtained for varying periods – 2 days: £8; 3 months: £29; 1 year: £59; and 1 year concessionary membership: £40.
Safety: All staff are trained and qualified in first aid.
Affiliations: BHPA.

Tariffs: 1-day introductory course (for groups of 4+ only): £60. 2-day introductory course: £110; 4-day Student Pilot course: £205; 4-day Club Pilot course: £210; Advanced Club Pilot course: £100 (free if equipment bought at centre). Group discounts available.
Booking: Deposit of £10 per person per day required. Balance due at least 21 days in advance. Cancellations received more than 14 days in advance charged 50% of deposit. If received less than 14 days in advance, deposit is forfeited and balance may only be applied to later course. If flights cancelled due to bad weather, refunds are not available but flights will be rebooked for a later date. Bookings are normally made in advance, but late bookings are sometimes accepted if space available. (Weekends usually require at least 2–3 weeks' advance notice, 48 hours for weekdays.) Cheques and credit cards accepted.
Access: Centre is in Hawes, off the A684. Nearest train station is Garsdale Junction, on the Settle–Carlisle line, and pick-ups can be arranged from station. Buses not available. Contact centre for more details.

---

par avion paragliding

Elm Tree Park
Manton
Marlborough
Wiltshire
SN8 1PS
Tel (01672) 861 380
Fax (01672) 861 580

One of 2 paragliding schools operating on the Marlborough Downs (see also Wiltshire Hang-gliding and Paragliding Centre p. 319), Par Avion offer 8-hour-per-day courses and can take people from beginner to pilot level. They also arrange trips abroad for experienced paragliders to the Alps, South Africa and Turkey. Courses at the Marlborough school are all around 4 days in length, unless you take one of the single-day or weekend 'tasters'. Those only casually interested can also take tandem flights. Accommodation is not provided, but the centre will arrange it nearby, at whatever budget, and pick you up each morning for training.

Season: Open all year.
Accommodation: No on-site accommodation. Centre will provide help in obtaining local accommodation.
Food: Not provided.
Children: Over 14 only; anyone under 18 must have consent of parents.
Disabled Facilities: None.
Insurance: Clients must obtain third-party insurance by joining BHPA, arranged on arrival at centre. Membership can be obtained for varying periods – 2 days: £8; 3 months: £29; 1 year: £59; and 1 year concessionary membership: £40.
Safety: All instructors certified in first aid.
Affiliations: BHPA; Association of Free Flight Professionals.
Tariffs: Tandem (2-person) flight: £40; 1-day introductory course: £55; weekend introductory course: £110; 4-day Student Pilot course: £200; 4–5-day Club Pilot course: £220 (50% refund if canopy bought through centre).
Booking: Deposit required: £60 for 4-day course, £45 for weekend course, £30 for 1-day course. If cancellation notice received less than 7 days in advance, 10% charge made. If flights cancelled due to bad weather, will be rebooked for a later date. Bookings are normally made in advance, but bookings up to 24 hours in advance can sometimes be accepted.
Access: 2 miles from Marlborough on the A4. Trains and buses available to Marlborough; pick-ups can be arranged by centre. Contact them for more details.

paramania

15 Broad St
New Radnor
Powys
LD8 2SP
Wales
Tel (01544) 350 375

The long high ridges of the Radnor Hills dividing England and Wales are excellent soaring country. Paramania is based at the foot of the hills and offers courses from introductory level up to Club Pilot. It also runs the Welsh Borders Paragliding Club, which offers more informal tuition on to higher levels. Paramania is quite party-oriented – while the training is serious, the après-soaring is riotous. You can get good beer in New Radnor. The only drawback is that you need your own transport to get to and from the flight sites each day. Once you become really good, you can sign up for one of Paramania's paragliding holidays in Spain. If you decide to buy your own paraglider, the school also operates as a dealership, for both new and second-hand equipment, and will help you get kitted out with the right level of gear.

Season: April to October.
Accommodation: Camping or B&B arranged locally. Prices not included in course tariffs.
Food: Not provided.
Children: Over-16s only.
Disabled Facilities: None.
Insurance: Clients must obtain third-party insurance by joining BHPA. Membership can be obtained for varying periods – 2 days: £8; 3 months: £29; 1 year: £59; and 1 year concessionary membership: £40.
Safety: First-aid-trained staff. Clients driven to hospital if necessary.
Affiliations: BHPA.
Tariffs: 2-day introductory course costs £117 or £145 if you want it to include a Student Pilot licence, which may be taken within 3 months of starting the course. A straight 4-day Student Pilot course costs £195. A 4–6-day Club Pilot course costs £52 per day.
Booking: Full payment 14 days before start date of course. If you cancel, a handling charge of 10% will be deducted from the refund. Group discounts are available: 5% for groups of 5 and over, 10% for groups of 10 and over.
Access: New Radnor is signposted from the A44 between Leominster and Pen y Bont. Clients must have their own transport.

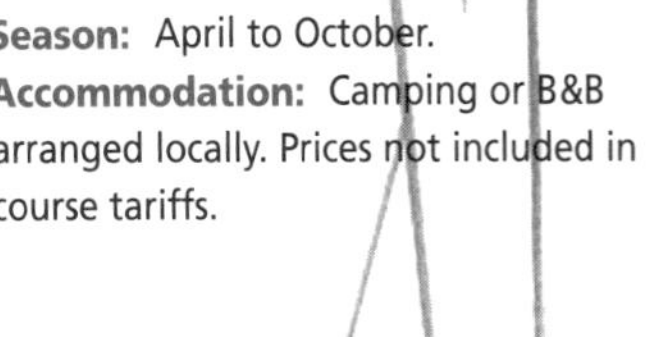

peak paragliding school

161 Abbey Brook Drive
Sheffield
S8 7UT
Tel & Fax (0114) 274 8796

This school has been open for 10 years now and its courses include 7 hours of tuition per day. A BHPA-affiliated school, it gets you flying over the Derbyshire Peaks, about 15 minutes away from the centre by car. Although the school has no accommodation, it will arrange local accommodation at any budget and pick you up for the day's tuition. You provide your own lunch on the hill.

This is a serious school. For example, its 4-day beginners' course includes a short exam on flight theory as well as the practicalities of flying, but the standards are reputedly very high. If you are thinking of taking the sport up seriously or becoming an instructor, this is a good place to go.

Season: Open all year.
Accommodation: No on-site accommodation. Centre will provide help in obtaining local accommodation.
Food: Not provided.
Children: Anyone under 18 must have consent of parents.
Disabled Facilities: None.
Insurance: Clients must obtain third-party insurance by joining BHPA. Membership can be obtained for varying periods – 2 days: £8; 3 months: £29; 1 year: £59; and 1 year concessionary membership: £40.
Safety: All instructors are St John's-certified.
Affiliations: BHPA; Royal Aero Club; Fédération Aéronautique Internationale.
Tariffs: 1-day taster: £55 (including insurance); 2-day course: £90; 4-day course: £180. (Discounts for group bookings.)
Booking: Booking at least 24 hours in advance; 50% deposit required. If cancellation notice received at least 7 days in advance, deposit may be applied to a later booking (no refunds). If flights cancelled due to bad weather, will be rebooked for a later date but no refunds will be given. All bookings are valid for 1 year.
Access: Centre is in Sheffield, but meeting point for flights is on Hope Valley Road (A625). Trains available to Hope station, and pick-ups can be arranged by centre. Contact them for more details.

sheffield hang gliding and paragliding centre

Cliffside
Church Street
Tideswell
Derbyshire
SK17 8PE
Tel & Fax (01298) 872 313

Stephen Hudson, the chief flying instructor at the Sheffield centrel, has been para- and hang-gliding for about 12 years and has competed for Britain. He offers the standard 'taster' weekend, recommended before you sign up for the 5-day Elementary Pilot certificate. All equipment is included in the tariffs.

The Sheffield centre flies over the Peak District National Park – one of 3 hang-gliding and paragliding outfits in the area. Courses are offered to all levels, including cross-country courses. There are no residential courses – you stay in local B&Bs and are picked up by minibus each morning for the 5-mile drive to the training slopes. If you don't have transport, Stephen will pick you up from the train station at Hope, on the Manchester–Sheffield line.

The Sheffield centre also sells the full range of equipment, new and second-hand, as well as operating a repair and overhauling service.

Tariffs: 2-day taster courses and 5-day Elementary Pilot courses available. Tuition is £45 per day, including use of equipment. Group discounts available.

See Hang-gliding (p. 193) for full details.

sussex hang gliding and paragliding ltd

16 Scarborough Road
Brighton
Sussex
BN1 5NR
Tel (01273) 888 443
Fax (01273) 880 572

A handy place to reach from London and the south-east, this school on the South Downs offers beginner, recreational and BHPA pilot certificate courses up to Club Pilot level. With a clubhouse and office in Brighton, it is a fairly large school, employing between 10 and 12 instructors depending on the season. You get about 6 hours of tuition per day. They claim that from the first morning of a course 'you will be harnessed into a paraglider and you will achieve your first tethered flights', i.e. catch an up-draught off a slope but stay in one place, held there by ropes while your teacher shouts instructions.

There are weekend and 3-day introductory courses, 5-day Elementary and Club Pilot courses. The school will help you to find accommodation in Brighton, and will drive you out to the training slopes each morning from the clubhouse on Crescent Road.

Tariffs: Fees include instruction and use of equipment. 1-day taster: £65 (includes insurance); 2-day taster course: £100; 5-day Elementary Pilot or Club Pilot certificate: £215 / £240.

See Hang-gliding (p. 195) for full details.

wiltshire hang-gliding and paragliding centre

The Old Barn
Rhyls Lane
Lockeridge
Marlborough
Wiltshire
SN8 4EE
Tel (01672) 861 555

This school offers courses from beginner level to Club Pilot on flights over the Marlborough Downs. With 3 full-time BHPA-qualified instructors, this is a good place to head for from London or Bristol, being a short drive from the M4 and the rail network. There is no accommodation, however, although the school will arrange accommodation for clients in Marlborough, whether hotel, B&B or camping, and pick them up free of charge, taking them by minibus up onto the downs.

Courses range from 1-day 'tasters' to 4-day Student Pilot certificates. Remember to wear boots with ankle support and to pack your own lunch each day.

Tariffs: 1-day introductory course: £65 (£55 weekdays); 2-day introductory course: £120 (£100 weekdays); 4-day Student Pilot course: £220 (£190 weekdays); Club Pilot courses: £55 per day (£45 weekdays).

See Hang-gliding (p. 197) for full details.

kitting yourself out

Almost all the BHPA-accredited schools sell kit, so if you decide to take up paragliding seriously you can buy all you need through the school where you are taking your pilot courses. As with the tariffs for courses, kit prices are fairly constant from school to school.

The most important item of equipment is the canopy, and this is a big expense. A good canopy will cost between £2,000 and £3,000. Canopies differ slightly in the 'heaviness' or 'lightness' of their braking systems, and this is the criterion by which most people make their choices. Good brands to buy are the UP Range (German-made), the Nova Range (also German) and Airwave (British-made). Once you have bought a canopy, you will need to have it inspected about once every 6 months at a BHPA-accredited school.

Next you will need a harness. Recommended for comfort is the French Sup'air design, so successful that it is now used by many different companies. A good Sup'air harness will cost between £200 and £450.

Getting the right flying suit is important. What you're looking for is warmth, as even in summer it can be very cold up at cloud base. Many instructors swear by the Skywear (German) and Skysystems (British) suits. An unlined suit costs around £100, while a fully lined one will set you back about £250. With the suit you will need a helmet. The main choice here is between open-face or full-face; for a good design choose anything in the Fly range (Italian). An open-face helmet costs around £60, and a full-face between £100 and £150.

It is definitely safer, though not compulsory, to carry a reserve parachute. This is particularly useful if flying abroad in higher mountain ranges where the thermals are stronger and the air currents more turbulent. There is a very broad range of reserve parachutes to choose from, so it is best to ask your instructor for his or her particular recommendation. Expect to pay £350+. You should have the reserve parachute inspected once a year at a good school.

Although first-timers can get away with good hiking boots, if you're planning to fly seriously, it's best to buy proper paragliding boots, which have extra ankle support, are waterproof and have no hooks or laces. Salomon, who also manufacture ski boots, offer good flying boots for around £110 a pair.

Finally, if you're intending to try for any records, or if you simply want to know how high you have been, you can buy an electronic altimeter. The best of these have audio and visual indications and come with a barograph, which will produce an on-screen graph for you after your flight, showing exactly how high and how far you have been. Altimeters cost about £200+ for a basic model, and around £600 with the barograph. Again, get your instructor to recommend a particular brand, as there are several good ones on the market.

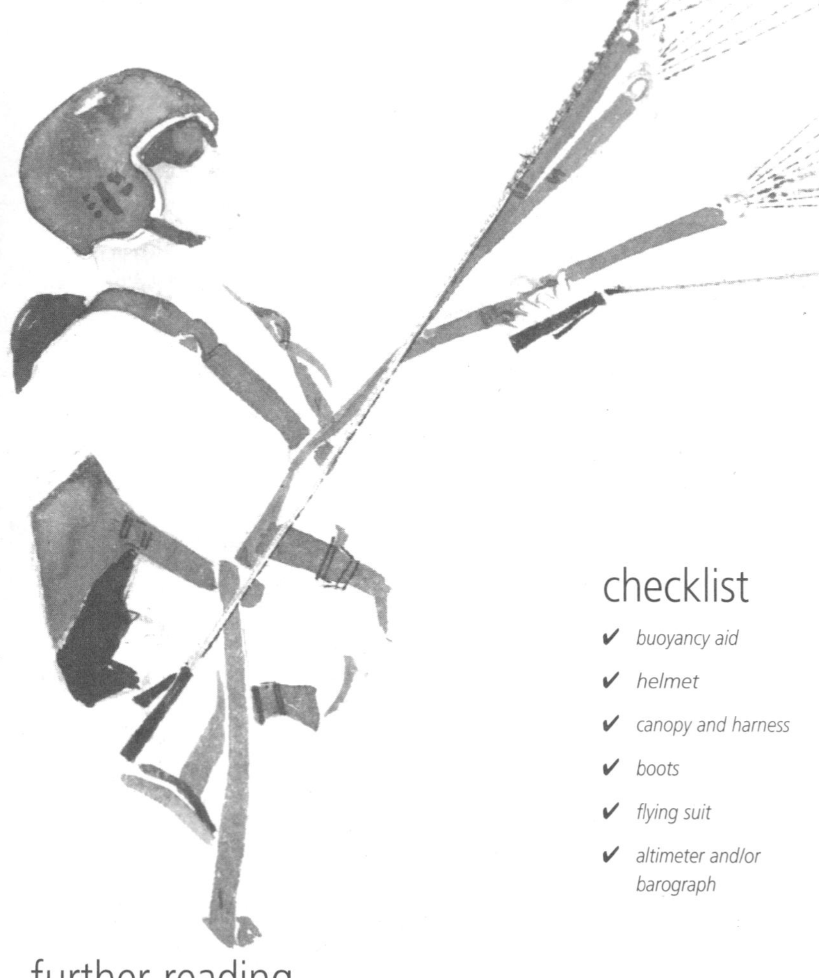

checklist

- ✔ *buoyancy aid*
- ✔ *helmet*
- ✔ *canopy and harness*
- ✔ *boots*
- ✔ *flying suit*
- ✔ *altimeter and/or barograph*

further reading

A Beginner's Guide to Airsports, Keith Carey, A & C Black, 1994; *Paragliding: The Complete Book*, Noel Withall, Springfield Books, 1993; *Touching Cloudbase*, Ian Currer, Air Supplies, 1996; *Hang Gliding Flying Skills*, Noel Whittall, Springfield Books, 1993.

governing body

The Royal Yachting Association (RYA)
RYA House, Romsey Road, Eastleigh
Hampshire SO50 9YA
Tel (01703) 629 962
Fax (01703) 629 924

photo: Andrew Holt

powerboating

Powerboats are basically designed for taking divers far out to sea and bringing them back again quickly. They are also used in rescue and recovery work, as security back-ups to non-motorized sea-going craft such as sea canoes and windsurfers, and as water ski and parascending tow boats.

Handling a powerboat is not easy, and can be dangerous. For this reason, the Royal Yachting Association (RYA) has devised a series of proficiency courses to limit the number of cowboys on the water. There are 4 certificates, known as RYA Levels 1–4. Level 1 is a 1-day introductory course and is usually taken as part of a Level 2 course, which involves picking up a mooring, anchoring, man overboard procedure, handling at speed, and a first introduction to navigation and piloting.

Level 3 (the Safety Boat Course) covers techniques for rescuing dinghies, windsurfers and canoes. It is applicable to drivers of safety boats at sailing clubs or sailing schools who may be required to rescue individual sailors and their craft or whole fleets of boats.

Level 4, the Advanced Course, is designed for experienced drivers who wish to use their boats in more challenging conditions than are catered for in the Level 2 course. It covers subjects such as high-speed and rough-weather boat-handling, pilotage at night, and passage-planning.

selected centres

calshot activities centre

Calshot Spit
Fawley
Southampton
Hampshire
S04 1BR
Tel (01703) 892 077
Fax (01703) 891 267

Calshot's powerboating weekends are aimed at taking you in 2 days through one of the RYA's powerboating certificates, from Level 1 – the introduction to powerboating – to powerboat instructor. The courses are aimed at prospective boat owners and teach not only boat handling but maintenance and emergency procedures.

You can either stay at the Calshot centre – in shared bunkrooms eating rather institutional food – or arrange, by yourself or through the centre, for accommodation to suit your own budget. The powerboating courses are held in the sheltered waters of the Solent and are ideal if you live in the South and are looking for a weekend break.

Season: April to November.
Affiliations: RYA.
Tariffs: Course fees are either non-residential (NR) (including tuition, equipment, lunch and dinner), or residential (R) (including tuition, equipment, accommodation and full board). 1-day introductory course: £65; weekend courses: £135 (NR) / £150 (R). 3-day instruction course: £185 (NR) / £210 (R).

See Windsurfing (p. 456) for full details.

falmouth school of sailing

The Boat Park
Grove Place
Falmouth
Cornwall
TR11 4AU
Tel (01326) 373 203 / 211 311

This Falmouth school offers powerboating courses from RYA Level 1 to Level 4, including training and assessment for the relevant certificates. You can also sit an International Certificate of Competence exam if you plan to sail abroad. This is for people who have already attained RYA Level 4 and have bought and equipped their own boat. The certificate is required if you wish to charter a powerboat in a foreign country.

The centre has various types of on-site accommodation, but can also help you find alternative places to stay. You will need your own transport to get to and fro.

Affiliations: RYA.
Tariffs: Prices include tuition and use of equipment. Prices vary according to season. 1-day RYA Level 1 course: £85–90; 2-day Level 2 course: £150–160; advanced 2-day course: £155–165.

See Sailing (p. 347) for full details.

the island cruising club

Island Street
Salcombe
Devon
TQ8 8DR
Tel (01548) 843 481
Fax (01548) 843 929

This is a big sailing outfit, with up to 30 instructors in the height of the summer season. The powerboat courses are something of a sideline, but are nonetheless very well run, with instruction up to RYA Level 4. All courses are run over 2 days mid-week or weekends and are fully residential – the club can accommodate up to 100 people in its comfortable double rooms. As well as the RYA certificate courses, once you have attained Level 3 you can sit the International Certificate of Competence, which entitles you to charter a powerboat anywhere in the world.

Affiliations: British Canoe Union; RYA.
Tariffs: Prices include tuition, equipment, insurance and full-board accommodation. Prices vary according to season. RYA Level 1 and 2 powerboat course (2 days): £100–120; RYA Level 3 Club Rescue course (2 days): £100–120; RYA Level 4 Fleet Rescue course (2 days): £100–120; RYA First Aid course (1 day): £80.

See Sailing (p. 351) for full details.

lea valley watersports centre

Banbury Reservoir
Greaves Pumping Station
North Circular Road
Chingford
Essex
E4 8QB
Tel (0181) 531 1129
Fax (0181) 527 0969

Based just outside East London, this centre offers powerboating from beginner to instructor level – 6 courses in all (non-residential), 1–3 days. The basic RYA certificates may be taken from Levels 1–4. After that, the instructor course is open to those with several years' powerboating experience, while the International Certificate of Competence allows you to charter boats abroad. The centre has been running for 23 years and employs up to 13 instructors.

Affiliations: RYA – Powerboating.
Tariffs: All prices include tuition and use of equipment. RYA Level 1 (1 day): £50; RYA Level 2 or 3 (2 days): £100; RYA Powerboat Instructor course (3 days): £155; RYA First Aid course (1 day): £25; Junior Introduction to Watersports course (2 days): £55. Discounts for club members.

See Water Skiing and Wet Biking (p. 440) for full details.

national watersports centre, cumbrae

Burnside Road
Largs
North Ayrshire
KA30 8RW
Scotland
Tel (01475) 674 666
Fax (01475) 674 720

Cumbrae's powerboating courses take people from complete beginners and, over 3 sets of 2-day residential courses, up to RYA Level 4 powerboat handlers. From this point they can organize private tuition with the school for training in rescue and fleet control – important qualifications for anyone wanting to get into sailing or diving instruction. Tuition is given in 4.5m and 5.5m Tornadoes, Commandos and an 8.1m launch.

Children: Must be 14 or older.
Affiliations: RYA.
Tariffs: All prices include tuition, equipment and full-board accommodation. 2-day Level 2 course: £125; 2-day Level 3 / 4 course: £85.

See Sailing (p. 355) for full details.

peninsula watersports

Higher Coombe Park
Lewdown
Okehampton
Devon
EX20 4QT
Roadford Lake, Devon
Tel (01409) 211 507
Stithians Lake, Cornwall
Tel (01209) 860 301
Upper Tamar Lake, Cornwall
Tel (01288) 321 712
Siblyback Lake, Cornwall
Tel (01579) 346 522

Of Peninsula's 4 West County centres, Roadford, Stithians and Siblyback offer powerboating, with courses for RYA Levels 1–3. Almost all the courses are run at weekends: a Level 1 course usually takes 2 days, while more advanced courses take up the weekend plus an extra day, and can be taken intensively or spread out over a series of evenings. Group and individual bookings are welcome.

None of the centres has accommodation, but they are happy to help you arrange it locally. You will need your own transport to get to and fro.

Affiliations: RYA – Powerboating.
Tariffs: All prices include tuition and use of equipment. RYA certificate courses: £40 per day. Group and family discounts available.

See Windsurfing (p. 465) for full details.

queen mary sailsports

Queen Mary Reservoir
Ashford Road
Ashford
Middlesex
TW15 1UA
Tel (01784) 244 776 / 248 881
Fax (01784) 252 772

Convenient for Londoners who lack the time to travel further afield, this school on the huge Queen Mary Reservoir in London's western industrial area offers 4 very good powerboating courses. The 1-day Introduction to Powerboating course takes you to RYA Level 1, the 2-day National Powerboat Certificate course to Level 2, and the 1-day Club Rescue

Coxswain course to Level 3. If you want to go beyond, the school also offers a Fleet Rescue course (RYA Level 4) over several weekends in the year. Personal tuition can be arranged at any time.

Queen Mary Sailsports is not a residential school, drawing most of its clientele from London and the surrounding area. Therefore most 2-day courses, if not held over weekends, are broken up into a series of evening sessions to make up the requisite hours.

Affiliations: RYA.
Tariffs: Prices include tuition and use of equipment. RYA Level 1: £60; RYA Level 2: £120; RYA Safety Boat: £120. Personal instruction (including equipment): £29 per hour. Group and sibling discounts available.

See Windsurfing (p. 467) for full details.

rockley point sailing centre

Hamworthy
Poole
Dorset
BH15 4LZ
Tel (01202) 677 272
Fax (01202) 668 268

The wide, sheltered waters of Poole Harbour make an ideal training ground for learning to handle a powerboat. Rockley offers a full range of courses from RYA Levels 1 to 4. Level 1 and 2 courses can be taken over a single day, Levels 3 and 4 over 2 or more days. The centre also offers an RYA Small Craft First Aid day course covering the principles of rescue and treatment on the water. If you are in a hurry to get up to a high level of skill, you should consider one of Rockley's Intensive Training courses of 14 to 18 weeks during which you can go beyond the basic RYA levels and gain up to 3 instructor qualifications as well. Otherwise Junior Instructor, Assistant Instructor and Instructor courses are offered in their own right, lasting between 7 and 20 days each.

Affiliations: RYA.
Tariffs: Prices include instruction and use of equipment. 1-day powerboat course: £130; 2-day powerboat course: £195; 1-day Level 2 assessment: £60.

See Sailing (p. 362) for full details.

shadwell basin project

Shadwell Pierhead
Glamis Road
London
E1 9EE
Tel (0171) 481 4210
Fax (0171) 481 0624

Based in London's Docklands, this has to be one of the cheapest places anywhere at which to learn powerboating. Beginners start with a 3-day introductory course (held over 3 successive evenings), which gains them their RYA Level 1 and 2 certificates, then move on to RYA Level 3 (coxswain), also over 3 days.

The courses are non-residential, and you will have to arrange your own transport to get to and fro.

Tariffs: 3-day RYA Level 1 course: £50; RYA Level 2: £100; RYA Level 3 (coxswain): £110; personal instruction by the hour: £30. Prices include equipment and tuition only.
Booking: Deposit required, non-refundable. 50% of course fee due if cancellation notice received less than 4 weeks in advance. Late bookings accepted if space available.

See Child and Youth Sports (p. 72) for full details.

uist outdoor centre

Cearn Dusgaidh
Lochmaddy
Isle of North Uist
Western Isles
PA82 5AE
Scotland
Tel (01876) 500 480

Although primarily a diving, sea canoeing and climbing centre, Uist also offers boat-handling courses in its own 5.8m Fury inflatable, which is equipped with a 90hp engine. You can take a powerboating course lasting anything from a day to a week, with instruction on the open ocean and in sea loch conditions. The centre has its own bunkhouse overlooking a small sea loch (look out for otters through the kitchen window), but can arrange local accommodation to suit your budget should you need it.

Season: Open all year.

Tariffs: Prices include instruction, equipment and accommodation. 1-week holiday (boat-handling only or combined with other centre activities): £220 (self-catering) / £270 (with full board). Day visitors: £25.

See Sub-Aqua Diving (p. 397) for full details.

windsport international ltd

Mylor Yacht Harbour
Falmouth
Cornwall
TR11 5UF
Tel (01326) 376 191
Fax (01326) 376 192

Windsport's Falmouth centre offers powerboating both as part of a general multi-activity package that includes water skiing, sailing, windsurfing and surfing, and on its own as specialist group courses lasting 5 days. You can also obtain private tuition towards the various RYA powerboating certificates, choosing between lessons on student-to-instructor ratios of 1:1 or 2:1.

The courses are run either residentially or non-residentially as you like, and there is a variety of accommodation: a sliding scale of course fees reflects the level of comfort you want – from B&B to camping.

Tariffs: Powerboating is one of the activities offered in the centre's multi-activity packages. 5-day family, child or adult course: £125 (adult), £95 (child); weekend family course: £48 (adult), £38 (child); 1-day family or child course: £25 (adult), £20 (child); 1-day adult course: £48. Residential packages are also available (including tuition, equipment and accommodation); prices vary according to level of accommodation chosen (hotel, guest house, farmhouse or camping). 5-day course (6 nights' accommodation): £365–545; weekend course (2 nights' accommodation): £220–280. Group discounts available.

See Sailing (p. 366) for full details.

kitting yourself out

There are three main types of powerboat – small inflatables (usually called RIBs), slightly larger Doreys (flat-bottomed fibreglass boats), and big launches of 16ft or over.

The two main RIB boats available in the UK are Avon Sea Riders and Zodiacs. These cost about £2,000 with a 50hp engine (Honda, Kawasaki, Johnson, Mariner or Mercury). Doreys, which are usually around 13ft long, are made by Dell Quay or WITH and also take a 40–50hp engine. Prices for new Doreys and an engine start at around £3,000. Larger launches are very expensive – you won't get away with much less than £6,000–7,000 for a hull and engine. There is such a variety of hulls available that it is best to speak to someone at a powerboating centre and discuss your specific needs before buying. These boats have inboard motors, but you still have to buy them separately if you are buying new. Beta Marine, also known as Kabota, are widely recommended.

Second-hand powerboats are obviously a cheaper option, and technically it is possible to kit yourself out with a RIB or Dorey in goodish nick for around £1,500. However, as always there are pitfalls. Buy through a school and have any craft vetted by your instructor.

An anchor and rope from a good chandler's cost around £250, while a decent buoyancy aid – America's Cup are popular among instructors – retails at something over £50. Tool kits for the motor (including spare oil filters and spark plugs – these are a must), with paddles and a good torch, can be bought from a boat dealership or through a school and together cost around £100. For safety, carry a pair of hand-held red flares in the tool kit – price around £40.

For VHF radios – and you should not own your own boat until you have taken an RYA VHF radio course – try the ICOM range. Expect to pay around £250 for a decent hand-held model.

checklist

- ✔ *tool kit*
- ✔ *boat and motor*
- ✔ *torch*
- ✔ *anchor and rope*
- ✔ *paddles*
- ✔ *buoyancy aid*
- ✔ *wet bags*
- ✔ *VHF radio*

photo: Acorn Activities

related activities

bog snorkelling
human bowling
base jumping
gut barging
dwyle flunking
cheese rolling
naked sports
rap diving
paintball
catapulting
bridge swinging

bungee jumping

WAAAAAAAAAAAAAAAAAAAAAAAAAAH! Quite what draws people to this simulation of suicide is a question for the psychologist. But bungee jumping is definitely addictive, despite the utterly indescribable fear that it inspires. Even fairly seasoned jumpers admit to wishing they hadn't put themselves in this situation when standing on the brink of the void.

According to veteran jumpers, bungee jumping soon palls, so several variations have evolved in recent years – among them mountain biking off a bridge or tower on a bungee cord, bungie catapulting, and bridge swinging.

selected centres

uk bungee club

Battersea Wharf
Queenstown Road
Battersea
London
SW8 4NP
Tel (0171) 720 9496
Fax (0171) 627 8861

You don't have to be in London to do the jump – though the club has a permanent jump tower on the south side of Chelsea Bridge. Jumps are also organized at various locations around the country, along with catapulting and extreme abseiling from 350ft. The club also organizes trips to France for canyon jumping, and to Zimbabwe for the famous Zambezi Bridge jump – the highest in the world. If you really want to get into the sport, you can also train through the club for the annual Extreme Games, which took place last year in New Zealand. These include freestyle events such as jumping with a mountain bike or surfboard. Mad, but something else to do because it's there. A jump costs £50. Discounts for club members and groups. Visa, Mastercard, Access and American Express cards accepted.

acorn activities

PO Box 120
Hereford
Hereford & Worcester
HR4 8YB
Tel (01432) 830 083
Fax (01432) 830 110

Acorn offer a choice of ordinary bungee jumping and, for real suicideros, bungee catapulting, in which you are fired 100ft into the air with, according to the brochure (the editor having been too chicken to try it), an acceleration greater than that of a Formula 1 racing car. Yikes! If you decide to be a stick-in-the-mud and go for the traditional jump, you will fall 180ft before bouncing. The first jump/catapult costs £40; a second jump/catapult costs £20.

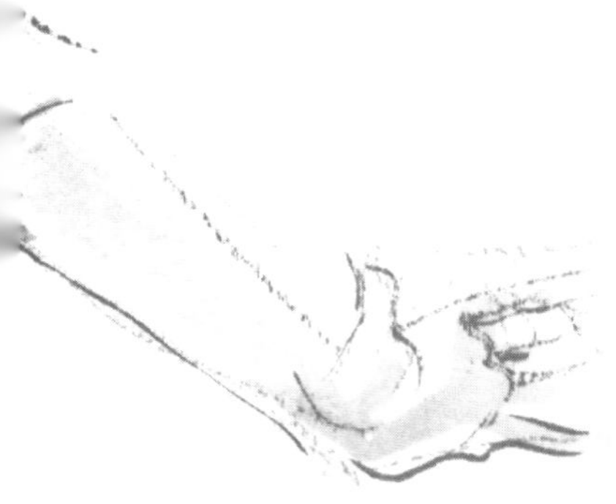

As far as gear is concerned, all you have to bring is yourself, at a minimum of 6.5 stone, and a maximum of 30 stone. If you are under 18 you need a parent or guardian present, or to have written permission from them.

The location for the jumps sometimes changes; it is usually in the Hereford & Worcester/Shropshire area, but sometimes in mid-Wales. Call Acorn for the latest details.

As if bungee jumping and catapulting were not enough, there is also bridge swinging, which involves bungeeing off a bridge to the side, rather than straight down. The idea is to build up sufficient velocity and momentum to swing underneath the bridge and up again on the other side. How you stop yourself from concertina-ing yourself Looney Tunes-style the instructors will no doubt tell you. Presumably it must be possible. There are no organized centres offering the sport, only a club. Contact the Brigsters Bridgeswinging Club, 79 Stricklandgate, Kendal, Cumbria LA9 4LT, tel (01539) 740 088.

bog snorkelling

Every August bank holiday, people flock from all over Wales (and, increasingly, from England) to enter the Neuadd Arms Hotel bog snorkelling race. The original bog has had a 60m-long trench cut into it and competitors must swim 2 lengths, face down and using only a snorkel to breathe, through the water, which Mr Green, the owner of the hotel, describes as 'pretty dirty'. You are expected to provide your own snorkel and flippers and to be in reasonably good physical shape. You'll need to be to win: the fastest time so far is 2 minutes, 11 seconds for the 2 lengths – a record set by a member of an English all-girl underwater hockey (octopushy) team. Octopushy, as a discipline related to bog snorkelling, has taken off in recent years, and there is now a national league – so be aware that you'll be up against semi-professional competition when you enter the bog. The contact address is Red Kite Activity Centre, Neuadd Arms Hotel, Llanwrtyd Wells, Powys LD5 4RB, tel (01591) 610 236.

human bowling

A bit of a joke, this one: one player climbs inside the ball, is strapped securely into the seat with a body harness, and is rolled at a set of pins standing 15 feet away, knocking over as many as possible. This is done in an indoor barn at an outdoor centre in Cumbria. They have all the equipment; just bring yourself and your friends, and try to do it on an empty stomach.

As with bog snorkelling, at the time of writing there was only one place the editor could find offering human bowling, but things may have changed by the time of publication. The Rookin House Centre may be able to find you a more local venue. The contact address is Rookin House Farm Riding & Activity Centre, Rookin House Farm, Troutbeck, Penrith, Cumbria CA11 0SS, tel (017684) 83561, fax (017684) 83276.

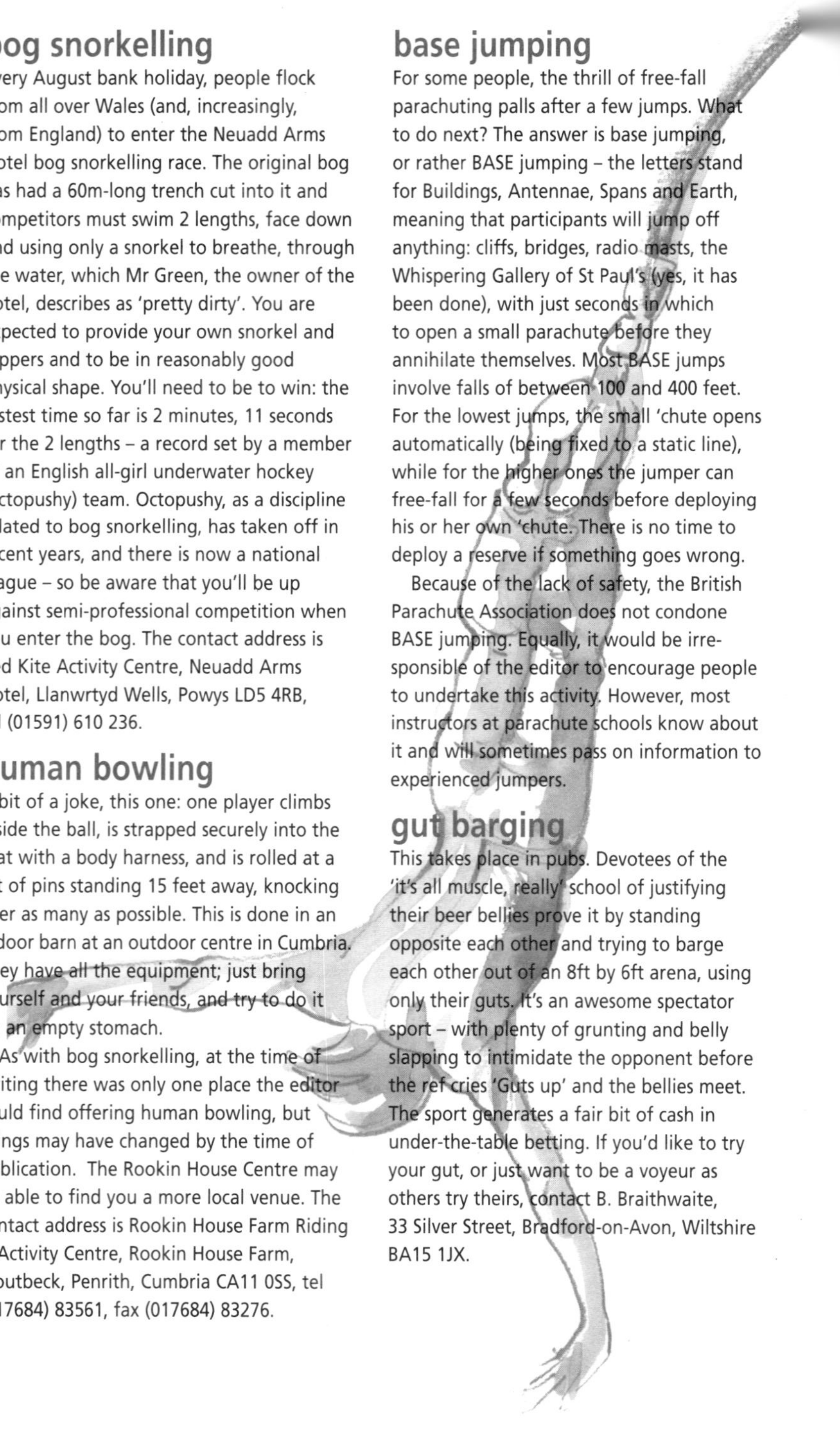

base jumping

For some people, the thrill of free-fall parachuting palls after a few jumps. What to do next? The answer is base jumping, or rather BASE jumping – the letters stand for Buildings, Antennae, Spans and Earth, meaning that participants will jump off anything: cliffs, bridges, radio masts, the Whispering Gallery of St Paul's (yes, it has been done), with just seconds in which to open a small parachute before they annihilate themselves. Most BASE jumps involve falls of between 100 and 400 feet. For the lowest jumps, the small 'chute opens automatically (being fixed to a static line), while for the higher ones the jumper can free-fall for a few seconds before deploying his or her own 'chute. There is no time to deploy a reserve if something goes wrong.

Because of the lack of safety, the British Parachute Association does not condone BASE jumping. Equally, it would be irresponsible of the editor to encourage people to undertake this activity. However, most instructors at parachute schools know about it and will sometimes pass on information to experienced jumpers.

gut barging

This takes place in pubs. Devotees of the 'it's all muscle, really' school of justifying their beer bellies prove it by standing opposite each other and trying to barge each other out of an 8ft by 6ft arena, using only their guts. It's an awesome spectator sport – with plenty of grunting and belly slapping to intimidate the opponent before the ref cries 'Guts up' and the bellies meet. The sport generates a fair bit of cash in under-the-table betting. If you'd like to try your gut, or just want to be a voyeur as others try theirs, contact B. Braithwaite, 33 Silver Street, Bradford-on-Avon, Wiltshire BA15 1JX.

dwyle flunking

Every year in the village of Pill in Somerset local young men from rival communities engage in ritual combat for possession of a beer-soaked rag (the dwyle), upon which the honour of each village depends. The archaic and cryptic scoring system was too complicated for the editor's limited brain to grasp. We advise you to leave well alone, but if you are of a psychotic disposition, contact Adrian Lovett-Turner at the White Swan pub in Twickenham, London, to find out how to join in.

cheese rolling

Less violent than dwyle flunking but stranger, this involves rolling great round Double Gloucester cheeses downhill. The one whose cheese goes furthest wins all the cheeses. No doubt it has its roots in some prehistoric earth ritual. The annual event takes place at the village of Painswick near Gloucester. Head into any of the pubs down there and they'll be glad to tell you how to enter.

naked sports

Despite global warming, Britain's climate is unkind to the unclothed. While the regular hot summers on the Continent have produced a nudist culture that no longer raises eyebrows (or anything else) over there, with plenty of nude sporting activity – especially windsurfing, water skiing and other water sports – on offer, Britain's climate cannot be relied upon. Those who go outside without clothes on therefore risk all kinds of danger, from assault to arrest – or a simple cold.

However, there are a few informal groups which get together for nude hillwalking in North Yorkshire and the Lakes. Similarly, there are a few nude canoers getting together along the coasts and rivers. There is also at least one company known to the author offering nude scuba diving, but as only a PO box address is given, the author invites readers to inform him as to whether this involves trips in Britain or abroad.

In the interests of security, this guide cannot supply any direct contact numbers for British naked adventure sports, but anyone seriously interested should phone a nudist outdoor publishing company called Coast and Country on (01723) 503 456. However, you should expect to undergo a fairly rigorous vetting process before being put in touch with anyone.

rap diving

This is abseiling in reverse – that is, instead of going down feet first, you go down head first, trying to balance yourself horizontally on the rock-face using your feet. Not good for people with vertigo. For more details, contact Scope, a charity that organizes rap diving for fund-raising purposes, on (01345) 69769.

paintball

Ever wanted to play soldiers? Now's your chance. Paintball has all the attributes of comic-book war – battle without death, atrocity, bombed cities, dead civilians and the like – based on running about in the woods (or in a warehouse) with a gun, firing pellets of paint at your opposing 'team'. These pellets can hurt when they hit, and for this reason you wear a mask and are told not to fire at close range – though everybody does.

Your objective is to capture the opposing team's flag, killing as many of them as is necessary. It's great fun, but don't wear your best clothes.

There are now dozens of centres around the country offering both indoor and outdoor paintballing. The average cost of a day is about £17–20 per person, but group bookings often get discounts. Standard extras are 100 paintballs at £7–10 and hire of more sophisticated guns at £3–5. Contact *Paintball International* magazine to find out who is in your area.

As yet there is no central governing body for paintball, but you can ensure your own safety by only booking with a centre that is a member of the British Safety Council.

governing body

Royal Yachting Association (RYA)

RYA House, Romsey Road, Eastleigh
Hampshire SO50 9YA
Tel (01703) 629 962
Fax (01703) 629 924

photo: Acorn Activitie

sailing

dinghies
yachts
catamarans
keelboats

Like, say, riding or falconry, there is something vocational about sailing – at its highest level it's not really something you do part-time. Learning the mysteries of ocean and wind, sea navigation and survival is a lifetime's work. And then there's the jargon – sailing is another pursuit that has its own language, understood only by the priesthood who practise it. However, it is becoming increasingly possible to practise recreational sailing – especially in dinghies – as a hobby rather than as a religion. What grabs everyone is the aesthetic – the shape of the boats, the tall mast and sails, the endless battle with the weather and the moods and colours of the water.

Probably the best way to start is in a dinghy, a small, fast boat designed for both open water and tidal creeks, which offers real bend-back-out-over-the-water excitement when running before the wind. There are probably as many inland reservoir dinghy schools now as there are coastal ones. Always pick a school that is recognized by the Royal Yachting Association (RYA). The organization has formulated a set of 5 certificate courses that coax you from unversed novice (what's a gybe, then, or a bilge for that matter?) to relatively skilled sailor, able to skipper your own dinghy. It's worth investing in the RYA's 3 course textbooks if you're planning to get through the various levels smoothly.

Children can learn to sail as well as any adult, and junior certificates are offered by the RYA: Young Sailor Stages 1–4 (advanced), or Optimist Grades 1–3. An Optimist is a junior-sized dinghy that can be safely handled by a beginner or raced by a more experienced young sailor.

After sailing dinghies for a bit, you might decide to try bigger boats, at a school that offers the RYA Assessment Cruises for Competent Crew, Day Skipper and Coastal Skipper certificates. If you attain the RYA's Yachtmaster's Offshore or Yachtmaster's Ocean certificates, you will sit on the right hand of God as far as other sailors are concerned. To pass you must have logged at least 2,500 hours in tidal waters, lived on board a cruising yacht for a minimum of 50 days, have made 5 passages of more than 60 miles, acting as skipper on 2 of them, with 2 other passages being overnight.

Or, if you don't want to work that hard, you could take a charter cruise. Either of these can get you sailing 33ft yachts, catamaran dinghies and other stylish craft and really exploring coastal waters. Once you've learned something about a variety of craft, you might want to go back to a Laser dinghy and try for a RYA Racing certificate, which teaches you specific speed techniques such as roll turning, boat-tuning and how to read a course. If you have your sights set on teaching, the 6-day RYA Instructor's course teaches you how to handle powerboats as well as learner-sailors. If you are already an experienced sailor and want to have instruction in your own boat, then a sailing school with experienced Yachtmaster instructors will be able to help you improve your skills.

selected centres

adventure sports

Carnkie Farmhouse
Carnkie
Redruth
Cornwall
TR16 6RZ
Tel (01209) 218 962 / (0589) 427 077

Dinghy Sailing

Carnkie offers a general introduction to dinghy sailing rather than specialist courses and holidays. The centre is therefore a good place at which to get a feel for the sport, but is not somewhere to go if you're intent on getting through the various RYA certificates. Sailing here is offered as part of a multi-activity package that includes windsurfing, surfing, rock climbing and abseiling, water skiing and/or paragliding. There are 2-day, 5-day and 7-day holidays on offer, all self-catering, and the centre has 3 full-time instructors (RYA-qualified) who offer 8 hours of tuition per day. The clientele is mainly drawn from people in their mid-20s. The centre will pick up people without their own transport from Falmouth, for a small charge.

Tariffs: Sailing is one of the activities offered in the centre's multi-activity package deals (accommodation included). Prices are variable, depending on season and type of accommodation desired: £44–78 for 2 nights / 2 activities; £150–195 for 5 nights / 5 activities; £154–273 for 7 nights / 7 activities. Group, long-term-stay, and previous-customer discounts available. Single persons desiring their own room must pay a 30% surcharge.

See Paragliding and Parascending (p. 310) for full details.

alba yacht services ltd

Dunstaffnage Yacht Haven
Oban
Argyll & Bute
PA37 1PX
Scotland
Tel (01631) 565 630 / 564 004
Fax (01631) 565 620

Yachts

Alba operate as both a sailing school and a yacht charter company. Their RYA sailing courses run over a week at a time and can take you through the first few certificates – Competent Crew, Day Skipper and Coastal Skipper. If you are already an experienced yachtsperson, it's worth chartering one of Alba's fleet for a journey up to the Inner and Outer Hebrides. There is quite a choice of craft: Moodys, Westerleys, Beneteaus and Sigmas. If you are qualified, you can skipper the yacht yourself. Otherwise, take along one of Alba's instructors.

Season: April to September.
Accommodation: Guests sleep in berths on board the yachts.
Food: Full board provided on RYA courses. Some de luxe cruises offer gourmet cuisine. Yacht charters are self-catering, although frozen meals can be ordered.
Children: Must be 21 to hire boats, but welcome as passengers.
Disabled Facilities: None.

Insurance: Holiday insurance is compulsory for clients; premium is added to invoice.
Safety: All staff trained in first aid.
Affiliations: RYA.
Tariffs: RYA practical courses – Competent Crew, Day Skipper and Coastal Skipper (including tuition and full-board yacht accommodation): £300–500 per person, depending on yacht. Another option is to charter a yacht (self-catering) and hire an RYA instructor for sailing tuition. Instructor fee: £420 per week. 10 different yachts are available for charter. Prices vary between boats and between seasons. Some sample prices are – £400 per week for an 8.1m yacht (2 adult / 2 child berths, early April); £1,100 per week for a 10.3m yacht (7 berths, August); £2,000 per week for a 12.3m de luxe yacht (10 berths, late June). Weekend charters and family rates available; contact centre for details.
Booking: Deposit (paid when booking): £200–600. Security deposit for charters (paid 2 weeks before charter): £200–600. Cancellation charges vary; contact centre for details. Advance booking required. Access and Visa cards accepted.
Access: From Glasgow take the A82 then the A85 to Dunstaffnage, near Oban. Trains and buses to Oban. 2-mile walk (or £3 cab fare) to harbour from stations.

bradwell outdoor education centre

Bradwell Waterside
Southminster
Essex
CM0 7QY
Tel (01621) 776 256
Fax (01621) 776 378

Yacht and Dinghy Sailing

This county council-run centre on the Essex coast runs beginners' and improvers' courses in Wayfarers, Toppers, Oysters and Bradwell 22s, mostly learning in the calm seas of Bradwell Waterside, with a safety boat in attendance. Offshore and continental yacht cruising are also offered on the centre's own Sigma 33 auxiliary sloop. RYA dinghy sailing certificate courses are also available up to Level 5, as well as yacht sailing courses up to Yachtmaster level – contact the centre for details – though in general the centre caters for first-timers. School groups are particularly welcome, and take priority over adult bookings. Because the centre receives government funding, it can afford to keep its prices lower than average. In fact, its only drawback is the ugliness of the building itself – a terrible piece of 1960s concrete-block architecture.

Affiliations: British Canoe Union.
Tariffs: 5-day sailing course (includes tuition, equipment and full-board accommodation): £78; offshore sailing weekend: £90; day activity (includes tuition and equipment): £22. Group and youth discounts available.

See Child and Youth Sports (p. 55-6) for full details.

bray watersports centre

Bray Lake
Monkey Island Lane
Windsor Road
Maidenhead
Berkshire
SL6 2EB
Tel (01628) 38860
Fax (01628) 771 441

Dinghy Sailing, Catamarans

This Thames Valley school offers 2 sets of year-round courses – one set for adults and another for children. The adult courses go from RYA Level 1 up to Level 4, beyond which you can join the centre's sailing club and take advanced tuition. Most of the courses are 2-dayers, run over weekends or, in summer, spread out over evening sessions. Junior courses are run up to RYA Level 3, and are generally run over a series of 4 or 5 half-day sessions, usually at weekends. If you already have some sailing experience, you can take lessons in a lightweight 'Hobie Cat' on an hourly basis. You can also hire Topper and Wayfarer dinghies by the hour, half-day or day.

As most of the centre's clientele come from the Thames Valley and outer West London, the centre has no accommodation. However, if you are passing through and want to sign up for an intensive course, the centre will help you book local accommodation to suit your budget. They also operate as a sales dealership, for both new and second-hand boats and gear.

Children: Junior courses available for children under 14; must be water-confident. Anyone under 18 must have consent of parent or guardian.
Affiliations: RYA.
Tariffs: Prices include tuition and equipment. RYA Level 1: £69; RYA Level 2: £150; RYA Level 3 or 4 course: £180. Junior RYA Stage 1: £16; Junior RYA Stage 2: £55; Junior RYA Stage 3: £60. Hobie lessons: £15–25 per person per hour. Group and youth (14–18) discounts available.

See Windsurfing (p. 455) for full details.

calshot activities centre

Calshot Spit
Fawley
Southampton
Hampshire
S04 1BR
Tel (01703) 892 077
Fax (01703) 891 267

Dinghy Sailing

If you want to learn dinghy sailing, the sheltered waters of the Solent make an ideal base. Calshot Activities Centre runs weekend and 5-day courses for beginners, taking you through RYA Levels 1 and 2 and teaching you how to handle a Topper. There are then individual weekend courses to take you through levels 3 and 4, where you learn basic racing techniques. If you already hold Level 3, you might like to try one of their Laser 2 training weekends, where you learn how to handle a faster boat and are introduced to boat-tuning, trapezing and spinnaker handling skills.

The Advanced Skills course (RYA Level 5) takes people on from recreational sailing and prepares them for the RYA instructor awards, combining racing with the chart work and navigation needed for dinghy cruising.

Calshot also offers instructor courses lasting between 1 and 5 days using Wayfarers and Toppers, and weekend sailing courses for children.

Season: April to September.
Affiliations: RYA.
Tariffs: Course fees are either non-residential (NR) (including tuition, equipment, lunch and dinner), or residential (R) (including tuition, equipment, accommodation and full board). Weekend courses: £95 (NR) / £110 (R); 5-day courses: £210 (NR) / £245 (R). Expedition course: £125. 6-day instructor courses: £190 (NR) / £220 (R). (Special courses for children available at reduced rates.)

See Windsurfing (p. 456) for full details.

---

clyde offshore sailing centre

Kip Marina
Inverkip
Inverclyde
PA16 0AS
Scotland
Tel (01475) 521 210
Fax (01475) 521 572

Yachts

Clyde Offshore operates both as a yacht sailing school and a chartering service for experienced sailors. The full range of RYA courses is on offer: Competent Crew, Day Skipper, Coastal Skipper and Yachtmaster, as well as family sailing courses and own-yacht tuition. As for chartering, Clyde Offshore runs a fleet of 6 small yachts (Elans, Sigmas, Sun Charms and Moodys) for sailing around the Isles. Corporate day cruises are also offered, with sailing out to the islands of Bute and Cumbrae and to Kintyre.

Season: March to November.
Accommodation: Guests sleep in berths aboard yachts.
Food: Full board included; vegetarian and special diets catered for upon request.
Children: Must be 16 or older unless accompanied by parent.
Disabled Facilities: None.
Insurance: Clients should arrange their own holiday insurance.
Safety: All instructors trained in first aid.
Affiliations: National Federation of Sailing Schools; RYA; Sail Scotland; Yacht Charter Association.
Tariffs: Prices include instruction and full-board accommodation on the yachts. Prices vary according to season. 2-day Helmsman motor cruising course: £165–195; 4-day Skipper motor cruising course: £290–400; 5-day RYA sail courses (Competent Crew, Day Skipper or Coastal Skipper): £190–260; 7-day RYA Yachtmaster sail course: £275–350. Discounts for groups and for early bookings.
Booking: 25% deposit required, non-refundable. Balance due 30 days before start of course. In the event of cancellation, client liable for full fees if place not resold. Bookings normally made well in advance, but late bookings accepted if space available. Visa and Access cards accepted.
Access: Off the A78 at Inverkip, between Gourock and Largs. Trains and buses to Inverkip, easy walk to marina.

cornish cruising

Falmouth Yacht Marina
North Parade
Falmouth
Cornwall
TR11 2TD
Tel (01326) 211 800
Fax (01326) 331 809

Yachts

Cornish Cruising operates both as a sailing school and as a pleasure-cruising service, with additional yacht chartering for experienced sailors. The RYA courses take you right from beginner level to the to: 2-day introductory courses, 5-day Competent Crew, Day Skipper and Coastal Skipper courses, week-long Experience and Techniques courses, and finally the Yachtmaster course. The courses can be shore-based or taken intensively aboard. The school employs 5 instructors and aims to give students about 12 hours of tuition per day. There is seldom a student-to-instructor ratio of more than 4:1.

The cruises run from the coast of Cornwall over to Brittany or south-west Ireland. These can be treated as learning breaks or complete holidays, just as you like. As for yacht chartering, the school runs a variety of craft for hire: choose between Van der Stadt and Sadler 34s, a Bavaria 390, a Westerley Merlin 28, an Oysterman 4.5, a Colvic Countess Ketch, an Etap 28i, a Sadler 26, a replica of an old Colin Archer gaff cutter, and a Robert Clark 72ft ketch.

Season: Open all year.
Accommodation: Accommodation is on board yacht for practical courses. Local accommodation can be arranged for shore-based courses.
Food: Full board for practical courses; vegetarian and special diets can be catered for.
Children: Must be 16 or over.
Disabled Facilities: None.
Insurance: Clients should arrange their own holiday insurance; can be arranged through centre.
Safety: Staff are trained in first aid and air/sea rescue.
Affiliations: National Federation of Sea Schools; RYA; Yachting Charter Association.
Tariffs: All prices include on-board accommodation, food and tuition (except shore-based courses). Prices vary according to season (low season: 6 January–7 April and 7 October–15 December; mid season: 8 April–14 July and 9 September–6 October; high season: 15 July–8 September). A large range of yachting courses is offered; some examples are – 2-day introductory course: £125–156; 5-day RYA Competent Crew or Day Skipper course: £286–360; 6-day RYA Coastal Skipper course: £343–434; RYA Yachtmaster preparation and exam (5 days, exam fees not included): £405–535; 6-day shore-based courses: £228–307; 1-day specialist courses (e.g. first aid, meteorology): £45. Group discounts available. Fleet of yachts also available for charter; contact centre for details.
Booking: 25% deposit required. No cancellation charge if notice received 8 weeks in advance, half the deposit lost if received 4–8 weeks in advance, and after that time the full deposit will be lost unless places can be refilled. Balance due 14 days before courses start. Bookings should be made well in advance, but late bookings sometimes accepted if space available. Access and Visa cards accepted.
Access: From Truro take the A39 to Falmouth. Trains from Truro to Falmouth. Pick-ups from station can be arranged by centre.

croft-na-caber

Kenmore
Loch Tay
Perthshire & Kinross
PH15 2HW
Tel (01887) 830 588
Fax (01887) 830 649

Dinghies, Keelboats and Catamarans

Loch Tay is a good place to get to grips with dinghy sailing. Croft-na-Caber provides training from complete beginner standard up to courses equipping you to race dinghies, keelboats – one step down from yachts – and catamarans.

Choose between half-day introductory courses, full-day RYA Level 1 and 2 courses and longer 2–5-day courses for the higher RYA levels. The centre offers accommodation at various budgets, and pretty competitive prices – it is an affordable place to take a sailing holiday. The centre runs a small fleet of dinghies: Wayfarers, Lasers, Toppers, as well as a Drascombe longboat, a Solung 26ft keelboat and a catamaran.

Boat hire for experienced sailors can be arranged, but you will need to provide proof of experience, either from an up-to-date logbook or a relevant RYA certficate.

Season: Year round.
Tariffs: Half-day sailing: £32; full day: £46; 2-day courses: £79; 5-day courses: £162. Prices include equipment and tuition but not accommodation or food. Boat hire for dinghies: £8–12 per hour; £16–24 for 3 hours; £24–36 full day; £12–14, £24–28, £36–42 for larger craft.

See White-water Rafting and Coracles (p. 447) for full details.

down yachts

37 Bayview Road
Killinchy
Newtownards
County Down
BT23 6TW
Northern Ireland
Tel & Fax (01238) 542 210

Yachts

The *Sundowner of Down* is an 8-berth sloop with a 35hp auxiliary engine. Sea-based courses for Competent Crew, Day Skipper and Coastal Skipper are offered in the north Irish Sea and Strangford Lough, with cruising to Scotland and the Western Isles. Most courses last 5 days, but specialist weekend or daily courses can also be arranged. The instructor-to-student ratio does not exceed 1:5.

Season: March to November.
Accommodation: Guests sleep in berths aboard yachts.
Food: Full board included; vegetarian and special diets catered for upon request.
Children: Must be 16 or older unless accompanied by parent.
Disabled Facilities: None.
Insurance: Clients should arrange their own holiday insurance.
Safety: All instructors trained in first aid.
Affiliations: RYA.
Tariffs: Prices include instruction and full-board accommodation on the yachts. Prices vary according to season. 5-day course £220 (low season) or £250 (high season).
Booking: £50 deposit required, non-refundable. Balance due 14 days before start of course. In the event of cancellation, client liable for full fees if place not resold. Bookings normally made well in advance, but late bookings accepted if space available. Payment by cash or cheque.
Access: Based in Bangor and Strangford Lough. Contact centre for full details.

eagle quest

Lowgrove Farm
Millbeck
Keswick
Cumbria
CA12 4PS
Tel (017687) 75351
Fax (017687) 75763

Dinghy Sailing for Beginners

This is a good place at which to try out sailing, to see if you like it before investing in a proper course. Eagle Quest offers dinghy sailing in Cumbria's Lake District, but as part of a general multi-activity programme rather than as a course proper. You can try sailing by the half-day or day or as part of a weekend, 5-day or 7-day multi-activity package. Eagle Quest's courses are residential – you can stay either in the centre's old stone farmhouse or in cheaper chalets or camp. Tariffs reflect the level of comfort you want. If you don't have transportation the centre will pick you up from the bus station in Keswick for a nominal charge.

Children: Courses open to all ages.
Tariffs: Sailing is one of the activities offered in the centre's multi-activity package deals. Prices vary according to level of accommodation desired (ranging from no accommodation to B&B) – 2 days of activities / 2 nights' accommodation: £60–99; 5 days of activities / 5 nights' accommodation: £160–225; 7 days of activities / 7 nights' accommodation: £200–299.

See Paragliding and Parascending (p. 311) for full details.

elie watersports

Elie Harbour
Elie
Fife
KY9 1BY
Scotland
Tel (01333) 330 962 / (0131) 343 2050

Dinghy Sailing

Elie is a small, friendly sailing school, with 3 full-time instructors offering tuition at all levels in the sheltered waters of Elie Bay. Instead of a structured course system, you can arrange a set of lessons aimed either at general proficiency or to get you through the RYA's Levels 1–5 certificates. Experienced sailors can hire Lasers, Toppers and Wayfarers by the hour, half-day or day.

The centre caters mainly to locals and summer holidaymakers coming to Elie beach. Although it has no accommodation, it is happy to make arrangements for you to suit your budget. However, you will need to get to and from the centre yourself.

Affiliations: RYA.
Tariffs: Hire and group instruction: £15 per hour.

See Windsurfing (p. 458) for full details.

fairlands valley sailing centre

Six Hills Way
Stevenage
Hertfordshire
SG2 OBL
Tel (01438) 353 241
Fax (01438) 743 483

Dinghy Sailing for Beginners

Set in a country park near Stevenage, with an 11-acre lake used for sailing, this school is a good place at which to get your first grounding in dinghy sailing, with courses offered up to RYA Level 2 using Wanderers, Wayfarers, Bosuns, Gulls, Toppers, or Optimists. The school has 3 permanent instructors and offers courses tailored to adults and children, organized groups and individuals. After you master the basics, craft are available for hire all year, with tuition offered on a 1:1 basis. Informal dinghy racing is arranged on Sunday mornings. There are no residential courses – the school caters mostly to locals living in and around Stevenage. You need your own transport to get to and from the lake. Fairlands Valley Sailing Centre has been running since 1972.

Season: Open all year.
Accommodation: Not provided.
Food: Café at centre.
Other Activities: Windsurfing (see p. 458).
Children: Centre offers special youth courses during school breaks. Play area with paddling pools (in summer). Reduced prices on boat hire for juniors.
Disabled Facilities: Challenger trimaran available for disabled sailors. Reduced prices on boat hire for registered disabled. Café and toilets are wheelchair-accessible.
Insurance: Clients should arrange personal insurance.
Safety: All staff trained in first aid.
Affiliations: National School Sailing Association; RYA.
Tariffs: Prices include instruction and use of equipment. 1½-hour taster session: £12; adult dinghy Level 1 course (3 days): £70; adult dinghy Level 2 course (2 days): £48; racing course (1 day): £42; Junior Certificate course (5 days): £60. Concessionary rates available.
Booking: £10 non-refundable deposit required. Balance due 2 weeks in advance of course. Late bookings accepted if space available.
Access: Off the A1 near Stevenage. Trains to Stevenage, local buses from Stevenage to park entrance (or can walk from station).

falmouth school of sailing

The Boat Park
Grove Place
Falmouth
Cornwall
TR11 4AU
Tel (01326) 373 203 / 211 311

Yacht and Dinghy Sailing

The Falmouth School of Sailing has been going since 1982, offering dinghy, keel-boat (halfway between a dinghy and a yacht) and yacht training for sailors of all degrees of competence. The school's fleet ranges from single-hander dinghies to a 35ft ocean cruiser. Children, adults and certain levels of disability can all be catered for.

There are 5 dinghy and keelboat courses available, from beginner to advanced level, which include assessment for the relevant RYA certificates, as well as 'taster' sessions for those who want to give the sport a try. Cruiser courses are also offered, and these too come with RYA certificate assessment for Competent Crew, Day Skipper, Coastal Skipper and, finally, Yachtmaster. Five-day sailing holi-days aboard any craft can be arranged for recreational sailors.

The centre has its own cottages, caravans and camping site, or you can stay outside. However, if you do this you will need your own transport to get to and from the centre.

Season: Open all year.
Accommodation: School has self-catering cottage (£140–210 per week) and a camping site (£2.50 per night) available, or will help arrange local accommodation.
Food: Meals available at clubhouse, including vegetarian selections.
Other Activities: Powerboating (see p. 324).
Children: Minimum age 8. Special courses for juniors under 16.
Disabled Facilities: Disabled clients can be accommodated, particularly the physically disabled and blind.
Insurance: Clients should arrange personal insurance cover, available through centre.
Safety: All staff trained in first aid.
Affiliations: RYA.
Tariffs: Prices include tuition and use of equipment, and vary according to season. A wide range of sailing courses is available; some examples are – taster dinghy sailing session: £10; taster keelboat sailing session: £15; 2-day RYA Level 1 dinghy course: £78–88; 3-day Level 3 dinghy course: £130–140; 5-day Level 4 dinghy racing course: £150–165; 3-day RYA Level 2 keelboat course: £120–130; 3-day Level 4 keelboat racing course: £135–145; 5-day RYA Competent Crew cruising course: £270–290; Coastal Skipper cruising course: £320–345; 6-day shore-based Yachtmaster course: £170; weekend yacht cruise (including food and on-board accom-modation): £180 plus £23 per person; 5-day multi-sailing holiday: £260. Group and family discounts available.
Booking: Booking fee of £20–75 is required (included in course fees). Balance due 4 weeks before course starts. Booking fee not refunded if cancellation notice received less than 4 weeks before start date. Late book-ings accepted if space available.
Access: Off the A39 at Falmouth. Trains and buses available to Falmouth; pick-ups from stations can be arranged by centre.

galloway sailing centre

Loch Ken
Castle Douglas
Dumfries & Galloway
DG7 3NQ
Scotland
Tel & Fax (01644) 420 626

Dinghy Sailing

Catering for all ages – from 8 to 80 – and from the total beginner to the experienced sailor, Galloway offers dinghy sailing courses on a large loch in the western Scottish Borders. Novices start at RYA Level 1 and can take a series of courses up to Level 4, which qualifies the sailor to handle racing craft. If you already have RYA Level 4 and want to hire a boat, the centre has a small fleet of Wayfarers, Toppers, Lasers, Gulls and Optimists, which can be taken out solo or sailed under supervision, whether as a group or on a one-to-one basis. Sailing can also be tried as part of a general multi-activity course or holiday along with canoeing, powerboating and windsurfing. Single adults or groups, families and unaccompanied children are all welcome.

Galloway Sailing Centre is affiliated to the Duke of Edinburgh's Award scheme. Children who need to gain points towards the Physical Activities section of their award can get their books marked up as follows: dinghy sailing or windsurfing to RYA Level 1 – 6 points; dinghy sailing or windsurfing to Level 2 – 12 points; dinghy sailing or windsurfing to Levels 3 and 4 – 18 points.

Season: April to October.
Accommodation: Camping on grounds with use of clubhouse facilities. Self-catering and full board available in new accommodation chalet (bunk rooms).
Food: Full board or lunches and dinner available.
Other Activities: Windsurfing (see p. 459).
Children: Clients must be 8 or over for residential courses.
Disabled Facilities: Disabled clients can often be accommodated; contact centre for more details.
Insurance: Clients should arrange personal insurance cover if desired.
Safety: All instructors trained and qualified in first aid.
Affiliations: RYA; Sail Scotland, Dumfries and Galloway; Scottish Canoe Association.
Tariffs: Prices vary according to high/low season (high season is from 27 May to 3 September), and include tuition and use of equipment. Half-day course: £24 / £20; day course: £38 / £34; weekend course: £62 / £55; 5-day course £130 / £120; 5 days of full-board accommodation: £130. Discounts for under-16s and for groups.
Booking: Deposit required (amount from £10–30). Deposit retained in event of cancellation, but may be applied to later date. Bookings usually made in advance, but late bookings accepted if space available.
Access: Off the A713 near Parton. Trains to Dumfries, buses to Castle Douglas. Pick-ups free from Castle Douglas, £13 from Glasgow Airport.

great glen school of adventure

South Laggan
Nr Spean Bridge
Highland
PH34 4EA
Scotland
Tel (01809) 501 381
Fax (01809) 501 218

Dinghy Sailing

Sailing on the sheltered waters of Loch Oich is offered to beginners wanting to start from scratch in a safe environment. Weekend and 5-day courses can take you up to RYA Level 2 or 3. Accommodation is in log cabins built by the loch shore.

If you are more experienced, the school hires out dinghies by the hour for supervised sailing sessions. For specific techniques you can hire an instructor as well.

Tariffs: Boat hire: £18 per hour. Instruction: £20 per person (2 hours).

See Paragliding and Parascending (p. 313) for full details.

hamble dinghy sailing

Wayfarer Lodge
Welbourn
Lincolnshire
LN5 0QH
Tel & Fax (01400) 273 003

Dinghy Sailing

Hamble run 2 dinghy sailing centres – one at Hamble (south of Southampton) and another in Falmouth – from a head office in Lincolnshire. Tuition on their dinghy sailing courses is intensive, with one senior instructor per course and one lower-level instructor per boat, and around 7 hours of tuition per day. RYA courses up to Level 5 are offered as single weekends, 3-weekend packages, and intensive 5-day courses. Individuals, groups and families can all be catered for. They also specialize in sailing courses for children.

Season: April to October.
Accommodation: Accommodation in local B&B available (£25 per night). Full-board camping available for children's courses (£95 for 5 nights).
Food: Not provided by centre (except for children's camps).
Other Activities: Child & Youth Sports (see p. 60).
Children: Special children's courses, camps and multi-activity holidays available. Child care available.
Disabled Facilities: Staff qualified in disabled instruction – by arrangement.
Insurance: Clients must arrange their own; can be arranged through centre.
Safety: Instructors qualified in first aid. Rescue boats accompany student boats in case of emergency.
Affiliations: National Federation of Sea Schools; RYA; British Marine Industries Federation.
Tariffs: Prices include instruction and equipment. Weekend course: £90; 5-day course: £189; Falmouth or Solent sailing week: £249 (£189 for children); 5-day sailing camps for 10–16-year-olds: £259; sailing weekend for 7–12-year-olds: £69.
Booking: Non-refundable deposit required, £20–60. Balance due 35 days in advance. No refunds of fees if cancellation made less than 5 weeks in advance. Access and Visa cards accepted. Late bookings up to 48 hours in advance are occasionally accepted if space available.
Access: Off the B3397 at Hamble village. Trains available to Southampton Parkway. Cab to centre approximately £7.

howtown outdoor centre ltd

Ullswater
Penrith
Cumbria
CA10 2ND
Tel (01768) 486 508
Fax (01768) 486 875

Dinghy Sailing

Howtown sits on the eastern shore of Ullswater – an ideal place at which to learn sailing owing to the 10mph restriction on all powered boats, which eliminates the noise and wash you normally suffer when wind- and motor-powered craft share the same waters.

Teaching beginners and improvers in its fleet of Topper dinghies is the centre's speciality, and a sailing course may be taken on its own or as part of a more general multi-activity programme. However, more advanced courses up to and beyond RYA Level 5 can also be arranged, as can training to instructor level. Contact the centre for details. Courses are residential, with accommodation in shared rooms overlooking the lake.

Affiliations: RYA.
Tariffs: Prices include tuition, equipment, insurance and full-board accommodation. VAT is not included. 1-day introductory sailing course (no accommodation): £45; 5-day sailing course: £250; 7-day sailing course: £295. Sailing is also one of the sports offered in the centre's youth multi-activity holiday weeks: £195. Group and unemployed discounts available.

See Child and Youth Sports (p. 61) for full details.

iris activity breaks

29 Alandale Drive
Pinner
Middlesex
HA5 3UP
Tel (0181) 866 3002

Dinghy Sailing for Beginners

Iris offer weekend introductory sailing breaks off the Hampshire coast or on a large reservoir in Cambridgeshire. The Hampshire course can also be tailored to more experienced sailors. The courses get you through the very basics – RYA Level 1 using Wayfarers and Toppers and introducing you to the complex terminology of this obsessive sport. All accommodation, local transport and equipment are supplied.

Accommodation: B&B in Hampshire or Cambridgeshire.
Tariffs: Weekend courses include 2 nights' B&B: from £130–145.

See Ballooning (p. 13) for full details.

the island cruising club

Island Street
Salcombe
Devon
TQ8 8DR
Tel (01548) 843 481
Fax (01548) 843 929

Dinghy and Keelboat Sailing

With up to 30 instructors' Island Cruising has grown from strength to strength since it was founded 44 years ago. Beginners and experienced sailors wishing to specialize, adults, children and families, people wanting to buy or fix up their own craft – all can be accommodated through one of the club's residential holidays or courses. Short, shore-based dinghy sailing courses (usually lasting 2 days) are offered from RYA Level 1 to 3, but there are weekly courses at the same level and beyond, with advanced and racing instruction thrown in as part of the package. Instructor training and assessment are also offered.

The yachting holidays are slightly different. You can opt for straight holidays with incidental crewing instruction, lasting from a weekend to a week or more, visiting Brittany and the Isles of Scilly. One particular holiday, the Music Cruise, lasts a weekend and is aimed at sailors who play an instrument.

More serious sailing courses include the Disaster Weekend, which teaches the correct procedures for emergencies at sea, weather and navigation weeks and, of course, the RYA's various yachting certificate courses. If you are already experienced try courses tackling basic sea survival, radar and electronic navigation, diesel engines, the night sky and VHF radio.

Season: Open all year.
Accommodation: Double and single rooms provided on board the *Egremont*, a converted ferry; space available for 60 guests.
Food: Full board provided; vegetarian and special diets catered for upon request.
Other Activities: Powerboating (p. 325).
Children: Minimum age 7. Sailing holidays and courses for unaccompanied children aged 10 and over.
Disabled Facilities: Twice a year dinghy/keelboat sailing is offered for visually impaired adults (£200 for 5-day course).
Insurance: Comprehensive holiday insurance is included in fees.
Safety: Staff trained in first aid and rescue.
Affiliations: British Canoe Union; RYA.
Tariffs: Prices include tuition, equipment, insurance and full-board accommodation. Prices vary according to season. Some examples are – RYA Level 1 dinghy/keelboat weekend course: £100–120; RYA Levels 1 & 2 combined dinghy/keelboat course (5 days): £215–330; RYA Level 3 dinghy/keelboat course (5 days): £215–330; advanced skills dinghy/keelboat course (6 days): £390; RYA Sailing Instructor course (6 days): £230–390; 2-day yacht handling course: £100–115; weekend yachting disaster training course: £100–115; 5-day RYA Competent Crew yachting course: £220–285; 6-day RYA Day Skipper yachting course: £320–355; 5-day RYA Coastal Skipper yachting course: £200–285; 1-day VHF radio course: £50; 2-day Radar & Electronic Navigation course: £150.
Booking: 25% deposit required. Balance due 28 days in advance of holiday, or stage payment plan available. Cancellation covered by holiday insurance policy. Late bookings accepted if space available. Visa, Access, Mastercard and Eurocard accepted.
Access: Off the A381 at Salcombe. Trains to Totnes or Newton Abbot stations, buses to Salcombe. Minibuses pick up from Totnes or Newton Abbot by arrangement (£7 and £11 respectively).

killowen outdoor education centre

Killowen Point
Rostrevor
Newry
County Down
BT34 3AF
Northern Ireland
Tel (01637) 38297

Dinghy Sailing

Killowen Point is at the southernmost edge of Ulster's coast, about 40 miles south of Belfast. It is a good place at which to learn basic dinghy skills: RYA Levels 1 to 3 are taught on the centre's Lasers, Optimists and Mirrors. The Level 1 and 2 courses can be combined, but it is quite a step to go from RYA Level 2 to 3 and some personal sailing is necessary between the courses if you want to gain the certificate, so it would be unreasonable to expect to go from Level 1 to Level 3 during a short holiday.

Multi-activity courses are also available, combining sailing with climbing, archery and canoeing, and special courses and holidays for children and youth groups are run in the summer.

Season: Open all year.
Accommodation: Bunkhouse accommodation on site.
Food: Full board provided; vegetarian and special diets catered for upon request.
Other Activities: Canoeing (see p. 24); Child and Youth Sports (p. 62); Climbing and Abseiling (p. 102).
Children: Minimum age 7. Sailing holidays and courses for unaccompanied children aged 10 and over.
Disabled Facilities: Some disabled students can be accommodated; contact centre for full details.
Insurance: Comprehensive holiday insurance is included in fees.
Safety: Staff trained in first aid and rescue skills.
Affiliations: British Canoe Union; RYA.
Tariffs: Prices include tuition, equipment, insurance and full-board accommodation, and vary according to season. A wide range of courses is offered; some examples are – RYA Level 1 dinghy weekend course: £100; RYA Level 1 & 2 combined course (3 days): £150; RYA Level 3 dinghy course (3 days): £100. Reduced rates for children; prices on application.
Booking: Full fee payable on booking. Refund only if booking cancelled more than 2 weeks before start date. Late bookings accepted if space available. Payment by cheque, cash or postal order.
Access: On the north shore of Carlingford Lough, 2 miles on the Kilkeel side of Rostrevor. Contact centre for full details.

lea valley watersports centre

Banbury Reservoir
Greaves Pumping Station
North Circular Road
Chingford
Essex
E4 8QB
Tel (0181) 531 1129
Fax (0181) 527 0969

Dinghy Sailing

Easy to reach from East London, this centre offers non-residential dinghy sailing courses up to RYA Level 4, with additional instructors' training and assessment. Courses last between 2 and 5 days, and there are programmes for both adults and juniors. Once you have really mastered the basics, specialist courses, such as Laser 'Masterclass', 'Gaffer', Spinnaker Improvement and VHF radio can also be arranged. The centre also runs a sailing club where you can consolidate and improve your skills while hiring their dinghies under supervision. They can also help you if you want to buy your own craft.

Affiliations: RYA.
Tariffs: All prices include tuition and use of equipment. RYA dinghy Level 1 (2 days): £60; RYA dinghy Level 2 (3 days): £80; RYA dinghy Level 3 (5 days): £95; RYA dinghy instructor course (5 days): £175; RYA first aid course (1 day): £25; junior Introduction to Watersports course (2 days): £55; junior introductory dinghy course (2 days): £40; junior improver/refresher course (4 days): £85. Discounts for club members.

See Water Skiing and Wet Biking (p. 440) for full details.

loch insh watersports & skiing centre

Insh Hall
Kincraig
Highland
PH21 1NU
Scotland
Tel (01540) 651 272
Fax (01540) 651 208

Dinghy Sailing

Loch Insh's sailing packages are run on the loch itself and on the wider stretches of the River Spey, with comfortable bunkhouse accommodation by the waterside. The courses follow the official RYA syllabus, teaching Levels 1–5 under the supervision of RYA-qualified instructors – student/instructor ratios follow the RYA guidelines. There are also 2-hour introductory sailing courses that you can take to see if you like the sport. Back-up is provided by safety boats, and life jackets and buoyancy aids are compulsory. All students should be able to swim 50m.

You can take an RYA Level 1 or 2 course over a weekend or a 5-day course that takes you up to Level 3 – you should be taking the helm of a single-hander by the last day, partaking in some friendly races. Courses for more advanced sailors can be organized by arrangement. The school has a fleet of Wayfarers, Seafarers, Toppers, Lasers, Mirrors, Enterprises and Fireballs (all dinghies) and a Challenger catamaran for disabled sailors.

Season: April to October.
Affiliations: RYA.
Tariffs: Instruction: £15 per hour. 2-day course: £49; 2-day course (with accommodation and full board): £97. 5-day course: £121; 5-day course (with accommodation and full board): £242. Prices increase about 10% in high season (7 July–27 August). Discounts for under-16s of around 25%.

See Skiing (p. 378) for full details.

medina valley centre

Dodnor Lane
Newport
Isle of Wight
PO30 5TE
Tel (01983) 522 195
Fax (01983) 825 962

Yachts and Dinghy Sailing

This is a sailing centre with a difference – a Christian sailing centre. It's very successful, having been open since 1963, and while its requirements for good behaviour might put off would-be buccaneers, it is nonetheless a well-regarded sailing school. Adult dinghy courses are offered from RYA Level 1 right through to instructor level, and there are specialized sailing courses for children and for the disabled. As for yachting, you can pleasure-cruise either by the day, week or fortnight with a view to learning, or just as a holiday, or you can take the RYA's 5-day yachting certificate series from Competent Crew up to Coastal Skipper level. If you hold a Yachtmaster's certificate, you can charter one of the centre's own yachts. Families are welcome on any course or cruise.

Season: April to September.

Accommodation: Twin, single and bunk-bed rooms available on-site.

Food: Residential courses include full board.

Other Activities: Child and Youth Sports (see p. 64); Disabled Activities (p. 135).

Children: Minimum age 8; unaccompanied children must be at least 14. Special youth courses available. Games facilities at centre.

Disabled Facilities: Boats designed for use by the disabled.

Insurance: Personal cover included as part of fees.

Safety: Instructors trained in first aid.

Affiliations: RYA.

Tariffs: Tariffs include instruction, equipment, accommodation and full board (unless otherwise noted). 5-day sailing course: £304 (£237 child); 5-day non-residential sailing course (includes lunch): £182 (£152 child); 6-day instructors' course: £309; 6-day multi-activity holidays from £263. (Some courses are slightly more expensive in high season, 29 July–26 August.)

Booking: Contact centre for booking details.

Access: Cars should take the ferry to the Isle of Wight from Portsmouth or Southampton. Trains to Portsmouth. Buses to Portsmouth and Southampton.

mylor sailing school

Mylor Harbour
Falmouth
Cornwall
TR11 5UF
Tel (01326) 377 633
Fax (01326) 372 120

Dinghy and Keelboat Sailing

One of several sailing and water sports schools based at Falmouth, Mylor has been going for 20 years and offers non-residential 5-day holiday courses, during which you can sit RYA dinghy sailing certificates Levels 1–4, as well as keelboat cruising days (purely recreational) and individual tuition. All age ranges are catered for, and any level of expertise, but groups are kept small – a maximum of 20 people split up among different instructors.

Season: Easter to end October.

Accommodation: No on-site accommodation, but centre will help book local places to suit your budget. Groups can be ferried to and fro by minibus for the cost of the petrol. Individuals and couples will need their own transport.

Food: Not provided.
Children: Minimum age 8; unaccompanied children must be at least 14. Special youth courses available. Games facilities at centre.
Disabled Facilities: Boats designed for use by the disabled.
Insurance: Clients should have their own personal accident cover.
Safety: Instructors trained in first aid.
Affiliations: RYA.
Tariffs: Prices include instruction and equipment only. 2-day introductory dinghy sailing course: £125 for 1 adult, £175 for 2; 5-day beginner and improver courses: £220–308; 7-day holiday course: £170–315; adult all-in packages: £270–498; 2-day introductory keelboat/cruiser courses: £150–199; 5-day beginner/improver courses: £295–375. Reduced rates for children. Contact centre for details.
Booking: 25% deposit must be paid when booking, balance payable 2 weeks prior to course start date. Payment by cash or cheque.
Access: If arriving by car, take the A39 from Truro towards Falmouth, then turn onto the B390 to Penryn and follow the signs to Mylor Churchtown. Clients arriving by bus or train should go direct to Falmouth, from where a cab to the centre will cost about £5.

national watersports centre, cumbrae

Burnside Road
Largs
North Ayrshire
KA30 8RW
Scotland
Tel (01475) 674 666
Fax (01475) 674 720

Dinghies, Catamarans and Yachts

This is a big concern. Whichever branch of sailing you are interested in, this centre can probably cater for you. Dinghy sailing courses for adults and juniors are run from RYA Levels 1 to 5, usually as separate 2-day courses. They can, however, be run together to form more intensive packages of a week or 2 weeks to speed you through the certificates. It's hard work, though. Instructor courses are also offered.

Introductory catamaran courses get the adrenalin going with really fast trapezing. These usually last for 2 days but, again, more intensive courses can be arranged to suit your needs. As for yachting, you can choose between pleasure cruises to the Hebrides, with incidental crewing tuition; proper courses (RYA Day Skipper, Coastal Skipper and Yachtmaster); or, for the very experienced, charter your own yacht and voyage around the Isles.

Season: April to October.
Accommodation: Twin rooms in 4 chalets, accommodating up to 48.
Food: Full board included; vegetarian and special diets catered for upon request.
Other Activities: Powerboating (see p. 326); Sub-Aqua Diving (p. 393); Windsurfing (p. 462).
Children: Junior courses for 9–14-year-olds available.
Disabled Facilities: 1 chalet is wheelchair-accessible; sailing instruction for the disabled.
Insurance: Clients should arrange their own holiday insurance.
Safety: All staff trained in emergency first aid.
Affiliations: RYA.
Tariffs: All prices include tuition, equipment use and full-board accommodation. Prices sometimes vary between low (April–May) and high (June–October) season.
A broad range of sailing courses is available; examples will be given for yachting, dinghy and catamaran sailing. Yachting: 5-day course for Competent Crew or Day Skipper qualifications: £255–275; weekend cruises: £102–108; 5-day Yachtmaster or Coastal

Skipper cruises: £255–275; West Highland racing week: £385; 1-day VHF operators' course (non-residential): £25; 5-day Day Skipper theory course (non-residential): £160. Dinghies: 2-day Level 1 course: £102; 5-day Level 2 course: £255: 5-day Level 5 course: £255; 2-day Advanced Single Handed course: £102; 4-day junior beginners' or improvers' course: £175; 5-day instructor course: £155. Catamarans: 2-day sailing course: £113. 1-day small craft first aid course (non-residential): £33.
Booking: £40 deposit required, non-refundable if cancellation received less than 6 weeks in advance. Bookings normally made in advance, but late bookings accepted if space available.
Access: Take the A434 or A760 to Largs. Trains and buses to Largs, ferries from Largs to Isle of Cumbrae.

---

newton ferrers sailing school

Westerly
Yealm Road
Newton Ferrers
Devon
PL8 1BJ
Tel & Fax (01752) 872 375

Dinghy Sailing

This 40-year-old dinghy sailing school on the Yealm estuary in Devon offers courses and holidays for all levels of competence. Sailing takes place on the estuary, in a nearby bay and on the open sea. For beginners and improvers the centre runs 2 different courses: the Elementary, which teaches basic handling of the sail, rigging, knots, wind direction, rules of the road, safety, and management of the helm; and the Intermediate, which takes the inexperienced helmsman through entering harbours, mooring and anchoring, and basic navigation and seamanship. If time permits, rudderless sailing is also taught, along with spinnaker and trapezing techniques.

The centre also runs junior courses at elementary and intermediate level for children between 8 and 15 years old. Single-handed Toppers are used – lively but safe craft for learner sailors to handle.

Those who want to progress beyond the intermediate course level can sit the full range of RYA certificates – up to Level 5. Contact the centre for full details. All courses are residential (though cheaper accommodation can be booked nearby if necessary), and usually last for 1 week. Longer or shorter breaks can also be organized. Accommodation is in a private house overlooking Newton and Noss Mayo creeks.

Season: April to September.
Accommodation: 3 double rooms at centre (£15 per night).
Food: Breakfast included (full board option for juniors).
Children: Must be 8 or older. Special courses for under-16s, youth discounts.
Disabled Facilities: None.
Insurance: Clients should arrange their own holiday insurance.
Safety: Staff trained in first aid.
Affiliations: National Federation of Sea Schools; RYA; West County Tourist Board.
Tariffs: Prices include tuition and use of equipment. 6-day courses: £162; 5-day courses: £125; weekend courses: £78.
Booking: Deposit required, £35 per person per week. Balance due 4 weeks in advance of holiday. Fees will be refunded in the case of cancellation if place can be refilled. Visa and Barclaycard accepted.
Access: Off the B3186 at Newton Ferrers. Trains to Plymouth, buses from Bretonside station to Newton Ferrers. Pick-ups from stations can be arranged by centre.

oban sea school

Mount Stuart
Gallanach
Oban
Argyll & Bute
PA34 4QH
Scotland
Tel (01631) 562 013

Yachts

Robert Kincaid's Oban Sea School specializes in yacht sailing, aimed at the beginner and recreational sailor, all of it under Robert's expert eye – he holds an RYA Yachtmaster's licence. Courses and cruises are run on board a well-equipped certified sail training vessel, with 3 main courses on offer: the RYA Competent Crew, Day Skipper and Coastal Skipper certificates. All courses last for a minimum of 5 days aboard. The Oban Sea School also offers straight cruising holidays off the west coast of the Highlands. The most exciting are the 10-day cruises which either go right up to the Orkney Islands or across to remote St Kilda. The bird-watching and whale-watching are superb, and the group on board is encouraged (and helped) to take full charge of the yacht: planning passages, pilotage and navigation to suit wind and weather and where the group feels like going. The ratio of students/guests to instructor is never more than 4:1.

Season: Late March to early October.
Accommodation: 5 berths aboard yacht.
Food: Meals provided, special diets can be catered for.
Children: Minimum age 10 if accompanied by adult, 16 if unaccompanied.
Disabled Facilities: Courses can be run for the mildly disabled; contact centre for details.
Insurance: Clients should arrange their own holiday insurance.
Safety: Staff trained in first aid.
Affiliations: RYA.
Tariffs: 5-day RYA courses (including tuition and full-board accommodation on yacht): £260–290; 6-day RYA courses: £346.
Booking: £50 non-refundable deposit. Balance due 6 weeks before start date. 10% cancellation charge (provided place can be resold). Late bookings accepted if space available.
Access: Take the A85 to Oban. Trains and buses also available to Oban. Boat is met on pier.

outdoor activities association

Marine Walk
Roker
Sunderland
Tyne & Wear
SR6 0PL
Tel (0191) 565 6662 / 565 7630
Fax (0191) 514 2873

Dinghy Sailing

This urban-based outdoor school offers dinghy sailing courses from beginner to RYA Level 3. Courses can either be taken as intensive residential 2-day breaks or spread over evenings and weekends so as to fit in with a school or work schedule. Open-sea sailing to Whitburn can also be arranged, as well as trips to nearby lakes and reservoirs. The school has its own fleet of GP14s, Toppers and single-handers.

Affiliations: RYA.
Tariffs: Prices include tuition and use of equipment. Introduction to Sailing course: £30; Introduction to Sailsports: £40; RYA courses Levels 1, 2, or 3 (2 days): £55.

See Windsurfing (p. 463) for full details.

outward bound

PO Box 1219
Windsor
Berkshire
SL4 1XR
Tel (01753) 731 005
Fax (01753) 810 666
Outward Bound Scotland, Loch Eil
Tel (01397) 772 866
Outward Bound Wales, Aberdovey
Tel (01654) 767 464
Outward Bound Ullswater, Penrith
Tel (017684) 86347

Dinghy and Yacht Sailing

Dinghy sailing is offered either as part of Outward Bound's multi-activity breaks (usually 7 days) or as specialist courses entitled Sea Voyages (in cutters), which last from 7 to 12 days. The Viking Wayfarer sea voyage (for 16–24-year-olds only) is run from the Scottish centre and takes in the rugged coastline of the Western Isles. Travelling in 28ft traditionally rigged cutters, you are taught basic sailing skills and navigation along with campcraft and cooking. Nights are spent ashore in tents. Towards the end of the course you will be given the opportunity to take sole charge of the vessel on its homeward leg. A second Scottish sea voyage, the West Coast Passage (open to anyone over 25), lasts 7 days and is conducted on 2 open-rigged gaff cutters, teaching navigation, sail handling, pilotage and weather. Again, on the homeward leg you are encouraged to take sole charge of the vessel for set periods. By night you camp on remote beaches and wild peninsulas. A third course, based on the same west coast passage route, is specially tailored to people of 50 and over, and qualifies you for the RYA Keelboat certificate.

Much less ambitious is the 5-day introductory Dinghy Sailing course, open to anyone over 14, and run from Outward Bound's Welsh centre. You learn basic sailing skills on the Dovey estuary and, if conditions allow, on the open sea. At the end of the course you have the opportunity to sit the RYA Level 2 award.

Affiliations: RYA.
Tariffs: All prices include tuition, equipment, full-board accommodation and transport during programme. Prices do not include VAT. Introduction to Dinghy Sailing course (Wales, 5 days): £250; Water Skills course (Wales, 7 days): £325; Introductory Water course (Wales, Ullswater, weekend): £130; Viking Wayfarer expedition (Scotland, 12 days, 16–24): £399; West Coast expedition (Scotland, 7 days, 25+): £325. Sailing is also included as part of the multi-activity holidays offered by centre (for 14–24-year-olds unless otherwise stated). 7-day multi-activity programme (Scotland, Wales, Ullswater): £249; 12-day multi-activity programme (Wales, Ullswater): £399; Outward Bound Classic (Scotland, Wales, Ullswater, 19 days): £499–599; weekend breaks (Wales, Ullswater, 25+): £130; 7-day programme (Scotland, Wales, Ullswater, 25+, 50+): £325; 12-day programme (Wales, Ullswater, 25+): £470.

See Walking (p. 426) for full details.

pugneys country park

City of Wakefield MDC
Asdale Road
Wakefield
West Yorkshire
WF2 7EQ
Tel (01924) 302 360
Fax (01924) 302 362

Dinghy Sailing

Pugneys Country Park near Wakefield in south-west Yorkshire contains a natural ox-bow lake formed from the River Calder. Apart from its outdoor activities, the place is interesting in its own right – the name derives from the Old English 'Pugnals', meaning goblin's nook, and the lake is overlooked by the ruins of Sandal Castle. Today Pugneys houses one of Britain's best-equipped water sports centres.

Dinghy sailing courses for adults and children are offered, starting with 'taster' evenings for those who want to give the sport a try, and graduating through all the RYA's basic certificates (Levels 1–3) and on to instructor training. Courses last for 14 hours, split into 2 sessions over both days of a weekend. The centre runs a small fleet of Wayfarers, Toppers, Mirrors and Lasers: experienced sailors can hire these for supervised sailing by the hour, half-day or day.

The centre caters mainly to individuals and groups in the South Yorkshire area and so has no accommodation. They can help you to find local B&B if you are passing through the area for a while, but you will need your own transport to get to and from the centre.

Children: Junior courses for 11–14, 15–18-year-olds.
Disabled Facilities: Toilets wheelchair-accessible.
Affiliations: RYA.
Tariffs: All prices include tuition and use of equipment.
RYA Level 1 course (2 days): £45;
RYA Levels 2–5 courses (40–50 hours): £100;
RYA Instructor course (6 days): £135.
Junior RYA Stage 1 & 2 course (20 hours): £38;
Junior RYA Stage 3 course (40–50 hours): £70;
Junior Improvers course (40–50 hours): £70.
Sailing also offered as part of centre's Junior Multi-activity course (5 3-hour sessions): £35.
(Note: These are 1996 prices; check with reception for any tariff or course changes.)

See Windsurfing (p. 466) for full details.

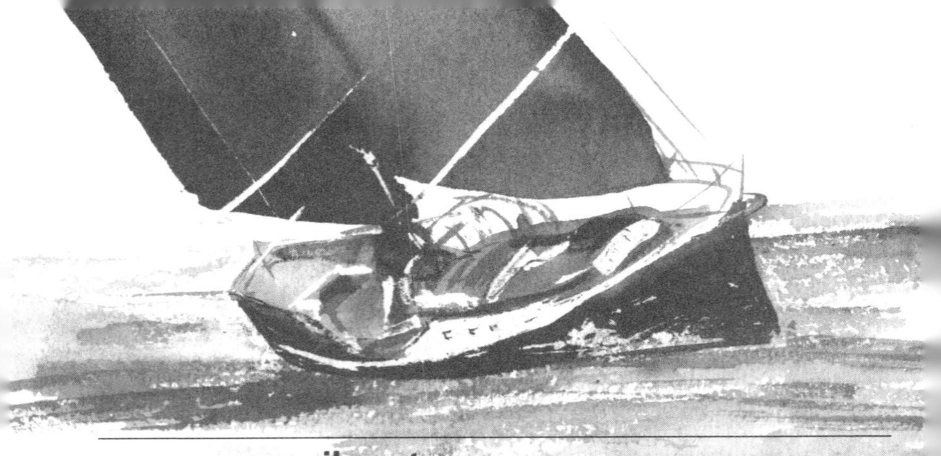

queen mary sailsports

Queen Mary Reservoir
Ashford Road
Ashford
Middlesex
TW15 1UA
Tel (01784) 244 776 / 248 881
Fax (01784) 252 772

Dinghy Sailing

Situated within the Greater London area, Queen Mary Sailsports offers non-residential courses and private tuition in most aspects of dinghy sailing. Supervised hiring of various craft can also be arranged: Optimists, Toppers, Lasers, Wayfarers and Comets.

If you're a total beginner, try the Learn to Sail course, either held over 5 consecutive days mid-week or broken up into 5 weekend sessions. The course teaches handling of single-handers, Wayfarers or keelboats and takes you through to RYA Level 2. Alternatively you can attend an intensive beginners' day course and get your RYA Level 1 certificate. Once you have obtained your Level 2 you can join the school's regular Saturday morning or Wednesday evening groups for sailing under supervision. These prepare you for your RYA Level 3 certificate, as do a variety of day courses on sailing faster craft, spinnaker handling, trapezing and learning to race. Those who have taken a long break between their certificate examinations can attend a number of 'improver' and 'refresher' days aimed at getting your hand in again. If all this is old hat to you, then the Advanced Racing weekends might be more interesting, along with the 2-hour High Performance one-to-one tuition sessions which get you handling very fast craft such as Laser 4000 and 5000, Dart 18 and Laser 2 or 505.

Queen Mary Sailsports also runs courses aimed at children aged 9 to 13 and teenagers of 14 to 18, both of which offer tuition to RYA Level 3. These youth courses are held either as regular Saturday morning sessions, or over more intensive 5-day or weekend periods.

Children: Minimum age 8. Special courses offered for juniors (8–13) and teens (13–18).
Disabled Facilities: Some disabled clients can be accommodated; contact centre for details.
Affiliations: RYA.
Tariffs: Prices include tuition and use of equipment. RYA Level 1 & 2 combined course (5 days): £235; Trial Sailing Day: £55; Improver/Refresher Days: £55; High Performance Days: £59; Start to Race Days: £50; Junior and Teen RYA courses (Levels 1–3, Advanced, Racing): £120. Personal instruction (including equipment): £75 per half-day, £140 per full day. Group and sibling discounts available.

See Windsurfing (p. 467) for full details.

rockley cruising school

Rockley Point
Hamworthy
Poole
Dorset
BH15 4LZ
Tel (01202) 665 310
Fax (01202) 668 268

Yachts and Dinghies

Rockley Point offers a very good series of courses for both beginners and serious sailors starting the long slog to their RYA Yachtmaster certificate. With 20 qualified instructors and 20 years of experience as a yachting school, Rockley is recognized as one of the premier schools in southern England. Courses are open to all ages – families and unaccompanied children are specially catered for on their own courses, learning to sail Optimist and Topper dinghies, while adults can take RYA yachting and dinghy courses either by the day or as intensive 2- or 5-day packages. Most of the sailing takes place in Poole Harbour, whose sheltered waters allow learner sailors to travel from quay to quay over fair distances without too much threat of bad conditions blowing up. Adults sail Wayfarer, Topper, Laser and Dart dinghies, with courses from RYA Levels 1 to 5, and on to Racing and Instructor level. Once you have reached RYA Level 3 on the dinghies, you have the option of trying your hand at yacht sailing in one of Rockley's week-long programmes. If you decide to go on with the yachts, you can sign up for the full range of 5–7-day RYA courses: Competent Crew, Day Skipper, Coastal Skipper and Yachtmaster, learning on Sadler 34s with no more than 5 students to 1 instructor.

The school also runs dinghy and catamaran sailing holidays in France, with courses from RYA Levels 1 to 5. Sailing takes place on several lakes west of Bordeaux.

Season: Open all year.
Accommodation: Practical courses provide accommodation in cabins of yachts. Local accommodation can be arranged for shore-based courses.
Food: Prices include all meals on board. Vegetarian and special diets can be accommodated upon request.
Other Activities: Rockley Cruising School is run in close association with Rockley Point Sailing School (see p. 362).
Children: Instruction for children available.
Disabled Facilities: None.
Insurance: Clients should arrange their own holiday insurance; packages available through centre.
Safety: Staff trained in first aid. Safety boats accompany fleets when out.
Affiliations: British Activity Holiday Association; British Marine Industries Federation; RYA.
Tariffs: Prices include instruction, equipment, meals on board and accommodation on board for practical courses. Fees vary according to season. A wide range of courses is available; some sample tariffs are: 7-day Competent Crew practical course: £350–420; 2-day Day Skipper practical course: £100–120; 3-weekend Coastal Skipper shore-based course: £200; 5-day Ocean Yachtmaster shore-based course: £180.
Booking: £30–75 deposit required, non-refundable. Balance due 6 weeks before start date. Cancellation charges: 4–6 weeks in advance: 70% of total; less than 4 weeks: 100% of total. Access and Visa cards accepted. Late bookings accepted if space available.
Access: Poole is off the A35. Trains and buses available to Poole. Taxi fare to school approximately £5.

rockley point sailing school

Hamworthy
Poole
Dorset
BH15 4LZ
Tel (01202) 677 272
Fax (01202) 668 268

Dinghy and Yacht Sailing

With 20 full-time instructors, this sailing school in Poole Harbour can cater for groups and individuals of any level of experience. The residential courses can be taken as weekend breaks, week-long blocks or spread over 3 weekends – for example, for RYA Levels 1–3, with the weekends consecutive or not, according to your schedule. Rockley Point offers tuition right up to racing level (Level 5) and also offers basic yachting weeks which you can use towards an RYA Competent Crew certificate. The school has several types of on-site accommodation (see below), or you can book your own nearby. However, those not staying on-site will need their own transport to get to and from the school.

Season: Open all year.
Accommodation: Choice of self-booked accommodation, on-site double rooms, singles or dorms, or local accommodation can be arranged with families, in B&Bs or caravans.
Food: Meals included in some holiday packages.
Other Activities: Child and Youth Sports (see p. 71); Powerboating (p. 327); Windsurfing (p. 468). Rockley Point Sailing School is run in close association with Rockley Cruising School (see p. 361).
Children: Centre specializes in teaching youths from 8 and up, with junior residential courses for 10–17-year-olds. Special evening activities organized for youths.
Disabled Facilities: None.
Insurance: Clients should arrange their own holiday insurance; packages available through centre.
Safety: Staff trained in first aid. Safety boats accompany fleets when out.
Affiliations: British Marine Industries Federation; Federation of Sea Schools; RYA; Southern Tourist Board.
Tariffs: Prices include instruction and equipment, and vary according to season. A wide range of courses is available; some sample tariffs are: 7-day sailing course: £240–280; 2-day sailing weekend: £90–95; 5-day sailing holiday (includes B&B plus lunch): £240–260; 13-night junior residential course (includes full-board accommodation): £220; 6-day Level 4 Blue Racing course: £240; 1-day Small Craft first aid course: £60.
Booking: £30–75 deposit required, non-refundable. Balance due 6 weeks before start date. Cancellation charges: 4–6 weeks in advance: 70% of total; less than 4 weeks: 100% of total. Access and Visa cards accepted. Late bookings accepted if space available.
Access: Poole is off the A35. Trains and buses available to Poole. Taxi fare to school approximately £5.

shadwell basin project

Shadwell Pierhead
Glamis Road
London
E1 9EE
Tel (0171) 481 4210
Fax (0171) 481 0624

Dinghy Sailing

If you're stuck in central London but have the evenings free, this Docklands centre offers good introductory sailing courses lasting 6 days (held over successive evenings), taking you through the first 3 RYA certificates. If you decide to go further, you can join Shadwell's sailing club and come in for regular sessions that count towards higher RYA qualifications. The staff can also give advice on buying a dinghy and can store and maintain boats for club members.

The courses are not residential and you will need to get to and from Shadwell Pierhead by yourself.

Affiliations: RYA.
Tariffs: 6-day introductory and advanced courses: £95. 1-day small craft first aid course: £30. 5-day multi-activity course (canoeing, climbing, sailing and windsurfing): £75. Annual memberships also available in sailing club for £70 per year (£35 concession).
Booking: Deposit required (no set amount), non-refundable. 50% of course fee due if cancellation notice received less than 4 weeks in advance. Late bookings accepted if space available.
Access: Short walk from Wapping tube station.
See Child and Youth Sports (p. 72) for full details.

sinbad charters

Aidenkyle House
Aidenkyle Road
Kilcreggan
By Helensburgh
Argyll & Bute
G84 0HP
Tel & Fax (01436) 842 247

Yachts

Sinbad is a particularly good place at which to start your career with yachts. Most of their courses are tailored to beginners and novices, although they also offer full facilities for more advanced sailors, including the RYA Yachtmaster assessment (by arrangement) and yacht charter, both skippered and on-your-own. The courses are run as on-board holidays of a week – as an introductory cruise on which you learn to crew while enjoying yourself, or during which you may be taught and examined for an RYA Competent Crew, Day Skipper or Coastal Skipper certificate (Coastal Skipper may take longer than just a week's course).

Groups are limited to 5 people and accompanied children are welcome. All tuition is undertaken by Mr Waddington, the owner of Sinbad Charters, who holds the RYA Yachtmaster Instructor and Professional Yachtmaster qualifications.

Season: April to October.
Accommodation: 5 berths on yacht.
Food: Self-catering for groups, groceries provided for single-berth bookings (approximately £5 per day).
Children: Families with young children are asked to book entire boat.
Disabled Facilities: None.
Insurance: Clients should arrange their own holiday insurance.
Safety: Skipper qualified in first aid and sailing rescue.

Affiliations: RYA; Associated Scottish Yacht Charters.
Tariffs: Prices include instruction, and vary according to season: £200–250 per week per berth, or £800–1,000 per week for whole boat (5 berths).
Booking: 25% deposit required. Balance due 1 month in advance. In case of cancellation, skipper will try to refill berths and deposit will be refunded minus £50 administrative charge. If berths cannot be filled, client liable for total fees. Late bookings sometimes accepted if space available.
Access: Rhu Marina is near Helensburgh off the A82. Trains from Glasgow to Helensburgh, buses available from Helensburgh to marina. Pick-ups can be arranged from train station.

---

tighnabruaich sailing school

Tighnabruaich
Argyll & Bute
PA21 2BD
Scotland
Tel (01700) 811 396

Dinghy and Keelboat Sailing

Established in 1965, this sailing school runs a fleet of 35 craft to suit all levels of expertise: Wayfarers, Laser 16s, Laser 2 Regattas, International 420s, Toppers and various single-handers are all on offer. There's an equally varied range of courses for adults and juniors. Most last a week and include assessment for and award of the relevant RYA qualification – up to RYA Level 5. Own-boat instruction and hire of craft can also be arranged, as can instructor training. The school is particularly well known for its advanced and racing dinghy training. It is 2 hours' drive from Glasgow.

Season: May to September.
Accommodation: Centre offers a variety of accommodation options, including youth hostels, camping, private accommodation and hotels.
Food: Meals available at most of the accommodation venues.
Other Activities: Windsurfing (see p. 469).
Children: Minimum age 8. Junior courses and youth discounts available.
Disabled Facilities: None.
Insurance: Clients should arrange their own holiday insurance.
Safety: All instructors trained in first aid. Safety boats on hand.
Affiliations: RYA.
Tariffs: Fees include instruction and use of equipment. Prices slightly higher in peak season (25 June–6 August). 1-week basic sailing course: £135–140; 1-week improver, intermediate, advanced or racing course: £141–147; 1-week combined windsurfing and sailing course: £135–140. Half-week courses available: £69–72. Group, family and youth discounts available.
Booking: £20 non-refundable deposit required. Balance due 28 days in advance of course. Refunds for cancellations only given if space can be refilled. Late bookings accepted if space available. Credit cards accepted.
Access: 2 hours by car from Glasgow. Trains from Glasgow to Gourock, ferry to Dunoon. Buses from Dunoon to Tighnabruaich.

ulster cruising school

The Marina
Carrickfergus
County Antrim
BT38 8BE
Northern Ireland
Tel (01960) 368 818

Yachts

Ireland's first recognized yachting school, run by instructors who have rounded Cape Horn, has a superb cruising ground, with cruising down the Irish coast, up the Clyde, to the Hebrides and the Isle of Man. Any level of sailor is welcome: for the experienced there are courses in advanced pilotage, navigation and specialist own-boat instruction and women-only courses. Shore-based RYA courses include VHF radio, and Diesel and Navigation. The full range of RYA Skipper certificates is also offered.

The school runs a Jeanneau Attalia 32ft. The instructor-to-student ratio on courses does not exceed 1:5.

Season: All year.
Accommodation: Centre offers a variety of accommodation options, including youth hostels, camping, private accommodation and hotels.
Food: Food provided on yacht-based courses. Special diets by arrangement.
Children: Over-16s only.
Disabled Facilities: None.
Insurance: Clients should arrange their own holiday insurance.
Safety: All instructors trained in first aid. Safety boats on hand.
Affiliations: RYA.
Tariffs: Fees include instruction and use of equipment. Prices slightly higher in peak season (25 June–6 August). An average 5-day course costs £250–270.
Booking: A 50% non-refundable deposit to be paid on booking. Balance payable 14 days before course start date (though some late bookings available). Payment by cash or cheque.
Access: Half an hour from the Carrickfergus ferry and airport. Free collection.

viking sail

6 Chapelton Drive
Largs
North Ayrshire
KA30 8RE
Scotland
Tel (01475) 673 652

Yachts

George Rich, the principal and chief instructor at Viking Sail, is an RYA examiner, which makes Viking's courses about as thorough as you could wish for. The full range of RYA certificates – Competent Crew, Day Skipper, Coastal Skipper and Yachtmaster – together with shore-based navigation, VHF radio, diesel and other practical courses, is on offer. There are also recreational cruises along some of the old Viking sailing routes. Most courses and holidays last 5–6 days, with weekends by arrangement, though longer Hebridean cruises and Ocean Yachtmaster passages, or straight boat charter, are also available. Based at Largs Haven, Viking Sail runs 2 boats – a Moody 31 and a Moody 336. The maximum instructor-to-student ratio is 1:4.

Season: March to October.
Accommodation: Centre offers a variety of accommodation options, including youth hostels, camping, private accommodation and hotels.

Food: Food provided on yacht-based courses. Special diets by arrangement.
Children: Over-16s only.
Disabled Facilities: None.
Insurance: Clients should arrange their own holiday insurance.
Safety: All instructors trained in first aid. Safety boats on hand.
Affiliations: RYA.
Tariffs: Fees include instruction and use of equipment. Prices slightly higher in peak season (25 June–6 August). An average 5-day course costs £285–295.
Booking: A 50% non-refundable deposit to be paid on booking. Balance payable 14 days before course start date (though some late bookings available). Payment by cash or cheque.
Access: Based at Largs Haven. Contact centre for full details.

---

wight water

19 Orchardleigh Road
Shanklin
Isle of Wight
PO37 7NP
Tel & Fax (01983) 866 269

Catamarans

Although Wight Water is not a sailing school per se, it is RYA-affiliated and is a good place at which to get a general grounding before going on to another school or sailing club to begin the long process of getting the RYA's proficiency certificates. You can have lessons by the hour or as a package spread over 5 days. If you already have some experience, Wight Water will hire you one of their light catamarans for supervised sailing in the bay. You can also try catamaran sailing as part of a more general water sports package that includes windsurfing, kayaking, wave skiing and surfing. Accommodation is either at the Saunders Hotel, or arranged by you locally. You will need your own transport to get to and from the centre.

Children: Discounts for youths under 19.
Insurance: Clients should obtain personal insurance cover.
Affiliations: RYA.
Tariffs: Catamaran hire: £14 per hour. Catamaran instruction: £20 per hour. Catamaran sailing is also one of the sports included in the centre's 5-session multi-activity package: £60. Group and youth discounts available.

See Windsurfing (p. 469) for full details.

---

windsport international ltd

Mylor Yacht Harbour
Falmouth
Cornwall
TR11 5UF
Tel (01326) 376 191
Fax (01326) 376 192
Falmouth Centre, Cornwall
Tel (01326) 376 191
Grafham Centre, Cambridgeshire
Tel (01480) 812 288
Rutland Centre, Rutland
Tel (01780) 722 100

Dinghy Sailing and Catamarans

Windsport is a big concern, running 3 centres in the East Midlands and the West Country – at Falmouth, and Grafham and Rutland Waters. Their sailing programme covers dinghies and catamarans – the same programme for each centre. You can begin learning to sail on either a catamaran or a dinghy course (or combine the two), or get a taste for the sport as part of a wider multi-water-sports programme.

Whichever you choose, you get around 6 hours of qualified tuition each day from one of the centres' qualified instructors (each centre has between 4 and 10 depending on the season). Experienced sailors can take their certificate courses or sail under supervision on a client-to-instructor ratio of 1:1 or 2:1. Courses last from 1 hour to 5 days and can be residential or non-residential. There's a variety of accommodation available and course fees are charged on a sliding scale depending on the level of comfort you want.

The Windsport schools are particularly recommended for anyone wanting to learn to sail Lasers – racing dinghies or catamarans. Their 5-day Cat Safari is one of the most exciting sailing courses on offer anywhere. For the regular RYA certification courses, RYA Levels 1–5 are offered for both dinghies and cats, and can be taken in 5-day intensive blocks or split up over a longer period of time to suit your schedule.

Season: Open all year.
Accommodation: Accommodation in choice of local hotel, guest house or farmhouse is included in residential packages. Self-catering chalets, caravans, camping and dormitory accommodation are also available; contact centre for details.
Food: Breakfast included in residential packages.
Other Activities: Child and Youth Sports (see p. 76); Land Yachting (p. 236); Powerboating (p. 328); Surfing (p. 409); Water Skiing (p. 442); Windsurfing (p. 470).
Children: Must be 8 or older. Special multi-activity courses for children and families. Youth (13–16) and junior (8–12) sailing courses available.
Disabled Facilities: None.
Insurance: Clients should arrange personal insurance cover. Can be provided by centre.
Safety: Staff trained in first aid. Rescue-boat drivers on hand.
Affiliations: British Canoe Union; British Federation of Sand and Land Yachting Clubs; RYA; West Country Tourist Board.
Tariffs: All prices include tuition and use of equipment. A large range of sailing courses is offered; some examples are – introduction to cat/dinghy (1 hour): £25; RYA cat/dinghy course Levels 1–5 (5 days): £275; personal cat/dinghy coaching: £25 per hour, £135 per day; junior dinghy course (5 days): £245; youth cat/dinghy course (5 days): £245; professional cat/dinghy racing (2 days): £120 per boat; Cat Safari (5 days – Falmouth only): £275. Sailing is also one of the activities offered in the centre's multi-activity packages. 5-day family, child, or adult course: £125 (adult), £95 (child); weekend family course: £48 (adult), £38 (child); 1-day family or child course: £25 (adult), £20 (child); 1-day adult course: £48. Residential packages are also available (including tuition, equipment and accommodation); prices vary according to level of accommodation chosen (hotel, guest house or farmhouse). 5-day courses (6 nights' accommodation): £365–545; 2-day courses (2 nights' accommodation): £220–280. Group discounts available.
Booking: Non-refundable deposit required: £100 (course only); £150 (residential course). Balance due 6 weeks before start date. Cancellation charge if notice received 5–8 weeks in advance: 50% of total; 2–4 weeks in advance: 70%; less than 2 weeks: 100%. Bookings normally made in advance, but late bookings accepted if space available. Visa and Access cards accepted.
Access: Varies according to location chosen; contact centre for details.

kitting yourself out

Not until you have passed your Competent Crew certificate should you even consider buying a boat, whether a dinghy or a yacht. When you buy a boat, you have the choice of buying something brand new that is too advanced for your experience, or of buying a second-hand dud that looks great but which will provide a nice hole for you to throw money into. Buying a boat is similar to buying a horse or a second-hand car, or anything else that requires specialist knowledge in order to understand what you see and know how to look beyond the glamour of first impressions. There are two ways around this. The first, if money is no object, is to consult your instructor and buy a new boat, taking him or her along to the dealer to make sure that you get what you have been advised to get, not what the salesman wants to sell you. The second way, if money *is* an object, is to sail for your first few years on rental boats – flotilla holidays are the best option – then trawl the classified ads of the sailing and yachting magazines under the benevolent supervision of an instructor. If you are prepared to spend several months, if necessary, finding the right craft, then all should be well. If you're in a hurry you are almost certain to take a big bath and end up hating your first boat.

A brand-new beginner's (single-hander) Optimist or Laser dinghy costs between £1,000 and £2,000 depending on the model, with prices going up quickly for double-handers and racing models, and a brand-new small yacht anything from £20,000 upwards. Larger craft can cost up to £300,000. However, yacht charter – the way most people do it – costs considerably less, usually about £500 per person for a large (say 6-berth) yacht for a week's hire. Light catamarans such as Hobie13s cost about £3,000 new, while a good-condition second-hand Hobie13 costs around £1,500. A good deal for a second-hand beginner's Optimist or Laser in reasonable condition would be about £500–1,000. Small yachts are harder to pin down, but if you pay less than £15,000 for your first 30ft boat, the chances are you are buying a dud. Any cheaper second-hand yacht will probably cost at least an additional £5,000 to make really seaworthy, and will almost certainly cost about the same per year to maintain.

A small-dinghy trailer costs around £200 new, though second-hand bargains exist, while dinghy sails cost from about £300 for a single spinnaker or £600 for a full suit (this is second-hand – there is no reason to buy new).

The other chandlery accessories like sailsuits, dry suits and tarpaulins are too numerous to go into here, especially for yachts. Suffice it to say that none of it is cheap.

In short, unless you are very wealthy, you cannot own a yacht as a hobby, and even dinghies are not cheap. If you are on a more modest budget and want to own a boat, you had better feel passionate enough about the sport to want to make it a way of life.

further reading

Sailing in a Week, Wendy Fitzpatrick, Hodder & Stoughton, 1990;
Pass Your Yachtmasters', Farhall and Peyton, Nautical Books, 1989.

checklist

- ✔ *dinghy, yacht or catamaran*
- ✔ *trailer, sail(s) and other chandlery*

British Mountain Council / photo: R. Payne

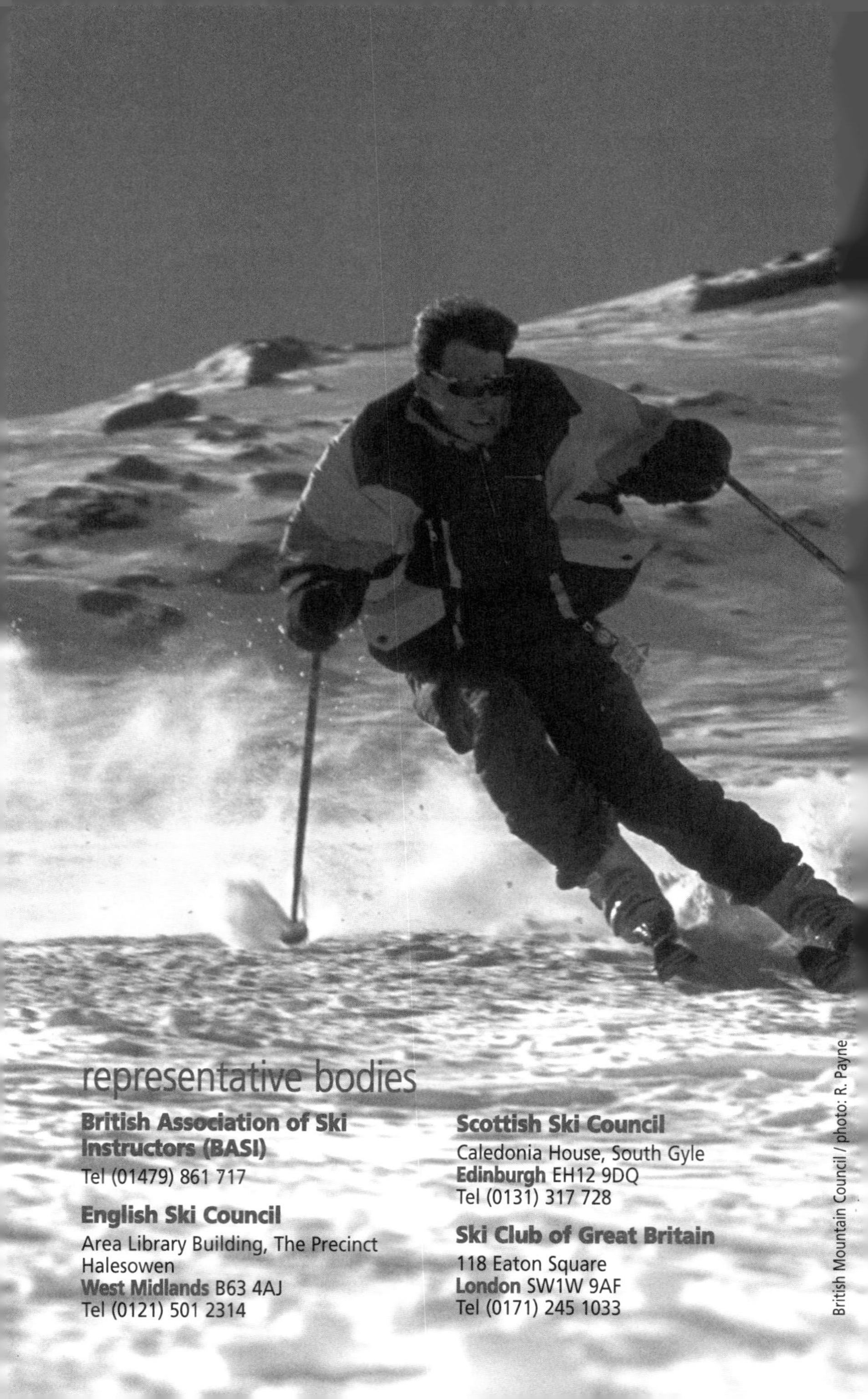

representative bodies

British Association of Ski Instructors (BASI)
Tel (01479) 861 717

English Ski Council
Area Library Building, The Precinct
Halesowen
West Midlands B63 4AJ
Tel (0121) 501 2314

Scottish Ski Council
Caledonia House, South Gyle
Edinburgh EH12 9DQ
Tel (0131) 317 728

Ski Club of Great Britain
118 Eaton Square
London SW1W 9AF
Tel (0171) 245 1033

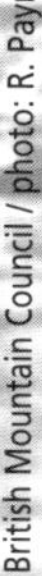

skiing downhil cross-country (nordic) ski touring snowboarding

Britain may not have the regular sunshine and powder conditions of the Alps, but in the highest uplands in Sçotland it does snow regularly enough to enable one to hone one's technique and have fun, provided one is not coping with the frequent white-outs, blizzards, howling winds, twists of heather poking up from the snow, or sheet ice. It has been said that if you can learn to ski well in Scotland you can ski anywhere. And there are many different disciplines to try. The downhill skier can now choose between a number of schools using prepared pistes and ski lifts. Aviemore, Ben Nevis, Glencoe, the Lecht and Glenshee are the main centres.

Ski mountaineers and Nordic (cross-country) skiers have a wider range, and can take guided trips, sometimes of up to several days. Both these disciplines allow you to ski uphill as well as down, and get you closer to the wildlife that shuns the noisy ski-lift areas. Of the two, ski mountaineering offers more fast descents but more slog on the uphill climbs, because your heel is locked into the ski, and you can only shuffle forward. Nordic skiing uses lighter boots and free-heel bindings that allow you to swish along on the flat and climb fairly easily but make going downhill difficult; as the skis are long and narrow the turning techniques are far harder to master. However, a good compromise is ski touring, where you use heavier Nordic equipment that allows for ease of glide on the flat but is easier to turn on, especially if you learn the telemark turn – a Norwegian technique involving dropping to one knee and extending one foot in front of the other, so that instead of two skis side by side you effectively have one continuous ski. Needless to say, this takes a lot of practice to perfect.

Real adrenalin-seekers should try snowboarding – you are limited to prepared pistes, but the stunts you can pull are almost unlimited, provided you're prepared to spend several seasons perfecting your technique. Many downhill ski schools offer snowboarding; where appropriate the two disciplines are listed together.

selected centres

bowles outdoor centre

Eridge Green
Tunbridge Wells
Kent
TN3 9LW
Tel (01892) 665 665
Fax (01892) 669 556

Downhill and Snowboarding (Dry-slope)

If you can't get to the snow but want to learn, then this ski school in Kent will get you prepared for the pistes. It has 9 full-time instructors, and several part-time, and offers residential courses with on-site B&B or bunkhouse accommodation. Courses run over Wednesdays, Fridays and Saturdays at 4 levels, with Level 1 aimed at people starting from scratch and Level 4 aimed at those who can use the tow lift and know how to snowplough.

Bowles also offers courses for intermediate skiers designed to improve skills and teach parallel turning, after which you can attend the advanced sessions. If you join up as a club member you can sign up for informal coaching sessions, and there are additional courses in snowboarding at beginner and improver level. Private lessons in either skiing or snowboarding are also available by arrangement.

In addition, Bowles organizes ski courses abroad in the French Alps and Colorado.

Season: Open all year for group bookings. Ski and snowboard courses for individuals October to March. Multi-activity courses April to August.
Accommodation: A new lodge has 8 double rooms (£20 per person per night + VAT) and 8 single rooms (£30 per night + VAT). 70 bunk beds are also available in dormitories for groups only, full board included (contact centre for details).
Food: Bar on site, meals provided.
Other Activities: Child and Youth Sports (see p. 55).
Children: Minimum age 9. Young people's ski courses and club sessions every Saturday afternoon from October to March. Children's birthday parties can be arranged.
Disabled Facilities: Adapted equipment is available for skiers with disabilities. If someone wishes to learn to ski and is prevented by the nature of their disability from joining conventional courses, the centre will offer private tuition at the same price as a course. Lodge has full wheelchair access and a lift.
Insurance: Clients should arrange personal insurance cover if desired.
Safety: All instructors qualified in first aid.
Affiliations: English Ski Council; British Association of Ski Instructors (BASI); British Snowboarding Association.
Tariffs: Group ski instruction sessions are 2 hours long and range from beginner to advanced – 1 session: £19; 2 sessions: £36; 3 sessions: £52; 4 sessions: £69. 1-day, 5-hour beginners' course: £46. Snowboarding instruction at beginner and intermediate levels is also available: £24 per 2-hour session. Private ski or snowboard instruction: £25 per hour for 1 person, £10 for each additional person (maximum 4). Special packages for youth, student and adult groups (including instruction, accommodation and full board) are available – contact centre for details.
Booking: £20 non-refundable deposit required per person. Balance is due 2 months before start date of course. Late bookings are sometimes accepted if space is available.
Access: Off the A26 between Tunbridge Wells and Brighton, 5 miles south of Tunbridge Wells. Trains and buses run from London to Tunbridge Wells. Pick-ups from station can be arranged by centre.

braemar nordic ski centre

Invercauld Road
Braemar
Aberdeenshire
AB35 5YP
Scotland
Tel (013397) 41242
Fax (013397) 41496

Nordic Skiing

Braemar is an attractive town and convenient for the slopes up at Glenshee. The Nordic ski courses on offer here are run either as 5-day intensives or over weekends. Basic cross-country tuition is on offer at beginner and intermediate level, while for the more experienced the Telemark Weekend teaches the finer points of cross-country downhill technique. Although accommodation is not included for these courses, all equipment and local transport are thrown in and the instructor-to-student ratio does not exceed 1:6.

Season: Open all year, but courses in winter only.
Accommodation: Not provided, but can be booked through the centre in local bunkhouses, B&Bs and hotels in Braemar.
Food: Not provided.
Children: Over-13s only.
Disabled Facilities: None.
Insurance: Clients should provide their own holiday insurance.
Safety: All instructors are trained in first aid.
Affiliations: British Association of Ski Schools (BASS).
Tariffs: Cross-country skiing per group per day: £80 for 1–2 people, £100 for 3–6 people. The Basic Cross-country Skiing 5-day course is £160, the Basic Weekend £75. The Intermediate Cross-country Skiing 5-day course costs £160, while the Intermediate Weekend is £75. The Telemark Weekend is also £75 and the Winter Hills Weekend £80.
Booking: 50% deposit required, balance to be paid on arrival. No charge for cancellations made 4 weeks in advance. Loss of deposit if cancellation between 1 and 4 weeks, and full balance due if cancellation within 1 week. Late bookings accepted if space available.
Access: In the centre of Braemar, a short walk from Braemar bus stand.

brathay exploration group

Brathay Hall
Ambleside
Cumbria
LA22 OHN
Tel & Fax (01539) 433 942

Nordic Skiing

Brathay Hall is an expedition centre aimed at young people (aged 18–25) who want to gain experience in a variety of mountaineering and eco-related sports. Their Introduction to Nordic Skiing week runs in the Cairngorms in February, from a set of comfortable chalets near Aviemore. No previous ski experience is necessary – the course is primarily aimed at beginners or near-beginners – but you should have a good standard of general fitness. The course introduces you to basic ascent and descent on Nordic skis, as well as skating and diagonal gliding along the flat. There is a client-to-instructor ratio of no more than 4:1 and each day includes about 7 hours out on skis. Equipment hire is not included in the general course price – it's another £40 on top – and you will have to get yourself to Aviemore. Once there, however, all food, accommodation and local transport are covered.

Season: February.
Accommodation: In chalets adjacent to homes of instructors.
Food: Food supplied to make up breakfast and packed lunches, evening meal provided.
Tariffs: Prices include full-board accommodation and instruction. Ski hire and lift passes not included. 1-week Introduction to Nordic Skiing course: £195.

See Eco-Sports (p. 144) for full details.

---

cairnwell mountain sports ltd

Gulabin Lodge
Glenshee
By Blairgowrie
Perthshire & Kinross
PH10 7QE
Scotland
Tel (01250) 885 255 / 885 256
Fax (01250) 885 255

Downhill and Snowboarding

The high Cairngorms are Britain's best and most reliable natural snow grounds. Cairnwell, at Glenshee ski resort, has access to some of the best of the Cairngorm snow. With a pool of instructors qualified up to BASI Grade I, the school offers downhill tuition, ski racing and snowboarding. Because the centre offers a variety of mountain sports – including hang-gliding and paragliding as well as hillwalking, climbing, canoeing and mountain biking – there is enough to keep you going should there be no snow when you arrive.

You can ski by the day, hiring equipment from the centre and skiing either by yourself or under instruction, or opt for 5-day skiing or snowboarding courses at full board right by the ski slopes.

Season: Open all year.
Accommodation: 16 beds on-site. B&B: £12 per night; £2 per night weekend supplement. Hotels, B&Bs, camping and caravan sites available close to centre.
Food: Breakfast available. Self-catering facilities.
Other Activities: Hang-gliding (see p. 188).
Children: All ages accepted.
Disabled Facilities: Access to all ground-floor facilities, toilets, accommodation, shop, etc. Specialized instruction can be arranged.
Insurance: Clients should arrange their own holiday insurance.
Safety: All instructors are trained and certified in first aid.
Affiliations: BASS.
Tariffs: Downhill and snowboard group lessons (maximum class size 8): £12 per 2-hour session. Discounts available for juniors. Private instruction: £18 per hour for 1 person, £20 per hour for 2 people, £25 per hour for 3 people, £30 per hour for 4 people. Race instruction including slalom pole hire and timing: £120 per half-day and £200 per full day. 5-day packages including accommodation, equipment and 2 hours per day instruction available from £145 for skiing and £178 for snowboarding. Nordic instruction for £16 per day. Packages including hire and instruction from £20 per day.
Booking: 50% deposit required, balance payable on arrival. No charge for cancellations made 4 weeks in advance. Loss of deposit if cancellation received within 1–4 weeks, and full amount payable if received within 1 week. Bookings normally required in advance, but late bookings accepted if space available.
Access: Off the A93 between Blairgowrie and Braemar. Trains available to Pitlochry, Perth and Dundee. Buses between Aberdeen and Braemar, or Dundee/Perth and Blairgowrie. Taxi fare to centre approximately £20.

glenmulliach nordic ski centre

Stronavaich
Tomintoul
Aberdeenshire
AB37 9ES
Scotland
Tel (01807) 580 356

Nordic Skiing

Cross-country ski enthusiasts will enjoy these small group courses (maximum 8 people) run on the hills of Tomintoul or, if there is no snow low down, up on the windswept wastes of the Ladder Hills by way of the Lecht – a nearby downhill ski resort.

The courses are aimed at everyone – from complete beginners' weekend courses that teach basic diagonal flat touring and kick turns for gentle descents, to intermediate weekends to improve these techniques and 5-day beginner and experienced-skier packages. Families are welcome, as are school groups. If you're really good, there is specialist cross-country downhill tuition that includes telemark.

The centre has no accommodation of its own, but the packages include local B&B and transport as well as equipment hire and a free pass to the centre's own machine-cut cross-country trails in the local forest and hill country.

Season: Approximately January to the end of March.
Accommodation: Centre will provide local B&B accommodation (plus lunch) for package holidays only. Otherwise clients can choose from a variety of local accommodation.
Food: Breakfast and packed lunches for package holidays. Restaurants within a few miles of centre.
Children: All ages welcome. Discounts available.
Disabled Facilities: None.
Insurance: Clients need their own holiday insurance.
Safety: Instructor trained in first aid and carries radio and first-aid kit.
Affiliations: Aberdeen and Grampian Region Tourist Boards.
Tariffs: Instruction charges – half-day: £15; 1 day: £20; 2 days: £35. (Nearly half off for children under 15). Holiday packages (including B&B accommodation, lunch, instruction and equipment hire) – 2 days: £90 (adults), £85 (12–15), £75 (under 12); 5 days: £180 (adults), £160 (12–15), £150 (under 12).
Booking: 10% non-refundable deposit required. Balance due 21 days in advance of course. Late bookings accepted if space available.
Access: Take the A9 to Aviemore, then the A95 and A939 to Tomintoul. Trains and buses available to Aviemore; pick-ups can be arranged by centre (approximately £20).

highland guides

Inverdruie
Aviemore
Highland
PH22 1QH
Scotland
Tel (01479) 810 729
Fax (01479) 811 153

Nordic Skiing

Founded in 1969, Highland Guides was the first centre to introduce commercial Nordic skiing to the UK. It teaches basic cross-country, ski touring, specialist cross-country downhill and telemarking – even ski jumping on Nordic equipment. Courses and holidays are run over weeks and weekends, mostly in Scotland, but with guided trips abroad to Norway too. The largest instructor-to-student ratio is 1:8 and courses are divided into 4 standards – Basic, Intermediate, Nordic Downhill and Telemarking. Family courses are also offered, as well as extreme-ground steep skiing and specialist school and youth courses. Up to 16 instructors are available through the main winter season.

Season: Approximately January to the end of March.
Accommodation: Not provided.
Food: Not provided.
Children: Accompanied children welcome at reduced rates. Minimum age 8 for family courses.
Disabled Facilities: None.
Insurance: Clients must have their own personal accident cover.
Safety: All instructors first-aid-trained. Mountain rescue on hand.
Affiliations: BASI.
Tariffs: For 4-day courses including equipment and instruction: £87 per adult, or £65 for under-15s. Instruction only for the same period costs £55 per adult or £38 for under-15s.
Booking: Last-minute bookings often taken; ring to see if there's a cancellation. Otherwise booking should be made 6 weeks in advance, with a deposit of 25%, balance payable on arrival. Access and Visa accepted.
Access: Inverdruie is on the Aviemore–Glenmore road, about 2 miles east of Aviemore. Clients arriving by train at Aviemore will be collected on request. Aviemore also has a coach stop.

hillend ski centre

Biggar Road
Edinburgh
EH10 7DU
Scotland
Tel (0131) 445 4433
Fax (0131) 445 5549

Downhill Skiing and Snowboarding (Dry-slope)

As a dry slope, Hillend warrants entry as the 'longest and most challenging in Europe', at least according to their official literature. Certainly, it is longer than most dry slopes and is a good place at which to prepare for the pistes. Being in the Pentland Hills just south of Edinburgh, the slope does get a fair smattering of snow in the winter, which makes the experience a little more real. They also offer a good ski repair service. Three slopes are on offer – a 400m main piste, a 300m low slope and a 200m 'fun' slope, as well as a 50m nursery for beginners. Hillend is a big business, employing 54 instructors and offering various types of tuition for individuals, groups, children and the disabled. Skiing is by the day only and you will need your own transport to get to and from the slope.

Season: Open all year (except the last 2 weeks in June).

Accommodation: Centre can provide help in obtaining local accommodation.

Food: Centre has restaurant offering vegetarian selections.

Children: Minimum age 6. Discounts for juniors. Snocats club for 7–12-year-olds.

Disabled Facilities: Disabled clients can often be accommodated. Centre is wheelchair-accessible and special skiing aids are available. Discounts for disabled skiers.

Insurance: Clients should arrange personal insurance cover.

Safety: Staff trained in first aid.

Affiliations: British Ski Federation; British Ski Slope Operators Association; Scottish National Ski Council.

Tariffs: Prices include instruction, use of lifts and equipment hire. 1-hour skiing class: £7.40 per person; private lessons for skiing or snowboarding (1–2 persons): £27.50 per hour; 2-hour Snowboard Taster session: £15; advanced snowboard instruction classes (1½ hours teaching, half-hour practice): £15.

Booking: Full payment required at time of booking. Late bookings accepted if space available. Visa, Access and Switch cards accepted.

Access: Off the A702 in Hillend Country Park. Trains to Waverly station in Edinburgh, buses to Hillend. Walking distance from bus stop to centre.

loch insh watersports & skiing centre

Insh Hall
Kincraig
Highland
PH21 1NU
Scotland
Tel (01540) 651 272
Fax (01540) 561 208

Downhill and Nordic Skiing

Basic downhill and Nordic skiing courses are both available at Loch Insh near Aviemore. You can choose between self-catering and full-board residential ski packages from 2 to 7 days' duration. The course fees include instruction, a ski pass and ski hire. Transport to and from the slopes is by arrangement (they are 20 minutes' drive away). Accommodation is in log chalets. Just behind the chalets is a dry slope for you to practise on between runs up at Aviemore.

If you opt for Nordic skiing, one definite advantage is getting away from the bustle of Aviemore's ski lifts to the quiet fastnesses of Glenfeshie and the Monaliadth Mountains – snow permitting. You learn basic flat techniques and step turns for negotiating downhill, but there is no specialist cross-country downhill tuition. If the snow miraculously disappears during the week you have booked, Loch Insh offer an alternative programme of mountain biking, orienteering, hillwalking and archery – or there are the water sports that the centre also specializes in. Multi-activity packages to include as many of these activities as possible can be arranged too – especially for children and youth groups.

Season: December to May.
Accommodation: 16 double rooms, 3 single rooms, 1 dormitory and log chalets for families available.
Food: Licensed restaurant on-site. Vegetarian meals and special-diet meals can be arranged.
Other Activities: Canoeing (see p. 25); Sailing (p. 353); Windsurfing (p. 462).
Children: Minimum age 8, 12 if unaccompanied by adult. Games room at lodge. Child discounts offered. Special youth courses and equipment.
Disabled Facilities: Most buildings accessible, 1 chalet with disabled facilities.
Insurance: Clients must arrange their own insurance cover.
Safety: All instructors trained in first aid.
Affiliations: Association of Ski Schools in Great Britain; BASI; Highlands of Scotland Tourist Board; Scottish Tourist Board.
Tariffs: Prices vary according to season – low season December/January, high season February/March/April. Full-board packages for downhill (including instruction, ski hire and accommodation) – 2-day: £63 low, £81 high (ski pass extra); 5-day: £211 low, £236 high (includes ski pass); 7-day: £271 low, £306 high (includes ski pass). Full-board packages for cross-country (including instruction, ski hire and accommodation) – 2-day: £61 low, £79 high (ski pass extra); 5-day: £173 low, £198 high (includes ski pass); 7-day: £212 low, £257 high (includes ski pass). Packages for instruction, ski hire and accommodation only (5 days): from £107 for juniors. Reduced child rates on request.
Booking: 25% deposit required, non-refundable. Balance payable 6 weeks before start of holiday, no refunds if cancellation notice received less than 28 days in advance. Visa cards accepted.
Access: Off the A9 between Aviemore and Kingussie. Trains and buses available to Aviemore; pick-ups from station can be arranged by centre.

lyncombe lodge

Churchill
Nr Bristol
Avon
BS19 5PQ
Tel (01934) 852 335
Fax (01934) 853 314

Downhill Skiing and Snowboarding (Dry-slope)

Set into a wooded slope of the Mendip Hills, Lyncombe Lodge's dry slope offers instruction by the hour – for downhill and snowboarding – or longer packages spanning a weekend or a week. Special skiing holidays are also available for school groups and unaccompanied children. It's a good place at which to learn, or to brush up on skills before heading off for a skiing holiday.

The weekend and week-long courses include accommodation and half-board, with guests sleeping in the lodge itself – a large converted farmhouse now used as an outdoor centre. You will need your own transport to get here.

Affiliations: British Ski Slope Operators Association.
Tariffs: Prices include equipment and instruction. 1-hour beginners' lesson: £10; private instruction: £12–25 per hour per person; snowboarding private lessons: £16–25 per hour per person; 2-day ski holiday (including accommodation and half-board): £120 + VAT. Skiing is also one of the sports offered in the centre's multi-activity package deals (including accommodation and half-board). 6-day holiday: £275–315 + VAT (according to season); 2-day holiday: £120 + VAT. (Discounts for children under 16.)

See Horse Sports (p. 217) for full details.

the mountain ski school

Aviemore Mountain Resort
Aviemore
Highland
PH22 1PF
Scotland
Tel & Fax (01479) 811 707

Downhill

Aviemore's Mountain Ski School operates both as a dry ski slope and a snow ski area, so that if the pistes are closed owing to the weather lessons are given on the centre's own dry slope. There is a variety of packages on offer here, from 1 to 3 days, including all equipment, ski passes and 4 hours of instruction per day. Alternatively, you can rent equipment and ski on your own or take lessons by the day according to your experience and fitness. There are also 3–7-day ski holidays for all levels of skier. School group packages of 2–6 days can also be arranged.

This is traditional downhill skiing, with 30 qualified instructors working at the school, making it the largest in Scotland, with access to all types of run. The only drawback to the school is that the Aviemore pistes can become very crowded during school and Christmas holidays. Try to come outside these times if you want to avoid queues, ice build-up on the runs and snow wear-out, i.e. heather poking through the surface.

Season: December to April.
Accommodation: No on-site accommodation, but school is associated with Balvatin Cottages in Newtonmore, a 15-minute drive away, where self-catering cottages can be hired from £170–550 per week (depending on cottage and season). Ski packages are also available with hotels and guest houses.

Food: Meals available in and around Aviemore.

Children: Special classes for 4–7-year-olds offered during holiday periods. Special group lessons for 7–12-year-olds at reduced rates. Children under 7 only accepted in group lessons if they have skied previously. Discounts available for youths under 17. Full-board ski packages available for school groups.

Disabled Facilities: None.

Insurance: Personal insurance cover can be arranged through school.

Safety: On-site medic, all staff trained in first aid.

Affiliations: Association of Ski Schools of Great Britain.

Tariffs: Prices for instruction, equipment rental and ski passes are separate unless purchased in package deals. Some examples of prices are – 1 day of group instruction (2½-hour sessions): £15; 5 days of group instruction (2½-hour sessions): £60; 1½-hour private lesson: £40 for 1–3 skiers. 1-day ski pass: £17; 6-day ski pass: £77 (under 17 half-price). 1-day standard ski rental (skis, sticks, boots): £11; 3-day premium ski rental: £31; 6-day standard ski rental: £39. Big Value Package (includes 5 days' ski hire, 4 days' instruction and 5-day lift pass): £141; Mini-Break Package (includes 3 days' hire and instruction): £64. Total ski holidays are also available (including accommodation, ski hire, instruction and passes): prices on application.

Booking: £20 non-refundable deposit required. Advanced booking only required for groups, otherwise late bookings accepted if space available. Credit cards accepted.

Access: Off the A9 at Aviemore. Trains and buses available to Aviemore.

---

outward bound

PO Box 1219
Windsor
Berkshire
SL4 1XR
Tel (01753) 731 005
Fax (01753) 810 666
Outward Bound Scotland, Loch Eil
Tel (01397) 772 866

Downhill

Outward Bound's Scottish centre runs a good beginner's course for downhill skiing. The tuition lasts for 5 days and introduces you to the equipment, progressing through snowplough and stem turns to linked turns and side-stepping and the beginnings of parallel turning. The last day has you skiing solo down a slalom course. The ski holiday is run at Aonach Moor, Scotland's newest ski resort, and the course fee covers a full lift pass.

Affiliations: Mountain Leaders Training Board.

Tariffs: Course fee of £295 per person includes tuition, equipment, full-board accommodation, local transport during programme and a ski pass. Price does not include VAT.

See Walking (p. 426) for full details.

scottish norwegian ski school

Speyside Sports
Grampian Road
Aviemore
Highland
PH22 1PD
Scotland
Tel (01479) 810 656 / 872 309
Fax (01479) 873 415

Downhill and Nordic Skiing

Another Aviemore-based centre, this one is slightly different to its competitors in that it offer Nordic as well as downhill skiing – with tuition to advanced level in both disciplines.

As is usual with resort-based ski schools, you can choose between instruction and equipment packages, renting equipment and skiing on your own, or booking a fully inclusive ski holiday from 2 to 7 days' duration. Bad-weather days can be made up for by dry-slope ski training, mountain biking or walking.

The downhill courses take you through the usual progression of stages from basic snowploughing to step turns, parallel turns and then to faster techniques as you get better. But of particular note are the courses dealing with telemarking – the most difficult of the cross-country (Nordic) downhill techniques to learn. It's very elegant when you get it right, though it takes a while. The telemark courses run either through weekends or over 5 days. To have any hope of really consolidating your technique you should go for the latter.

Season: January to April.
Accommodation: Residential ski packages available in association with the Cairngorm Hotel.
Food: Restaurants available in the Cairngorm Ski Area and at the Cairngorm Hotel.
Children: Instruction available for small children (4–7) and juniors (7–18). Youth discounts available.
Disabled Facilities: Disabled skiers can be accommodated; contact centre for details.
Insurance: Clients must arrange personal holiday insurance.
Safety: Instructors trained in first aid. Ski patrol on hand.
Affiliations: BASS.
Tariffs: Prices for ski packages include 4 hours' instruction per day, equipment hire and lift pass. 2 days: £73; 3 days: £100; 4 days: £125; 5 days: £145; 6 days: £165; 7 days: £180. Residential ski packages include B&B accommodation, lift pass and either equipment hire or tuition (£11 per day supplement for both). 2 days / nights: £99; 3 days / 2 nights: £119; 3 days / nights: £139; 5 days / nights: £199. Telemarking courses also available, including instruction and lift pass. Weekend: £60 (ski hire £18 additional); 5 days (includes video analysis): £99 (ski hire £36 additional). Tuition, equipment hire and lift passes can be purchased separately if desired.
Booking: £20 deposit required, non-refundable. Late bookings accepted if space available. Credit cards accepted.
Access: Take the A9 to Aviemore. Trains and buses to Aviemore. Can walk to centre from stations.

kitting yourself out

Experienced skiers are obsessed by ski gear and are constantly updating their equipment. This section is aimed at first-timers just beginning the odyssey of bewildered digging into the pocket that comes with buying your own equipment.

For downhill beginners, a pair of short (175–185cm) Rossignol VC3 downhill skis will set you back about £185. More expensive, but aimed at the same level of skill, are the K2 8100 Equipe 2S, which cost around £310, or the Salomon Force 9 3S at about £335. Both these more expensive skis give you better turning control, even when technique is lacking. Expect to add another £100 to the cost of your skis when the bindings are added. Ask your retailer and/or instructor which type of bindings you should buy.

Then you'll need boots. A pair of good downhill boots (Rossignols, Nordicas and Langes are reliable manufacturers) will cost between £180 and £250, and a good, properly insulated ski suit about £200–250: Nordica, Skila and K2 produce good stuff. Downhill ski poles cost about £30 for a basic, solid pair. Leki, Salomon, K2 and Volkl poles are recommended.

Once you start getting into the other forms of skiing, the equipment becomes more complicated. As a rule, it is a good idea to buy gear that can be used for a variety of things – for example, if you are taking up cross-country skiing with touring in mind it is advisable to buy heavy metal-edged cross-country skis such as Asne Telemarks (between £200 and £350 per pair, plus another £100 or more for the bindings), and their attendant heavy boots (good ones are Garmont Tour boots, at about £120–180 per pair), because these will allow you to both glide on the flat and turn more easily on descents, functioning well both on prepared pistes and tracks and for trail-breaking through new snow. Cross-country ski poles vary in price from basic Rossignols (about £20 a pair) for light track work to adjustable Leki Wanderfreunds (about £30 a pair) for heavy touring.

However, if you don't want to spend so much money, you can kit yourself out for straight cross-country for under £150. Several places offer all-in equipment packages for cross-country, cross-country downhill and telemarking. The Highland Guides ski school at Aviemore offers several such packages, starting at £119 for the most basic cross-country gear, suitable only for gliding along prepared, fairly level tracks, and £139 for slightly more adaptable skis, boots and poles, jumping to £350 all-in for touring equipment such as the Asne skis and Garmont Tour boots listed above. Highland Guides also offers a specialized telemark equipment package for £480, including Asne Mountain Extreme skis, Garmont Telemark boots and Rottefella Riva II bindings. But only a specialist should invest in this, for the gear is similar to ski mountaineering equipment and unworkable for touring.

If you're planning to take up ski mountaineering you should expect to pay about £150–200 for a good pair of good beginner's skis and bindings, such as Rossignol or Salomon, and about £175 for a pair of solidly made boots, (again Rossigols and Salomons are good). Ski mountaineering poles need to be able to take very heavy pressure and so are expensive – for example, a mid-range pair such as Leki Powders will set you back about £45.

As for clothing, the heavily insulated downhill suits and trousers are too hot for cross-country or ski touring. You'll need a good jacket (good names are Mountain Range, Karrimor, Mountain Equipment, Bradsport, Phoenix and Berghaus), which costs between £130 and £200; an inner fleece jacket, such as a Polartec or Reco Fleece at about £60–90; walking or ski breeches (try the Rohan brand, at about £45 a pair); Gore-Tex leg gaiters and thermal gloves, underwear and hat. Hold off buying other cross-country accessories, such as waxes that you apply to the bottom of the ski for extra glide and adhesive 'skins' for getting uphill, until you know the exact conditions of the area or areas where you plan to ski.

further reading

Learn to Ski in a Weekend, Bartelski and Neillands, Dorling Kindersley, 1991;
The Skiing Handbook, Karl Gamma, Pelham, 1992.

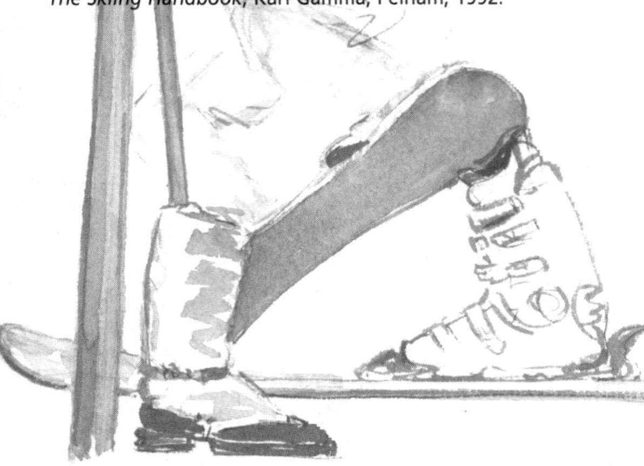

checklist

- ✔ *ski suit (for downhill only)*
- ✔ *skis and bindings*
- ✔ *ski breeches with weatherproof jacket and gaiters (for cross-country, telemark and ski mountaineering only)*
- ✔ *poles*
- ✔ *boots*
- ✔ *hat, gloves and thermal underwear*

governing body

British Sub-Aqua Club (BSAC)

Telford's Quay, Ellesmere Port
South Wirral
Cheshire L65 4FY
Tel (0151) 357 1951
Fax (0151) 357 1250

photo: Andrew Holt

sub-aqua diving

Almost every public swimming pool in Britain has a resident sub-aqua school, offering to get you qualified over a period of months. These are, unfortunately, too numerous to list here, but you can find some in your local Yellow Pages. This chapter notes only those schools that offer residential diving courses that take you into the ocean, and centres offering diving trips to the more experienced.

All centres are affiliated to the British Sub-Aqua Club (BSAC), which has laid down the series of qualifications that must be taken by all British divers. These are Novice Diver, followed by Novice Diver II, Sport Diver, Dive Leader, Advanced Diver and finally First Class Diver. There is a specific course for each qualification, teaching sea charts, currents and tides, the basic physics of air pressure and the human body, and the functioning of equipment – from aqualungs and air compressors to the correct water temperatures for different types of wet and dry suits. Signing up for a BSAC course gives you automatic BSAC membership (and with it third-party liability insurance), and the qualifications are recognized by the World Underwater Federation – useful when taking trips abroad. It's worth picking up the official BSAC manual, *Sport Diving*, which acts as both a textbook and a reference for the courses from Novice to Advanced Diver.

Sub-aqua diving has certain physiological requirements. Before you can register for a course you will have to pass a BSAC medical. Also, no one under the age of 14 may take a Novice Diver course.

As well as belonging to the BSAC, your instructor should be a member of the Professional Association of Diving Instructors (PADI). All the centres listed in this chapter use PADI instructors. Those interested in becoming instructors may take qualifications once they have passed a BSAC Sports Diver course. There are 4 grades of instructor: Assistant, Club, Advanced and National.

selected centres

acorn activities

PO Box 120
Hereford
Hereford & Worcester
HR4 8YB
Tel (01432) 830 083
Fax (01432) 830 110

Acorn offer a combined Novice Diver I & II course (over 5 days) in mid-Wales, and an Open Water Diver course (also over 5 days) in North Wales. Both include some pool and classroom work, but you spend most of your time diving in the sea or local lakes (depending on the weather). Certificates are given at the end of the course, and all equipment is supplied, as well as transport to and from the dive sites. A medical will be conducted on the first day of the courses, and Acorn warn that no one suffering from asthma, epilepsy or any respiratory difficulties should come on either course: there are no refunds if you do not pass the medical. Acorn suggest that you take a medical with your own GP before signing up for the course.

Accommodation: Not included in price. Arranged by Acorn in local farmhouses or hotels.
Tariffs: Half-day introductory course: £50; 5-day Novice Diver or Open Water course: £375.

See Walking (p. 414) for full details.

andark

256 Bridge Road
Lower Swanwick
Southampton
Hampshire
SO31 7FL
Tel (01489) 581 755

Although Andark's 3-day Novice Diver course takes place in an indoor pool, their 5-day Sport Diver is taught in open water, as are their PADI courses, from Open Water I right through to Divemaster. Andark's diving grounds are excellent – trips go out into the Solent and other areas of the South Coast, where there are wrecks a-plenty. It's up to you whether you sign up as a group, join a group, or take individual tuition. Specialist courses in boat handling and oxygen compressor management, as well as twice-weekly recreational dives and equipment hire, are all offered alongside the regular courses. Andark is also a dive equipment dealership.

Season: Open all year.
Accommodation: No on-site accommodation. Centre will provide help in obtaining local accommodation.
Food: Not provided.
Children: Minimum age 14; anyone under 18 needs consent of parent or guardian.
Disabled Facilities: None.
Insurance: BSAC cover included in course price.
Safety: All instructors trained in first aid and sub-aqua rescue.
Affiliations: BSAC; PADI.
Tariffs: Prices include all tuition and equipment hire. Introduction to Diving 1-day course: £40. BSAC Novice Diver I & II 4-day course: £250. BSAC Sport Diver 5-day course: £280. Dive Leader training: £65 per

day. Guided dives: £12 per dive or £20 per day. Advanced courses by arrangement; contact centre for price details.
Booking: Bookings normally made in advance, but late bookings sometimes accepted if space available. A non-refundable deposit of £25 must be paid on booking. Payment by cash, cheque or credit card.
Access: Lower Swanwick is on the A3024 about 8 miles south-east of Southampton town centre. It has its own railway station, and a cab fare from there to the centre is about £3.

---

anglesey diver training specialists

Porthdafarch Road
Holyhead
Anglesey
Gwynedd
Wales
LL65 2LP
Tel (01407) 764 545

This is one of the best-equipped dive schools in Britain and a good place to go as a beginner. As with the North Wales and Dyfed coast, the waters around Anglesey are very clean and full of marine life, including some exotic species that drift up on the Gulf Stream in summer. Seals, dolphins and porpoises are common diving companions. Although the centre is not residential, there is any number of B&Bs or local campsites available, often within easy walking distance of the centre. Apart from the certificate and specialist courses (such as chart work, air compressor management, oxygen administration and boat handling), the centre also offers charters and guided dives for individuals and groups at a number of sites off the island.

Season: Open all year.
Accommodation: No on-site accommodation. Centre will provide help in obtaining local accommodation.
Food: Not provided.
Children: Minimum age 14; anyone under 18 needs consent of parent or guardian.
Disabled Facilities: None.
Insurance: BSAC cover included in course price.
Safety: All instructors trained in first aid and sub-aqua rescue.
Affiliations: BSAC; PADI.
Tariffs: Prices include all tuition and equipment hire. Introduction to Diving 1-day course: £40. BSAC Novice Diver I & II 3-day Course: £250. BSAC Sport Diver 5-day course: £280. Dive Leader training: £65 per day. Guided dives £12 per dive or £20 per day. Advanced courses by arrangement; contact centre for price details.
Booking: Bookings normally made in advance, but late bookings sometimes accepted if space available. A non-refundable deposit of £25 must be paid on booking. Payment by cash, cheque or credit card.
Access: Anglesey is reached via the Menai Bridge (A5), and Holyhead is at the far western end of the island. The town has a train station and a cab from there to the centre costs about £3.

chester school of diving

67 Brook Street
Chester
Cheshire
CH1 3DZ
Tel (01244) 314 204

Although this school is based in the town, it offers a Learn to Dive in 6 Days course (Novice Diver I & II) that includes 5 open-water dives. The full range of PADI international qualifications is also on offer, including Advanced, Divemaster, Rescue and speciality courses in boat handling and air compressor management. Boat charter and guided dives to local wrecks are available to experienced recreational divers. Trips further afield – mostly to the North Wales coast – are also offered.

Season: Open all year.
Accommodation: No on-site accommodation. Centre will provide help in obtaining local accommodation.
Food: Not provided.
Children: Minimum age 14; anyone under 18 needs consent of parent or guardian.
Disabled Facilities: None.
Insurance: BSAC cover included in course price.
Safety: All instructors trained in first aid and sub-aqua rescue.
Affiliations: BSAC; PADI.
Tariffs: Prices include all tuition and equipment hire. BSAC Novice Diver I & II 5-day course: £260. BSAC Sport Diver 5-day course: £280. Dive Leader training: £65 per day. Guided dives: £12 per dive or £20 per day. Advanced courses by arrangement; contact centre for price details.
Booking: Bookings normally made in advance, but late bookings sometimes accepted if space available. A non-refundable deposit of £25 must be paid on booking. Payment by cash or cheque.
Access: The school is in central Chester. Clients arriving by bus or train can be met for a small charge to cover petrol.

cornish diving and watersports

Marine Crescent
Bar Road
Falmouth
Cornwall
TR11 4BN
Tel (01326) 311 265

This centre offers open-water tuition and guided dives off the Cornish coast, with around 7 hours of tuition/diving per day. Groups of up to 10 people can be accommodated (there are 3 instructors), but individual tuition is also available. Boat charter can be arranged, along with a dive skipper, for any qualified diver. The full range of BSAC courses is taught – from Novice Diver I and II through Sport Diver and beyond – with specialist Nitrox and Technical Nitrox courses for would-be instructors. Courses are non-residential and vary between 1 and 5 days in length. Cornish Diving has been running for over 15 years.

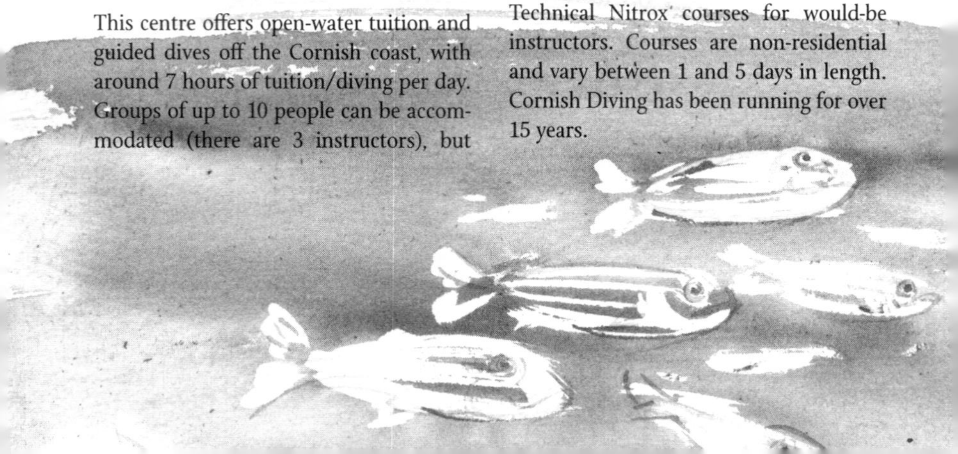

Season: Open all year.
Accommodation: No on-site accommodation. Centre will provide help in obtaining local accommodation.
Food: Not provided.
Children: Minimum age 14; anyone under 18 needs consent of parent or guardian.
Disabled Facilities: None.
Insurance: BSAC cover included in course price.
Safety: All instructors trained in first aid and sub-aqua rescue.
Affiliations: BSAC; PADI.
Tariffs: Prices include all tuition and equipment hire. Introduction to Diving 1-day course: £40. BSAC Novice Diver I & II 4-day course: £250. BSAC Sport Diver 5-day course: £280. Dive Leader training: £65 per day. Guided dives: £12 per dive or £20 per day. Advanced courses by arrangement; contact centre for price details.
Booking: Bookings normally made in advance, but late bookings sometimes accepted if space available. A non-refundable deposit of £25 must be paid on booking. Payment by cash, cheque or credit card.
Access: If arriving by car, head through Falmouth town centre's 1-way system towards the docks and look out for Cornish Diving on the right as you near the water. Falmouth has a train station – change at Truro from InterCity. The station is close to the school – ring them for exact directions. There is also a local bus stop nearby. Ask to be set down at the taxi rank.

---

divers down

The Pier
High Street
Swanage
Dorset
BH19 2NT
Tel (01929) 423 565

This is the oldest recognized dive school in England, whose consistently high standard of tuition and dive leading has kept it in business for over 20 years. Their Learn to Dive in 6 Days (BSAC Novice I & II) course comes highly recommended, but the school also runs the full range of BSAC and PADI courses right up to Divemaster. Also available are specialist boat and compressor handling courses, private dive leading, boat charter to local wrecks, and a well-stocked dive shop.

Season: Open all year.
Accommodation: Centre will provide help in obtaining local accommodation.
Food: Not provided.
Children: Minimum age 14; anyone under 18 needs consent of parent or guardian.
Disabled Facilities: None.
Insurance: BSAC cover included in course price.
Safety: All instructors trained in first aid and sub-aqua rescue.
Affiliations: BSAC; PADI.
Tariffs: Prices include all tuition and equipment hire. Introduction to Diving 1-day course: £40. BSAC Novice Diver I & II 4-day course: £250. BSAC Sport Diver 5-day course: £280. Dive Leader training: £65 per day. Guided dives: £12 per dive or £20 per day. Advanced courses by arrangement; contact centre for price details.
Booking: Bookings normally made in advance, but late bookings accepted if space available. A non-refundable deposit of £25 must be paid on booking. Payment by cash, cheque or credit card.
Access: Swanage is on the Isle of Purbeck in Dorset, at the end of the A351 from Wareham. It has a railway station, and a cab from there to the centre costs around £3.

dv diving

138 Mountstewart Road
Newtownards
County Down
BT22 2ES
Northern Ireland
Tel (01247) 861 686
Tel/Fax (01247) 464 671

The lough shores of County Down are some of Britain's best dive sites – crammed with intact wrecks and sub-tropical marine life that drifts up on the warm Gulf Stream waters during the summer. DV Diving run trips to Belfast Lough, Strangford Lough and along the Ards Peninsula, including the Copeland Islands and Rathlin. Apart from dive holidays and courses, the centre offers boat charter and all equipment hire. Complete packages, including travel from mainland Britain, can be arranged. Course holidays for combined BSAC Novice Diver I and II run as a 5-day package, as does one for Sport Diver. More advanced training is charged on a daily basis.

Season: Open all year.
Accommodation: No on-site accommodation. Centre will provide help in obtaining local accommodation.
Food: Not provided.
Children: Minimum age 14; anyone under 18 needs consent of parent or guardian.
Disabled Facilities: None.
Insurance: Liability cover included in course price; clients should arrange personal holiday insurance if desired.
Safety: All instructors trained in first aid.
Affiliations: BSAC; PADI; Technical Diving International.
Tariffs: Prices include all tuition and equipment hire. Introduction to Diving 1-day course: £40. BSAC Novice Diver I & II 4-day course: £250. BSAC Sport Diver 5-day course: £280. Dive Leader training: £65 per day. Guided dives: £12 per dive or £20 per day. Advanced courses by arrangement; contact centre for price details.
Booking: Fees are 50% refundable if cancellation notice received 28 days in advance. Bookings normally made in advance, but late bookings sometimes accepted if space available.
Access: On Mountstewart Road between Ballywalter and Newtownards.

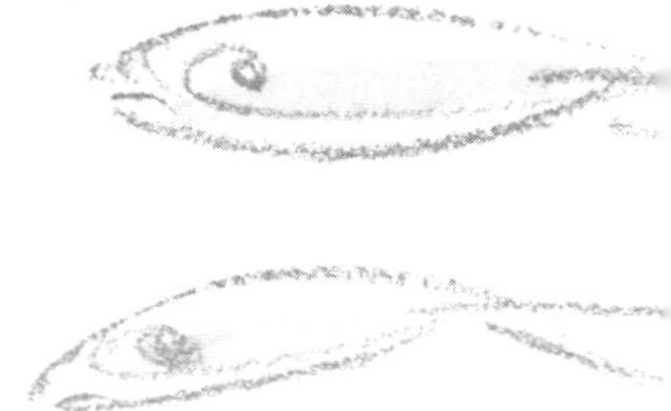

falmouth underwater centre

Maenporth Beach
Falmouth
Cornwall
TR11 5HN
Tel (01326) 250 852 / (03859) 36801
Fax (01326) 250 852

Tuition for all levels of experience is offered here, including short introductory evenings that let you try out the equipment, either in a pool or in a sheltered cove, followed by the range of BSAC and PADI courses: Open Water Diver, Advanced Open Water, Novice Diver, Novice Diver II, Sport Diver, Dive Leader, and Advanced Diver, as well as individual training and accompanied dives for any level of competence. Most of these courses last 4–7 days and are run every week, year round. There are even concessions for benefit claimers and full-time students.

Specialist courses for would-be professionals, such as Oxygen Administration, Practical Rescue Management, Dive Planning and Marshalling, Boat Handling, Advanced Diving Techniques and Search and Recovery, are also taught – all of them in one 8-day package, should you wish it. Boat diving and charter are also available, whether by the day or in 5-day holiday packages. The school, which has been running 12 years, has 6 full-time instructors plus various part-timers as necessary. All equipment is included in the course fees, but not accommodation, which you arrange locally through the centre.

Season: Open all year.
Accommodation: No on-site accommodation. Centre will provide help in obtaining local accommodation.
Food: Café on-site.
Children: Minimum age 14; anyone under 18 needs consent of parent or guardian.
Disabled Facilities: Disabled persons accepted subject to medical clearance – building has no special facilities.
Insurance: Clients are covered by centre's insurance.
Safety: All instructors trained in first aid.
Affiliations: BSAC; PADI; Royal Yachting Association; City and Guilds.
Tariffs: Diving charter: £12 per dive; £20 per day; £90 for 5-day dive package; £120 for 5-day dive package (including cylinder, weight belt and air). Trial dives from £10. Qualification courses from £100.
Booking: Fees are refundable if cancellation notice received 14 days in advance, minus 10% handling charge. Bookings normally made in advance, but late bookings sometimes accepted if space available.
Access: Off the A39 at Maenporth Beach in Falmouth. Trains and buses to Falmouth, cab to beach costs around £3.

guernsey school of diving

Castle Emplacement
St Peter Port
Guernsey
Channel Islands
GY1 1AU
Tel (01481) 722 884
Fax (01481) 714 162

If you find yourself in the Channel Islands, this diving school offers open-water trial dives and novice courses as well as the usual advanced courses and charter services to local wrecks. They also run sea fishing trips. Courses are non-residential. With 3 full-time instructors and 8 years of experience, the school can also offer specialist courses in boat handling and chart work.

The diving school is part of an older organization called Sarnia Skin Divers – one of the few skin diving centres in Britain. It operates as a club, but will take out visitors who are competent swimmers, and preferably experienced snorkellers.

Season: Open all year.
Accommodation: No on-site accommodation. Centre will provide help in obtaining local accommodation.
Food: Not provided.
Children: Minimum age 14; anyone under 18 needs consent of parent or guardian.
Disabled Facilities: None.
Insurance: Clients should have their own personal accident cover.
Safety: All instructors trained in first aid.
Affiliations: BSAC.
Tariffs: Try-dives: £25; Novice Diver I & II: £225. Contact centre for tariffs of other courses.
Booking: Fees are refundable if cancellation notice received 14 days in advance, minus 10% handling charge. Booking normally made in advance with a 20% deposit, but late bookings sometimes accepted if space available.
Access: The centre is 5 minutes drive from the town centre on the sea front.

island underwater safaris

'Nowhere'
Old Town
St Mary's
Isles of Scilly
Cornwall
TR21 ONH
Tel (01720) 422 732

The ocean around the rocky coastline of the Isles of Scilly is known for its warm-water diving (at least in summer). Mark Groves, who runs the 'safaris', is a trained instructor with a background of Caribbean and Red Sea reef diving. He offers dives for all levels of experience, including total beginners – even for children aged 10 and over – getting you into the water, after some basic instruction, to marvel at the abundance of sea life in these clean coastal waters. All equipment is provided, and no previous experience is necessary. You do need to be a good swimmer, though. Groups are limited to a maximum of 6 people. There is no on-site accommodation, but you can book it locally to suit your budget through the centre.

Among the highlights of Mark Groves's underwater safaris is the possibility of playing with seals and, occasionally, with dolphins. If you don't want to go under the water, snorkelling forays with the seals can also be arranged.

Experienced divers (anyone with BSAC Sport Diver or equivalent) can dive to any number of wreck sites in the area, or to the more remote reefs. A purpose-built 22ft catamaran and 18ft dinghy get you to the dive sites. The rest is up to you.

Season: Easter to October.
Accommodation: Centre can provide help in arranging local accommodation, from camping to hotels.
Food: Not available.
Other Activities: Eco-Sports (see p. 146).
Children: Over-10s only.
Disabled Facilities: None.
Insurance: Should be arranged by clients.
Safety: Instructors trained in first aid.
Affiliations: PADI.
Tariffs: Diving safari (includes instruction and equipment): £28. Wreck or reef boat dives (including equipment and boat hire): £30 for 1 day, £128 for 6 days.
Booking: Deposit required. Late bookings accepted if space available.
Access: Ferry or plane from Penzance to St Mary's.

national watersports centre, cumbrae

Burnside Road
Largs
North Ayrshire
KA30 8RW
Scotland
Tel (01475) 674 666
Fax (01475) 674 720

This centre offers one of the few introductory diving courses that take place in the open water. The diving off Cumbrae is highly recommended, with very clear waters and some warm-water marine life travelling up on the Gulf Stream through the summer months.

Experienced divers can also organize dive-boat charter through the centre. Ring them for the full range of options.

Children: Must be 12 or older.
Affiliations: Course run in conjunction with Scuba Experience, a 5-star PADI diving centre.
Tariffs: All prices include tuition, equipment and full-board accommodation. 5-day beginners' course: £440.

See Sailing (p. 355) for full details.

nervous wreck diving centre

Ganavan Sands
Oban
Argyll & Bute
PA34 4YD
Scotland
Tel & Fax (01631) 566 000

With over 150 dive sites to choose from, Nervous Wreck offers some of the most varied diving on the west Highland coast. If you are already an experienced diver, then the wrecks, reefs and shoals are yours. If you want to learn to dive, the centre offers 5-day courses, aimed at getting you through your first PADI certificates. There are 2 courses, one for beginners, which gets you your PADI Open Water licence, and for those who already hold this qualification, Advanced Open Water. If you want to go for a higher licence, you can take the centre's 7-day Divemaster.

There are also specialized courses: the Medic First Aid, lasting 1 day, teaches rescue procedures, how to unblock obstructed airways, control of bleeding, shock management, and illness and injury assessment; there are also Wreck Diver, Deep Diver, Night Diver, Boat Diver, Dry Suit Diver, Underwater Photographer, RYA Boat Handler, and VHF Radio courses. In short, Nervous Wreck can take you from being an absolute novice right through to experienced instructor level – given time, of course.

Unfortunately, there is no on-site accommodation, but the centre will book it for you locally, at whatever budget. All equipment and transport to dive sites are included in the course fees.

Season: Open all year.
Accommodation: Centre will provide help in finding local accommodation in hostels, B&Bs or hotels.
Food: Restaurant and bar at centre.
Children: Must be 12 or older. Junior open-water courses available.
Disabled Facilities: None.
Insurance: Clients should arrange their own holiday insurance.
Safety: Staff trained in first aid.
Affiliations: BSAC; PADI.
Tariffs: All prices include tuition, but do not include use of equipment unless stated otherwise. A wide range of courses is available; samples include – 5-day Open Water course (equipment included): £300 (£290 for juniors); 2-day Advanced Open Water course: £195; 7-day Divemaster course: £295; 2-day Deep Diver course: £80; 2-day Night Diver course: £60; 2-day Wreck Diver course: £85; diving taster session: £30; Guided Shore Dive: £25.
Booking: 25% non-refundable deposit required. Bookings normally made 2 weeks in advance, but late bookings accepted up to 48 hours in advance if space available. Visa cards accepted.
Access: Take the A85 to Oban Bay. Contact centre for public transport details.

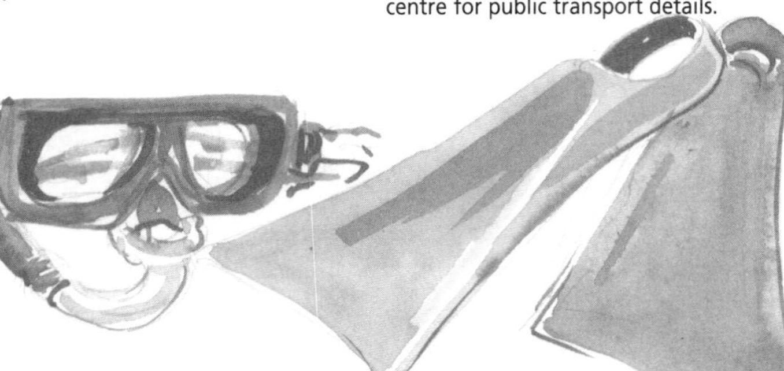

st martin's diving services

Highertown
St Martin's
Isles of Scilly
Cornwall
TR25 0QL
Tel (01720) 422 848

The Isles of Scilly have more wrecks and reefs than you could explore in a single season. These, combined with warm, clear waters and abundant sea life, make the little archipelago one of Britain's best general dive sites. At St Martin's diving school, beginners can take their BSAC certificate courses (there is accommodation), while more experienced divers can arrange guided dives, or charter a boat themselves. The centre has 2 boats, one of which can take 12 people, the other 6.

If you want to become an instructor and need to learn specialized skills, St Martin's also offers courses in boat handling, compressor operation, chart work and other topics necessary for the aspiring professional or dive leader.

All equipment is included in the course fees, but accommodation is extra. St Martin's has been operational for 8 years.

Season: March to October.
Accommodation: Self-catering flat for 6–8 divers (bring your own linen): approximately £250 per week. Rental of additional flats, camping or local B&B can be arranged by centre.
Food: Hot drinks supplied on dives.
Children: Minimum age 14.
Disabled Facilities: None.
Insurance: Clients must arrange their own insurance (BSAC members are covered).
Safety: Transport provided to nearest decompression chamber if needed. Staff trained in first aid, diver rescue and oxygen administration.
Affiliations: BSAC.
Tariffs: 3-hour introductory course: £27. Seal snorkelling trip: £28. Charter dive prices (based on 2 dives a day for 6 days) vary according to group size. Daily fees from £18.50 per person (group of 8) to £14 per person (group of 12). Daily boat hire from £148 (group of 8) to £168 (group of 12). Self-catering accommodation from £50 per person per week.
Booking: Non-refundable deposit required (contact centre for details). Bookings normally made in advance, but late bookings sometimes accepted if space available.
Access: The Isles of Scilly are accessible by ferry, leaving from Penzance.

scuba-tech

8 Owen Road
Skerton
Lancashire
LA1 2AR
Tel (01524) 381 831

Become a qualified diver in 5 days, with inshore open-water diving in the Lake District. This BSAC Novice Diver I & II course can be followed up with Sports Diver or the full range of PADI courses right up to Divemaster. Although lake diving is not as exciting as diving in the sea, these courses are convenient for people living in the north-west, and can be combined with mountain-related activities such as hillwalking, climbing and mountain skills.

Season: Open all year.
Accommodation: No on-site accommodation. Centre will provide help in obtaining local accommodation.
Food: Not provided.
Children: Minimum age 14; anyone under 18 needs consent of parent or guardian.

Disabled Facilities: None.
Insurance: Clients are covered by centre's insurance.
Safety: All instructors trained in first aid.
Affiliations: BSAC; PADI.
Tariffs: £220 for 5-day learn-to-dive package. Prices for more advanced courses on application.
Booking: Fees are refundable if cancellation notice received 14 days in advance, minus 10% handling charge. Bookings normally made in advance, but late bookings sometimes accepted if space available. Payment by cheque.
Access: Courses take place at various locations in the Lake District. Contact centre for full details. Pick-ups from local train and bus stations can be arranged.

---

69 diving ltd

Sunseeker International Marina
West Quay Road
Poole
Dorset
BH15 1HX
Tel (01202) 677 427
Fax (01202) 682 744

This centre runs interesting adventure diving courses and holidays off the South Coast and the Isle of Purbeck, with trips out to local wrecks and rock shelves teeming with marine life. Learn-to-dive courses of 2, 3, 4 or 7 days are offered, along with boat charter and equipment hire. New and second-hand equipment sales are also available.

Season: Open all year.
Accommodation: No on-site accommodation. Centre will provide help in obtaining local accommodation.
Food: Not provided.
Children: Minimum age 12; anyone under 18 needs consent of parent or guardian.
Disabled Facilities: None.
Insurance: Clients are covered by centre's insurance.
Safety: All instructors trained in first aid.
Affiliations: British Sub Aqua Club (BSAC), Professional Association of Diving Instructors (PADI), International Association of Nitrox and Technical Divers (IANTD).
Tariffs: Diving charter: £12 per dive, £20 per day; £250 for 5-day Learn-to-dive package. Prices for more advanced courses on application.
Booking: Cancellation notice in writing 14 days prior to start date Payment by cheque or credit card (no Amex). Bookings normally made in advance, but late bookings sometimes accepted if space available. Payment by cheque.
Access: Poole can be reached via the A31 and A3049. There is also a train station. A cab from there to the centre costs around £4.

uist outdoor centre

Cearn Dusgaidh
Lochmaddy
Isle of North Uist
Western Isles
PA82 5AE
Scotland
Tel (01876) 500 480

The Outer Hebrides are magical no matter what time of year you visit them, or for what reason. The Uist Outdoor Centre sits squarely in the middle of the long archipelago and through Neil, the owner, and his team of 3 full-time instructors, the whole chain of islands and the waters around them are yours to explore.

The diving here varies between ocean and sea loch. Courses cater for everyone from the beginner upwards, with really experienced divers able to charter the centre's 5.8m Fury RIB powerboat.

The local waters are particularly interesting for those of an ecological bent – the Outer Hebrides lie at the centre of an oceanographic 'mixing zone'. The warm Gulf Stream brings in warm-water species such as mako shark, sunfish, sea slugs, soft corals and anemones. Seals abound in the area, as do porpoise, dolphin and orca (killer whales).

The centre overlooks a sea loch and has its own bunkhouse, or can arrange other accommodation to suit. All equipment is included in the course fees, as are accommodation and pick-up/set-down from the ferry terminal.

Season: Open all year.
Accommodation: 20 dormitory beds at centre. (Guests can also stay at centre without participating in sporting activities: £8 per night.)
Food: Self-catering or full-board options. Vegetarian and special diets catered for upon request.
Other Activities: Canoeing (see p. 36); Climbing and Abseiling (p. 109); Eco-Sports (p. 151); Powerboating (p. 328); Walking (p. 432).
Children: Minimum age 8 unless accompanied by adult.
Disabled Facilities: Centre has disabled access.
Insurance: Clients covered by centre's insurance.
Safety: Staff trained in first aid.
Affiliations: Scottish Tourist Board.
Tariffs: Prices include instruction, equipment and accommodation. 1-week holiday (diving only or combined with other centre activities): £220 (self-catering) / £270 (with full board). Day visitors: £25.
Booking: 10% non-refundable deposit required. Balance due 28 days before start date. Late bookings accepted if space available.
Access: Cars must take ferry from Kyle of Lochalsh to Uig (on Skye), then to North Uist. Trains available to Kyle of Lochalsh, buses available to Uig. Pick-ups from ferry terminal on Uist can be arranged by centre.

kitting yourself out

If you're diving off Britain, the cold waters make a dry suit with an 8mm membrane practical. If you want to dive in warmer waters, a wet suit with a membrane of between 2mm and 6mm is ideal. Make sure your suit is of good quality neoprene and tight-fitting – in a loose one you'll chill. For dry suits, try the Northern Diver, Beaver, RoHo, DUI or Poseidon ranges, which cost from £200 to £320 new. For wet suits, the Viking, Hydrotech, Bermuda and Typhoon ranges are good. Expect to pay from £100 for a 2mm suit to £180–200 for a 6mm one.

Next comes the mask. It's important to choose one with a good angle of vision, both horizontally and vertically. Masks come in 3 basic types: standard, silicone and low-volume. Ask your instructor which you should have. IST are good manufacturers.

After a mask, you'll need fins, or flippers. With these you have a choice of full-shoe for cold water (you wear booties underneath, price around £25), and heel-strap fins for warm water, worn over bare feet. Both Wenoka and Sea Style make good fins; prices in the £30–50 range. No matter what water you're diving in, you'll also need a weight belt. The Polar Bear, Dive 2000, Hydrotech and Oceanic ranges have many adherents and prices start from about £18.

Finally, there's the most vital piece of equipment – an aqualung set (jacket and cylinders) and air regulator. These are highly specialized and vary according to what type of dive you're planning. However, always good are Aqua-Lung UK, Buddy, Scubapro or Oceanic for aqualungs, and Spiro, Scubapro, Apeks or Mares for regulators. Prices are in the £500–700 range for aqualung and regulator.

A dive computer (worn on the wrist), to regulate depth, decompression, ascent rate and to give a variety of other useful information, is a good idea if you're serious about the sport. Aladdin, Suunto, Datamaster, Monitor and Scubapro produce good computers. A very basic model costs about £150 new, with prices going up to around £350.

If you find the prices of new sub-aqua gear rather frightening , there is a thriving market in second-hand stuff, mostly sold through the BSAC clubs – and this is how most people get going. Get your instructor to come with you and vet any equipment you're planning to buy.

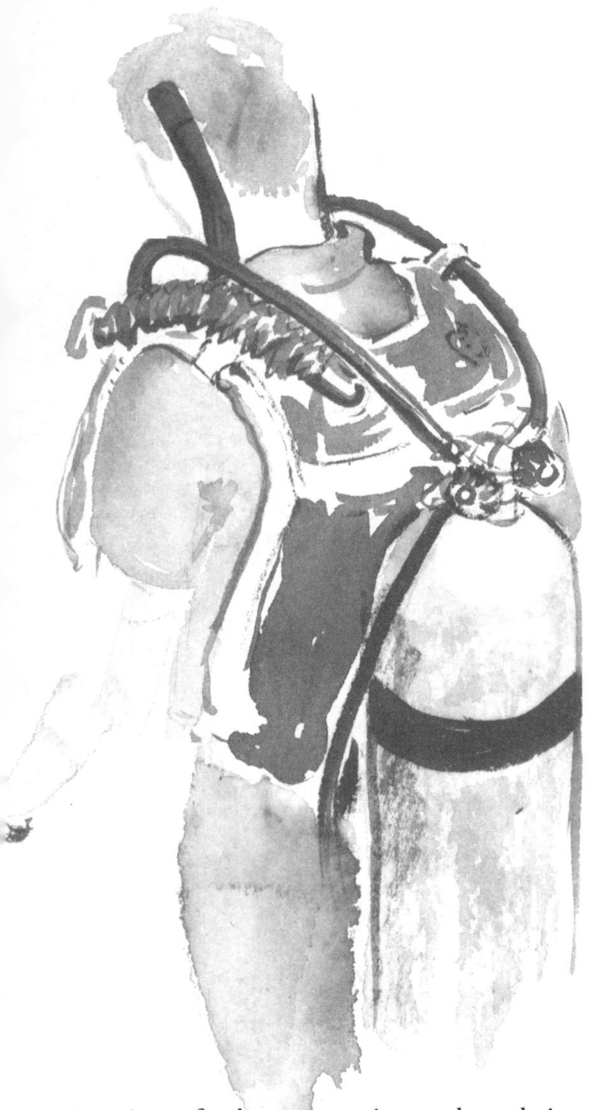

checklist

- ✔ *wet suit or dry suit*
- ✔ *weight belt*
- ✔ *mask*
- ✔ *aqualung set and regulator*
- ✔ *fins*
- ✔ *computer*

A variety of other accessories, such as knives, dive bags, underwater compasses and cameras, gloves and hoods, can hike up your total bill considerably. But these are not generally necessary for a beginner.

further reading

Sport Diving – The Official BSAC Manual from Novice Level to Advanced Diver Certificate, Stanley Paul, 1995.

photo: Andrew Holt

governing body

British Surfing Association (BSA)
Champion's Yard, Penzance
Cornwall TR18 2TA
Tel (01736) 60250
Fax (01736) 331 077

surfing

It looks impossible to do, and actually it is bloody difficult to learn, but surfing is a sport most people can master given enough time and dedication. It is quite a physically demanding sport – as the rippling bodies of regular surfers testify – and before taking it up you should be able to swim 50m in open water without tiring. Before using a surfboard, it is also a good idea to mess about with a body board (also called a boogie board) to get an idea of how waves work. Most surfing centres will hire these out for very little money.

Having decided that you want to surf, sign up for lessons; don't just head into the water blindly with a hired board. Even relatively close to shore the sea is dangerous. You will notice that surfers generally enter the water in the same place, avoiding local currents and rocks. Always use a surfboard with an ankle leash, which prevents you losing it when you wipe out and stops it from hitting someone further down the wave. Also, practise paddling the board out to waves, lying on your stomach and using your arms as paddles. This is tiring and the more you do it, the stronger you will become.

When you and the instructor are in position, wait for him to tell you to start paddling back towards the beach. A wave will be coming up behind you. As it catches you it will lift the board. Grab the sides, tense your stomach and thigh muscles, and try to stand up, with one foot under your chest and the other foot just over 12 inches behind, both at right angles to the centre of the board. At the same time, make sure the nose of the board is out of the water, or it might 'pearl' – dive down like a dolphin, taking you with it. This will almost certainly happen to you on your first few attempts. However, many people do manage to stand up at the end of their first day. If you take a 3- or 5-day course, you should be standing fairly confidently by the end, and your muscles will be on the way to Baywatchdom.

Another form of surfing – wave skiing – involves sitting on a narrow board (or 'ski') and paddling with a type of kayak double paddle to catch the wave. Details are given at the end of the chapter.

selected centres

acorn activities

PO Box 120
Hereford
Hereford & Worcester
HR4 8YB
Tel (01432) 830 083
Fax (01432) 830 110

The surfing off the Dyfed coast is not as famous as that in Cornwall, but aficionados recommend it for beginners: it has gentler waves than Cornwall and an all-year surfing season – though you'd have to be a bit of a masochist to go into the Atlantic in winter. Accredited British Surfing Association (BSA) instructors take you for either a 2-day introductory course (they reckon it's feasible for you to stand up on the board during your first day), or a 5-day power-wave course. Acorn will arrange accommodation to suit your budget, and you can book courses for any week of the year you like.

Note that Acorn offer a variety of water sports among their adventure holidays, including sailing, windsurfing, power-boating and water skiing. Contact them to find out more about these activities, and see Walking (p. 414) for a list of the adventure sports offered by Acorn that are featured in this guide.

Accommodation: Local accommodation can be arranged through centre. Choose your own budget.
Tariffs: The 2-day course costs £80 and the 5-day course £200. Both tariffs include tuition and equipment, but not accommodation.

See Walking (p. 414) for full details.

adventure sports

Carnkie Farmhouse
Carnkie
Redruth
Cornwall
TR16 6RZ
Tel (01209) 218 962 / (0589) 427 077

You can either concentrate on surfing only here or learn it as one aspect of a multi-activity holiday. Surfing is offered by the day, over a weekend or 2-day break, or as 5- or 7-day holidays. The farmhouse centre has been running for 12 years and aims its holidays at people in their mid-20s. Tariffs include accommodation – the prices are set on a sliding scale from double rooms down to camping. All holidays are self-catering. All local transport is provided and the centre will pick you up from Falmouth if you don't have transport for a charge of £2.

Affiliations: BSA.
Tariffs: Surfing is one of the activities offered in the centre's multi-activity package deals (accommodation included). Prices are variable, depending on season and type of accommodation desired: £44–78 for 2 nights / 2 activities; £150–195 for 5 nights / 5 activities; £154–273 for 7 nights / 7 activities. Group, long-term stay and previous-customer discounts available. Single persons desiring their own room must pay a 30% surcharge.

See Paragliding and Parascending (p. 310) for full details.

atlantic pursuits

11 Priestacott Park
Kilkhampton
Bude
Cornwall
EX23 9TH
Tel (01288) 321 765

Run by ex-special-forces instructors, Atlantic Pursuits is a small, efficient centre offering non-residential half-day and day courses or packages of 3–5 days that concentrate on getting you familiar with the board and at home in the surf. Those who already have experience can hire equipment for the day; those who sign up for courses get 4 hours of intensive tuition daily – enough to get you good and tired. Private tuition to any standard can be arranged.

Season: 1 March to 30 November.
Accommodation: Centre will help to book local accommodation – camping, B&B or hotel.
Food: Not provided.
Other Activities: Canoeing (see p. 19).
Children: Surfing instruction available for children aged 10 and over.
Disabled Facilities: None.
Insurance: Third-party insurance must be obtained by joining the BSA: £2 per year.
Safety: Instructors first aid and lifesaver trained.
Affiliations: BSA; British Canoe Union; Surfing Life Saving Association.
Tariffs: Prices include instruction and equipment – half-day course: £10; full day: £20; 3-day: £55; 5-day: £90. Groups of 10 or more can take advantage of discounted rates – £15 per person per day.
Booking: Same-day bookings can be taken subject to availability, but in general longer courses should be booked at least 14 days in advance. 20% deposit required, non-refundable if you cancel less than 48 hours before course starts. Balance payable on arrival. Payment by cash or cheque.
Access: Ring centre for details.

headland hotel

Fistral Beach
Newquay
Cornwall
TR7 1EW
Tel (01637) 872 211
Fax (01637) 872 212

The Headland Hotel is an unlikely venue for surfing. A relic of the short-lived days of the English Riviera, its staid Edwardian façade (and, to some extent, clientele) seems at variance with the anarchic image of surfing. But the Headland has survived, presumably, by being able to adapt, and despite its stiff-looking decor and staff it provides some of the best surfing tuition in Britain. It is also the venue for one of our major surfing competitions, the Headworx Professional Surfing Championships, which draws entrants from all over the surfing world. Fistral, the hotel's beach, is renowned for its excellent surfing conditions in summer, and the tutors claim that 70% of beginners learning here manage to stand on the board during their first lesson.

You can take half or full days of tuition, or longer 2-day, 5-day and fortnight intensive courses if you are really serious. The hotel sells and hires surfing gear and includes all equipment in the price of tuition.

Season: May to early October.
Accommodation: Many double and single rooms available in this grand Victorian hotel (£37–64 per night depending on room, season and board options).
Food: Restaurant at hotel. B&B or half-board options. Vegetarian and special diets can be catered for.
Children: Hotel has playroom, outdoor playground, baby listening devices and other facilities for children of guests. Child discounts available. Surfing instruction available for children 6 and over.
Disabled Facilities: Hotel is wheelchair-accessible.
Insurance: Third-party insurance must be obtained by joining the BSA: £2 per year.
Safety: Lifeguards on beach.
Affiliations: None.
Tariffs: Prices include instruction and equipment – half-day course: £15; full day: £25; 2-day: £45; 5-day: £100; fortnight: prices on application. 10% discount for hotel guests.
Booking: For guests of the hotel, there is a non-refundable deposit of £50 per person. If cancellation notice received 29–55 days in advance, guest liable for 40% of total charge; 1–28 days, 80% of total; same day, 100% of total. Credit cards are accepted, cheques by prior arrangement only. Although bookings normally made in advance, late bookings are accepted if space available.
Access: Off the A3059 at Newquay. Trains and buses to Newquay; pick-ups can be made by hotel (£4 charge).

national surfing centre

North Fistral Beach
Newquay
Cornwall
Tel (01637) 850 737 (May–Oct)
Fax (01736) 331 077

Postal Address:
British Surfing Association
Champions' Yard
Penzance
Cornwall
TR18 2TA

Run under the direct auspices of the BSA, this school offers some of the most competitive rates in the UK and has instructors employed directly by the BSA. Courses are open to all ages and abilities (assuming you are reasonably fit), from half-day to 5-day courses with tuition, boards and wet suits thrown in. The centre is just behind the beach car park next to the Surf Life-Saving Club.

Season: May to early October.
Accommodation: Not provided, but the centre will help you book it locally.
Food: Not provided.
Children: Children 8 and over welcome.
Disabled Facilities: None.
Insurance: Third-party insurance must be obtained by joining the BSA: £2 per year.
Safety: Instructors trained in surf rescue.
Affiliations: BSA.
Tariffs: Prices include instruction and equipment – half-day course: £15; full day: £25; 2-day: £45; 3-day £60; 5-day: £100.
Booking: If booking in advance, a 25% deposit should be paid with the booking, balance payable on arrival. Payment by cash or cheque.
Access: In Newquay, behind the North Fistral Beach car park, next to the Surf Life-Saving Club. Clients arriving by bus or train can be picked up for the cost of the petrol.

outdoor adventure

Atlantic Court
Widemouth Bay
Nr Bude
Cornwall
EX23 0DF
Tel (01288) 361 312
Fax (01288) 361 153

Outdoor Adventure has been running since 1981, offering surfing holidays designed for both beginners and experienced surfers. With a superb beach right on the doorstep, in a bay visited by dolphins, the centre has access to a continuous Atlantic swell that provides waves for all levels of surfer, all fronting the same stretch of sand.

There are 10 instructors here, and it's up to you to tell them what you want to learn. Rich Gill, the head instructor, tries to tailor each holiday/course to suit the needs of the group or individual rather than following a rigid syllabus. However, if you really get the bug and want to progress, Outdoor Adventure can lay on a structured BSA award course that will get you your certificate of competence and, if you are an aspiring professional, set you on the way to becoming an instructor. If weather conditions turn against you, the centre will lay on mountain biking, canoeing, sailing, windsurfing or indoor climbing at no extra cost. Alternatively, you can opt for a multi-activity holiday including these other sports. The holidays and courses are run as weekend, 3-day and 7-day packages.

The centre occupies a large, rambling cottage on a small cliff overlooking Widemouth Bay and all holidays/courses include accommodation here (double, single or dorm rooms) and full board. They will also pick you up free of charge from Bude if you arrive by public transport.

Season: March to November.
Accommodation: Sea front centre with 8 twin rooms, 1 4-bed room, 2 3-bed rooms, 1 single.
Food: Home-cooked meals provided. Vegetarian and special diets catered for.
Other Activities: Windsurfing (see p. 464).
Children: Minimum age 16.
Disabled Facilities: None.
Insurance: Clients should take out personal insurance cover; can be arranged through the centre.
Safety: All staff trained in first aid and life-saving.
Affiliations: British Activity Holiday Association; British Canoe Union; BSA; Mountain Leaders Training Board; Royal Yachting Association.
Tariffs: Prices for surfing courses or multi-activity holidays include full-board accommodation, instruction, use of equipment and wet suit. Weekend break from £123; 3-day holiday from £177; 5-day holiday from £288.
Booking: Non-refundable deposit required: £100. Balance due 60 days before start of holiday. Access, Visa, Mastercard and Eurocard accepted (5% surcharge applies). Although bookings normally made in advance, late bookings sometimes accepted if space available.
Access: From Exeter, take the A30 to Okehampton and Launceston, then the A395 to Hallworthy. Join the A39 towards Bude, then the coastal road to Widemouth Bay. Trains and buses available from Exeter to Bude; centre will arrange pick-up.

surf's up surf school

The Valley Caravan Park
Old Polzeath
Cornwall
PL27 6SS
Tel (01208) 862 003

With surfing lessons for people of all ages, this school runs introductory half-days and/or half-day improvers' sessions as well as longer residential and non-residential 'developer' courses for those with some surfing experience. These can be for a weekend or a whole week. The Surf's Up school offers very competitive rates and is keen to dispel the 'cool' image that prevents some people trying the sport – the youngest person they have taught is 8 years old, and the oldest 67.

Course tariffs include use of wet suits and boards and also advice on buying your own gear. They do not include accommodation, which is arranged off-site to suit your budget.

Season: April to December.
Accommodation: No on-site accommodation, but centre can arrange a variety of local accommodation, from camping to hotels. Residential packages in caravan park are also available.
Food: Not provided.
Children: Must be 8 years old and water-confident. Surfing and rookie lifeguard courses available for children.
Disabled Facilities: Special-needs clients are welcome and courses will be adapted where necessary. Contact centre for details.
Insurance: Clients should arrange personal insurance cover.
Safety: Qualified lifeguards and life-savers on beach.
Affiliations: BSA.
Tariffs: All prices include tuition and use of equipment. 2½-hour introductory session: £13; 2½-hour improvers' session: £13; 5-session developer course: £50; 2-day residential course (including accommodation): £45; 7-day residential course (including accommodation): £90. Group discounts available.
Booking: Deposit required if course pre-booked. No charge in case of cancellation. Late bookings accepted if space available (48 hours' notice usually needed in peak season and for children's courses).
Access: Take the A39 to Wadebridge, then follow signs to Polzeath. Trains to Bodmin Parkway then bus to Polzeath (via Wadebridge). Buses to Wadebridge and local buses to Polzeath.

tolcarne beach

Narrowcliff
Newquay
Cornwall
TR7 2QN
Tel (01637) 872 489 (summer)
(01209) 719 172 (winter)

This small beach-side centre employs 3 instructors and offers tuition at all levels as well as board hire for people wanting to surf independently. On-site self-catering accommodation can be included in the course/holiday fee, or arranged elsewhere in the beach town, to be paid for separately. Clients do not have to surf just on Tolcarne beach – the centre has equipment hire outlets on Fistral North and South beaches, as well as on Towan and Great Western. By mid-1997, the centre plans to have built a new surf school with more accommodation and a lecture room. Ring them to see how far work has progressed.

Season: Open all year, but main season is April to October.
Accommodation: Self-catering beach bungalow available for 4–6 persons (£201–429 per week). Local B&B can also be arranged.
Food: Café on beach; vegetarian selections available.
Children: All ages welcome.
Disabled Facilities: None.
Insurance: Clients should arrange their own holiday insurance.
Safety: Staff trained in rescue and first aid.
Affiliations: None.
Tariffs: Prices include tuition and equipment hire. Full day of surfing: £15. Group and weekly discounts available.
Booking: Deposit required for advanced bookings. Same-day bookings accepted if space available.
Access: Trains to Newquay station, buses to Tolcarne Beach; both stations are a short walk from centre.

wight water

19 Orchardleigh Road
Shanklin
Isle of Wight
PO37 7NP
Tel & Fax (01983) 866 269

Wight Water offer lessons by the hour, a package of 5 daily sessions, or surfing by yourself on a hired board. There is also an option to try surfing as part of a multi-activity programme that also includes catamaran sailing, wave skiing, windsurfing and canoeing.

Accommodation is either at the Saunders Hotel, or arranged by you locally. You will need your own transport to get to and from the centre.

Children: Discounts for youths under 19.
Insurance: Clients should arrange personal insurance cover.
Affiliations: BSA.
Tariffs: 5-session surfing course (BSA Fin Awards): £40. Surfing is also one of the sports included in the centre's 5-session multi-activity package: £60. Group and youth discounts available.

See Windsurfing (p. 469) for full details.

windsport international ltd

Mylor Yacht Harbour
Falmouth
Cornwall
TR11 5UF
Tel (01326) 376 191
Fax (01326) 376 192

Windsport is a big company and runs 3 centres across the country, that in Falmouth being the only one that offers surfing as part of a multi-activity water sports package. The other sports include catamaran and dinghy sailing, powerboating, water skiing and, if you want it, land yachting. Multi-activity packages are run either as 'fun days' or, more usefully, over 5 days, where there is really time to learn. Bookings are divided between various types of group: individuals may sign up for a general adults' course, while others are run specifically for families, unaccompanied children and corporate groups. However, if you decide that you want to concentrate on surfing only, private tuition on a student-to-instructor ratio of 1:1 and 2:1 is offered.

Courses can be residential or non-residential – whatever suits you. There is also a variety of accommodation available, and fees are charged on a sliding scale reflecting the level of comfort you choose.

Season: Open all year.
Tariffs: Surfing is one of the activities offered in the centre's multi-activity packages. 5-day family, child or adult course: £125 (adult), £95 (child); weekend family course: £48 (adult), £38 (child); 1-day family or child course: £25 (adult), £20 (child); 1-day adult course: £48. Residential packages are also available (including tuition, equipment and accommodation); prices vary according to level of accommodation chosen (hotel, guest house or farmhouse). 5-day courses (6 nights' accommodation): £365–545; 2-day courses (2 nights' accommodation): £220–280. Group discounts available.

See Sailing (p. 366) for full details.

kitting yourself out

checklist

- ✔ *buoyancy aid*
- ✔ *leash and rail saver*
- ✔ *board*
- ✔ *wet suit*

There are 3 basic kinds of surfboard: custom, soft and pop-out. Beginners should use the soft board, made from a foam that lacks the hard fibreglass finish of other boards. It is less dangerous if it hits you or anyone else. Expect to pay about £160 for a new soft board – best to buy it new as they tend to get knackered quickly and are seldom in good nick when sold second-hand. A custom board is hand-crafted and is made to your specifications. As an experienced surfer you will know what type you want – thruster, swallow-tail, single-fin or whatever. They cost about £300 new and can be bought through most surf schools. Get your instructor to advise you if you're a first-timer. Pop-out boards are cheaper, about £80–150, but they are heavier than custom boards and more limited in design.

The second-hand market is huge, and you can usually pick up a decent used custom board for around £100–120, but always get someone knowledgeable to vet the thing first. Points to watch out for are: water in the board – squeeze around any chips or dents to see if the foam core is taking in water; make sure that the fibreglass has not separated from the foam – the telltale clue is little bubbles of glass which go flat when you press them; check the fin to see if it is still firm in the board. If buying from a shop, discuss how much it will cost to put right any damage to a second-hand board.

Try to get a board that's 9 to 12ins longer than your height and about 20ins wide at the middle. The more width there is at each end, the easier it will be to catch a wave. The board should be about 3ins thick.

A surfboard leash stops the board running away from you and into other surfers when you wipe out. Leashes are ideally about 6ft long and cost about £15–20. A leash should come with a rail saver – a flat nylon strap a couple of inches wide and between 6ins and 8ins long, which stops the leash biting into the sides of your board in the underwater mêlée, at about £10.

Wet suits are necessary all year in Britain's waters. Summer suits come without legs or arms and are about 2–3mm thick. Winter suits have long arms and legs and are about 4–5mm thick. Double-lined suits are more hard-wearing. Make sure the suit fits snugly without being constrictive. Expect to pay from about £200 for a new full suit or £80–150 for a 'shortie'. Viking, Hydrotech, Bermuda and Typhoon are good.

wave skiing

The editors could not find any centres offering specific courses in wave skiing. There is, however, a number of wave skiing clubs around the country, all of which offer transport and tuition and will help in getting you kitted out. To find out who's in your area contact:

The British Wave Ski Association
30 Fairfield, Sampford Peverell,
Tiverton
Devon EX16 7DE
Tel & Fax (01884) 821 366
or
34 Greenham Wood, Bracknell
Berkshire RG12 7WJ

The association runs a series of coaching weekends every year, usually in October and November, for both beginners and would-be competition-standard wave skiers.

kitting yourself out

There are many manufacturers to choose from for both ski boards and paddles, but Pro Designs and Dirty Habits are reckoned to be two of the best for intermediate- to advanced-level boards (prices range between £200 and £400) and PowerBlades for paddles, which retail at about £35–50. Beginners should start with a standard, cheap polyurethane board for about £80–90.

There is a thriving second-hand market, however, with classified ads in the Wave Ski Association's newsletter. Beginners should be able to kit themselves out with ski board and paddle for around £100, and intermediate to advanced paddlers can do the same for around £250–280.

checklist

- ✔ *wave ski board (includes fins, belt and seat pad)*
- ✔ *double paddle*

representative body

The Ramblers Association

1-5 Wandsworth Road
London SW8 2XX
Tel (0171) 339 8500
Fax (0171) 339 8501

walking

country walking
hillwalking
munro-bagging
corbett-collecting

Britain is criss-crossed with innumerable public footpaths as well as scores of long-distance foot-trails, and covering even the latter could fill several volumes. For this reason this chapter lists only centres that offer organized walking holidays, whether led or self-guided, and it is divided into three categories: hillwalking (demanding upland treks); country walking (less demanding); and two of the more hard-core offshoots of hillwalking, Munro-bagging and Corbett-collecting – the Scottish obsession with climbing as many hills over 3,000ft (Munros) or 2,000ft (Corbetts) as possible. However, readers should note that these latter sports are practised by mad people – you have to be very fit and accept that there are severe weather risks involved.

Anyone interested in more specialized aspects of upland walking, such as navigation, orienteering, scrambling and winter precautions, will find them in the Mountain Skills chapter, and those wanting to combine their walks with wildlife-watching or botany will find all necessary information in the Eco-Sports chapter. Those wanting to get really close to nature – by actually living off the land they're walking through – should turn to the Woodlore chapter.

The other more eccentric offshoots of hillwalking – ridge-running, fell-running and night-time fell-running – are not included in this guide as they are too risky for any responsible operator to get involved in – the insurance premiums would be astronomical. If you want information on these sports, contact the mountain rescue organization for the area you are interested in.

selected centres

acorn activities

PO Box 120
Hereford
Hereford & Worcester
HR4 8YB
Tel (01432) 830 083
Fax (01432) 830 110

Country Walking and Hill-walking (Guided)

Acorn Activities run country walking and hillwalking packages along various routes in western England and Wales, specifically in Hereford & Worcester, Shropshire, Dyfed and Snowdonia.

For country walking the best option is probably their guided walking week along the Pembrokeshire Coastal Path. The route's cliffsides, sheltered bays, seals, porpoises, wild flowers and seabirds make this one of the most pleasant walks in Britain. One day of the walk is spent on an island just offshore, and the guide makes a point of taking you to Neolithic and Bronze Age sites along the way. You stay in a small hotel in the tiny cathedral town of St David's, one of our island's earliest-known pilgrimage centres. There are only 2 Dyfed walking weeks each year, leaving in the second weeks of May and September.

A little more demanding is the Offa's Dyke walk through the Welsh Marches, following the line of the great earthwork erected by the Saxon king Offa of Mercia during the 10th century to keep the wild Welsh out of his kingdom. The Offa's Dyke walk can be done as a 2-, 3-, 4-, 5- or 6-day walk, with accommodation in farmhouses along the way. You do the walk without a guide, but Acorn provide maps and transport, and your luggage goes ahead of you by car. The Offa's Dyke walk can be undertaken at any time of year.

Other country walking packages include the walking weekends in several areas around the Offa's Dyke path. Recommended are the Llandrindod Wells, Elan Valley and Radnor Hills walks, all in the Welsh Borders. These run from April to the end of October.

For hillwalking, try the 5-day 'Escape to Snowdonia' – a guided walk around Cader Idris, through some of Wales's wildest country, sleeping under canvas (this trip only runs in August). All you need to bring is a sleeping bag; everything else is provided. Lasting 4 nights, the Easter Weekend guided walk, which goes up into the Glascwm above Kington on the Powys/Hereford & Worcester border, is also strongly recommended – again all you need is a sleeping bag. Less strenuous is the guided walking week in the Brecon Beacons, which runs in the second weeks of June and October. Although the hills are steep, you only walk up to 8 miles per day; accommodation is in local B&Bs.

Season: Open all year.
Accommodation: Local accommodation provided.
Food: Full board included.
Other Activities: Ballooning (see p. 10); Bungee Jumping (Related Activities, p. 333); Canoeing (p. 18); Cycle Sports (p. 114); Eco-Sports (p. 142); Gorge Walking (p. 176); Horse Sports (p. 202); Sub-Aqua Diving (p. 386); Surfing (p. 402); White-Water Rafting (p. 446); Woodlore (p. 474).
Children: Children over 12 are welcome on walking trips when accompanied by a parent or guardian.

Disabled Facilities: None.
Insurance: Clients should arrange their own holiday insurance; may be arranged through centre.
Safety: All instructors are accredited with their own sports' governing bodies.
Affiliations: Heart of England Tourist Board; Wales Tourist Board.
Tariffs: Prices include accommodation and guide. Llandrindod Wells walking weekend: £120; Brecon Beacons walking week: £350; Pembrokeshire National Park walking week: £395; Snowdonia 5-day walk (camping): £130; Welsh Hills Bank Holiday Weekends: £150. Offa's Dyke Path walk (unescorted with luggage carried forward): £217–865; Wye Valley walk (unescorted with luggage carried forward): £278–1,060.
Booking: Non-refundable deposit of £10 per day is required. Balance due 60 days in advance. Cancellation charges (as percentage of total cost): 43–59 days in advance: 80%; 29–42 days: 85%; 15–28 days: 90%; 0–14 days: 100%. Late bookings welcomed if space available.
Access: Varies according to site chosen; contact centre for more details.

---

alba walking holidays

24 Lundavra Road
Fort William
Highland
PH33 6LA
Scotland
Tel (01397) 704 964

Hillwalking

Like Acorn Activities, Alba are not a centre but a holiday organizer – though on a more personal scale. Andrew Ravenhill personally guides the hillwalking, scrambling and climbing trips that he organizes into the mountains of Scotland's western Highlands. Groups are small – a minimum of 2 and a maximum of 8 people; no kids allowed – and although he welcomes any level of walker (trips are divided into Moderate and Strenuous), you will need to be at least halfway fit to enjoy one of these excursions. He particularly specializes in winter walking, with trips up onto the snowbound Munros around Fort William. However, his summer walking trips are also excellent, guiding you on day walks through the wild mountains around Torridon, Kintail, Knoydart and Kingussie. The Knoydart trip, which includes a foray into the very remote area around Loch Hourn (Gaelic for hell), is really spectacular, if hard going.

Season: All year.
Accommodation: B&B accommodation is included in holidays.
Food: Breakfast provided.
Other Activities: Climbing and Abseiling (see p. 91); Mountain Skills (p. 273).
Children: No special facilities.
Disabled Facilities: None.
Insurance: Insurance cover included in price of holidays.
Safety: Staff medic; all instructors trained in mountain first aid.
Affiliations: Association of Mountaineering Instructors.
Tariffs: All packages are a week long and include 5 days' guiding services, equipment and transport. Guests have the option of arranging own accommodation or 7 nights' B&B. Winter Munros: £200 / £325; summer walks: £185 / £310. (Group discounts available.)
Booking: £50 non-refundable deposit required. Balance due 4 weeks before start date, non-refundable. Late bookings accepted if space available.
Access: A82 to Fort William. Trains and buses available to Fort William; pick-ups arranged by centre.

avalon trekking scotland

Bowerswell Lane
Kinnoull
Perth
Perthshire & Kinross
PH2 7DL
Scotland
Tel & Fax (01738) 624 194

Hillwalking

Another holiday organizer, Avalon run guided walks all through Scotland. Their speciality is long treks, such as the Southern Upland Way through the beautiful Borders (14 days), the Northern Passage and Coast to Coast trips (14 days), the West Highland Way (8 days), the Speyside Way (5 days), Reivers Way (6 days), the Fife Coastal Path (5 days), and a tour through the Grampian Passes (6 days). There are also island trips in Argyll and Arran (5 days), the Isle of Mull and Iona (8 days) and on Skye (8 days). Some of the long routes in northern England, such as the Pennine Way and the Cumberland Way, are also offered.

Perhaps the most interesting of Avalon's trips are those through country the tourists seldom get to. These include: the Northern Passage from Fort Augustus to Cape Wrath via Easter Ross, Ben More and Strath Oykel; the Southern Upland Way through the wild mountains of Dumfries & Galloway, the Teviots and the Lammermuirs (Walter Scott country); and the Reivers Way, which crosses and recrosses the England/Scotland border through the Cheviots and the emptinesses of north Northumberland.

Routes are divided into grades – A, B and C. Grade A means walking up to 15 miles per day, Grade B 10–12 miles and Grade C 6–9 miles. All the 14-night walks are Grade A, as are the Reivers and Grampian trips. The island routes vary between Grade B and C. The good news is that you only have to carry a day pack – the rest goes on ahead of you by car. You provide your own walking boots and outdoor clothing.

Season: All year.
Accommodation: Local accommodation is provided in hotels and guest houses.
Food: Breakfast, dinner and packed lunch provided. Vegetarian or special diets catered for upon request.
Children: Lower age limit 18.
Disabled Facilities: None.
Insurance: Clients should arrange their own holiday insurance; inexpensive cover can be obtained through centre.
Safety: All staff trained in first aid.
Affiliations: Perthshire Tourist Board; Scottish Activity Holidays Association.
Tariffs: A wide range of walks available around Scotland and northern England; all include accommodation, full board, guide and transport of baggage between points along walk. Sample walks include: the Northern Passage (14 nights): £765; West Highland Way (8 nights): £435; Grampian Passes (6 nights): £405. Group discounts are available on all routes.
Booking: Non-refundable deposit of £50–100 per person required. Balance due at least 6 weeks prior to start. Cancellation charge if notice received more than 42 days in advance: deposit forfeited; 29–42 days: 25% of balance; 15–28 days: 50% of balance; 7–14 days: 75% of balance; 0–6 days: 100% of balance. Late bookings accepted up to 48 hours in advance if space available.
Access: Meeting points are at nearest train station or airport to site chosen.

black dragon outdoor experiences

7 Ethelbert Drive
Charlton
Andover
Hampshire
SP10 4EP
Tel (01264) 357 313

Hillwalking for Beginners

Black Dragon run walking tours in the Brecon Beacons National Park and Snowdonia, with trips aimed at most levels of fitness and all levels of expertise. The Introductory Mountain Walking holidays, which can be done as day trips, over a weekend or a longer period (by arrangement), are designed for people who have never been on the hill before. The walks are not too demanding, take in some very beautiful scenery, and introduce the basics of clothing and footwear, map reading, pacing yourself, accident procedures and personal safety, and general matters such as access, conservation and the environment.

If you are a little bit fitter and already have some experience, the Improvers holidays (also run as day trips, weekends or longer packages) take in some more demanding routes, steeper, longer ascents, and cover group safety, mountain hazards, mountain rescue, weather awareness, basic first aid, and route planning. For both holidays there is a leader-to-walker ratio of 1:4.

Black Dragon's holidays are open to individuals, groups and families. Bunkhouse accommodation, camping or B&B – whichever you prefer – can be arranged, and all local transport is laid on.

Tariffs: Day courses include instruction and equipment, weekend courses also include accommodation and full board. Mountain Walking day course: £28; Brecon Beacons Mountain Walking weekend: £137; Snowdonia Mountain Walking weekend: £147.

See Mountain Skills (p. 274) for full details.

chichester interest holidays

14 Bay View Terrace
Newquay
Cornwall
TR7 2LR
Tel (01637) 874 216

Country Walking

Chichester House is a small hotel in Newquay, Cornwall, that offers gentle walking for people who want time to explore and look around rather than survive the rugged upland trails. They have various routes over moorland, farmland, along rivers and estuaries and varied stretches of coastline. There is quite an emphasis on local archaeology, and the experienced guides will explain the differences between a fogou (a kind of Neolithic burial mound) and a barrow, and who was living in Cornwall during the Mesolithic or Iron Age. There are also flint-collecting trips to some of the richer local Stone Age sites. Excursions last for a week, unless you want to make a special trip by prior arrangement. All the walking is by the day only, returning to Chichester House by minibus for dinner and bed. Walking groups are limited to 10 people and the maximum length of any one walking day is 10 miles. When possible the minibus meets you with your lunch.

Season: Specific weeks March to June, September to October.
Accommodation: 3 double, 2 twin and 2 single rooms in guest house.
Food: Full board included; vegetarian and special diets catered for upon request.
Children: Must be able to walk 10 miles.
Disabled Facilities: None.
Insurance: Holiday cancellation insurance can be arranged through centre.
Safety: Staff trained in first aid.
Affiliations: English Tourist Board; West Country Tourist Board.
Tariffs: Price includes 7 nights' accommodation, full board (including packed lunches), guide and local transport: £190.
Booking: £30 deposit required. Contact centre for cancellation policy details.
Access: Take the A392 to Newquay. Trains and buses available to Newquay, centre within walking distance from stations.

dartmoor expedition centre

Rowden
Widecombe
Newton Abbot
Devon
TQ13 7TX
Tel (01364) 621 249

Hillwalking

This is one of Britain's longest-running outdoor centres, with 25 years behind it. Based in an old stone farmhouse, it has the whole of Dartmoor for a playground. All levels of sportsperson are catered for – courses range from beginner through recreational walking to instructor training, most lasting for 1 week, although they can be tailored to suit your needs.

The Moorland Explorers course prepares the hillwalker for mountaineering, introducing compass navigation (there's plenty of fog on Dartmoor to put these skills to the test), bivouacking in the open and interpreting contours. A little more serious is the Mountain Leader's Basic Training week, which covers the first part of the Leadership training certificate for would-be instructors – a good course for anyone planning to take groups into the hills. More varied is the Rovers course, an expedition across the open moor, camping on the hill, navigating over the tors and ending with a 2-day canoe journey down the River Tamar.

If you don't fancy things so organized, you can use the centre as a base for your own hillwalking trip on Dartmoor, guided or unguided.

Season: Open all year.
Accommodation: Bunkhouse accommodation in converted farmhouse. Camping away from the centre for some courses.
Food: Full board included.
Other Activities: Canoeing (see p. 21); Caving (p. 44); Climbing and Abseiling (p. 94); Orienteering (p. 177).
Children: Special courses for children 11+ and 14+; multi-activity holidays for unaccompanied children in the summer.
Disabled Facilities: None.
Insurance: Clients only need cover for their personal belongings.
Safety: Instructors trained in first aid and life-saving skills.
Affiliations: British Canoe Union; British Mountaineering Council (BMC); Mountain Leaders Training Board (MLTB); National Association of Outdoor Education Centres.
Tariffs: Prices include tuition, equipment and full-board accommodation. Rovers course (6 days): £200; Moorland Explorers course (6 days): £200; Mountain Leader's Basic Training course (6 days): £200. Walking is included in the multi-activity package offered by centre: £200 per week. An instructor for group walking trips can be hired for £90 per day.
Booking: Deposit required; contact centre for details. Bookings accepted up to 48 hours in advance if space available.
Access: Trains and buses to Newton Abbot. Pick-ups can be arranged by centre, or cabs can be taken (around £5).

---

edale yha activity centre

Rowland Cote
Nether Booth
Edale
Sheffield
S30 2ZH
Tel (01433) 670 302
Fax (01433) 670 234

Hillwalking

Edale runs hillwalking courses for recreational walkers and aspiring instructors and guides. The centre has a training and assessment course for would-be professionals, of 6 and 7 days' duration respectively, at the end of which you are qualified to lead groups anywhere in the British hill ranges.

Less formal is the 2-night Walk the Peak trip, a relatively undemanding weekend of hillwalking for people who want to leave route-finding to their guide.

Season: All year.
Children: Minimum age 16.
Tariffs: Prices include equipment, instruction and full-board accommodation – 2-day hill walk: £80; 6-day MLTB mountain leader course: £238. Walking is also one of the sports offered in the centre's multi-activity package deals: approximately £42 per day in high season (April–August), £32 in low season (November–February).

See Caving (p. 45) for full details.

first ascent - outdoor experience

Far Cottage
Church Street
Longnor
Nr Buxton
Derbyshire
SK17 0PE
Tel (01298) 83545
Fax (01298) 83897

Country Walking

First Ascent organize various kinds of walking holidays. Perhaps the best is the 'independent' option, where they book you into farmhouses, inns and hotels, transferring your luggage on by car while you meander 8–10 miles per day on foot through the valleys and escarpments of the southern Peak District National Park. The same package is offered for the byways and coastal paths of Anglesey and at the edge of the north Staffordshire moorlands. Walking holidays abroad are also offered – to Mallorca, Menorca, and in Nepal and Tibet, though these last are strenuous and require a much greater level of fitness than the British and European holidays.

Season: February to November.
Accommodation: 4 twin and 2 single rooms in stone-built cottage for Peak District holidays. Holidays elsewhere in England will have local B&B accommodation.
Food: All meals included in holiday price; vegetarian selections available.
Other Activities: Canoeing (see p. 23); Climbing and Abseiling (p. 97).
Children: Clients must be over 18.
Disabled Facilities: None.
Insurance: Clients should arrange personal insurance cover; can be arranged through centre.
Safety: All staff trained in first aid and emergency rescue.
Affiliations: British Canoe Union; BMC; MLTB.
Tariffs: Prices include guiding and full-board accommodation. A range of walks is available; some examples are – Sedate Strolling weekend: £130; Winter Walking (2 nights): £130; Walking the Trans-Pennine (7 nights): £390; independent walking weeks (including B&B accommodation, luggage transfer, route and maps): £225–245.
Booking: £40 non-refundable deposit required. Cancellation charges: 29–56 days in advance: 50% of total; 15–28 days: 75%; 14 days or less: 100%. Bookings accepted up to 48 hours in advance if space available.
Access: Off the B5053 near Longnor. Trains and buses to Buxton. Pick-ups can be arranged by centre (£5–10 charge).

hadrian mountaineering

19B Carnoch
Glencoe
Argyll & Bute
PA39 4HS
Scotland
Tel (01855) 811 472

Hillwalking, Munro-bagging, Corbett-collecting

These are demanding hill walks, run year-round for people who want to cross the line between hillwalking and mountaineering. The guided trips involve some scrambling, occasional ropework and navigation in the Black Cuillins of Skye and over the classic Munros of Glencoe and Lochaber. If you are thinking about qualifying as a mountain leader, Hadrian also offer the MLTB Mountain Leader (Summer) award course – a 5-day intensive slog which, if you pass, qualifies you to lead hillwalking trips for a living.

All Hadrian's trips include local accommodation, on a sliding scale that reflects the level of comfort you need – camping, bunkhouse, B&B or hotel. All local transport is provided.

Tariffs: Fees include instruction, equipment and in-course transport; arrange your own accommodation or full-board option available. 2-day (2-night) Cuillin Ridge Traverse: £149 / £179; 5-day (6-night) Winter hillwalking course: £199 / £349.

See Mountain Skills (p. 278) for full details.

high trek snowdonia

Tal y Waen
Deiniolen
Gwynedd
LL55 3NA
Wales
Tel & Fax (01286) 871 232

Hillwalking

Back to the hard stuff! High Trek Snowdonia lead some of the best guided trekking available in the mountains of North Wales. There is summer and winter hillwalking in packages of 7, 5 and 3 days (long weekends). Some of it is very tough (they provide the ice axes), but there are also more gentle routes, such as their 7-day Valleys and Villages walk, which children can cope with as easily as adults. In between these extremes are moderate routes such as the 7-day Castle to Castle trail from Caernarfon to Conway via Snowdonia. There are also various budgets on offer – some routes go between youth hostels, while others stay in B&Bs. Whichever one you take, High Trek provide all the equipment – all you need to bring is yourself, warm clothes and stout boots. You need only carry a day pack on the walks – your luggage is transported on for you each day, even on the hostels route.

Season: January to November.
Accommodation: Accommodation varies according to holiday chosen, ranging from hotels and B&B to camping.
Food: Full board included; meals taken at place of accommodation and packed lunches provided on the trail. Vegetarian meals can be arranged.
Other Activities: Climbing and Abseiling (see p. 100); Gorge Walking and Coasteering (p. 180); Mountain Skills (p. 279).
Children: Children welcome if accompanied by adults; discounts given on some walking breaks.
Disabled Facilities: None.
Insurance: Clients must arrange their own holiday insurance; inexpensive policies can be arranged through centre.
Safety: All guides and instructors trained in first aid.
Affiliations: Association of Mountaineering Instructors; Wales Tourist Board.
Tariffs: Long-weekend walking breaks (including accommodation, full board, equipment and guide): £189; 7-day trekking holidays (inclusions as above): £335–395.
Booking: Non-refundable deposit of £50 or £75 required. Balance due 4–6 weeks before start date. Cancellation charges: 75% of total cost if notice received 2–4 weeks before start, 100% if less than 2 weeks.
Access: Deiniolen is near Bangor off the A5 or A55. Trains and buses to Bangor; free pick-ups arranged by centre.

highlander mountaineering

Highlea
Auchnarrow
Tomintoul
Aberdeenshire
AB37 9JN
Scotland
Tel (01807) 590 250

Hillwalking, Munro-bagging, Corbett-collecting

If you're interested in learning the technicalities of mountaincraft while walking some of Britain's tougher trails, then this is the outfit for you. The trips run all year, some of them under canvas or in bothies, others staying in B&Bs, but all of them carrying a full pack – with the exception of Highlander's one gentle route, the 5-day Moray Coast and Speyside Way, for which luggage is transported.

Hard-core Munro-baggers can find nirvana on the Cairngorm 4,000-footers route, which ascends and descends 7 of the highest Munros in central Scotland, including Cairn Gorm itself, Ben Macdhui, Cairn Toul, Lochan Uaine and Braeirach, all of which top 4,000ft. If that's not enough punishment, there's the 5-day Across the Roof of Scotland route, all under canvas, which ascends a collective total of 20,000ft, taking in 17 Munros.

Although there is no rule proscribing children, in general the routes are aimed at fit young adults and anyone outside that category is unlikely to enjoy the trips. However, a plus is that these are among the best value-for-money hillwalking packages on offer.

Highlander Mountaineering also run Winter Survival and Navigation courses (see Mountain Skills, p. 279 for details of these).

Season: Open all year.
Accommodation: Guests stay in a choice of hotels in Tomintoul before setting off, then in B&Bs, under canvas or in bothies, depending on the route chosen.
Food: B&B or full-board options available; vegetarian meals available upon request.
Other Activities: Climbing and Abseiling (p. 100); Mountain Skills (p. 279).
Children: No special facilities.
Disabled Facilities: None.
Insurance: Clients must arrange their own holiday insurance.
Safety: All staff trained in first aid and rescue skills.
Affiliations: BMC.
Tariffs: Courses include guide, equipment, accommodation and meals (either B&B or full board). Sample tariffs include – 5-day Peaks Trek (full board): £165; summer hill-walking and navigation week: £295 (B&B) / £365 (full board); 2-day Cairngorm Munro trek: £75 (half-board); winter walking week-end: £95 (B&B) / £120 (full board).
Booking: Non-refundable deposit of 20% required. Balance due 28 days in advance. Cancellation charge: 100% of total cost if within 2 weeks of start date. Access and Visa cards accepted. Late bookings accepted if space available.
Access: A9 to Grantown-on-Spey, then A939 to Tomintoul. Trains and buses to Aviemore; centre will arrange pick-up from station (small charge to cover fuel).

kevin walker mountain activities

74 Beacons Park
Brecon
Powys
LD3 9BQ
Wales
Tel & Fax (01874) 625 111

Hillwalking

Kevin Walker has been running his Welsh-based mountaineering and hillwalking courses for 15 years and ranks as one of Britain's best instructors for getting people started in the hills and turning them into skilled mountaineers. He offers several walking packages: a basic introductory hillwalking trip through the Brecon Beacons over 1, 2 or 5 days; a Hillwalkers' Confidence course over 2 or 5 days for those who want to try something a little more demanding; a Mountain Navigation weekend course that deals with basic compass use, route-finding and interpretation of contours; Security on Steep Ground, a 1-day course for walkers who want to try screes and ridges; Wild Country Camping, a weekend dealing with equipment, techniques and skills on which you spend a night under canvas on the open hill; and Mountain Survival, another weekend that shows you what to do if you get stuck on the hill. All these courses have a student-to-instructor ratio of 4:1.

Beyond these recreational courses, there are others aimed at would-be instructors or instructors wishing to progress, including the 6-day MLTB Mountain Leader (Summer) training.

Season: Open all year.
Accommodation: Local accommodation can be arranged through centre.
Food: Not provided.
Other Activities: Caving (see p. 46); Climbing and Abseiling (p. 102); Mountain Skills (p. 281).
Children: Children under 18 must be accompanied by a parent or legal guardian.
Disabled Facilities: None.
Insurance: Clients must arrange their own holiday insurance. Inexpensive cover with the BMC can be arranged through centre.
Safety: All staff trained in first aid; medic on-site.
Affiliations: MLTB.
Tariffs: A large range of courses is available; prices include tuition and equipment. Some examples are – 1-day novice hillwalking course: £50; 5-day novice hillwalking course: £235; 2-day Hillwalkers' Confidence course: £95; 6-day Mountain Leader training course: £259 (includes self-catering accommodation).
Booking: £10 or 20% (whichever is greater) non-refundable deposit. Balance due 3 weeks before start date. Cancellation fees: 6+ weeks: deposit; 4–6 weeks: 30% of total; 2–4 weeks: 50% of total; less than 2 weeks: 100% of total. Late bookings sometimes accepted if space available.
Access: Courses are based either in Betws-y-coed or Crickhowell. From Shrewsbury take the A5 to Betws-y-coed. From Abergavenny take the A40 to Crickhowell. Trains available to Abergavenny; cab to Crickhowell is approximately £6. Trains and buses available to Betws-y-coed.

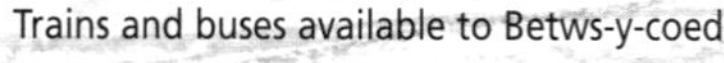

kingspark llama farm

Berriedale
Highland
KW7 6HA
Scotland
Tel (01593) 751 202

Walking, Bird-watching with Llamas

An eccentric one, this, and the editors were a little unsure as to whether it belonged with eco-sports or walking – probably both, so it's going in both. A llama farm up in the far north-east of Scotland, this centre hires its charges out as obliging pack animals for exploring the surrounding coast and mountains, whether as day trips or hikes of several days. A guide and experienced llama-wrangler accompanies you, pointing out things of interest along the way – wild flowers, wildlife and historic sites – eventually guiding you to one of several coastal bird-watching hides built by the RSPB. Presumably the guide is also on hand to wrestle down the pack beast should it become intransigent. You can either stay at the farm, taking different walks each day, or arrange for longer treks inland. Contact the farm for details.

Season: Open all year.
Accommodation: 2 single, 2 double and 1 family room available at farm (£14 per night). Camping is possible, but no ablution facilities.
Food: Breakfast included, evening meals can be arranged.
Children: All ages welcome.
Disabled Facilities: Disabled guests can be accommodated.
Insurance: Clients should arrange their own holiday insurance if required.
Safety: No special safety provisions.
Affiliations: None.
Tariffs: £12 per llama (can be shared).
Booking: Deposits only required for large groups, non-refundable. Late bookings accepted if space available.
Access: On the A9 north of Helmsdale. Trains to Helmsdale station, buses to llama farm available. Centre will pick up from train station (£10 return fare).

munros

c/o D. Currie
9 The Terrace
Boat of Garten
Highland
PH24 3BH
Tel (01479) 831 376

Munro-bagging, Corbett-collecting

Tackling remote Munros of Sutherland and the other outer regions of the Highlands, the more accessible ones of the Cairngorms and the western Highlands, and scrambling on the Cuillin ridges of Skye: Munros offer 5-day walking trips, with a base at the residential centre in the Spey Valley or in local bothies or under canvas. The centre offers a walker-to-leader ratio of no more than 6:1. Beginners and experienced walkers alike are welcome, with the walks taking place through the summer season.

Season: May to September.
Accommodation: Some courses entail camping in the hills (tents can be provided). Otherwise, centre will provide help in arranging hostel or B&B accommodation in the Spey Valley.
Food: Food is included on some courses.
Children: Must be 16 or over.
Disabled Facilities: None.
Insurance: Clients must arrange their own.
Safety: Staff trained in first aid.

Affiliations: None.
Tariffs: Prices include transport from the Speyside area. 5-day Remote Munros course (includes food): £180; 5-day residential course: £160; 5-day Skye Munros course (includes food): £250. Daily rates available (except for Remote Munros). Discounts for BMC members and groups, and concessionary rates.
Booking: 25% deposit required. Balance due 28 days in advance of course. Cancellation charges apply only if notice received very late (contact centre for details). Bookings up to 48 hours in advance accepted if space available.
Access: From Perth, take the A9 to Aviemore (this is the meeting point for trips). Trains and buses available to Aviemore.

---

north-west frontiers

Strathkanaird
Ullapool
Highland
IV26 2TP
Tel & Fax (01854) 666 229

Hillwalking

Ullapool lies at the southern edge of some of Scotland's wildest country, and North-West Frontiers have access to it: the rampart-like mountains of Dundonnel, Ben More, Loch Maree, Cape Wrath and north-west Sutherland, Lochinver and Assynt, the Isles of Harris and Rhum – these are areas that few visitors to Scotland ever reach. You need to be pretty fit for these trips. They last a week, are limited to 8 people, and are divided thus: Moderate – a leisurely pace, but walking for 5–6 hours per day with easy gradients on rough paths; Intermediate – 7 hours of walking per day with around 3,000ft of ascent; Strenuous – 8 or more hours per day with 3,000–5,000ft of ascent. Fortunately you only have to carry a day pack as you take circular walks each day from the same guest house or hotel. You also get a day off in order to rest.

The moderate and strenuous routes all take in Munros and Corbetts – in some cases, like the strenuous Dundonnel route, you can take in 8 or 9 of the beasts. Wildlife is also a priority, and red and roe deer, sea and golden eagles, puffin colonies, seals and, if you are very lucky, pine martens and wild cats are encountered on many of the routes.

As Ullapool is a difficult place to reach, the trips pick up and drop off in Inverness – so it is feasible to get an overnight train from the south and be in the remote hills the next day.

Season: Weekly trips, April to October.
Accommodation: Local B&B, guest house or hotel.
Food: Breakfast provided, packed lunches available for a charge (dinner provided with some packages). Vegetarian or special diets catered for upon request.
Children: Children under 18 must be accompanied by a parent or legal guardian.
Disabled Facilities: None.
Insurance: Clients must purchase their own; can be arranged through centre.
Safety: All staff qualified in first aid.
Affiliations: Greenpeace; John Muir Trust.
Tariffs: Prices include 7 nights' B&B, 5 days' guided walks, transport to/from the holiday base and for each walk: £295. Some holidays have the option of high-quality hotel accommodation ranging from £350–580. £165 per week for walking only.
Booking: £50 non-refundable deposit. Balance due 6 weeks before start of holiday. Access, Visa and Mastercard accepted. Late bookings accepted if space available.
Access: All holidays meet in Inverness; guests are then transported to the holiday base. Trains, buses and planes available to Inverness.

ossian guides

Sanna
Newtonmore
Highland
PH20 1DG
Scotland
Tel & Fax (01540) 673 402

Hillwalking, Munro-bagging

Ossian run a series of superb hillwalking weeks and occasional weekends through the summer and autumn, including a traverse of the high Cairngorms, a specialist Munro-bagger's ascent of Scotland's top three peaks of Ben Nevis, Ben Macdhui and Braeriach, and a trek through Knoydart, one of the wildest areas of the western Highlands, with a scramble over Munros such as Ladhar Bheinn. These trips, classed as 'moderate' but in fact requiring a reasonable level of fitness, are offset by 3 'easy' routes, all a week long, one following in the footsteps of Bonnie Prince Charlie after his army's defeat at the Battle of Culloden in 1746 – from Badenoch to the Atlantic mouth of Loch Shiel. Ossian also organize specialist photographic treks, their best being through Knoydart, with landscape and wildlife photography the priority.

Season: May to October.
Tariffs: All treks include guiding, equipment, accommodation and full board. A variety of treks is available; some examples of 7-dayers are – Cairngorm Experience: £389; Scotland's Top Three Trek: £349; Perthshire and Badenoch: £389; Classic Ridges: £389.

See Mountain Skills (p. 283) for full details.

outward bound

PO Box 1219
Windsor
Berkshire
SL4 1XR
Tel (01753) 731 005
Fax (01753) 810 666
Outward Bound Scotland, Loch Eil
Tel (01397) 772 866
Outward Bound Wales, Aberdovey
Tel (01654) 767 464
Outward Bound Ullswater, Penrith
Tel (017684) 86347

Hillwalking, Munro-bagging

Outward Bound's 3 centres are run by a trust that aims to get people from all walks of life out and doing, with a bewildering range of courses tailored for different types of individual or group – from unaccompanied children or school parties right through to instructors wanting to progress. Most of the courses/holidays are multi-activity (though there are some specialist courses) and are divided into the following age groups: 11–14, 14–15, 16–17, 18–24, 25+ and 50+. The children's courses are run as part of the Duke of Edinburgh's Award scheme. For the 18–24 age group, there is a 12-day hillwalking expedition across Skye. For the 25–50 age group there is a 7-day Highland Mountain Journey and another 7-dayer, the Welsh Wayfarer. There are 2 7-day hillwalking expeditions aimed at people of 50+, both in Scotland, one on the west coast, the other in the Highlands. Outward Bound also run a 7-day women-only expedition across the Lake District, and one women-only MLTB (Summer) instructor course.

These hillwalking trips are spent almost entirely on the hill, sleeping under canvas or in bothies, climbing the higher peaks (Munros) and learning navigation, mountain safety and weather awareness.

Season: Open all year.
Accommodation: Dormitory accommodation (single-sex); some camping nights away from centre.
Food: Full board included; vegetarian and special diets catered for.
Other Activities: Canoeing (see p. 28); Child and Youth Sports (p. 66); Climbing and Abseiling (p. 105); Cycle Sports (p. 119); Disabled Activities (p. 135); Mountain Skills (p. 284); Orienteering (p. 181); Sailing (p. 358); Skiing (p. 380).
Children: Specialized courses are for 14+-year-olds unless otherwise stated. There are multi-activity holidays for 3 youth age groups: 11–14, 14–15 and 16–17.
Disabled Facilities: Special programmes for disabled clients, including disabled youths.
Insurance: Basic accident insurance included in course fees.
Safety: Staff trained in first aid and rescue skills.
Affiliations: British Canoe Union; MLTB; Royal Yachting Association.
Tariffs: All prices include tuition, equipment, full-board accommodation, transport during programme. Prices do not include VAT. Summer Mountain Leader training (Scotland, Wales, Ullswater, 7 days, 18+): £270; Summer Mountain Leader assessment (Scotland, Ullswater, 7 days, 20+): £270; Winter Mountain Leader training (Scotland, 7 days, 18+): £295; Scottish Winter hillwalking (Scotland, 7 days): £245; walking expeditions (Scotland, 12 days): £325–399. hillwalking is also included as part of the multi-activity holidays offered by centre (for 14–24-year-olds unless otherwise stated). 7-day multi-activity programme (Scotland, Wales, Ullswater): £249; 12-day multi-activity programme (Wales, Ullswater): £399; Outward Bound Classic (Scotland, Wales, Ullswater, 19 days): £499–599; weekend breaks (Wales, Ullswater, 25+): £130; 7-day programme (Scotland, Wales, Ullswater, 25+ / 50+): £325; 12-day programme (Wales, Ullswater, 25+): £470.
Booking: Non-refundable deposit of £100. Balance due 4 weeks in advance of course. Cancellations only accepted if more than 6 weeks in advance, afterwards full course fee is payable. £14 fee for any booking changes. Bookings must be made in advance. Visa and Access cards accepted.
Access: Leaflet giving details of how to get to various centres will be mailed to clients upon booking.

pinnacle ridge mountain guiding

Croft 12
Portnalong
Isle of Skye
Highland
IV47 8SL
Scotland
Tel (01478) 640 330

Munro-bagging, Corbett-collecting

If you want to bag Munros this is the holiday for you. Pinnacle Ridge is a specialist guiding service for experienced hillwalkers, taking small groups (maximum 6 people) on 5-day trips up into the high Cuillins of Skye and through Torridon on the mainland. The walks cover a lot of ground, so you will have to be quite fit to enjoy them, and are aimed at getting the client to progress from hillwalking to scrambling and basic mountaineering. If you don't fancy being part of a group, you can hire Colin Threlfall, who runs the show and guides all the trips himself, to guide you personally, but that costs a fair bit more.

The hillwalking trips do not include accommodation. You will need to book this yourself, but Colin will advise you on what's available nearby at your budget. He will then pick you up each morning and deliver you back.

Season: April to October.
Tariffs: Prices are for guiding services only – 5-day Winter Walking course: £160; 5-day hillwalking course: £130; 5-day Cuillin Munros course: £160. Private guiding is available; contact organization for more information.

See Mountain Skills (p. 285) for more details.

preseli venture

Parcynole Fach
Mathry
Haverfordwest
Dyfed
SA62 5HN
Wales
Tel (01348) 837 709
Fax (01348) 837 656

Country Walking

Walking the coastal paths of the Pembrokeshire Coast National Park, or exploring the deep-cut lanes and open commons of the Preseli Hills, these walking holidays are not arduous, but they provide good exercise in softly beautiful surroundings. From 2 to 5 days long, with drop-offs and pick-ups in the centre's minibus so that you can do 1-way walks, these are great trips for independent country walkers. You return each night to the centre – a small Welsh cottage, accommodating only 16 people tops – for a hearty meal, and are given a packed lunch to take each day. It's up to you how far you want to walk. The centre provides route maps, taking in ancient sites, castles and good spots for seeing seals and seabirds.

Tariffs: Prices include drop off/collection service and full-board accommodation. 2-day holiday: £59; 3-day holiday: £88. Walking and coasteering are included as part of the centre's multi-activity packages – 2-day holiday: £129; 3-day holiday: £189; 5-day holiday: £285.

See Cycle Sports (p. 121) for full details.

red kite activity centre

Neuadd Arms Hotel
Llanwrtyd Wells
Powys
LD5 4RB
Wales
Tel (01591) 610 236

Country Walking

The Cambrian Mountain valleys of mid-Wales are one of Britain's least explored stretches of wild country, and are blessedly free of other walkers on all but their best-known paths. The walks from the Red Kite centre (actually rather a comfortable hotel) are not strenuous – you don't have to be an experienced walker and you are encouraged to bring children along. If you book in for a week's walking, you are guided into the local countryside for 5 days, and have 1 day off. No walk exceeds 10 miles.

The Neuadd Arms Hotel encourages bird-watchers to come walking in the winter, as this is the best time to see the rare red kite, and the valleys are often surprisingly sheltered and mild. A walking holiday here includes full board. By night there are local real ales to drink in the hotel bar.

The Neuadd Arms is also host to some more strenuous (and much sillier) activities, such as a bog-leaping, point-to-point on mountain bikes and Britain's bog snorkelling championship (see Related Activities, p. 334 for more details).

Season: Open all year.
Accommodation: 14 double, 6 single rooms. B&B £18–23 per day; full board £30 per day. Group discounts available. Dormitory-style attic accommodation also available at reduced rates.
Food: Hotel offers wide range of meals, including vegetarian or special diet selections when requested.
Other activities: Cycle Sports (see p. 122).
Children: Games room in hotel. Baby-listening devices available. Discounts on accommodation: children under 5 years free, 75% off for 5–12-year-olds, 40% off for 13–16-year-olds.
Disabled Facilities: None.
Insurance: Clients are covered by centre's insurance.
Safety: Nurse on-site, and all guides qualified in first aid.
Affiliations: Wales Tourist Board; Outdoor Wales Federation.
Tariffs: Small donation to local charity as entrance fee.
Booking: No advance booking required.
Access: A483 between Builth Wells and Llandovery. Trains available to Llanwrtyd Wells station on the Swansea–Shrewsbury line; pick-up from station can be arranged by centre.

snowgoose activities

The Old Smiddy
Station Road
Corpach
Fort William
Highland
PH33 7LS
Scotland
Tel & Fax (01397) 772 467

Hillwalking, Munro-bagging, Corbett-collecting

If you already fit and want to tackle some serious walks, you will enjoy a Snowgoose hillwalking trip. These are run in both summer and winter and, in some cases, cross the line between hillwalking and mountaineering, with some very exposed stretches of steep ground, occasional elementary ropework and, in winter, use of ice axe and crampons. Winter walks have a leader-to-walker ratio of 1:6.

You can choose how high or far you want to walk, with local Corbetts and Munros accessible year-round and a guiding service available for tailor-made trips into more remote areas than those covered on the 2- and 3-day hillwalking packages. Other than on the tailor-mades, you return every evening to Fort William to stay either in one of Snowgoose's self-catering apartments, in their bunkhouse, or in a B&B nearby. Groups staying in off-site accommodation can be ferried to and from the centre for about 50p a mile.

Affiliations: Association of Mountaineering Instructors.
Tariffs: All prices include instruction and use of equipment. Winter Mountain Walking (3 days): £105; Weekend Winter Hillwalking (2 days): £70; Corbett Mountain Day: £25; Munro Mountain Day: £30; Ridge Walking Day: £40; Winter Mountain Walking: £35. Walking is also offered as part of the centre's multi-activity courses (2–5 days): £30 per day. Group discounts available.

See Canoeing (p. 33) for full details.

summitreks adventure services

14 Yewdale Road
Coniston
Cumbria
LA21 8DU
Tel (015394) 41212
Fax (015394) 41055

Hillwalking Leadership Courses

Summitreks' hillwalking courses are run through the YHA and are specifically aimed at aspiring instructors rather than people walking merely for pleasure. Their British Hillwalking Leaders course (Certificates I and II) is held over 3 successive weekends and covers personal and group equipment, including maintenance, choice and cost, navigation – maps and compasses – group leadership, first aid, safety and survival, hazards and rescue, weather awareness, route-planning, insurance and the law, access and the environment. The course weekends run from May to October and are fully residential, with about 7 hours of practical teaching on the hill. Full board and local transport are provided.

Affiliations: Association of Mountaineering Instructors; BMC; YHA.
Tariffs: Prices include instruction, equipment and full-board accommodation. Winter hill-walking weekends: £95; Winter Hillwalking (5 days): £220; British Hillwalking Leaders weekend course: £99.

See Mountain Skills (p. 288) for full details.

tayside hilltours

26 North Loch Road
Forfar
Angus
DD8 3LS
Scotland
Tel & Fax (01307) 462 045

Hillwalking, Munro-bagging, Corbett-collecting

Tayside do the lot: hillwalking for beginners and intermediates, winter walking, and Munro-bagging for the extremists. All of the walks are guided and take place in the mountains of Scotland's eastern Highlands. They last a week (Sunday to Sunday) – apart from the day walking packages which you can arrange informally with the owners. They can supply equipment, but prefer you to bring your own. All groups are limited to a maximum of 9 people.

There is an emphasis on getting people out into the wilder places and the more remote glens. Tayside's guides really do know the hills, and are used to dealing with all levels of walker. The beginners' trips are limited to a maximum of 8 miles per day, the intermediate ones to 10 miles (with a couple of Munros thrown in towards the end when you've become fitter). The Munro-baggers' week averages about 15 miles per day. Beginners' trips have 2 rest days, the others 1. Please bear in mind that the winter walking trips run from January to April only.

Season: Open all year.
Accommodation: Accommodation provided in local guest houses.
Food: All meals included; vegetarian and special diets catered for upon request.
Children: Children under 18 must be accompanied by a parent or legal guardian.
Disabled Facilities: None.
Insurance: Clients must arrange their own holiday insurance. Inexpensive cover can be arranged through centre.
Safety: Transport to hospital provided if needed, but guides do not have specific paramedical or rescue training.
Affiliations: Scottish Tourist Board.
Tariffs: Week-long walking holidays include accommodation, meals, transport and guiding: £259 summer / £305 winter. Day walks (guiding and transport only): £14–22.
Booking: £25 non-refundable deposit required. Balance due 6 weeks before start date; full amount may be retained if cancellation made within 6 weeks of start. Late bookings accepted if space available.
Access: Forfar is 14 miles north of Dundee on the A90. Trains available to Dundee, buses available from Dundee to Forfar. Pick-ups can be arranged by centre for a fee (£5 from Dundee railway station, £25 from Edinburgh Airport, £20 from Aberdeen Airport).

uist outdoor centre

Cearn Dusgaidh
Lochmaddy
Isle of North Uist
Western Isles
PA82 5AE
Scotland
Tel (01876) 500 480

Hillwalking

The open bog moorland of North Uist or the rock-strewn, exposed hillsides of neighbouring Harris are your choices for guided hillwalking from this centre. These Hebridean landscapes are both wildly beautiful and testing – high winds, exposed ridge scrambles, alternating boggy low ground and steep uplands combining with plentiful wildlife, both land and marine (you are seldom out of sight of the sea), and more ancient sites than have yet been recorded. These include strange Celtic forts built in the middle of the inland lochs which must be approached via an ankle-deep causeway with a 'clapper' – a loose rock purposefully placed so that you tread on it and make a noise, warning the now-ghostly inhabitants of your coming. There are also stone circles and menhirs, dolmens, barrows, early Christian hermits' beehive huts, chapels and souterrains – Neolithic and Iron Age underground grain stores and refuges in time of war.

You can choose where to walk, and for how long, with nights under canvas or back at the centre's own bunkhouse (or local B&B if you prefer). Survival skills can also be incorporated into a guided walk.

Season: All year.
Tariffs: Prices include instruction, equipment and accommodation. 1-week holiday (walking only or combined with other centre activities): £220 (self-catering) / £270 (with full board). Day visitors: £25.

See Sub-Aqua Diving (p. 397) for full details.

whitewave activities

19 Linicro
Kilmuir
Isle of Skye
Highland
IV51 9YN
Scotland
Tel (01470) 542 414

Hillwalking

These 1-day and 5-day hillwalking trips over the remote Trotternish hills of Skye get you right away from the other tourists on the island and into the wilder uplands where few people ever go. There is a definite emphasis on ecology, with attempts to see rare birds such as corncrake, and identification of wild flowers and fungi. This is combined with informal tuition on hillwalking techniques such as basic map and compass navigation, weather awareness, route-finding and what to do in an emergency.

Tariffs: Explore Skye walking holiday (includes guide and 5 nights' full-board accommodation): £220. Guided walks can be arranged on a daily basis; contact centre for details. Group, family and youth rates available.

See Canoeing (p. 36) for full details.

further reading

The Backpackers' Handbook, Hugh McManners, Dorling Kindersley, 1995; *The Big Walks*, Wilson and Gilbert, Diadem, 1980; *The Corbetts and Other Scottish Hills*, Johnstone, Brown and Bennett, Scottish Mountaineering Association, 1990; *The First 50 – Munro Bagging without a Beard*, Muriel Grey, Mainstream Publishing, 1991.

kitting yourself out

A good backpack should be supported mostly from the waist, keeping the bulk of the weight high on your back, so that you do not get painful 'shoulder drag' after a few hours of walking. Other points to look for are an internal frame, Gore-Tex or similar semi-waterproof material, chest straps for distributing the weight, and about 75 litres of carrying capacity. A few tried and tested brands are Karrimor, Mountaincraft and Berghaus, whose large backpacks begin at about £70–80.

By contrast, a good day pack needs only about 25 litres of capacity. Again, Karrimor is a good brand, along with Mountaincraft and Berghaus. Prices begin at about £30.

Without a decent pair of boots, you will be going nowhere. Make sure you've worn them in a good week or two before setting off on a trail. Look for ankle support, good grip, waterproof material and, when trying them in the shop, a gap at the toes and the back of the heel wide enough for one finger to slip into. This will allow for foot swelling and sock expansion from moisture, and will usually mean you can wear 2 pairs of socks without cramping your feet. Never buy boots that feel tight across the instep when you lace them up. Look for brands such as Mountaincraft, Moac, Berghaus, Hi-Tec and Line 7. Good boots start at about £40–45 and go up to around £80 for all-weather models.

Thermal socks, gloves, hats and underwear are produced by a number of manufacturers, but Marks and Spencer are always reliable, and charge around £18 for a set of thermal long johns and top. For insulated waterproof jackets, walking breeches and Gore-Tex gaiters, see the Skiing equipment section (p. 382).

Ordnance Survey maps are quite expensive – about £5 each – but you need them, and that's that. Buy a plastic cover to stop them disintegrating in wind and rain.

If you're planning to camp, Mountaincraft make good-quality, reasonably priced dome tents that can take rough weather: a good 3-man model costs around £150–180. Other brands to look for are Vango, Phoenix, Khyam, Man Alive, Jack Wolfskin and Trigano. Don't skimp on your tent – a decent one lasts for years but an inadequate one is downright dangerous if it breaks or collapses in high wind, leaving you exposed on the hill.

If you plan to go winter camping in Scotland, invest in a Phoenix Phreak (about £240) or a Saunders Jet Packer Plus (about £220).

As for sleeping bags, there's a wealth of choice – usually graded by season – a cheapish summer sheet being a one-season bag, and so on. If you plan to camp from spring to autumn, look for a three-season bag. Try Snugpak, Mountaincraft, Hi-Gear, Vango and Ajungilak and expect to pay between £50 and £85. Only the die-hard winter mountaineers will need a four-season. Good brands are Rab, Mountain Equipment and Ajungilak. Prices are high – from £90–150.

Opinions are fiercely divided as to what is the best kind of stove. Butane stoves are easy to use but not very eco-friendly. The gas canisters don't last long either. But prices are low – from about £20–30, and they boil water very quickly. Unleaded petrol/paraffin/Coleman fuel-fired stoves are slightly trickier to use, but have a longer working life and the fuel lasts longer. They are more expensive to buy (from around £45to £85 or more) but they are cheaper to run and are much more economical if you're planning to do long trips.

You can buy special lightweight pots and pans for about £4 per unit. Make sure that you buy a pan grip for taking them on and off the stove. Also remember that it pays to buy a good knife – if not a Swiss Army model, then one of the better imitations. Get your camping store to advise you on this and be prepared to spend at least £20 for one that will last and stay sharp over the years. For safety, you should also carry a compass and bivvy bag in case you get lost, or need to wrap up someone who has fallen (see Mountain Skills, p. 290). And don't forget a torch. And chocolate.

checklist

- ✔ *day pack*
- ✔ *thermal long socks*
- ✔ *boots*
- ✔ *thermal underwear*
- ✔ *gore-tex jacket*
- ✔ *gore-tex gaiters*
- ✔ *backpack*
- ✔ *showerproof walking breeches*
- ✔ *ordnance survey maps*

camping gear

- ✔ *tent*
- ✔ *sleeping bag*
- ✔ *stove*
- ✔ *pots and pans*
- ✔ *knives*

390 City Road
EC1V 2QA
Tel (071) 833 2855
Fax (071) 837 5879

water skiing wet biking

Water skiing and wet biking (also called jet biking or jet skiing) are express tickets to an adrenalin rush – but both are much more difficult to learn than they appear. Although some people get it together quite quickly with water skiing, most are shocked by the violence of the pull and spend some time coping with this before they can stand up. However, if you persevere, the sport is highly rewarding, and much more physical than one might think. It is a real strain to hold the body at the correct angle to the water to maintain balance while going in a straight line, let alone carving turns or going over jumps. Many people just give the sport a try once and leave it at that, but it is worth taking an organized course – these usually last 3 days – so that you can progress and actually start having fun, rather than just getting wet and a little scared.

Wet biking is almost as difficult to learn. It looks as though it should be a piece of cake, but unlike a road, which stays still and is hard, water does not behave as one wants it to – especially when it throws up waves or capriciously swallows the bike's nose, sending you over the handlebars with a splosh. Most water sports centres with wet bikes hire them out for limited sessions of 15 minutes apiece. If you are serious about wanting to learn, booking several of these can become expensive. Ring a local centre and ask them for a bulk rate for serious tuition – they don't offer this as an official tariff, but most are willing to negotiate.

selected centres

adventure sports

Carnkie Farmhouse
Carnkie
Redruth
Cornwall
TR16 6RZ
Tel (01209) 218 962 / (0589) 427 077

Water Skiing

Carnkie offer water skiing either on its own or as part of a general multi-activity package that includes climbing and abseiling, surfing, windsurfing and/or paragliding. You can arrange for instruction either by the day, over a weekend or a 2-day break, or take longer holidays of 5 to 7 days. All holidays are self-catering and there is a sliding scale of fees depending on how much comfort you want. Carnkie will pick you up and drop you off at Falmouth bus or train station for a fee of just £2.

Tariffs: Water skiing is one of the activities offered in the centre's multi-activity package deals (accommodation included). Prices are variable, depending on season and type of accommodation desired: £44–78 for 2 nights / 2 activities; £150–195 for 5 nights / 5 activities; £154–273 for 7 nights / 7 activities. Group, long-term-stay and previous-customer discounts available. Single persons desiring their own room must pay a 30% surcharge.

See Paragliding and Parascending (p. 310) for full details.

docklands watersports centre

King George V Dock
Gate 14
Woolwich Manor Way
London
E16 2NJ
Tel (0171) 511 7000

Wet Biking

This is a recreational centre where Londoners can try their hands at wet biking, convenient to get to if you live in the city and want to get wet at the weekend – the centre is open on Sundays. Until recently, they also offered water skiing – to competition standard – and canoeing. It is worth asking if they intend to pick up these courses again if you want to get into other water sports. For the moment, however, it seems that the centre has decided to restrict its activities to wet biking only.

Season: Open all year.
Accommodation: Not available.
Food: Vending machines on site.
Children: Minimum age 8. Junior water sports courses available.
Disabled Facilities: Some disabilities can be catered for; contact centre for details.
Insurance: Clients should arrange personal insurance cover if desired.
Safety: All staff trained in first aid; rescue boats on hand.
Affiliations: British Water Ski Federation (BWSF); British Canoe Union.
Tariffs: Jet bike hire: £15 for 15 minutes. Discounts for club members.
Booking: Full payment required when booking. Refunds given (less £2.50 fee) if cancellation notice received more than 1 week in advance. Bookings cancelled more than 48 hours in advance will be given credit for later date; no credit or refunds if cancellation received less than

48 hours in advance. Late bookings accepted if space available. Visa and Access cards accepted.

Access: The centre is easily reached by public transport – either take the tube and get off at East Ham, or use BR's North Woolwich or Galleon's Reach stations.

elie watersports

Elie Harbour
Elie
Fife
KY9 1BY
Scotland
Tel (01333) 330 962 / (0131) 343 2050

Water Skiing, Wet Biking

Elie is a small, friendly sailing school, with 3 full-time instructors offering tuition at all levels in the sheltered waters of Elie Bay. Supervised jet bike hire is offered by the quarter- and half-hour.

Affiliations: Royal Yachting Association.
Tariffs: Hire and group instruction: £15 per hour.

See Windsurfing (p. 458) for full details.

great glen school of adventure

South Laggan
Nr Spean Bridge
Highland
PH34 4EA
Scotland
Tel (01809) 501 381
Fax (01809) 501 218

Water Skiing, Wet Biking

Loch Oich is a good place at which to learn to water ski, its sheltered waters offering calm conditions with enough wind to produce small waves, which make the ride a bit more fun. If you do not want just to water ski, you can combine it with wet biking or other water sports such as windsurfing and dinghy sailing over a weekend or 5-day break, staying in log cabins built on the loch shore.

Tariffs: Water skiing: £6 per tow (about 5 minutes). Instruction: £20 per person (2 hours). Jet bike hire: £10 per quarter-hour. Instruction: £20 per person (2 hours).

See Paragliding and Parascending (p. 313) for full details.

iris activity breaks

29 Alandale Drive
Pinner
Middlesex
HA5 3UP
Tel (0181) 866 3002

Water Skiing, Jet Biking

Iris offer a combined jet bike and water ski beginners' weekend on a large reservoir in Cambridgeshire, with B&B at a local hotel thrown in. After some basic tuition, you should be able to ride the jet bike unaided, hopping over the waves at up to 30mph. The water skiing involves rather more tuition, but the instructors aim to get you standing up on your first couple of goes.

As well as the B&B accommodation, Iris provide the equipment and local transport to and from the lake and hotel.

Accommodation: B&B at the Alconbury House Hotel, Huntingdon.
Tariffs: Weekend course includes tuition, equipment and 2 nights' B&B: approximately £110.

See Ballooning (p. 13 –14) for full details.

lea valley watersports centre

Banbury Reservoir
Greaves Pumping Station
North Circular Road
Chingford
Essex
E4 8QB
Tel (0181) 531 1129
Fax (0181) 527 0969

Water Skiing, Wet Biking

This centre, situated just outside East London, offers single ski rides that last about 5 minutes each, or full-day and half-day courses. If you get the bug, the centre can coach right through to slalom, jumping and trick skiing. You can also join the centre's ski club for reduced rates and more intensive tuition sessions. Ski boat drivers' courses and 'banana rides' (in effect 2 ski tows) complete the picture. Wet bike hire and tuition can also be arranged.

Season: Open all year.
Accommodation: Not available.
Food: Vending machines on site.
Other Activities: Powerboating (see p. 325); Sailing (p. 353); Windsurfing (p. 461).
Children: Minimum age 8. Junior water sports courses available.
Disabled Facilities: None.
Insurance: Clients should arrange personal insurance cover if desired.
Safety: All staff trained in first aid; safety boats on stand-by.
Affiliations: BWSF; Royal Yachting Association – Powerboating, Sailing, Windsurfing.
Tariffs: All prices include tuition and use of equipment. Water skiing or banana boat session: £10–14 (depending on season); water skiing course (half-day): £26; water skiing course (full day): £48; BWSF Instructor course (3 days): £155; Royal Yachting Association first aid course (1 day): £25; Junior Introduction to Watersports course (2 days): £55. Discounts for club members.
Booking: Full payment required when booking. Refunds given (less £2.50 fee) if cancellation notice received more than 1 week in advance. Bookings cancelled more than 48 hours in advance will be given credit for later date; no credit or refunds if cancellation received less than 48 hours in advance. Late bookings accepted if space available. Visa and Access cards accepted.
Access: Off the A406 in Chingford. Ring centre for public transport details.

loch lomond water ski club

North Hall Cottage
Church Road
Luss
Alexandria
Argyll & Bute
G83 8NZ
Scotland
Tel (01436) 860 632

Water-skiing

This is one of Britain's best-equipped water ski clubs, with 2 Mastercraft Tournament ski boats, a jump, slalom course, training boom, special junior training sessions and, unusually for a water ski centre, nearby accommodation that can be booked through the club. The centre is open to beginners and people training to high competition standard, and has 20 years' experience in coaching. However, you will need your own transport to get to and from the centre. If you join the club, the costs of training go down considerably, and special evening sessions for club members should help to improve your skills fairly quickly.

Season: Easter Saturday to September.
Accommodation: Hotel and lodge accommodation available at the marina where clubhouse is located. Camping and hostel nearby.
Food: Restaurant on-site.
Children: Minimum age 6; special junior training nights weekly.
Disabled Facilities: Disabled clients can sometimes be accommodated. Contact centre for details.
Insurance: Clients should arrange personal insurance cover if desired.
Safety: First-aid kits carried by instructors.
Affiliations: BWSF; West Dunbartonshire Sports Council; Greater Glasgow and Clyde Valley Tourist Board; Scottish Water Skiers' Association.
Tariffs: Price includes tuition and use of equipment. 15-minute run: £10 (adults), £7 (juniors under 16). Group discounts available.
Booking: Call (01384) 753 000 to make bookings. Payment by cash or cheque.
Access: Off the A82 at Cameron House Marina. Trains and buses to Balloch, walking distance to marina (or cab fare is approximately £3).

windsport international ltd

Mylor Yacht Harbour
Falmouth
Cornwall
TR11 5UF
Tel (01326) 376 191
Fax (01326) 376 192

Water Skiing

Windsport's Falmouth centre offers water skiing either as part of a multi-activity package that includes a whole bunch of water sports, or on its own with private tuition on a student-to-instructor ratio of 1:1 or 2:1.

The courses can be residential or non-residential as you like, and there is a variety of different types of accommodation, with fees charged on a sliding scale to reflect the level of comfort required.

Season: All year.
Tariffs: Water skiing is one of the activities offered in the centre's multi-activity packages. 5-day family, child or adult course: £125 (adult), £95 (child); weekend family course: £48 (adult), £38 (child); 1-day family or child course: £25 (adult), £20 (child); 1-day adult course: £48. Residential packages are also available (including tuition, equipment and accommodation); prices vary according to level of accommodation chosen (hotel, guest house or farmhouse). 5-day course (6 nights' accommodation): £365–545; week end course (2 nights' accommodation): £220–280. Group discounts available.

See Sailing (p. 442) for full details.

kitting yourself out

Water skiing can get very expensive if you want to be fully independent – i.e. owning a boat as well as the actual ski equipment. However, any good school or water sports centre will be able to give you a pull, as well as offer coaching, if you start to get very good and want to take the sport further. The cost of these probably works out far cheaper than buying, insuring, storing and maintaining your own ski boat.

Good water skis are made by Connolly and Sevylor (they both make good ropes too). A beginner's set costs about £100, plus £10 for the rope. Advanced skis go up to £500 and more. Water rings and bananas – fun things to get towed on if you become tired – are also made by Conolly and Sevylor, and cost around £100 each.

Good buoyancy aids for water skiing are made by America's Cup and cost about £50 or so. Wet suits from GULL cost about £100–300 new. Dry suits from Musto cost between £200 and £400.

Now for the really expensive bit – a boat and motor. The most basic type of boat is an RIB made of rubber. This, together with a Yamaha, Kawasaki, Johnson, Mariner or Mercury engine (must be above 50hp), costs about £1,500 new, or somewhere under £1,000 second-hand. A more expensive but more solid option is a fibreglass flat-bottomed Dory – with an engine it will cost around £4,000. Top of the range are the Fletcher Bay Liner ski boats which start at around £5,000.

Wet biking is also expensive if you want your own machine. Yamaha, Kawasaki, Sea-Doo and Polaris all make good ones for about £4,000–6,000 new. Second-hand machines can be had for as little as £1,500, but watch out – they need a lot of maintenance, and spare parts for old models can be a problem.

As with water skiing, you will also need a buoyancy aid worn over a wet or dry suit. See above for prices and manufacturers.

checklist

- ✔ *water skis*
- ✔ *water ring or banana*
- ✔ *ski rope*
- ✔ *wet suit or dry suit*
- ✔ *buoyancy aid*
- ✔ *boat*

photo: Andrew Holt

white-water rafting

Britain is not known for its thunderous rivers – one tends to assume that these are only encountered on continents where high mountains create a violent run-off from snow-melt. However, the Welsh Borders boast rivers – the Wye and some of its tributaries – that create conditions very similar to snow run-off simply through rainwater running off the Welsh hills. The rapids can become immensely exciting – especially through the winter and spring – with one or two of them reaching Grade 4. To put this in perspective, the highest grade of rapid that you are allowed to take people down commercially is Grade 5.

coracles

Also part of the Welsh Borders' white-water scene are coracles – round boats made to an ancient design, using an inverted oval 'bender' of flexible branches to make a frame over which cured skins or canvas sheets are stretched taut. The whole lot is then sealed with pitch and you have a boat. This is where the problems begin. Lacking a rudder, the coracle is near-impossible to steer – you have to use a single-bladed paddle in a specially adapted figure-of-eight motion, continually spinning the boat across the river's current.

A skilled coracler can navigate long stretches of river, even through stretches of white water. Some people even claim that you can cross the Channel in them. Certain regattas now include classes for coracles.

Coracles go back thousands of years. In Britain, Celtic fishermen used them on the fens and rivers and a few still survive in Wales. (Oddly enough, they are still in common use in southern India, of all places.) Several coracle builders in the Welsh Marches now offer 2–3-day courses in both constructing and propelling the craft on the Rivers Wye, Teme and Lugg. Once you've learned how to use the thing, you then have a boat that you can take anywhere, and which fits into the back of a small car. The courses are both physically and mentally demanding but great fun.

selected centres

acorn activities

PO Box 120
Hereford
Hereford & Worcester
HR4 8YB
Tel (01432) 830 083
Fax (01432) 830 110

Acorn organize white-water trips on all available rivers, sending you to whichever one is running best at the time you book. Wet suits, buoyancy aids and helmets are provided, along with B&B, but you will need your own transport to get to the sites. Water is guaranteed all year, but be aware that as water levels drop in the summer months, during high summer the rafting day is confined to a 2-hour session. The rest of the day you can fill with abseiling or an assault course. All raft sessions are led by qualified guides in paddle boats (you do the paddling) and each rafting day includes lunch.

If you don't fancy white water, Acorn also organize rafting days where you build and then launch your own raft under supervision, racing it across a lake or river.

Season: Open all year.
Tariffs: Price includes accommodation, guide, lunch and all equipment. A full day costs £40, with a minimum booking of 8 people. Half-day rafting costs £20.

See Walking (p. 414) for full details.

black mountain activities

PO Box 5
Hay-on-Wye
Hereford & Worcester
HR3 5YB
Tel (01497) 847 897

Running on the upper waters of the River Wye, Black Mountain operate several rafting routes of about 15 miles each, encountering several sets of large rapids, usually up to Grade 3, but sometimes higher if water levels change. The routes take roughly 4 hours. The centre uses paddle rafts (i.e. you do the paddling) that carry from 6 to 8 people. The season lasts from October to March only, and even then trips may occasionally be postponed if water levels are not high enough. If this happens, you can decide to rebook at a later date, or keep the same dates but replace the rafting with any of Black Mountain's other activities, which include caving, gorge walking, mountain biking and canoeing. When booking a rafting trip, ask for a route that includes the 'Hell Hole'.

Season: October to March.
Accommodation: Not provided. Black Mountain will arrange local accommodation to suit your budget.
Food: Packed lunch only.
Other Activities: Canoeing (see p. 19); Caving (p. 43); Climbing & Abseiling (p. 93); Mountain Biking (p. 116); Gorge Walking (p. 176).
Children: Only children over 10 may white-water raft.
Disabled Facilities: None.
Insurance: Clients should arrange their own travel insurance.
Safety: All river guides trained in first aid and water rescue.
Affiliations: British Canoe Union; Wales Tourist Board.

Tariffs: A day's white-water rafting costs £35 per person, including lunch, wet suit and instruction.

Booking: Advance booking essential, as trips are increasingly popular. Full tariff must be paid with booking. Late bookings accepted if space allows.

Access: Black Mountain assemble clients at a central pick-up point for transport to the launching site by minibus. Maps detailing how to reach the pick-up point will be sent on confirmation of booking. You will need your own car to reach the pick-up point.

---

croft-na-caber

Kenmore
Loch Tay
Perthshire & Kinross
PH15 2HW
Tel (01887) 830 588
Fax (01887) 830 649

Croft-na-Caber outdoor centre run rafting trips on the River Tay. Of the 3 runs they offer, the Grandtully is the most exciting, with some fairly serious rapids – the British white-water kayaking championships have been held at Grandtully. A gentler version takes in the rapids around Stanley Weir and the Cat's Hole – though this would be too gentle for real excitement-seekers. For a family trip, you can also sign up for the 'Chinese Run' – a slow float down the Tay with a few minor rapids, but mostly just taking in the scenery.

Rafting trips generally take about a half-day, including getting to the launching site, briefing, putting on wet suits, etc., as well as getting back to Croft-na-Caber at the end of the day. The centre has accommodation to suit most budgets.

If going down the rapids in a boat seems too tame, try hydro-boarding (also known as river sledging), which involves holding onto a body surfboard designed for one person and taking the rapids on your belly. Give this a go if you think you've tried it all.

Season: Year round.

Accommodation: Croft-na-Caber is a large stone-built Victorian lodge. Choose between full-board hotel-style accommodation (£40 per person per night), B&B (£20 per person), or self-catering log chalets (£50–60 per night for a 4–6-bed chalet).

Food: The centre can provide full or half-board, or you can self-cater. Special diets by prior arrangement.

Other Activities: Canoeing (see p. 21); Gorge Walking (p. 177); Sailing (p. 344).

Children: Grandtully run: minimum age 12; Chinese run: minimum age 10; hydro-boarding: minimum age 14.

Disabled Facilities: None.

Insurance: Clients should arrange their own personal accident cover.

Safety: All guides trained in river rescue. Helmets and buoyancy aids compulsory.

Affiliations: British Canoe Union (BCU); British Hang-gliding and Paragliding Association; Royal Yachting Association.

Tariffs: Grandtully or Stanley run: £24 per person; Chinese run: £18 per person; hydro-boarding: £29 per person.

Booking: Telephone to make a reservation and get a booking form, which should be returned with a 20% deposit within 7 days. Late bookings may be made if space permits.

Access: Croft-na-Caber is just out of Kenmore village, on the south shore road of Loch Tay. Kenmore is 6 miles from Aberfeldy on the A827 / A9 junction, 2 hours north of Edinburgh.

free spirits

5 Ballinlaggan
Acharn
Aberfeldy
Perthshire & Kinross
PH15 2HT
Tel (01887) 830 633

Another Tayside white-water operation, Free Spirits run 4-hour trips through the Grandtully and Stanley sections of the river's larger rapids. A small, family-run company, this is a good bet for people new to rafting who want to be looked after in a more personal way than many outdoor companies are able to do. Free Spirits also run trips for special-needs groups: they have successfully catered for people sent to them by the Scottish Prison Service and the Scottish Health Service. Unfortunately, however, white-water rafting is not suitable for the the disabled, as it requires almost total mobility. The company supplies equipment and guides, as well as transport to and from the river, but not accommodation. The owners are happy to book it for you, however, at any budget.

Season: Year round.
Accommodation: Not provided, but centre will book in the immediate area.
Food: Not provided.
Other Activities: Gorge Walking (see p. 179).
Children: Minimum age 12.
Disabled Facilities: None.
Insurance: Clients should arrange their own personal accident cover.
Safety: All guides trained in river rescue. Helmets and buoyancy aids compulsory.
Affiliations: BCU.
Tariffs: Grandtully or Stanley run: £24 per person.
Booking: Telephone to make a reservation and get a booking form, which should be returned with a 20% deposit within 7 days. Late bookings may be made if space permits.
Access: Rendezvous sites near the river will be given when booking. You will need your own transport to get from your accommodation to the rendezvous, or you can arrange a pick-up for an extra charge.

the greenwood centre

The Church Hall
Llanafan Fawr
Builth Wells
Powys
LD2 3PN
Tel/Fax (01597) 860 469

Tim Wade runs the Greenwood Centre near Builth (pronounced 'Bilth') Wells and offers a variety of courses in working non-seasoned wood for all sorts of things including furniture-making and willow basketwork. The most fun course, however, is the coracle-making. Over 2 days you are guided through the construction of your own boat, using specialist methods of woodworking such as steam bending. You then launch the thing and are taught how to handle it with a special 'figure of eight' motion of the paddle. When the course is over you can take your boat home with you.

Builth Wells is in the mid-Welsh Borders, amid some of the least touristy but most beautiful countryside in Britain. The coracle courses take you into some of the best of it along the River Wye.

Season: June and July.
Accommodation: Camping available at centre (£1.50 per night) or local accommodation can be arranged.

Food: Daily lunch and beverages provided, 1 evening barbecue.
Children: Children of all ages welcome.
Disabled Facilities: None.
Insurance: Clients should arrange their own holiday insurance.
Safety: Staff trained in first aid.
Affiliations: Wales Tourist Board.
Tariffs: Price includes tuition, materials, equipment, lunch and 1 dinner. 2-day course: £125.
Booking: 15% non-refundable deposit required. Balance due 28 days before start date. Late bookings accepted if space available.
Access: Off the A470 at Builth Wells. Trains to Llandrindod Wells. Buses to Builth Wells.

---

national white water centre

Canolfan Tryweryn
Frongoch
Bala
Gwynedd
LL23 7NU
Wales
Tel (01678) 521 083
Fax (01678) 521 158

This is Britain's most organized white-water option, but it's also the most expensive at £150–180 per trip; you have to divide it between 4–7 people (7 is the maximum a raft can take) to make it affordable. The runs last about 2 hours only, but they involve several trips down the centre's world championship course below the Celyn Dam in North Wales. If you don't fancy 2 hours there's also a 20-minute option of 1 run only. Expect big rapids. All equipment is provided – though wet suits must be hired at extra cost. Canoeing is also an option; contact the centre for more details.

Season: All year.
Accommodation: Not provided.
Food: Not provided.
Children: Over-12s only.
Disabled Facilities: None.
Insurance: Clients must arrange personal insurance cover.
Safety: All instructors qualified in first aid and water rescue.
Affiliations: Welsh Canoeing Association; Wales Tourist Board.
Tariffs: 2-hour run: £141 per raft (weekdays), £188 (weekends and holidays). Wet suit hire: £4 per person.
Booking: Advance booking essential – apply for a booking form. A deposit of £20 per raft is required. Total due 15 days before start date.
Access: Bala is half an hour north of Dolgellau and the same east of Porthmadog. Clients must supply their own transport.

peter faulkner coracles

24 Watling Street
Leintwardine
Shropshire
SY7 0LW
Tel (01547) 540 629

Also based in the Welsh Borders, these 4-day coracle courses involve building and then launching your own hide-bottomed round boat on the River Teme. Non-smokers can stay with the Faulkners (full board), or the family can help you find something in the village, either within walking distance or a short drive away. Alternatively, you can just show up for a visit and trial paddle to get the feel of these strange craft. Longer trips down the Teme are being planned (Peter Faulkner has navigated 85 miles of the river in a coracle), and anyone interested should telephone him for more details.

Season: Usually spring to late autumn.
Accommodation: Full board with the Faulkners or local B&B, camping, etc.
Food: Meals provided if living in, otherwise lunch snacks can be provided.
Children: Minimum age 18.
Disabled Facilities: The course work is physically demanding, so prospective disabled students should contact Peter Faulkner to discuss details.
Insurance: Clients should arrange their own holiday insurance. Note: coracling is not a water sport in the normal sense, but you should mention it to the insurance company.
Safety: Staff have no specific medical training.
Affiliations: The Coracle Society.
Tariffs: Price includes full-board accommodation, instruction, all materials and use of equipment. 4-day coracle-making course: £500.
Booking: Call centre for booking details.
Access: Leintwardine is 9 miles west of Ludlow on the A4113. Ludlow is the nearest train station. (You will, however, need a vehicle and roof rack to take your coracle home!)

kitting yourself out

For white-water rafting it is best to let the company supply all equipment – it is included in the price of the trip anyway. Even if you own your own wet suit, paddle, buoyancy aid or helmet, you are quite likely to damage or lose them on your way down the river and it isn't worth risking them.

Coracles are a different matter, however. There is little point in buying one of these strange craft unless you have learned the techniques of paddling the thing, for it is far from self-explanatory, and if you don't know what you are doing you just go round in circles. For this reason it is better to go on a coracle-building and paddling course like the 2 listed above than simply to buy a coracle. As it happens, however, the two coracle-makers who run the above-listed courses are the only British manufacturers the editor could find.

If you do decide to take one of these courses, you will not only end up with a coracle but you will also have benefited from a few days' tuition into the bargain, and all the materials – leather- or pitch-covered canvas, greenwood frame and paddle – will have been thrown in.

governing body

Royal Yachting Association
RYA House, Romsey Road, Eastleigh
Hampshire SO50 9YA
Tel (01703) 629 962
Fax (01703) 629 924

windsurfing

Windsurfing has become a lot easier in the last few years. It used to be like this: you'd surface and, for the hundredth time that afternoon, would splash wearily towards your board, struggle onto it and begin the whole business again – crouch, kneel, totter to your feet and start to haul the heavy rig out of the water where it has capsized. This has all changed. Recent innovations in equipment and training have made the whole process much easier. Not only is the kit much lighter to use these days, but most schools now guarantee that within half an hour you'll make your first basic sail, leaning back in balance with the sail and boom and sheeting in (taking the wind), gliding miraculously over the water thinking 'I can do it, I can...', then splash, and you're back in. But next time it gets a little easier, then easier still...

Windsurfing is perhaps the best way to learn the principles of sailing, as you are effectively your own craft, adapting your body to the vicissitudes of wind and water. And it's open to just about everybody: beginners don't have to be that fit to learn. Two-hour 'taster' sessions and intensive weekend courses are now being offered around the country. The taster sessions will give you the feel of windsurfing, while the weekend courses take you from the very basics – such as learning the correct terms for all the rigging, launching (getting on) and sailing away – to sailing up or downwind, tacking (sailing in a zig-zag upwind), gybing (going about) and steering.

The sport no longer requires the high levels of physical fitness that it used to – at least not at the purely recreational level. Most people now wear a harness that allows the weight of the sail to be taken on the waist and bum, allowing you to sail for long periods without undue strain. There is also a thriving racing scene at local club and school level, open to almost all levels of ability from relative beginner to Olympic standard.

Windsurfing is also open to any age group – from 7 to 70 – and the invention of the wet/dry suit has made winter sailing feasible, though most schools still operate only from April to October. It's always fun, but at its peak windsurfing can be one of the most exciting of all water sports – to the point where you can perform stunts such as looping 360 degrees in the air off a big wave, or surfing at 30–40mph.

For those who don't want to perform Herculean feats, the comparatively simple pleasure of windsurfing up and down in a calm reservoir or bay is just as rewarding; in the words of one regular pleasure sailor: 'Nothing is more meditative than tacking up and down a stretch of open water, feeling your body sing with the wind. Ten minutes and I've forgotten where I am . . .'

Splash!

selected centres

adventure sports

Carnkie Farmhouse
Carnkie
Redruth
Cornwall
TR16 6RZ
Tel (01209) 218962 / (0589) 427 077

Carnkie offer windsurfing as part of a multi-activity programme rather than as an end in itself. If you are looking for an introduction to the sport, then this is a good place to come to, but you won't find courses to take you through the RYA certificate programme. You can choose between weekend and 2-day courses or longer 5- and 7-day holidays that also include sailing, climbing and abseiling, surfing and paragliding. There is also a sliding scale of tariffs depending on how much comfort you want in your accommodation. All holidays are self-catering and the centre will pick up and drop off anyone without their own transport in Falmouth for a small charge. They cater mostly for people in their mid-20s.

Tariffs: Windsurfing is one of the activities offered in the centre's multi-activity package deals (accommodation included). Prices are variable, depending on season and type of accommodation desired: £44–78 for 2 nights / 2 activities; £110–195 for 5 nights / 5 activities; £154–273 for 7 nights / 7 activities. Group, long-term-stay and previous-customer discounts available. Single persons desiring their own room must pay a 30% surcharge.

See Paragliding and Parascending (p. 310) for full details.

bray watersports centre

Bray Lake
Monkey Island Lane
Windsor Lane
Maidenhead
Berkshire
SL6 2EB
Tel (01628) 38860
Fax (01628) 77144

Windsurfing courses are divided into 2 types at Bray – those for adults and those for juniors. For adults, you can start with a 10-hour Learn to Windsurf intensive course, spread over 3 days, with, hopefully, an RYA Level 1 certificate (covering basic handling skills and turning) at the end of it. A second 10-hour course, also spread out over 3 or 4 days, takes you to RYA Level 2 (coping with windier conditions and sailing between specific points), and following on from this the Introduction to Planing course (2 days) gives you the RYA Level 3 certificate (dealing with waves and basic racing techniques). For the highest basic levels – RYA 4 and 5 (racing, rough weather and rescue training) – there are advanced courses spread out over a week or more; you can choose when to have the training sessions.

The junior windsurfing courses are aimed at kids from 8 to 12 years old, with an emphasis on fun. They go up to RYA Level 3. During term time the course sessions are run after school, starting at 4.30 p.m. and lasting about 2 hours. During school holidays the sessions run at fixed times during the day.

Most of Bray's clientele are day visitors from Berkshire and outer West London, so there is no accommodation at the centre. However, if you're passing through and want to take a course, they will help you to book local accommodation to suit your budget. You will need your own transport to get to and fro. While you're at Bray, you can also try one of their canoeing, powerboating, sailing or multi-activity sessions.

Season: Open all year.
Accommodation: Centre will provide help in obtaining local accommodation.
Food: Snack bar at centre.
Other Activities: Sailing (see p. 341).
Children: Junior courses available for children 8–16 years old; must be water-confident. Anyone under 18 must have consent of parent or guardian.
Disabled Facilities: Centre is wheelchair-accessible and all courses can be adapted for the disabled.
Insurance: Clients should arrange personal insurance cover if desired.
Safety: All staff trained in first aid.
Affiliations: RYA.
Tariffs: Prices include tuition and equipment. RYA Level 1 or 2 course: £69; RYA Level 3 course: £100. Junior RYA Levels 1, 2 or 3: £49. Personal tuition also available for Levels 1–5. Instructor and Assistant Instructor courses run all year. Group and student discounts available.
Booking: Payment is due in full at time of booking. Money refunded upon cancellation only if notice received more than 1 week in advance. Late bookings accepted if space available. Visa and Access cards accepted.
Access: Off the M4 at Maidenhead (Junction 8/9 or 6). Trains and buses to Maidenhead.

calshot activities centre

Calshot Spit
Fawley
Southampton
Hampshire
S05 1BR
Tel (01703) 892 077
Fax (01703) 891 267

Calshot is a residential multi-activity centre specializing in water sports. They have a reputation as one of the best places at which to learn windsurfing, and offer 12 different courses in the sport. You can obtain each certificate (for example RYA Levels 1–3 and the RYA Instructor Levels 1–3) on separate 2-day courses, or you can take 5-day courses that give you 2 certificate levels. You have the choice of staying full-board at the centre or arranging (or getting them to arrange) your own accommodation if you don't fancy sleeping in bunk beds.

Calshot also run introductory day courses teaching basic techniques, or as sharpening-up clinics for more experienced windsurfers. There are also supervised sailing days where those who have already completed one of the RYA certificates can practise in safe, sheltered water on the centre's equipment and with their safety officers standing by.

Season: Windsurfing courses run May to August.
Accommodation: 150 bunk beds available.
Food: Meals provided; vegetarian and special diets can be catered for.
Other Activities: Canoeing (see p. 20); Child and Youth Sports (p. 56); Cycle Sports (p. 116); Powerboating (p. 324); Sailing (p. 341).
Children: Special children's courses, games available. Birthday parties can be arranged.
Disabled Facilities: Arrangements can be made to accommodate disabled people; contact centre for more details.
Insurance: If clients require personal insurance, inexpensive cover can be arranged through the centre.
Safety: All instructors trained in first aid.
Affiliations: RYA – Windsurfing.
Tariffs: Course fees are either non-residential (NR) (including tuition, equipment, lunch and dinner), or residential (R) (including tuition, equipment, accommodation and full board). 1-day course: £45; weekend courses: £95 (NR) / £110 (R); 5-day courses: £210 (NR) / £245 (R); 5-day coaching courses: £190 (NR) / £220(R). (Special courses for children available at reduced rates.)
Booking: £25 non-refundable deposit required. Balance payable 8 weeks before course starts. Access and Visa cards accepted. Bookings normally made in advance, but late bookings sometimes accepted if space available.
Access: Off the M27 near Southampton. Trains and buses available to Southampton; pick-ups can be arranged by centre (for adventure holidays only).

arsington sport and leisure

arsington Water
shbourne
erbyshire
E6 1ST
el (01629) 540 478
ax (01629) 540 666

These windsurfing courses on Carsington Water, just a few miles south of the Peak District, are run over a day or weekend, and go from RYA Level 1 to 3 for recreational windsurfers; they also offer Instructor Level 1. 'Taster' sessions are available for people who just want to give the sport a try. If you are already experienced, the centre hires out windsurfing equipment for supervised sailing by the hour, half-day or day.

The Carsington centre is non-residential and you will need your own transport to get to and from the waterside.

Season: Open all year, but courses run from April to October only.
Accommodation: Not available.
Food: Restaurant on-site.
Children: All ages welcome.
Disabled Facilities: None.
Insurance: Clients should arrange personal insurance cover.
Safety: Instructors trained in first aid.
Affiliations: RYA – Windsurfing.
Tariffs: All prices include tuition and use of equipment. Introductory windsurfing session: £12.50; RYA Level 1 course (12 hours): £60; RYA Level 2 course (12 hours): £65; RYA Level 3 course (14 hours): £65; Windsurfing Instructor course: £145; junior windsurfing courses: £50.
Booking: 10% non-refundable deposit required. Balance due 4 weeks in advance of course. Refunds only given on cancellation if place can be refilled. Late bookings accepted if space available. Visa and Access cards accepted.
Access: Off the B5035 at Carsington. Contact centre for public transport details.

elie watersports

Elie Harbour
Elie
Fife
KY9 1BY
Scotland
Tel (01333) 330 962 / (0131) 343 2050

Elie is a small, friendly windsurfing and sailing school, with 3 full-time instructors offering tuition at all levels in the sheltered waters of Elie Bay. You can choose between a structured 2-day course, or set of courses, aimed at getting you through the RYA's Level 1–4 certificates, or you can arrange for group or private beginners' or improvers' lessons by the hour. If you are already proficient, windsurfer hire by the hour, half-day or day is also available.

The centre caters mainly to locals and summer holidaymakers coming to Elie Beach, but although it has no accommodation, it is happy to make arrangements for you to suit your budget. However, you will need to get to and from the centre yourself.

Season: May to September.
Accommodation: Centre will provide help in arranging local accommodation at B&Bs or hotels.
Food: Not available.
Other Activities: Sailing (see p. 345); Water Skiing and Wet Biking (p. 439).
Children: All ages welcome.
Disabled Facilities: None.
Insurance: Clients should arrange their own holiday insurance.
Safety: Staff qualified in first aid and rescue boat skills.
Affiliations: RYA.
Tariffs: Hire and group instruction: £10 per hour, £14 per 2 hours. Private lessons: £12 per hour. 2-day RYA certificate course (Levels 1–4): £55.
Booking: No deposit required. Late bookings accepted if space available.
Access: Off the A917 at Elie. Contact centre for public transport details.

fairlands valley sailing centre

Six Hills Way
Stevenage
Hertfordshire
SG2 OBL
Tel (01438) 353 241
Fax (01438) 743 483

Day and 2-day courses in introductory windsurfing are offered on this 11-acre lake in a country park outside Stevenage. It's a good place at which to break into the sport – fairly low-key with 3 full-time instructors and various versions of the same courses tailored for adults, children, groups, etc. Once you have learned, you can hire equipment from the centre whenever you have time. You can also take individual lessons to improve, and eventually train for your RYA certificates. The school has been running since 1972.

Fairlands does not run residential courses – most of the centre's clientele is local. You will need a car to get to and from the lake.

Tariffs: Prices include instruction and use of equipment. 3-hour introductory session: £27; introductory course (1½ days): £70; 6-hour improver course: £48; half-day junior course: £15. Concessionary rates available.

See Sailing (p. 346) for full details.

galloway sailing centre

Loch Ken
Castle Douglas
Dumfries and Galloway
DG7 3NQ
Scotland
Tel & Fax (01644) 420 626

Catering for all ages – from 8 to 80 – and for the total beginner as well as the experienced sailor, Galloway offers windsurfing courses on a large loch in the western Scottish Borders. Novices start at RYA Level 1 and can take a series of courses up to Level 4, which qualifies the sailor to handle racing craft. If you already have RYA Level 4 and want to hire a boat, the centre has a small fleet of windsurfers which can be taken out solo or sailed under supervision, whether as a group or on a one-to-one basis. Windsurfing can also be tried as part of a general multi-activity course or holiday along with canoeing and windsurfing. Single adults or groups, families and unaccompanied children are all welcome.

Galloway Sailing Centre is affiliated to the Duke of Edinburgh's Award. Children who need to gain points towards the Physical Activities section of their award can get their books marked up as follows: dinghy sailing or windsurfing to RYA Level 1 – 6 points; dinghy sailing or windsurfing to RYA Level 2 – 12 points; dinghy sailing or windsurfing Levels 3 and 4 – 18 points.

Tariffs: Prices vary according to high/low season (high season is 27 May–3 September), and include tuition and use of equipment. Half-day course: £24 / £20; day course: £38 / £34; weekend course: £62 / £55; 5-day course: £130 / £120. 5 days of full board accommodation: £130. Discounts for under-16s and for groups.

See Sailing (p. 348) for full details.

great glen school of adventure

South Laggan
Nr Spean Bridge
Highland
PH34 4EA
Scotland
Tel (01809) 501 381
Fax (01809) 501 218

This centre offers learn-to-windsurf courses on the sheltered waters of Loch Oich from April to October. You can choose between a 2-hour 'taster' session (much falling in the water and general frustration) or a weekend or 5-day introductory course that gets the basics down properly and gives you the skill necessary to go it alone and/or take the RYA's 5 windsurfing award tests. More experienced windsurfers can hire equipment and sail by the hour, under supervision.

The centre has built several wooden A-frame chalets by the lochside, which are included as accommodation if you take a weekend or 5-day course. Alternatively, you can stay in a local B&B or hotel and the centre will arrange transport for you to and from the lochside if needed.

Season: April to October.
Tariffs: Rental of board and wet suit: £6 for 1 hour, £10.50 for 2 hours, £14 for 3 hours, £23 for 6 hours. Instruction: £20 per person (2 hours).

See Paragliding and Parascending (p. 313) for full details.

iris activity breaks

29 Alandale Drive
Pinner
Middlesex
HA5 3UP
Tel (0181) 866 3002

Iris organize learn-to-windsurf weekends on Lake Windermere aimed at total beginners. By the end of the weekend you should be able to rig, launch, sail and change direction (gybe). The courses are residential and include 2 nights' B&B at the Salutation Hotel, Ambleside. You will need your own transport to get to the hotel.

Although this course does not give you an RYA certificate at the end of the 2 days, it does provide a solid grounding in the basic skills and is recommended for anyone with a casual interest who wants to give the sport a try before committing themselves to learning for a test.

Accommodation: B&B at the Salutation Hotel, Ambleside.
Tariffs: Weekend course includes 2 nights' B&B: approximately £135.

See Ballooning (p. 13–14) for full details.

lea valley watersports centre

Banbury Reservoir
Greaves Pumping Station
North Circular Road
Chingford
Essex
E4 8QB
Tel (0181) 531 1129
Fax (0181) 527 0969

Based just outside East London, this centre offers non-residential windsurfing courses for beginners only, either as a half-day introduction or a full day, at the end of which you are assessed for your RYA Level 1 windsurfing certificate. Thereafter you may buy a windsurfing day ticket, but only using your own equipment, and provided you can supply proof of insurance. Anyone wanting to take more advanced RYA windsurfing courses will have to look elsewhere.

Affiliations: RYA – Windsurfing.

Tariffs: All prices include tuition and use of equipment. Half-day windsurfing course: £22; full-day windsurfing course: £46; RYA First Aid course (1 day): £25; Junior Introduction to Watersports course (2 days): £55. Discounts for club members.

See Water Skiing and Wet Biking (p. 440) for full details.

loch insh watersports & skiing centre

Insh Hall
Kincraig
Highland
PH21 1NU
Scotland
Tel (01540) 651 272
Fax (01540) 651 208

Loch Insh and the River Spey provide the water for these residential windsurfing courses aimed at taking you from complete beginner to intermediate level over a weekend course, or up to RYA Level 3 over a 5-day course. If you just want to try windsurfing out, the school also runs 2-hour introductory windsurfing lessons to get you started on the water.

All equipment is provided by the school – from child rigs to Tiga and Ten Cate Boards – and all courses are run under the supervision of RYA-qualified instructors and follow the association's recommended student-to-instructor ratio. Rescue boats are always on stand-by and buoyancy aids and life jackets are compulsory.

Season: April to October.
Affiliations: RYA – Windsurfing.
Tariffs: 2-hour introductory session: £19. 2-day course: £49; 2-day course (with accommodation and full board): £97. 5-day course: £121; 5-day course (with accommodation and full board): £242. Prices increase about 10% in high season (7 July–27 August). Discounts for youths of around 25%.

See Skiing (p. 378) for full details.

national watersports centre, cumbrae

Burnside Road
Largs
North Ayrshire
KA30 8RW
Scotland
Tel (01475) 674 666
Fax (01475) 674 720

This centre on the Inner Hebrides island of Cumbrae offers courses from RYA Level 1 to Level 4, broken up into 3 separate 2–3-day sessions. Board hire is also available for more experienced sailors, as is tuition in racing. The courses are fully residential.

Children: Junior courses for 9–14-year-olds.
Affiliations: RYA.
Tariffs: All prices include tuition, equipment and full-board accommodation. 3-day Level 1 course: £102; 3-day Level 2 / 3 course: £102; 3-day Level 3 / 4 course: £102; 5-day junior beginners' or improvers' course: £175.

See Sailing (p. 355) for full details.

outdoor activities association

Marine Walk
Roker
Sunderland
Tyne & Wear
SR6 0PL
Tel (0191) 565 6662 / (0191) 565 7630
Fax (0191) 514 2873

This urban outdoor centre is primarily designed for getting people from the inner city involved in outdoor adventure sports. The formal courses are aimed at beginners, with learn-to-windsurf evenings spread over as many as it takes to gain the basic skills. Once you have attained this level, you can go on to take the RYA courses from Levels 1 to 5, which can, again, be spread over as many evening or weekend sessions as it takes, so as to fit in with a school or work schedule. Windsurfing equipment can be hired by the hour for supervised sailing. Costs are low, but you will need your own transport to get to and fro. School groups and other organized bulk bookings are welcome.

Season: Open all year.
Accommodation: Not available.
Food: Not available.
Other Activities: Canoeing (see p. 26); Climbing and Abseiling (p. 104); Sailing (p. 357).
Children: All ages welcome; junior courses available.
Disabled Facilities: Bathrooms wheelchair-accessible; activities adaptable for disabled clients.
Insurance: Clients should arrange their own holiday insurance if desired.
Safety: Staff trained in first aid and rescue skills.
Affiliations: British Canoe Union; Mountain Leaders Training Board; RYA.
Tariffs: Prices include tuition and use of equipment. Introduction to Windsurfing: £30; Introduction to Sail Sports (2 days) £40; RYA Level 1, 2 or 3 courses (2 days): £55.
Booking: 25% non-refundable deposit required. Full fees due if booking cancelled less than 7 days before start date. Bookings must be made at least 1 week in advance.
Access: On the A183 at Roker, just north of Sunderland. Trains and buses to Sunderland; stations walking distance to centre.

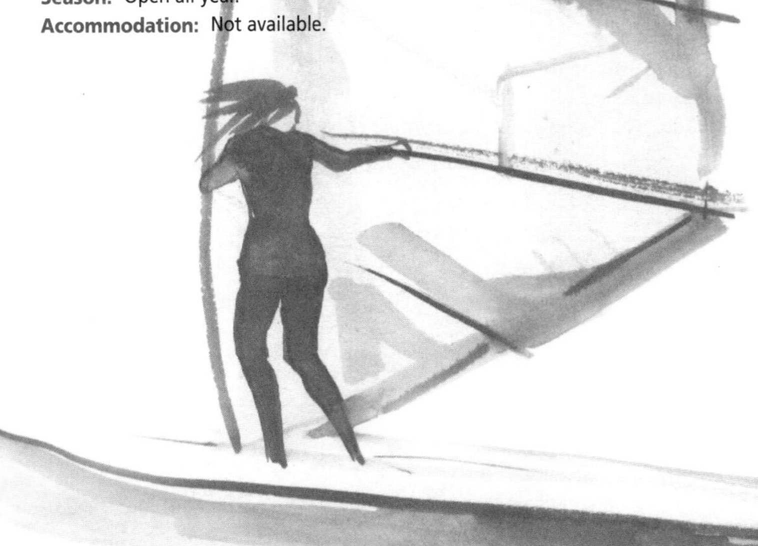

outdoor adventure

Atlantic Court
Widemouth Bay
Nr Bude
Cornwall
EX23 0DF
Tel (01288) 361 312
Fax (01288) 361 153

This is a beautiful place at which to learn to windsurf – in the waters of Widemouth Bay, with the Cornish cliffs rising either side of the sweep of sand, and with dolphins often playing in the surf. Outdoor Adventure is based in a large, rambling cottage just above the bay and offers windsurfing weeks, weekends and 3-day breaks with full board and accommodation thrown in. The holidays cater for all levels of experience – RYA Levels 1 to 5 – and you should go up a grade and receive a certificate at the end of each course, all being well. Friends of differing abilities can come on holiday at the same time, but are then split into the relevant groups while under instruction – which takes up 7 hours of each day.

There are varying types of accommodation on offer – double, single and dorm rooms – and the course tariffs are charged on a sliding scale to reflect your choice. Outdoor Adventure will also pick you up from Bude free of charge if you arrive by public transport.

Season: March to November.
Affiliations: British Activity Holiday Association; British Canoe Union; British Surfing Association; Mountain Leaders Training Board; RYA – Windsurfing.
Tariffs: Prices for windsurfing courses or multi-activity holidays include full-board accommodation, instruction, use of equipment and wet suit. Weekend break from £123; 3-day holiday from £177; 5-day holiday from £288.

See (Surfing p. 406) for full details.

peninsula watersports

Higher Coombe Park
Lewdown
Okehampton
Devon
EX20 4QT
Roadford Lake, Devon
Tel (01409) 211 507
Stithians Lake, Cornwall
Tel (01209) 860 301
Upper Tamar Lake, Cornwall
Tel (01288) 321 712
Siblyback Lake, Cornwall
Tel (01579) 346 522

Of Peninsula's 4 West Country centres, Roadford, Siblyback and Stithians specialize in windsurfing at all levels, while Tamar offers it only to RYA Level 3. The courses on offer are: at Roadford RYA windsurfing Levels 1–2 (no junior levels); at Stithians Levels 1–4 (juniors 1–3); at Tamar Levels 1–3 (juniors 1–3); at Siblyback Levels 1–5 (juniors 1–5). All centres offer windsurfing 'taster' sessions evenings and weekends. Most RYA courses last 2 days, either over a weekend or spread out over a series of evenings. Group and individual bookings are welcome. If you want to try out some other water sports, Peninsula also offer tuition in canoeing, powerboating and dinghy sailing.

None of the centres has accommodation, but they are happy to help you arrange it locally. You will need your own transport to get to and fro.

Season: April to October.
Accommodation: Centre will provide help in finding local accommodation.
Food: Light refreshments available.
Other Activities: Canoeing (see p. 29); Powerboating (p. 326).
Children: Must be 8 years old and water-confident. Junior windsurfing club/lessons for 8–13-year-olds.
Disabled Facilities: Toilets wheelchair-accessible; sailing tuition for disabled clients offered.
Insurance: Third-party insurance required only if you use your own equipment.
Safety: Staff trained in first-aid rescue techniques.
Affiliations: British Canoe Union; RYA – Sailing, Windsurfing and Powerboating.
Tariffs: All prices include tuition and use of equipment. 2-hour taster session: £15; 2-day RYA certificate course: £48. Hire rates on application. Group and family discounts available.
Booking: Deposits only required for group bookings (deposit lost if cancellation notice received less than 1 week in advance). Bookings normally made 1 week in advance for groups, 1 day in advance for individuals, but late bookings sometimes accepted if space available. Visa and Access cards accepted.
Access: Contact each centre individually for access details.

pugneys country park

City of Wakefield MDC
Asdale Road
Wakefield
West Yorkshire
WF2 7EQ
Tel (01924) 302 360
Fax (01924) 302 362

Pugneys Country Park near Wakefield in south-west Yorkshire contains a natural ox-bow lake formed from the River Calder. Apart from its outdoor activities, it is interesting in its own right – the name derives from the Old English 'Pugnals', meaning goblin's nook, and the centre is overlooked by the ruins of Sandal Castle. Today the lake has one of Britain's best-equipped water sports centres. Windsurfing courses for adults and children are offered, starting with 'taster' evenings for those who want to give the sport a try, and graduating through all the RYA's basic certificates (Levels 1–3) and on to instructor training. All the courses last for 14 hours, but the sessions are spread out over both days of a weekend.

The centre caters mainly to individuals and groups in the South Yorkshire area and so has no accommodation. They can help you find local B&B if you are passing through the area for a while, but you will need your own transport to get to and from the centre.

Season: Open all year. (Hire season 1 March to 30 November.)
Accommodation: Not available.
Food: Vending machines only.
Other Activities: Canoeing (see p. 31); Child and Youth Sports (p. 68); Sailing (p. 359).
Children: Junior courses for 8–16-year-olds. Junior boards and rigs available.
Disabled Facilities: Toilets wheelchair-accessible.
Insurance: Clients should arrange personal insurance cover.
Safety: All staff trained in first aid, life-saving and safety boat-handling.
Affiliations: RYA – Windsurfing, Sailing; British Canoe Union.
Tariffs: All prices include tuition and use of equipment. 2 introductory evening sessions: £25; 2-day RYA Level 1 or 2 course: £59; improvers' coaching session (4 hours): £20; Level 1 RYA Instructor course (6 days): £135; junior introductory sessions (2 half-days): £23; RYA Junior Certificate course (5 3-hour sessions): £54; junior improvers' coaching session (8 hours): £30. Windsurfing also offered as part of centre's Junior Multi-activity course (5 3-hour sessions): £35. (Note: These are 1996 prices; check with reception for any tariff or course changes.)
Booking: £10 deposit secures a course place. Bookings usually made in advance although late bookings accepted if space available.
Access: Off the M1 (Junction 39) near Wakefield. Trains and buses to Wakefield. Local buses from Wakefield go to centre.

queen mary sailsports

Queen Mary Reservoir
Ashford Road
Ashford
Middlesex
TW15 1UA
Tel (01784) 244 776 / 248 881
Fax (01784) 252 772

One of the most convenient schools for Londoners, Queen Mary Sailsports offer non-residential courses in a variety of sailsports. Their windsurfing training programme is aimed at all levels of competence. Those who already hold certificates can hire equipment (under supervision) or take private lessons in specific techniques. For beginners, the Learn to Windsurf course is recommended, run over 3 2½-hour evening sessions, which is convenient if you're working. By the end of it you should have attained RYA Level 1. Following on from this are the improvers' courses, run over 1 full day, which take you to RYA Level 2, the Introduction to Fun Boards (another 1-day course to RYA Level 3), which takes you into high-wind sailing, and various advanced programmes. These run at RYA Level 4 and aim at refining your technique. Almost all the advanced courses are held over 1 full day.

For children aged 9–13 there is a special Junior Learn to Windsurf course held over 5 3-hour sessions, as well as regular Saturday 'Improver' mornings. The children's courses go as far as RYA Level 2. Similar versions of these courses are held for teenagers (aged 14–18), but going on to RYA Level 3.

Season: Open 7 days a week June to August, Wednesday to Sunday rest of year.
Accommodation: Not available.
Food: Food is available in restaurant and bar.
Other Activities: Child and Youth Sports (see p. 68); Powerboating (p. 326); Sailing (p. 360).
Children: Minimum age 9 years. Special courses offered for juniors (8–13) and teens (13–18).
Disabled Facilities: Courses for the disabled are currently being developed.
Insurance: Clients should arrange their own personal accident insurance.
Safety: Staff qualified in first aid and rescue skills.
Affiliations: RYA – Sailing, Windsurfing, Powerboating.
Tariffs: RYA Level 1 course (includes equipment): £69; supervised 2-hour session (includes equipment): £22; RYA Level 2 course (includes equipment): £55; RYA Level 3 or 4 courses: £50 (equipment hire additional £10); RYA Junior and Teen Windsurfing Level 1 courses (including equipment): £69; RYA Teen Levels 2 and 3 courses (including equipment): £109. Personal instruction Levels 1 and 2: £17 per hour; Levels 3 / 4 / 5: £22 per hour. Group, early-booking and sibling discounts available.
Booking: Full payment must be made before course begins. Cancellation charge: 20% of total. Late bookings accepted if space available. Visa, Mastercard and Switch cards accepted.
Access: A few miles from either the M3 (Junction 1) or the M25 (Junction 13) at Ashford, Middlesex. Trains from Waterloo to Ashford or Sunbury, buses to Ashford. Cab fare from Ashford around £3.

rockley point sailing school

Hamworthy
Poole
Dorset
BH15 4LZ
Tel (01202) 677 272
Fax (01202) 668 268

The sheltered waters of Poole Harbour make for about as safe an environment as you could wish for learning to windsurf. Rockley's windsurfing courses are mainly aimed at beginners: they run a good 2-day introductory course that gives you an RYA Level 1 certificate. However, if you're really serious, the centre can whiz you through the various RYA Levels and give you up to 3 instructor certificates if you take one of their intensive courses, which last from 14 to 18 weeks. You can also book personal tuition or supervised sailing in a group by arrangement with the centre.

Season: 29 May to 4 June, 3 July to 27 August.
Affiliations: RYA – Windsurfing.
Tariffs: 2-day windsurfing course: £95.

See Sailing (p. 362) for full details.

rossendale valley water park

Clowbridge Reservoir
Clowbridge
Burnley
Lancashire
BB11 SPF
Tel (01282) 412 965

Rossendale Valley specialize in windsurfing beginner and improver courses (RYA Levels 1 and 2) for adults and children, and equipment hire for intermediate and advanced board sailors. The courses are run over half- and full days and are non-residential. You will need your own transport to get to and from the centre. Beginners' dinghy sailing sessions can also be arranged to fill up an extra half-day, as well as powerboating 'taster' sessions.

Season: Open all year.
Accommodation: Not available.
Food: Refreshments available at centre.
Children: Junior club and courses available.
Disabled Facilities: None.
Insurance: Clients should arrange personal insurance cover.
Safety: All instructors trained in first aid.
Affiliations: RYA.
Tariffs: Prices include instruction and use of equipment. 2-hour taster session: £25; RYA Level 1 course (2 day): £60; RYA Level 2 course (1 day): £45; improver session: £30: RYA Junior Level 1 course: £40.
Booking: 33% deposit required, no cancellation charges. Late bookings accepted if space available. Credit cards accepted.
Access: A682 south of Burnley. Buses available to Burnley area, short walk to centre.

tighnabruaich sailing school

Tighnabruaich
Argyll & Bute
PA21 2BD
Scotland
Tel (01700) 811 396

Just 2 hours' drive from Glasgow, this windsports school offers residential windsurfing courses to suit all ages and levels of expertise, as well as board hire by the hour or day. Most courses last a full week. For beginners, the Basic course takes you through to intermediate level (RYA Level 3), while advanced and racing courses (up to RYA Level 5) are also available for those who really want to hone their skills. The centre has a variety of accommodation, prices for which are included, on a sliding scale according to the level of comfort desired, in the course fee.

Tariffs: Fees include instruction and use of equipment. Prices slightly higher in peak season (25 June–6 August). 1-week windsurfing course: £135–140; 1-week combined windsurfing and sailing course: £135–140. Half-week courses available: £69–72. Group, family and youth discounts available.

See Sailing (p. 364) for full details.

wight water

19 Orchardleigh Road
Shanklin
Isle of Wight
PO37 7NP
Tel & Fax (01983) 866 269

This is a good place for beginners to start at, with lessons by the hour or the day, or as part of a 5-day course aimed at taking you up to RYA Level 3. You can also try out the basics as part of a multi-activity water sports programme that also includes catamaran sailing, surfing, wave skiing and canoeing. You will need your own transport to get to and from the centre.

Season: Open all year.
Accommodation: Centre will help find suitable accommodation at nearby campsites, or in B&B (plentiful in the area).
Food: None.
Other Activities: Canoeing (see p. 37); Cycle Sports (p. 126); Sailing (p. 366); Surfing (p. 408).
Children: Discounts for youths under 19.
Insurance: Clients should arrange personal insurance cover.
Affiliations: RYA.
Tariffs: 5-session windsurfing course (RYA Windsurfing Levels 1–3): £50. Windsurfing is also one of the sports included in the centre's 5-session multi-activity package: £60. Group and youth discounts available.
Access: Take ferry to Isle of Wight from Portsmouth, Southampton or Lymington. Centre will pick up from port.

windsport international ltd

Mylor Yacht Harbour
Falmouth
Cornwall
TR11 5UF
Tel (01326) 376 191
Fax (01326) 376 192
Falmouth Centre, Cornwall
Tel (01326) 376 191
Rutland Centre, Rutland
Tel (01780) 722 100

Windsport is a big company and has 2 centres, in Falmouth and Rutland, where you can learn to windsurf. The centres are predominantly sailing schools, but they also offer a good standard of windsurfing tuition as part of their multi-activity water sports packages. These also include catamaran and dinghy sailing, powerboating, water skiing and, if you want it, land yachting. These multi-activity packages are run either as 'fun days' or, more usefully, over 5 days, where there is really time to learn. Bookings are divided between various types of group: individuals may sign up for a general adults' course, while others are run specifically for families, unaccompanied children and corporate groups. However, if you decide that you want to concentrate on windsurfing only, private tuition on student-to-instructor ratios of 1:1 and 2:1 is offered.

Courses can be residential or non-residential – whatever suits you. There is also a variety of accommodation available, and fees are charged on a sliding scale reflecting the level of comfort you choose.

Affiliations: RYA.
Tariffs: Windsurfing is one of the activities offered in the centre's multi-activity packages. 5-day family, child or adult course: £125 (adult), £95 (child); weekend family course: £48 (adult), £38 (child); 1-day family or child course: £25 (adult), £20 (child); 1-day adult course: £48. Residential packages are also available (including tuition, equipment and accommodation); prices vary according to level of accommodation chosen (hotel, guest house or farmhouse). 5-day course (6 nights' accommodation): £365–545; weekend course (2 nights' accommodation): £220–280. Group discounts available.

See Sailing (p. 366) for full details.

further reading

Successful Windsurfing, Clive Boden, Sackville Books, 1989;
Learn to Windsurf in a Weekend, Phil Jones, Dorling Kindersley, 1992.

kitting yourself out

There are so many different types of board that the choice is often overwhelming. Also, the learning curve is now so steep that it's pointless to buy kit until you've settled at an advanced plateau of ability, or you'll be constantly having to change your equipment. BiC, Hi Fly, Mistral, Tiga, F2 and Fanatic are all good manufacturers of boards and sails, while Neil Pryde make sails only, which are considered the best. To kit yourself out for the first time with intermediate/advanced gear will cost from £600 to £1,000 for the sail and mast, board and harness (comes with the sail). However, you can do it second-hand a lot cheaper (see below).

When you get up to high-wind sailing (shortboarding), the choice narrows a little: really advanced sailors sometimes favour custom boards, such as Critical Section's Freeride range (from £600 for the board alone), while others swear by high-grade standard manufactured boards such as the BiC Veloce range and the advanced Hi Fly range. Some of these can top £1,000. Advanced sails and masts (usually made by the same manufacturers) can cost as much as the board.

Wet suits are not cheap if you buy them new. Prices vary from about £80 for a short-sleeved and -legged summer 'shortie' through to about £200–350 for a top-of-the-range all-season wet/dry suit that can be used even in winter. Recommended manufacturers of both summer and winter suits are GULL, Neil Pryde, Typhoon and Sparta. GULL and Neil Pryde also make good wet suit boots for £25–40.

As with many action sports, windsurfing has a huge second-hand market in equipment. Asking around at clubs or cruising the classifieds of *Windsurf* magazine is a good way to find cheap kit but, as always, make sure you get a second opinion from an instructor or experienced friend before buying. Boards that have been seriously knocked around often let in water and wet suits are often torn. However, you can get kitted out with a very good board, sail and mast for £150–200 and obtain wet suits for £40–50 through the clubs and classifieds.

checklist

- ✔ *board*
- ✔ *sail and mast*
- ✔ *wet suit - summer or winter*
- ✔ *wet suit boots*

woodlore

survival skills
identifying fungi

Living off the land is something most of us feel that we could do if we had to, but how many of us really have a clue? Even in summer, which of the many plants are edible, which are poisonous? In bare winter, how can we find and identify the few fungi, berries and roots that would keep us alive until the spring? And before we try and fill our bellies, how many of us would know how to build a rain-proof shelter from branches, or light a fire without using a match?

A number of places in Britain now run courses in woodlore, varying from relatively gentle guidance for identifying fungi, to all-out survival courses held in all seasons and all weathers.

You don't have to be super-fit or gung-ho to do a survival course: even the winter courses can be taken by just about anyone and are held over either a weekend or a week. But be warned; even two days living totally off the land can be a frighteningly alien experience. If you try a week of it, you will enter a whole other state of being, where your life's horizon narrows down to food, shelter and warmth. Oddly enough, this is often deeply relaxing – despite the challenges and obvious hardships, it is impossible to come away from such a course without a real sense of achievement, and a new perspective on day-to-day pressures.

selected centres

acorn activities

PO Box 120
Hereford
Hereford & Worcester
HR4 8YB
Tel (01432) 830 083
Fax (01432) 830 110

Survival Skills

Acorn's (rather gentle) Survival Weekends are held in July, August and October, although you can arrange your own, for a minimum of 6 people, at any time of year. The course is led by ex-special-forces instructors who teach both basic and advanced survival techniques. Learn how to eat wild fungi, barks and roots, build shelters, cook outside, and other skills. It must be said, however, that Acorn's survival weekends are not hard-core – there is no going hungry nor is there any great discomfort. People really wanting detailed tuition in natural survival may be disappointed, but anyone looking for a gentler introduction to the idea of living off the land will have a great time. Ring Acorn for this year's dates.

Season: All year round.
Tariffs: Survival weekend: £105.

See Walking (p. 414) for full details.

breakaway survival school

17 Hugh Thomas Avenue
Holmer
Hereford
Hereford & Worcester
HR4 9RB
Tel (01432) 267 097

Survival Skills

Breakaway Survival lead serious survival and team-building courses in the forests and moorlands of the Brecon Beacons and surrounding countryside, and offer both weekend and week-long trips. You are shown how to build your own shelter (meaning that after the demonstration you actually have to construct the thing), how to use a map and compass, how to navigate at night and start and maintain a fire. Vegans and vegetarians should be aware that you will be expected to catch, skin and prepare rabbits, pheasants and eels, as well as gathering wild plants and fungi.

In charge is Mick 'Ginge' Tyler, an ex-SAS man, who started Breakaway in 1982. Although his courses are challenging, they are not specifically physical tests, and the pace is deliberately slow – giving you time to look at the landscape properly so that you can understand how to survive in it. You are even allowed to visit the local pub when camping on low ground – but you have to navigate your own way there and back across country in the dark without a torch. However, you should be part-way fit, as there are mountain rescue exercises that demand a lot of steep hill work.

You need to bring walking boots, rucksack and sleeping bag and one change of clothing and footwear. You'll also need a knife, matches, candle, torch, water- and windproofs. Some chocolate doesn't go amiss either.

Season: Open all year.
Accommodation: You build it (plus tents and parachutes, as needed).

Food: You find it (and other provisions supplied).
Children: Minimum age 14.
Disabled Facilities: None.
Insurance: Clients are covered by school's insurance.
Safety: Instructors are qualified paramedics.
Affiliations: None.
Tariffs: Weekend introductory course: £60; 5-day basic course: £150; weekend advanced course: £60; 5-day advanced course: £150.
Booking: £20–40 deposit required, balance due on completion of course. In the case of cancellation, amount can be credited to an alternative course. Late bookings sometimes accepted if space available.
Access: From Brecon, take the A4059 to Penderyn. Trains and buses available to Hereford; pick-ups arranged by centre.

fly high sky sports

101 Heath Road
Barming
Maidstone
Kent
ME16 9JT
Tel (01622) 728 230 /
(0860) 351 130 (mobile)

Survival Skills

Fly High organize specialist survival weekends, primarily aimed at pilots or air crew who fly over uninhabited regions; nonetheless, the courses are open to all comers. The training is theoretical and practical, covering shelters and how to build them, fire-lighting with and without artificial aids, tracking and trapping, improvising tools and clothing, navigation, self-rescue and first aid. You can choose whether to stay in the school's comfortable bunkhouse by night or to rough it in your home-made shelter.

Season: All year.
Tariffs: 1-day course: £45; weekend course: £80.

See Paragliding and Parascending (p. 312) for full details.

kindrogan field centre

Enochdhu
By Blairgowrie
Perthshire & Kinross
PH10 7PG
Scotland
Tel (01250) 881 286
Fax (01250) 881 433

Identifying Fungi

Kindrogan is a general field studies centre housed in an old Victorian manor. Apart from its more botanical and wildlife-oriented activities, it runs 2 courses devoted to the identification of fungi – an invaluable study of wild food for any would-be survivalist. Kindrogan is not like other woodlore schools, where clients sleep rough and live off the land. You stay in comfort at the centre, with board and accommodation thrown in. But what it lacks in adventure, Kindrogan makes up for in expertise. With 50 years' experience behind them, the centre's courses are very reliable and come highly recommended by survivalists and botanists alike.

Tariffs: Prices include tuition, full-board accommodation and transport during course. Introduction to Fungi (3 days): £84; Fungi (1 week): £270.

See Eco-Sports (p. 147) for full details.

woodlore

77 Dillingburgh Road
Eastbourne
Sussex
BN20 8LS
Tel (01323) 648 517
Fax (01323) 738 356

Survival Skills

Raymond Mears, who runs Woodlore, learned his bushcraft from the Zairean pygmies and the Cherokees of the Great Smoky mountains of North Carolina. He offers a range of 2-day and 6-day courses. If you have only a weekend available, the Fundamental Bushcraft course covers a wide range of basic skills, and you will be living totally in the wild. If you have a bit more time, it is even more rewarding to take the 6-day Foundation Course which gives you time to put the skills really to the test. This course is not for vegetarians or vegans, as there is an emphasis on catching fish and game, as well as working hide, antler and bone. However, Mears is also big on the pygmy and Native American ethics of putting back what you take out, and explains their conservation philosophies. Combined with this is instruction on how to make flint tools and how to use plants for medicine as well as food.

Woodlore also offer several wilderness-related courses such as birch bark weaving, carving with knife and axe, bush cookery and nature awareness and animal tracking. You become so quickly and completely immersed in the detail of the woods and heathlands where the courses take place that you forget you're in the affluent, built-up south-east. Mears's courses are unforgettable.

Season: March to November.
Accommodation: Not provided (bring your own tent).
Food: Varies according to course.
Children: Minimum age normally 16; those under 18 require consent of parent of guardian. Special youth courses available.
Disabled Facilities: None.
Insurance: Clients should arrange their own holiday insurance.
Safety: Staff trained in first aid.
Affiliations: None.
Tariffs: A wide variety of woodlore courses is offered; some examples are – 2-day Nature Awareness & Animal Tracking course: £100; 2-day Bushcraft Cookery course: £100; 2-day Foraging for Fungi course: £150; 1-week Foundation course (includes food): £350; 1-week Journeyman course (includes food): £360.
Booking: £50 non-refundable deposit required. Balance due 6 weeks before start date. Cancellation charges: 4–6 weeks before start, 50% of total; 0–3 weeks before start, 100% of total. Late bookings sometimes accepted if space available.
Access: A22 to Eastbourne. Trains and buses available to Eastbourne; contact centre for more details.

further reading

The Commando Survival Manual, Hugh McManners, Dorling Kindersley, 1994.

kitting yourself out

For details on clothing, backpacks, sleeping bags and camping equipment (although on woodlore courses you generally aren't allowed a tent) please see Walking, p. 434, and for navigational equipment turn to Mountain Skills, p. 290.

The more specialized kit you need for learning woodlore must be constructed from material gathered in the wild: birch twigs or bracken to build your 'pick-up', dry sticks to rub together over dry grass to make fire. A really good woodsman knows how to make his or her own flint knife. With this you can skin animals caught in the dead-fall trap you have constructed. Rope and string can be made from birch bark. There's a whole world of knowledge to be gained. Provided you have good boots, waterproofs, a backpack and sleeping bag, you are ready for a woodlore course.

photo: Acorn Activities

indexes

activities listed by counties
centres and their activities
centres listed by counties
list of abbreviations

Index: activities listed by counties

England

Wales

Scotland

Northern Ireland

Index: centres and their activities

Index: centres listed by counties

England

Scotland

Northern Ireland

Wales

list of abbreviations

ABRS	Association of British Riding Schools
ARDS	Association of Racing Drivers Schools
ARKS	Association of Racing Kart Schools
BABO	British Association of Balloon Operators
BARS	British Association of Rally Schools
BASI	British Association of Ski Instructors
BASS	British Association of Ski Schools
BBAC	British Balloon and Airship Club
BCU	British Canoe Union
BFC	British Falconers Club
BFSLYC	British Fed. of Sand and Land Yacht Clubs
BFSS	British Field Sports Society
BGA	British Gliding Association
BHPA	British Hang Gliding and Paragliding Assoc.
BHS	British Horse Society
BMAA	British Microlight Aircraft Association
BMC	British Mountaineering Council
BOF	British Orienteering Federation
BPA	British Parachute Association
BSA	British Surfing Association
BSAC	British Sub-Aqua Club
BWSF	British Water Ski Federation
CAA	Civil Aviation Authority
MLTB	Mountain Leaders Training Board
MSA	Motor Sports Association
PADI	Professional Assoc. of Diving Instructors
RAC	Royal Automobile Club
RDA	Riding for the Disabled
RSPB	Royal Society for the Protection of Birds
RYA	Royal Yachting Association
SPSA	Single Pitch Supervisors Award
STB	Scottish Tourist Board
WTB	Wales Tourist Board
YHA	Youth Hostel Association